LIVING-ROOM

Withdrawn

LIVING-ROOM
MATSUNAGA-SAN
7

Keiko Iwashita

MATSUNAGA
SAN

LIVING-ROOM

Contents

Story

Family circumstances have wrested Meeko from an ordinary family life to her uncle's boarding house, where her unrequited feelings for her housemate Matsunaga-san only grow with each passing day. Thanks to Ryo-kun's machinations, Meeko and Matsunaga-san are able to spend an exciting day at her school festival together. Then they find out that Hattori-san is getting married and moving out, so everyone plans a surprise party, which ends up being a resounding success! Meanwhile, has Ryo-kun developed his own feelings for Meeko? And what is this confrontation with Matsunaga-san?

SAN

Characters

Boarding House

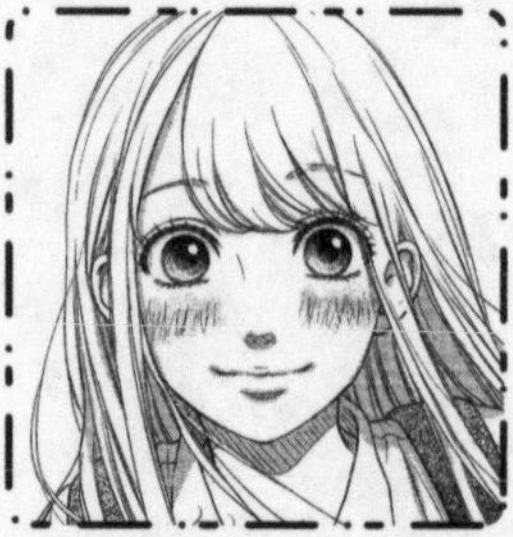

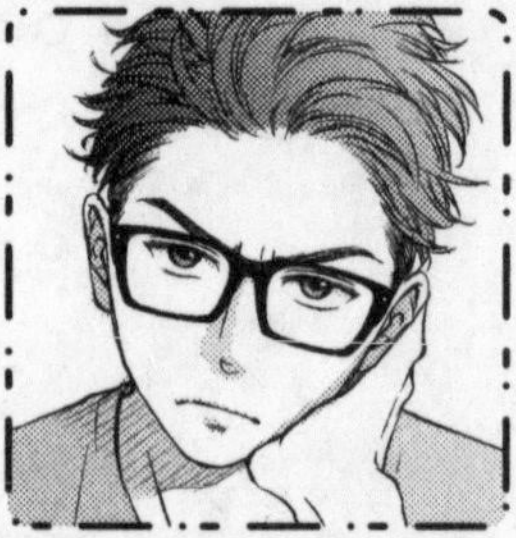

Miko Sonoda

A 17-year-old high school girl.
Only knows how to cook curry.
Pining for Matsunaga-san.

Jun Matsunaga

A designer who works from home.
28 years old.
Sharp-tongued but caring.

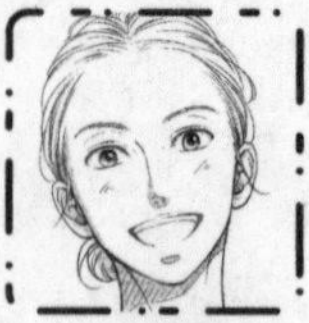

Kentaro Suzuki
A bartender.
Girl-crazy (?)

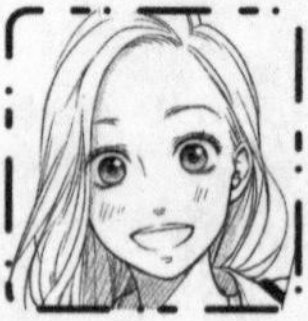

Asako Onuki
A nail artist.
Like a big sister.

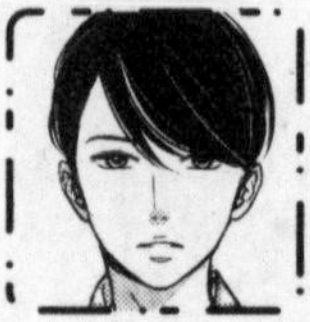

Ryo Hojo
A quiet college student.
Interested in Meeko?

School

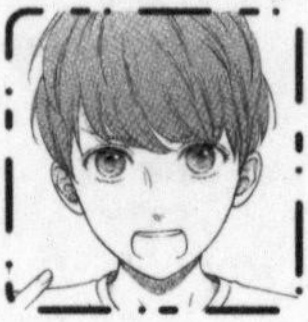

Natsumi Kobayashi
Meeko's homeroom teacher. A former resident of the boarding house and Matsunaga-san's ex.

MATSUNAGA

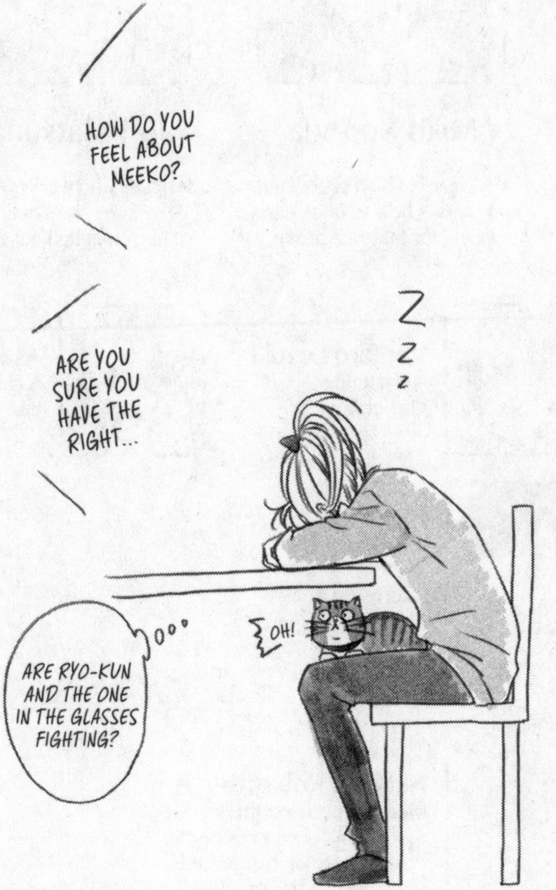
HOW DO YOU FEEL ABOUT MEEKO?
Z Z Z
ARE YOU SURE YOU HAVE THE RIGHT...
OH!
ARE RYO-KUN AND THE ONE IN THE GLASSES FIGHTING?

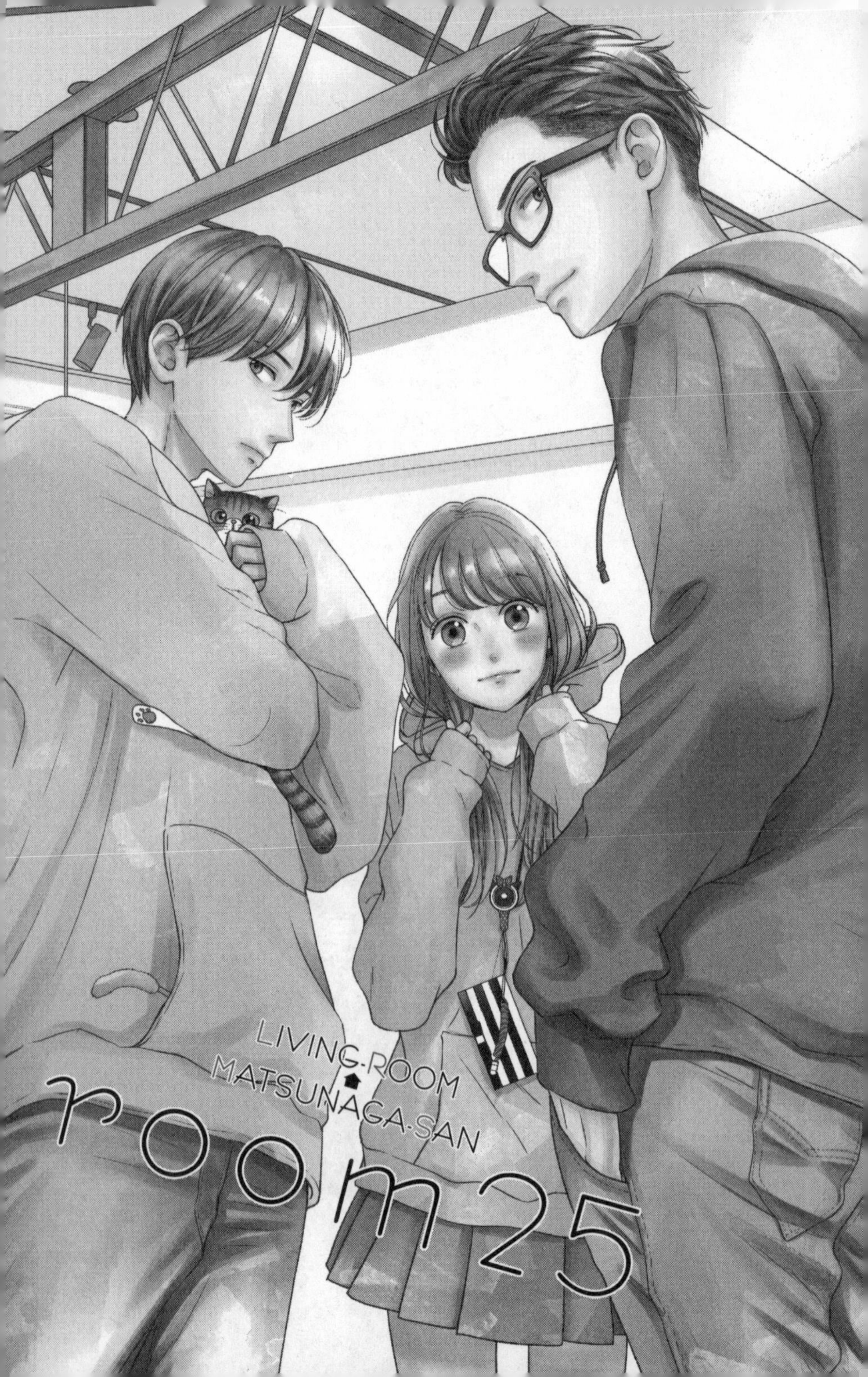
LIVING-ROOM MATSUNAGA-SAN
room 25

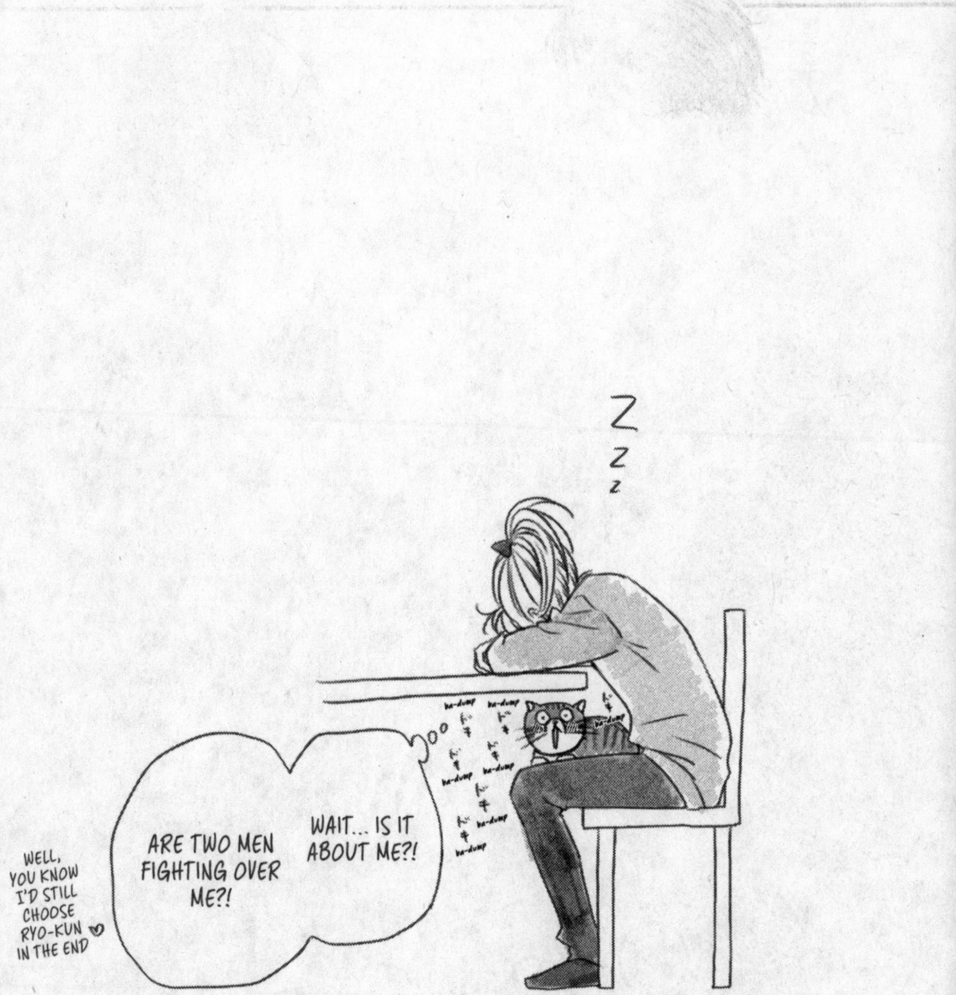
ZZZ
ba-dump ba-dump ba-dump ba-dump ba-dump ba-dump ba-dump
WAIT... IS IT ABOUT ME?!
ARE TWO MEN FIGHTING OVER ME?!
WELL, YOU KNOW I'D STILL CHOOSE RYO-KUN IN THE END

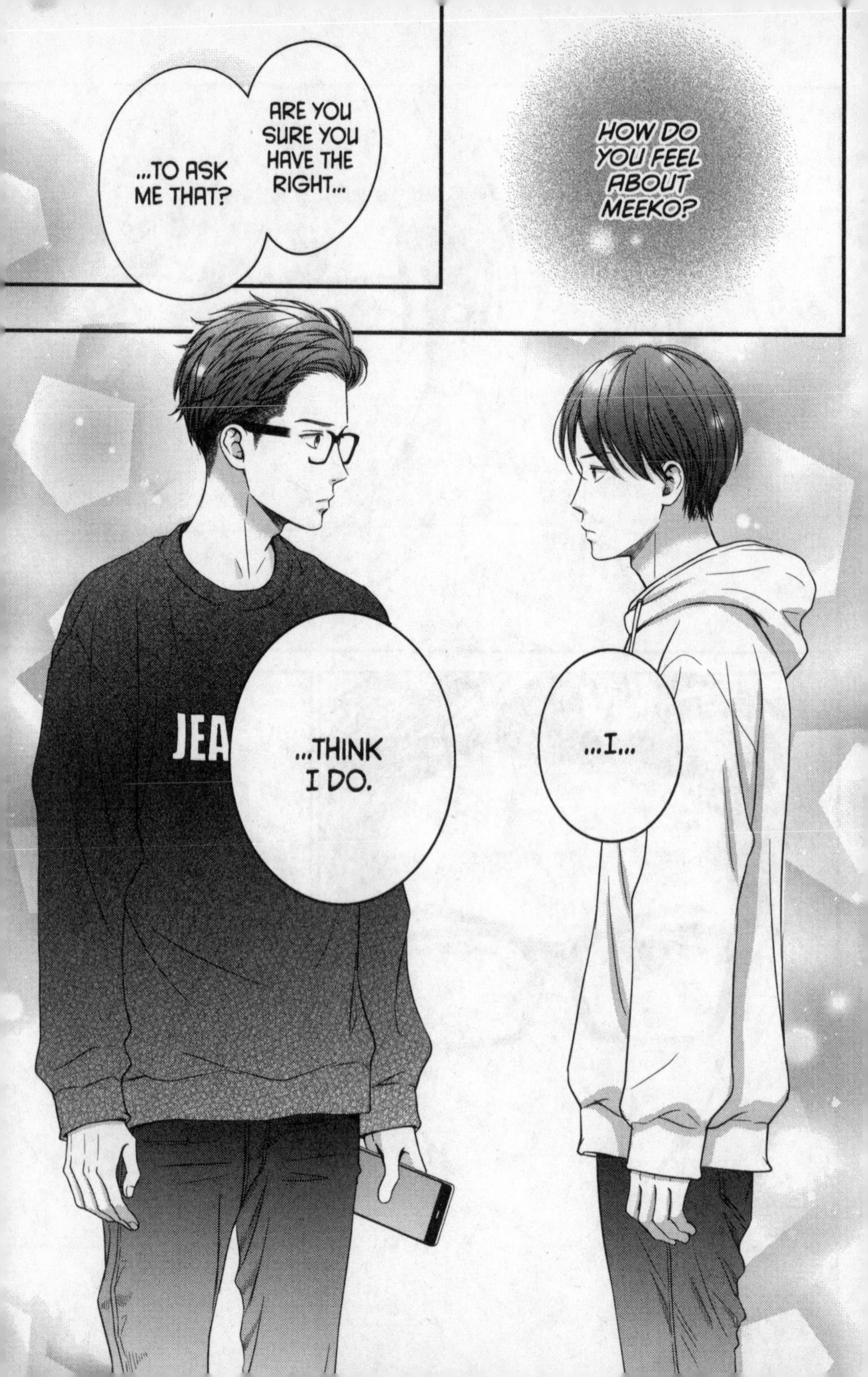
HOW DO YOU FEEL ABOUT MEEKO?
ARE YOU SURE YOU HAVE THE RIGHT...
...TO ASK ME THAT?
...I...
...THINK I DO.

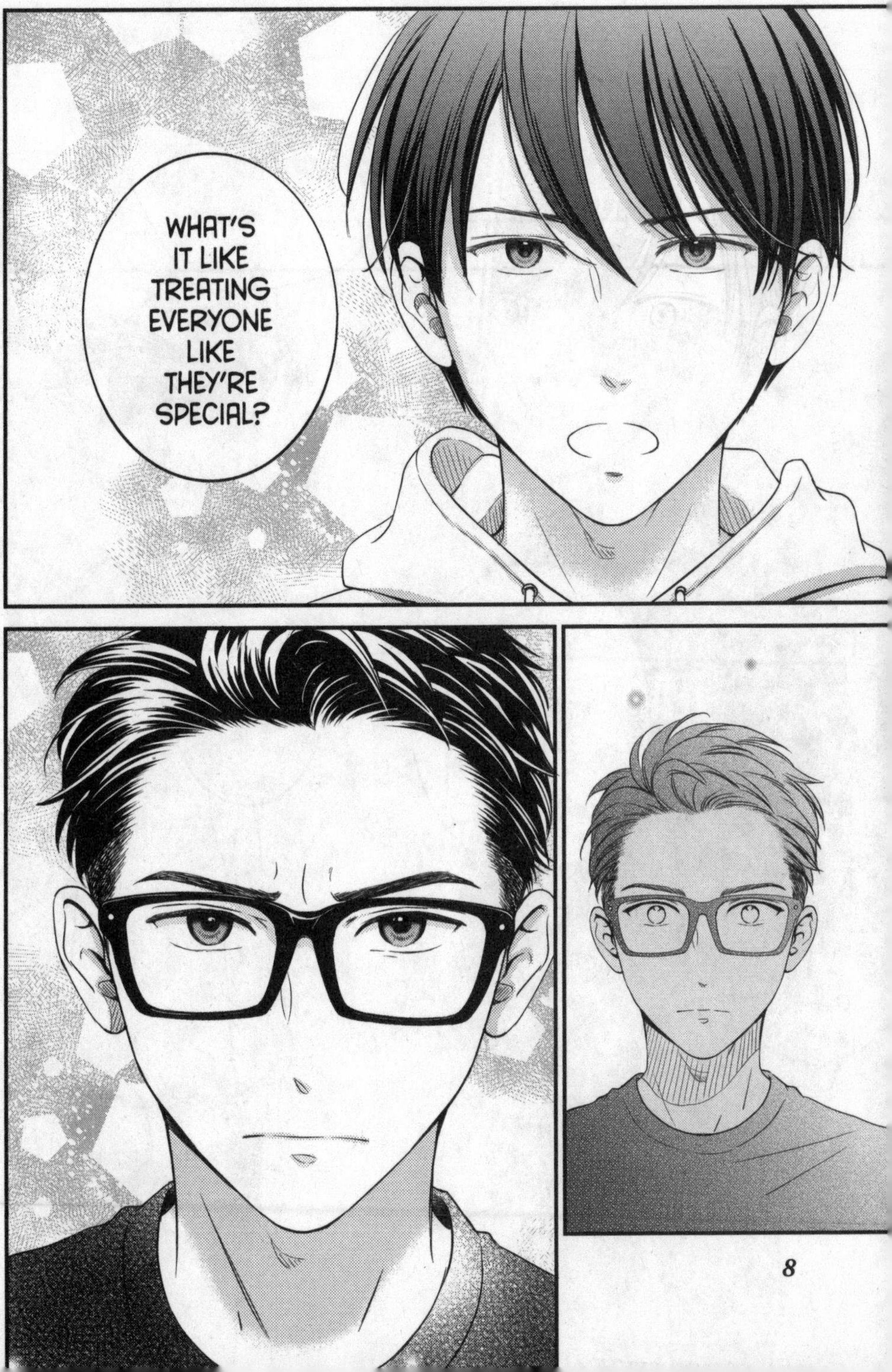
WHAT'S IT LIKE TREATING EVERYONE LIKE THEY'RE SPECIAL?

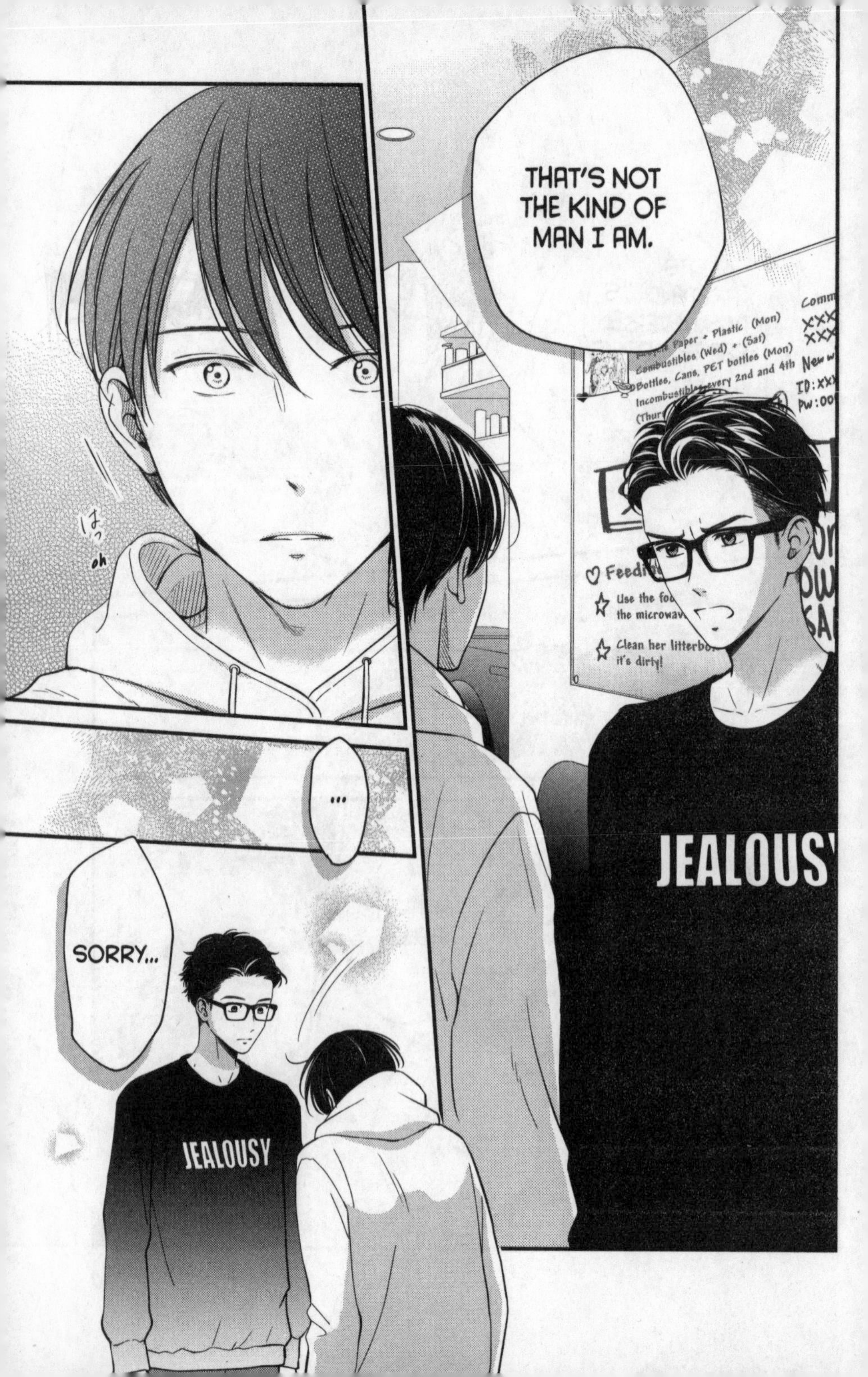
THAT'S NOT THE KIND OF MAN I AM.
Combustibles (Wed) + (Sat)
Bottles, Cans, PET bottles (Mon)
Clean her litterbo
it's dirty!
JEALOUS
はっ
oh
...
SORRY...
JEALOUSY

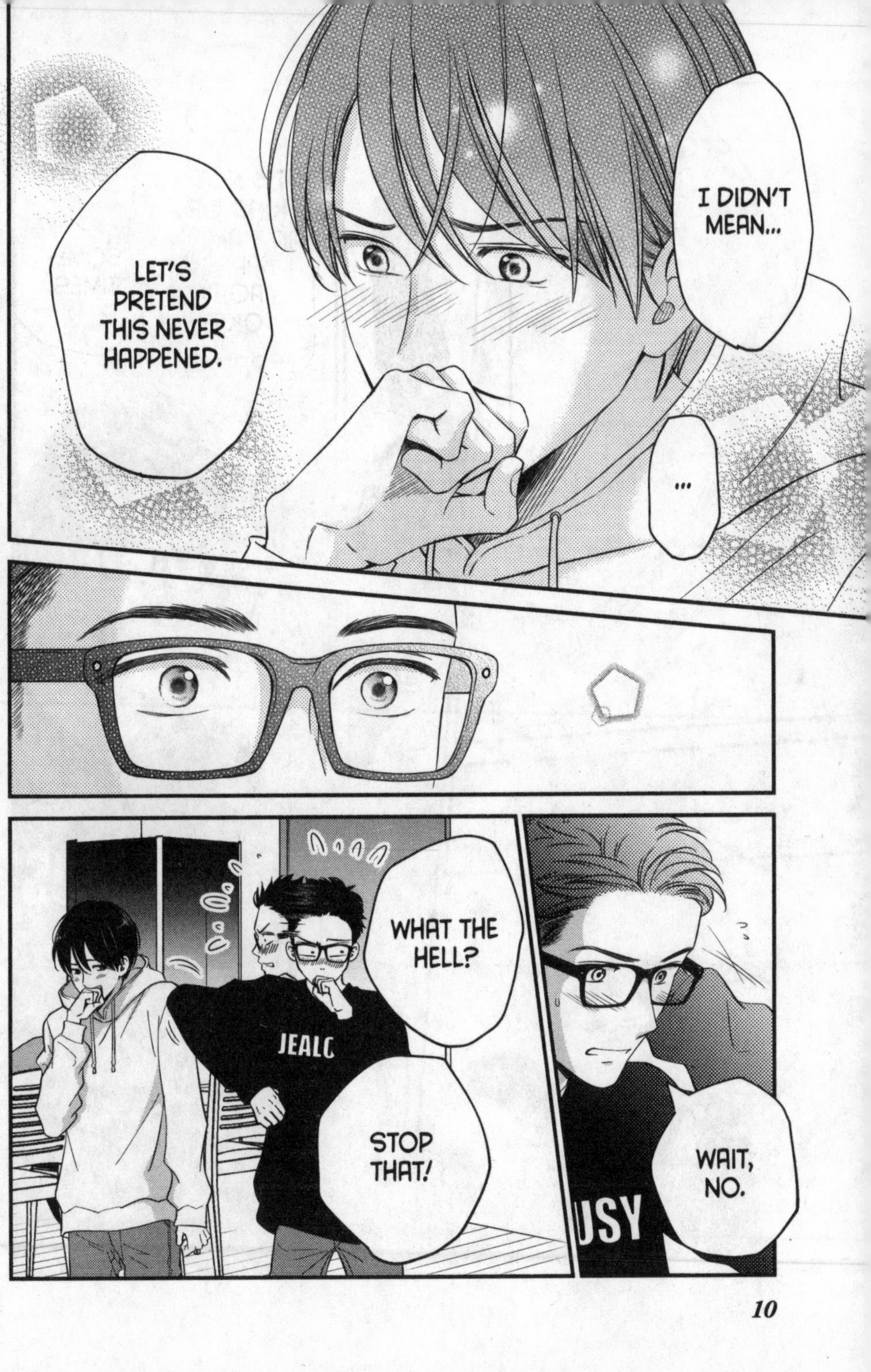
I DIDN'T MEAN...
...
LET'S PRETEND THIS NEVER HAPPENED.
USY
WAIT, NO.
WHAT THE HELL?
JEALC
STOP THAT!

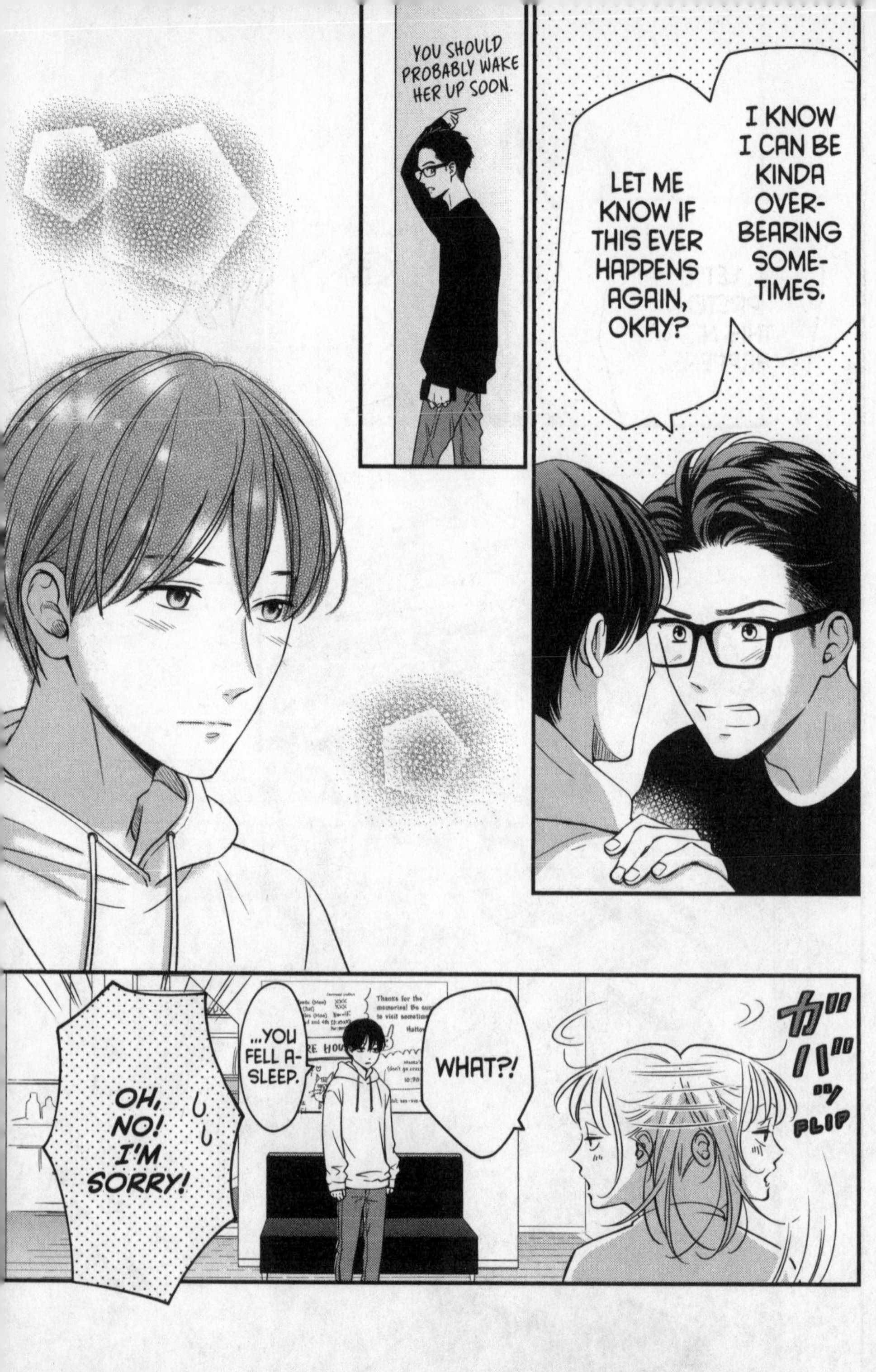
I KNOW I CAN BE KINDA OVER-BEARING SOME-TIMES.
LET ME KNOW IF THIS EVER HAPPENS AGAIN, OKAY?
YOU SHOULD PROBABLY WAKE HER UP SOON.
ガバッ
FLIP
WHAT?!
...YOU FELL A-SLEEP.
OH, NO! I'M SORRY!

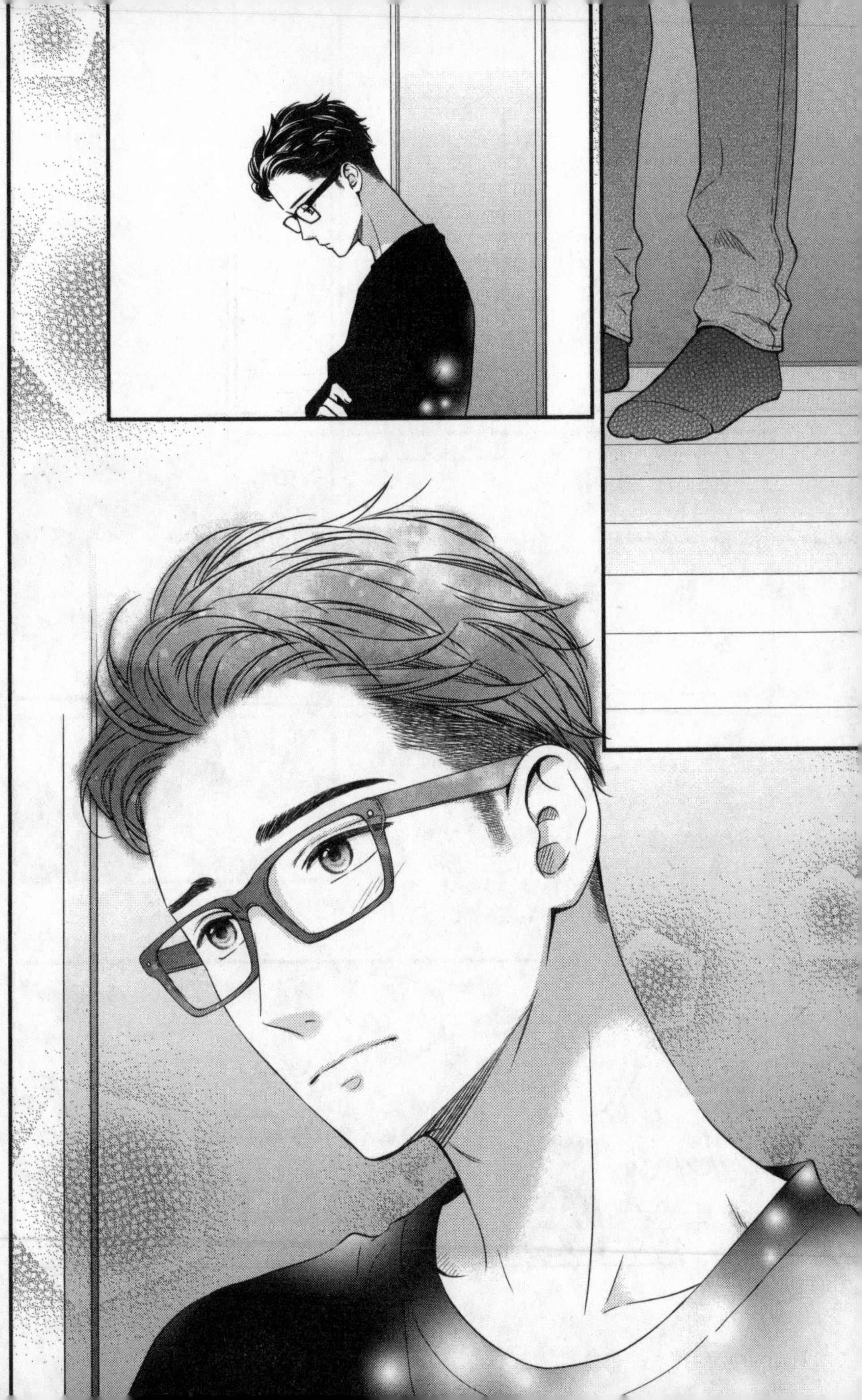

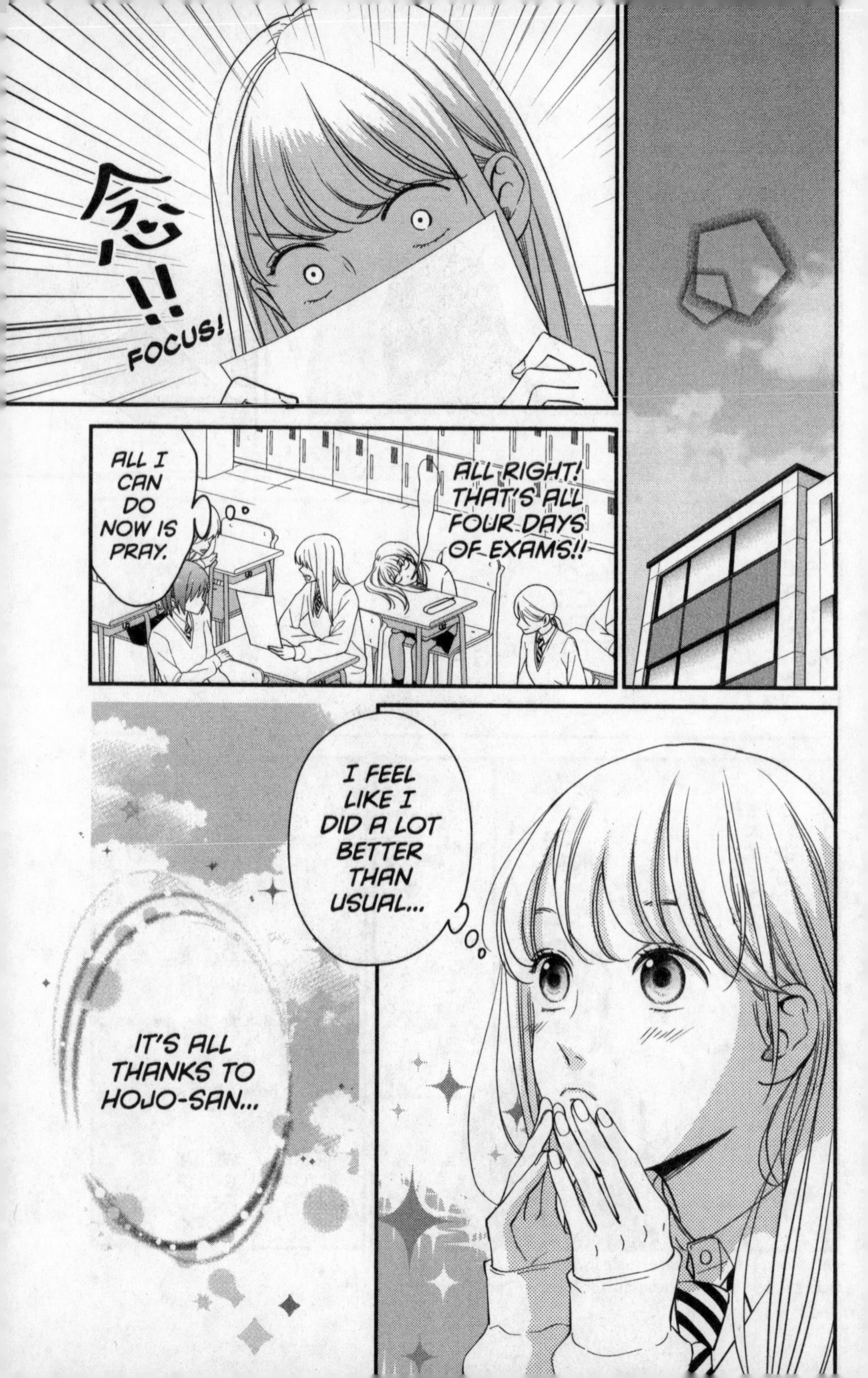
念!!
FOCUS!
ALL RIGHT! THAT'S ALL FOUR DAYS OF EXAMS!!
ALL I CAN DO NOW IS PRAY.
I FEEL LIKE I DID A LOT BETTER THAN USUAL...
IT'S ALL THANKS TO HOJO-SAN...

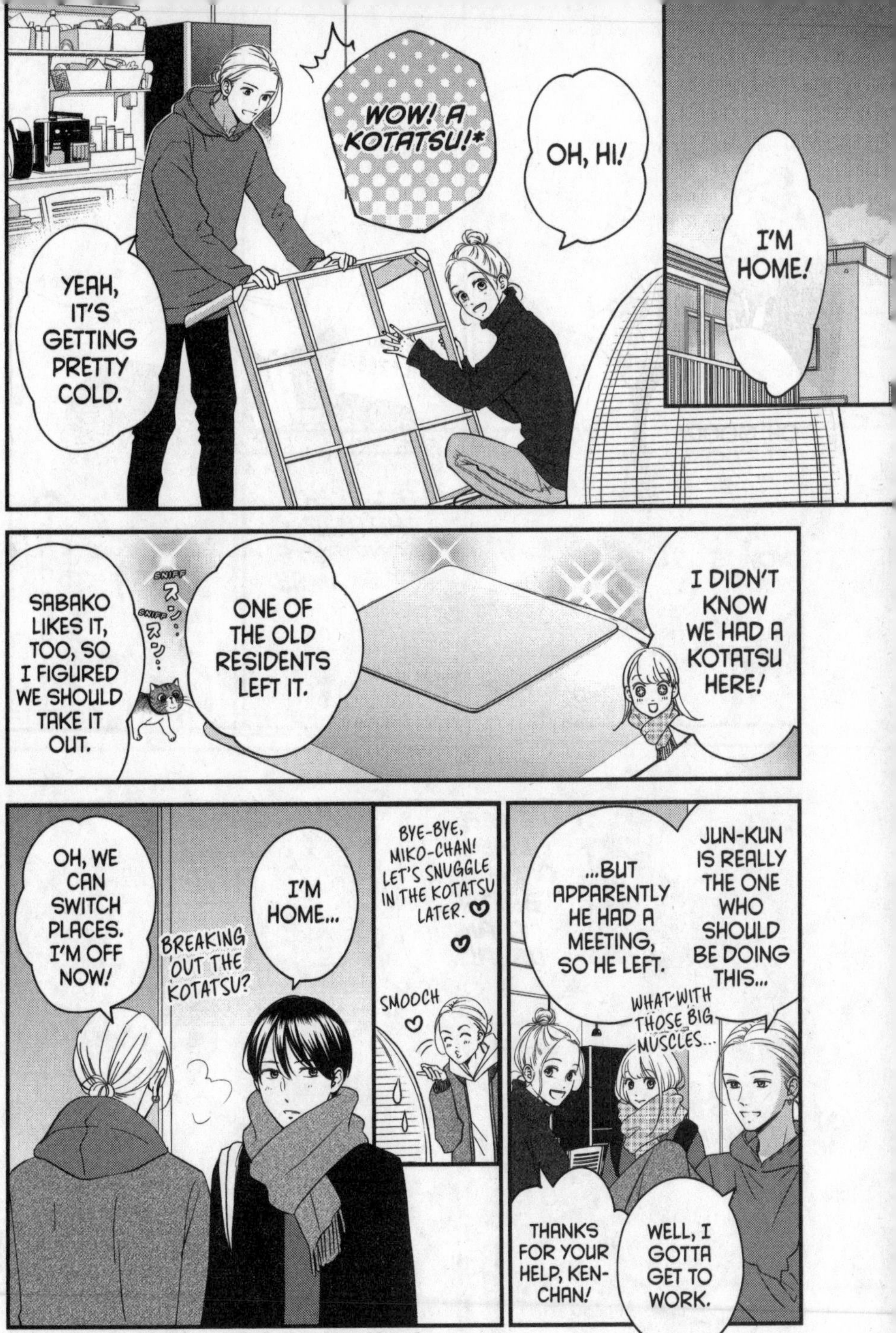
I'M HOME!
OH, HI!
WOW! A KOTATSU!*
YEAH, IT'S GETTING PRETTY COLD.
I DIDN'T KNOW WE HAD A KOTATSU HERE!
ONE OF THE OLD RESIDENTS LEFT IT.
SNIFF スン… SNIFF スン…
SABAKO LIKES IT, TOO, SO I FIGURED WE SHOULD TAKE IT OUT.
JUN-KUN IS REALLY THE ONE WHO SHOULD BE DOING THIS...
WHAT WITH THOSE BIG MUSCLES...
...BUT APPARENTLY HE HAD A MEETING, SO HE LEFT.
WELL, I GOTTA GET TO WORK.
THANKS FOR YOUR HELP, KEN-CHAN!
BYE-BYE, MIKO-CHAN! LET'S SNUGGLE IN THE KOTATSU LATER.
SMOOCH
I'M HOME...
BREAKING OUT THE KOTATSU?
OH, WE CAN SWITCH PLACES. I'M OFF NOW!

*A *kotatsu* is a low wooden table frame covered by a futon, under which there is a heat source. They are commonly used in winter.

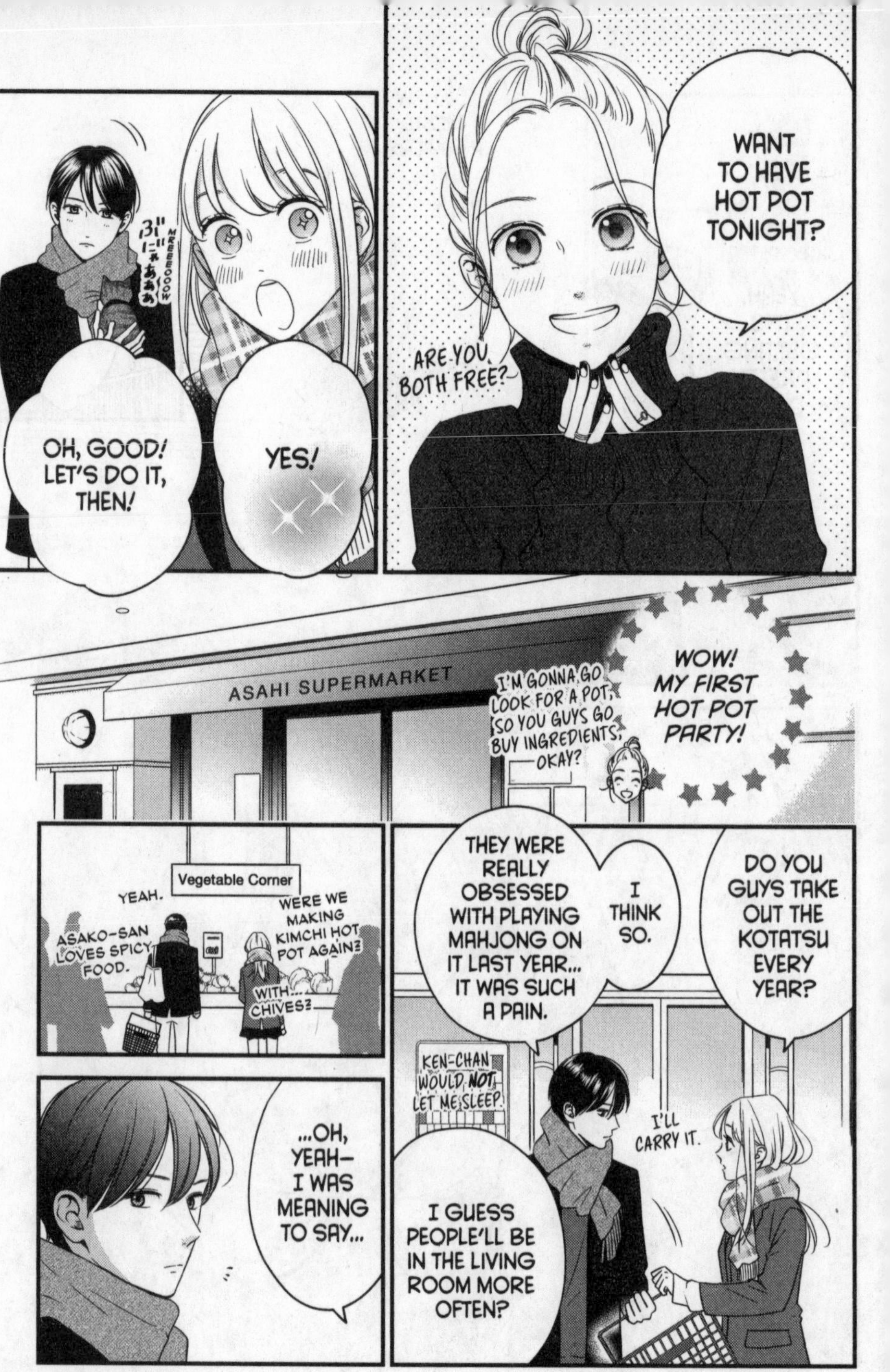
WANT TO HAVE HOT POT TONIGHT?
ARE YOU BOTH FREE?
MREEEOOOW
YES!
OH, GOOD! LET'S DO IT, THEN!
ASAHI SUPERMARKET
WOW! MY FIRST HOT POT PARTY!
I'M GONNA GO LOOK FOR A POT, SO YOU GUYS GO BUY INGREDIENTS, OKAY?
DO YOU GUYS TAKE OUT THE KOTATSU EVERY YEAR?
I THINK SO.
THEY WERE REALLY OBSESSED WITH PLAYING MAHJONG ON IT LAST YEAR... IT WAS SUCH A PAIN.
KEN-CHAN WOULD NOT LET ME SLEEP.
I'LL CARRY IT.
I GUESS PEOPLE'LL BE IN THE LIVING ROOM MORE OFTEN?
Vegetable Corner
WERE WE MAKING KIMCHI HOT POT AGAIN?
WITH... CHIVES?
YEAH.
ASAKO-SAN LOVES SPICY FOOD.
...OH, YEAH— I WAS MEANING TO SAY...

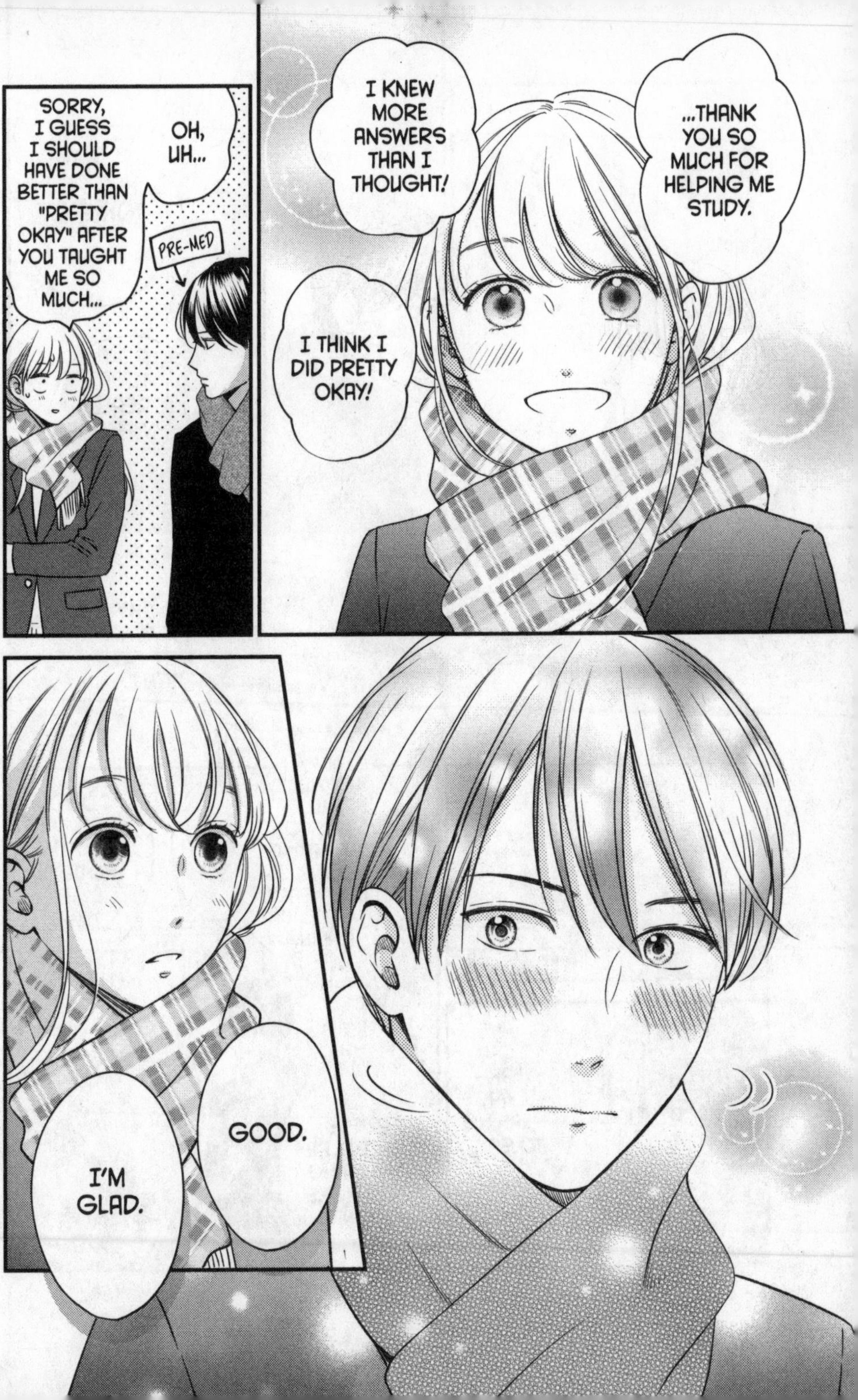
...THANK YOU SO MUCH FOR HELPING ME STUDY.
I KNEW MORE ANSWERS THAN I THOUGHT!
I THINK I DID PRETTY OKAY!
OH, UH...
PRE-MED
SORRY, I GUESS I SHOULD HAVE DONE BETTER THAN "PRETTY OKAY" AFTER YOU TAUGHT ME SO MUCH...
GOOD.
I'M GLAD.

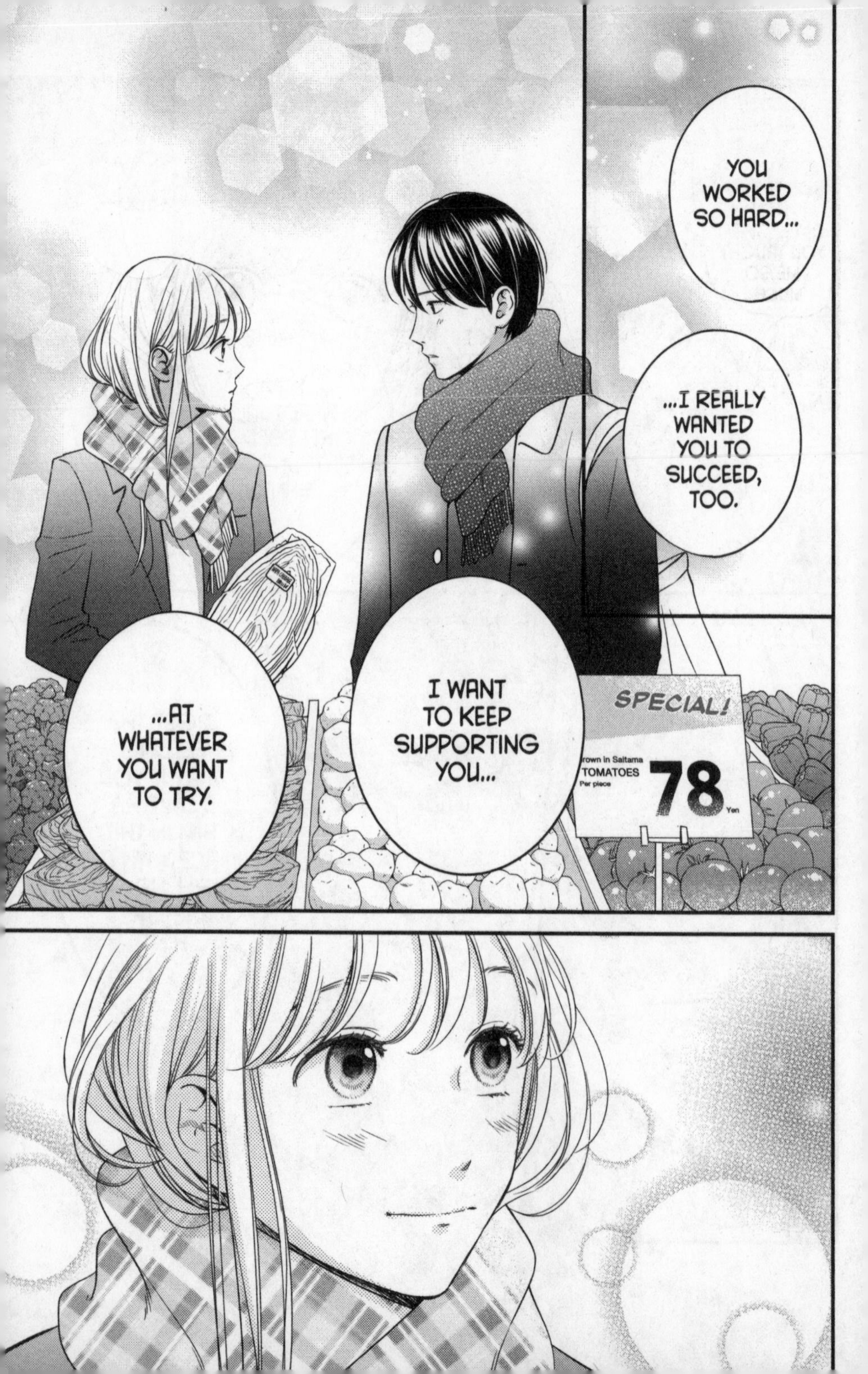
YOU WORKED SO HARD...
...I REALLY WANTED YOU TO SUCCEED, TOO.
I WANT TO KEEP SUPPORTING YOU...
...AT WHATEVER YOU WANT TO TRY.
SPECIAL!
rown in Saitama TOMATOES Per piece
78 Yen

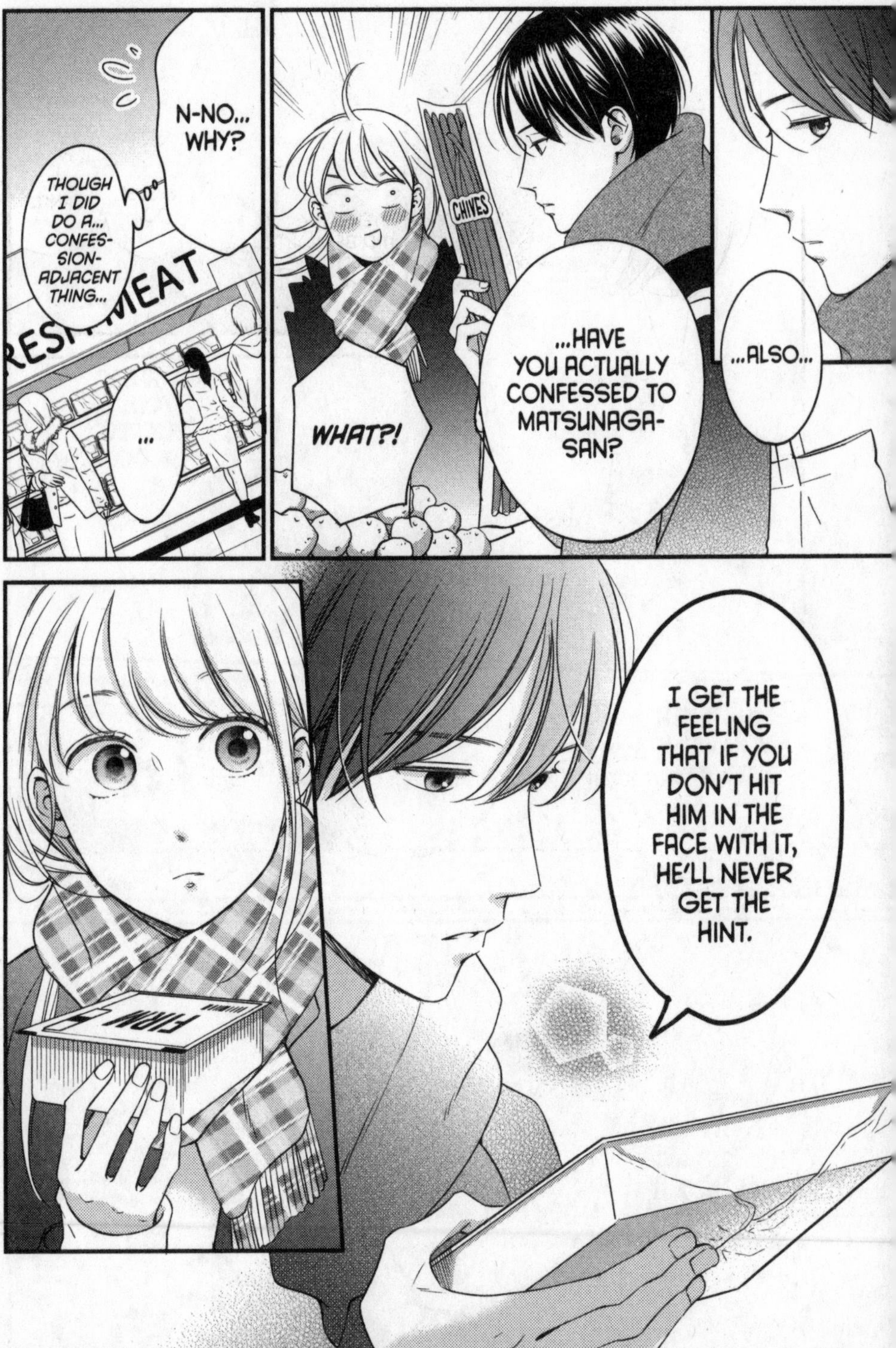
...ALSO...
...HAVE YOU ACTUALLY CONFESSED TO MATSUNAGA-SAN?
CHIVES
WHAT?!
N-NO... WHY?
THOUGH I DID DO A... CONFESSION-ADJACENT THING...
...
I GET THE FEELING THAT IF YOU DON'T HIT HIM IN THE FACE WITH IT, HE'LL NEVER GET THE HINT.
FIRM

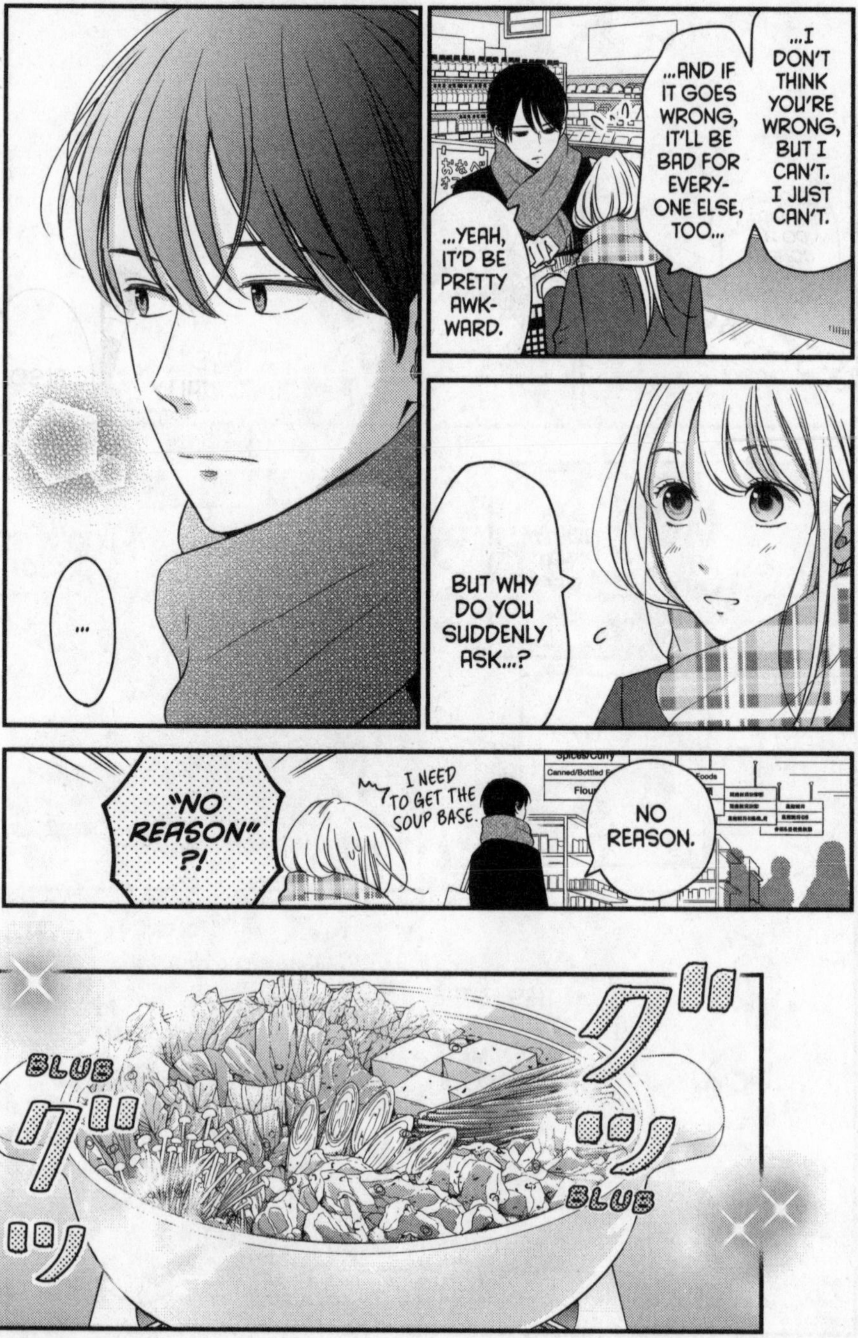
...I DON'T THINK YOU'RE WRONG, BUT I CAN'T. I JUST CAN'T.
...AND IF IT GOES WRONG, IT'LL BE BAD FOR EVERY-ONE ELSE, TOO...
...YEAH, IT'D BE PRETTY AWK-WARD.
BUT WHY DO YOU SUDDENLY ASK...?
...
NO REASON.
I NEED TO GET THE SOUP BASE.
"NO REASON"?!
BLUB
BLUB

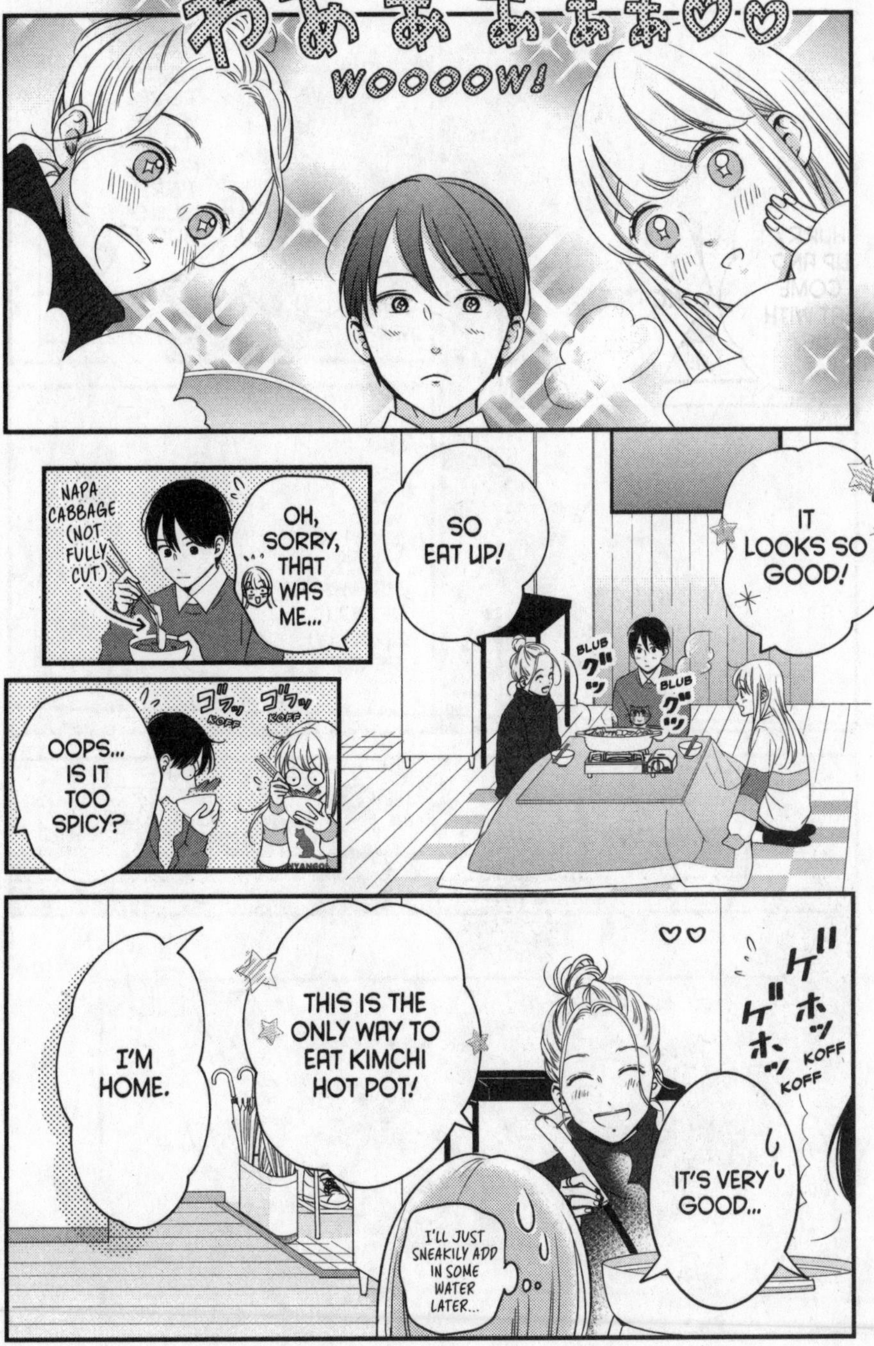
わぁぁぁぁぁ♡♡
WOOOOOW!
IT LOOKS SO GOOD!
SO EAT UP!
BLUB グツ
BLUB グツ
OH, SORRY, THAT WAS ME...
...
NAPA CABBAGE (NOT FULLY CUT)
ゴフッ KOFF
ゴフッ KOFF
OOPS... IS IT TOO SPICY?
ゲホッ ゲホッ KOFF KOFF
IT'S VERY GOOD...
I'LL JUST SNEAKILY ADD IN SOME WATER LATER...
THIS IS THE ONLY WAY TO EAT KIMCHI HOT POT!
I'M HOME.

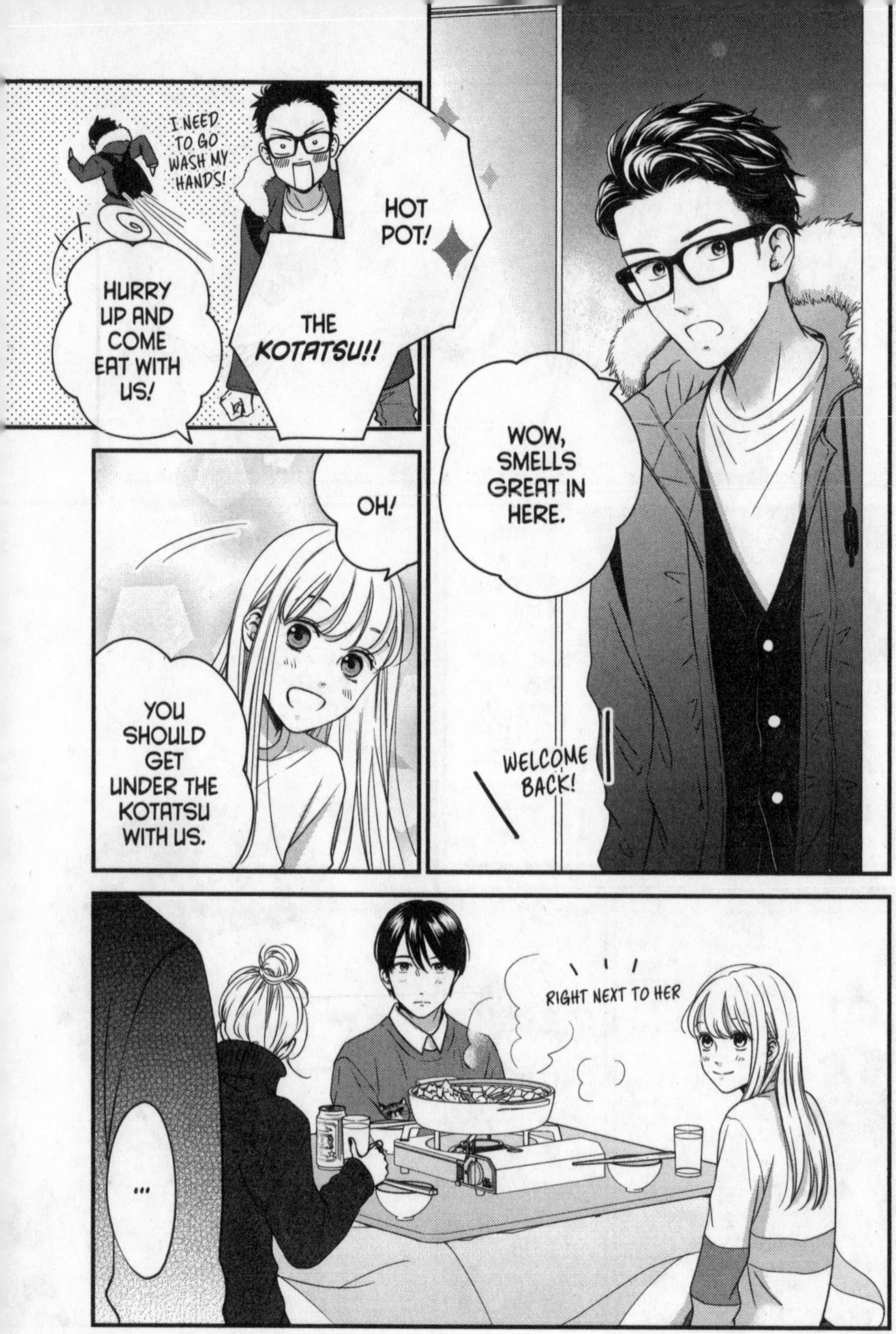
WOW, SMELLS GREAT IN HERE.
WELCOME BACK!
HOT POT!
THE KOTATSU!!
I NEED TO GO WASH MY HANDS!
HURRY UP AND COME EAT WITH US!
OH!
YOU SHOULD GET UNDER THE KOTATSU WITH US.
RIGHT NEXT TO HER
...

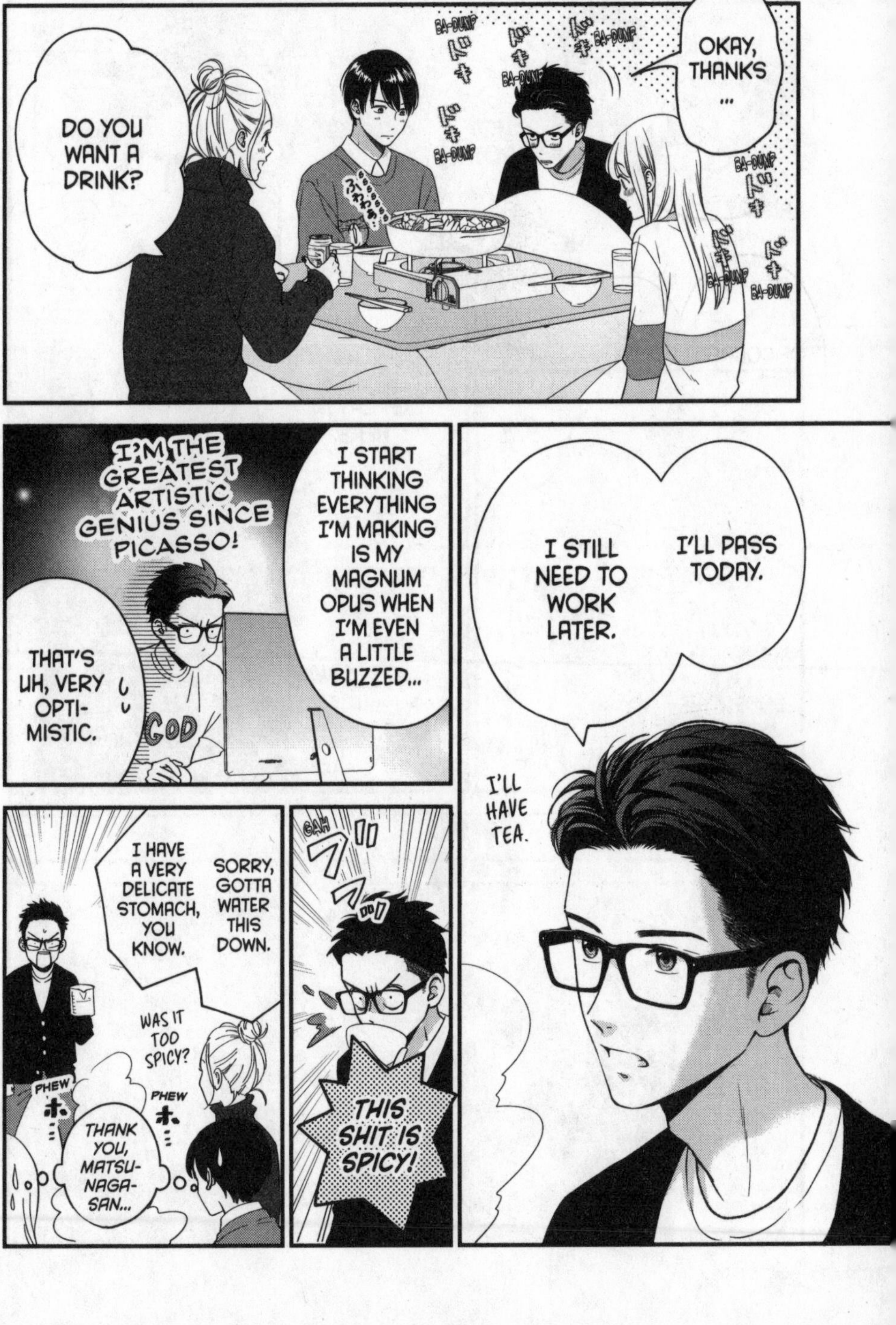
OKAY, THANKS ...
BA-DUMP
ドキ
BA-DUMP
ドキ
BA-DUMP
ドキ
BA-DUMP
ドキ
DO YOU WANT A DRINK?
I'LL PASS TODAY.
I STILL NEED TO WORK LATER.
I'LL HAVE TEA.
I START THINKING EVERYTHING I'M MAKING IS MY MAGNUM OPUS WHEN I'M EVEN A LITTLE BUZZED...
I'M THE GREATEST ARTISTIC GENIUS SINCE PICASSO!
THAT'S UH, VERY OPTI-MISTIC.
GOD
GAH
THIS SHIT IS SPICY!
SORRY, GOTTA WATER THIS DOWN.
I HAVE A VERY DELICATE STOMACH, YOU KNOW.
WAS IT TOO SPICY?
PHEW
ホ
PHEW
ホ
THANK YOU, MATSU-NAGA-SAN...

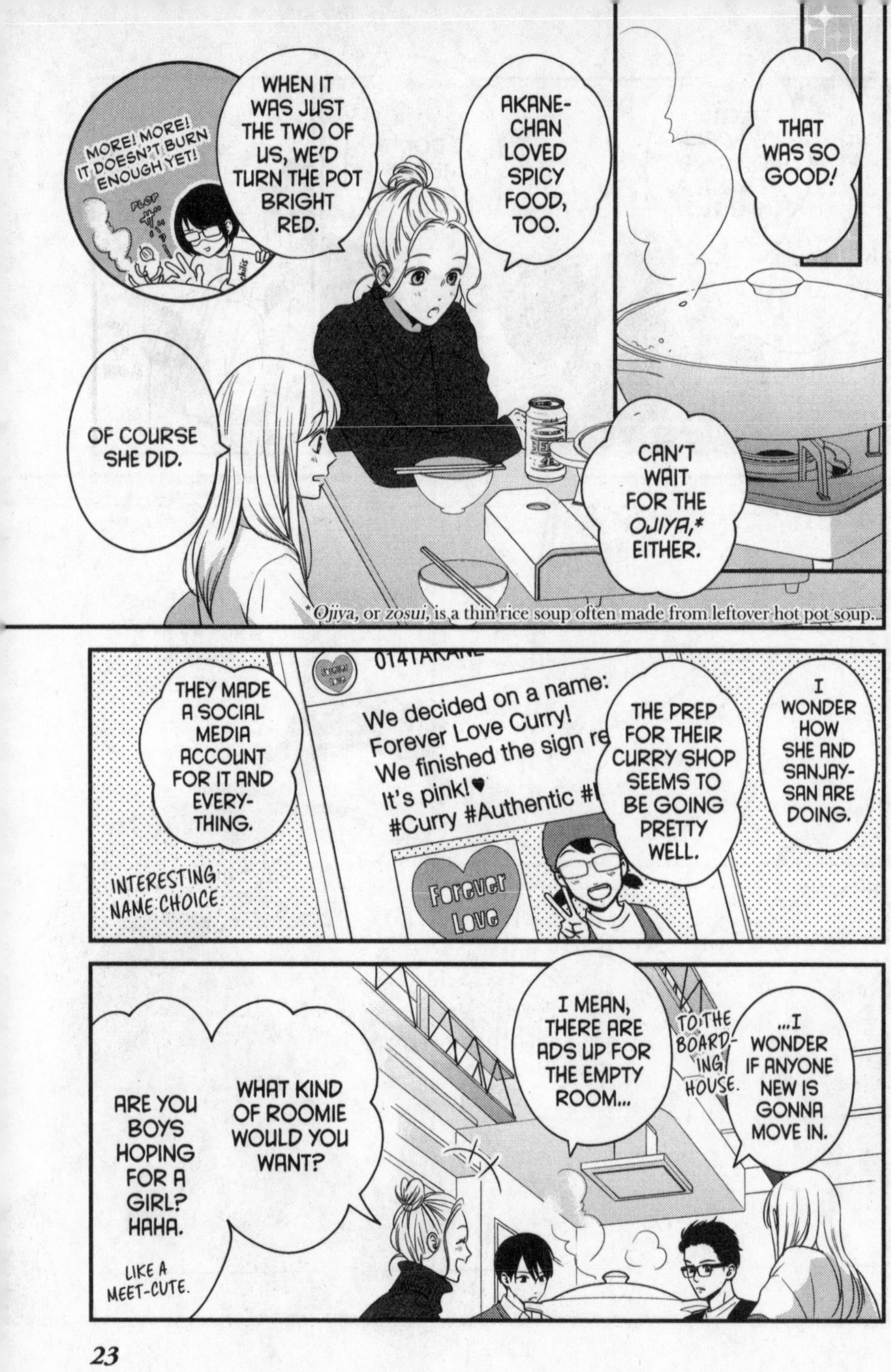
THAT WAS SO GOOD!
CAN'T WAIT FOR THE *OJIYA,** EITHER.
AKANE-CHAN LOVED SPICY FOOD, TOO.
WHEN IT WAS JUST THE TWO OF US, WE'D TURN THE POT BRIGHT RED.
MORE! MORE! IT DOESN'T BURN ENOUGH YET!
PLOP
OF COURSE SHE DID.
I WONDER HOW SHE AND SANJAY-SAN ARE DOING.
THE PREP FOR THEIR CURRY SHOP SEEMS TO BE GOING PRETTY WELL.
0141AKANE
We decided on a name:
Forever Love Curry!
We finished the sign re
It's pink!♥
#Curry #Authentic #
Forever Love
THEY MADE A SOCIAL MEDIA ACCOUNT FOR IT AND EVERY-THING.
INTERESTING NAME CHOICE.
...I WONDER IF ANYONE NEW IS GONNA MOVE IN.
TO THE BOARD-ING HOUSE.
I MEAN, THERE ARE ADS UP FOR THE EMPTY ROOM...
WHAT KIND OF ROOMIE WOULD YOU WANT?
ARE YOU BOYS HOPING FOR A GIRL? HAHA.
LIKE A MEET-CUTE.

**Ojiya*, or *zosui*, is a thin rice soup often made from leftover hot pot soup.

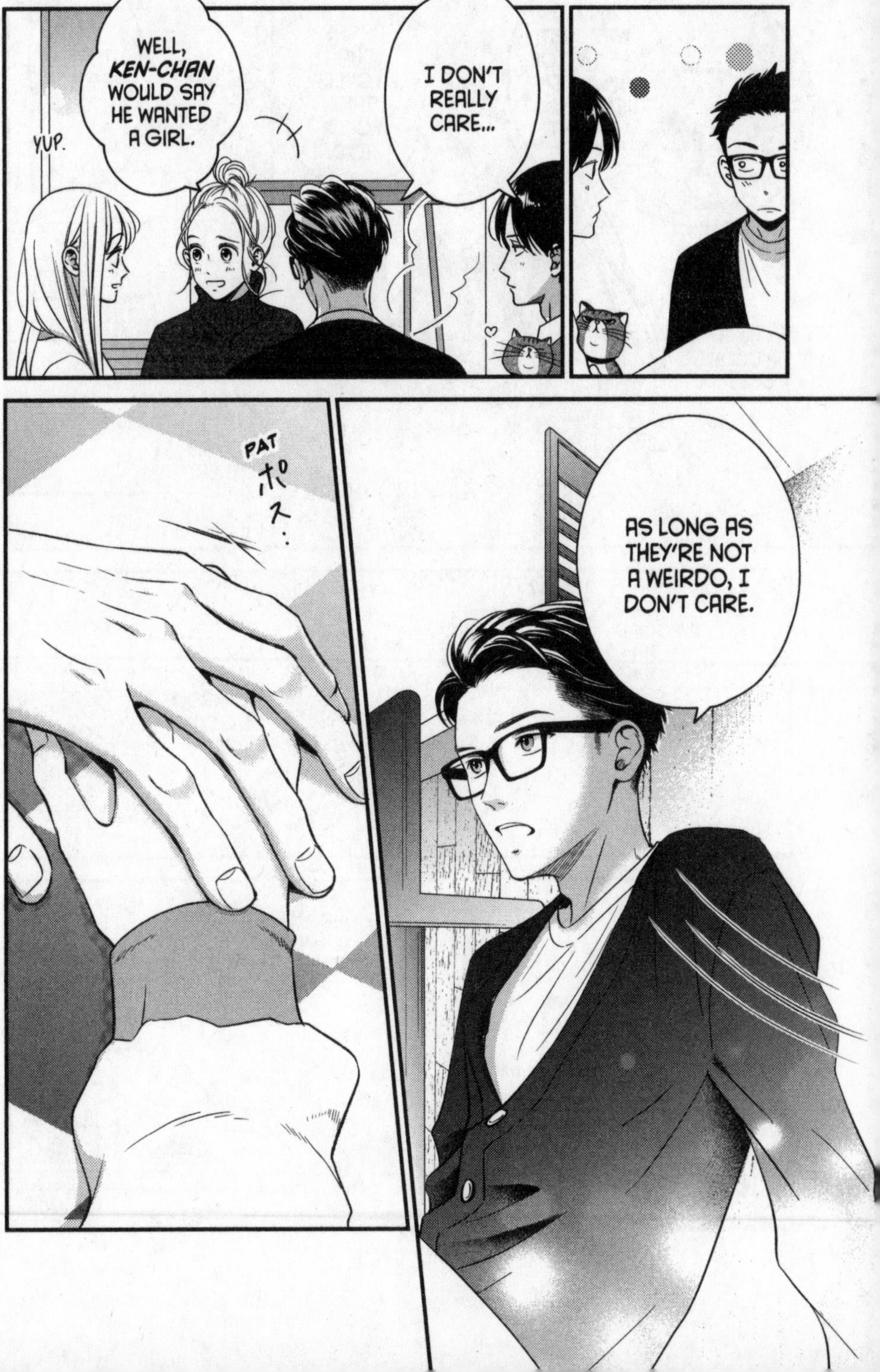
I DON'T REALLY CARE...
WELL, KEN-CHAN WOULD SAY HE WANTED A GIRL.
YUP.
AS LONG AS THEY'RE NOT A WEIRDO, I DON'T CARE.
PAT
ポス..

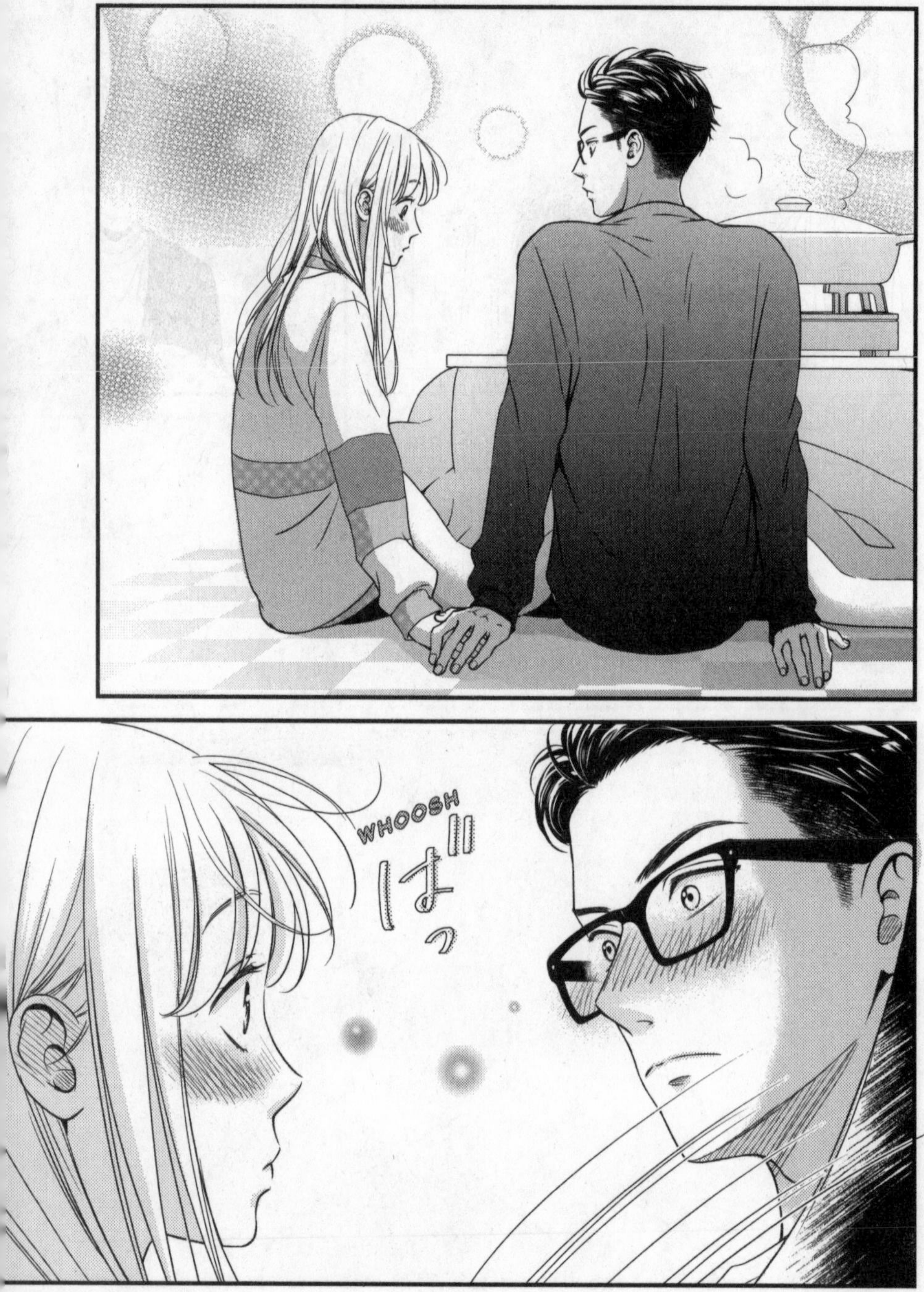
WHOOSH
ばっ

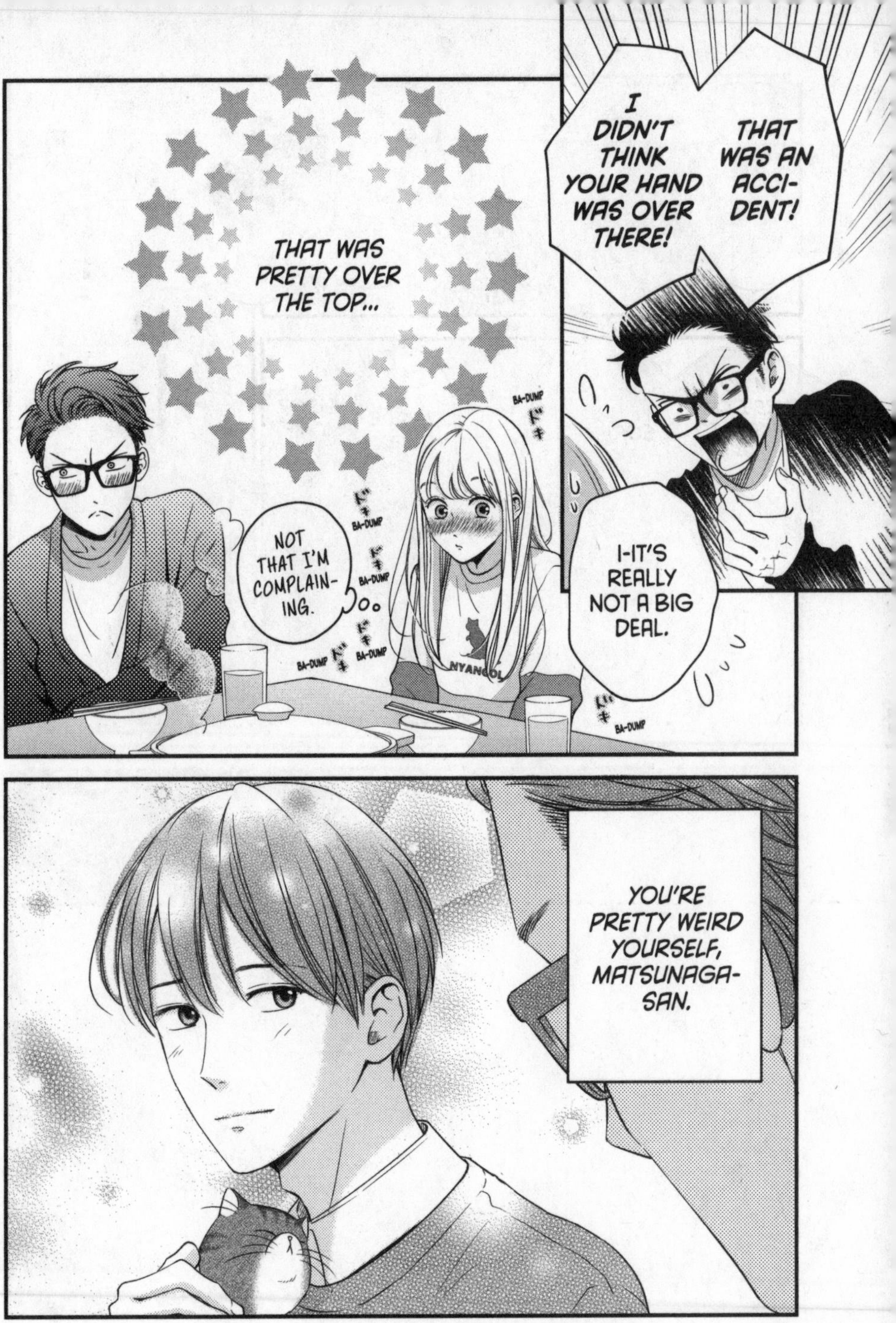
THAT WAS AN ACCIDENT!
I DIDN'T THINK YOUR HAND WAS OVER THERE!
I-IT'S REALLY NOT A BIG DEAL.
THAT WAS PRETTY OVER THE TOP...
BA-DUMP
BA-DUMP
BA-DUMP
BA-DUMP
BA-DUMP
BA-DUMP
NOT THAT I'M COMPLAINING.
YOU'RE PRETTY WEIRD YOURSELF, MATSUNAGA-SAN.

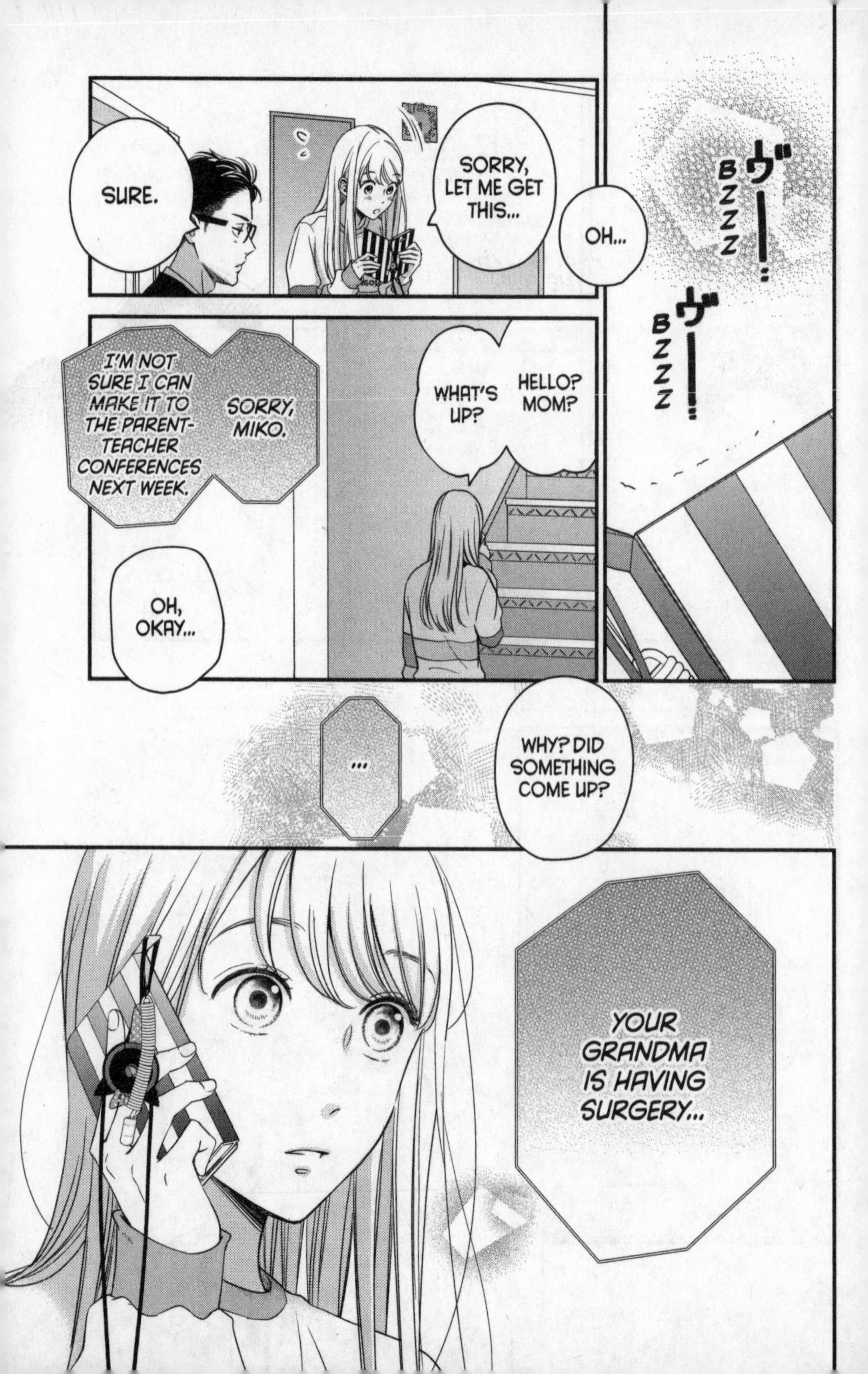
ヴー!!
BZZZ
ヴー!!
BZZZ
OH...
SORRY, LET ME GET THIS...
SURE.
HELLO? MOM?
WHAT'S UP?
SORRY, MIKO.
I'M NOT SURE I CAN MAKE IT TO THE PARENT-TEACHER CONFERENCES NEXT WEEK.
OH, OKAY...
WHY? DID SOMETHING COME UP?
...
YOUR GRANDMA IS HAVING SURGERY...

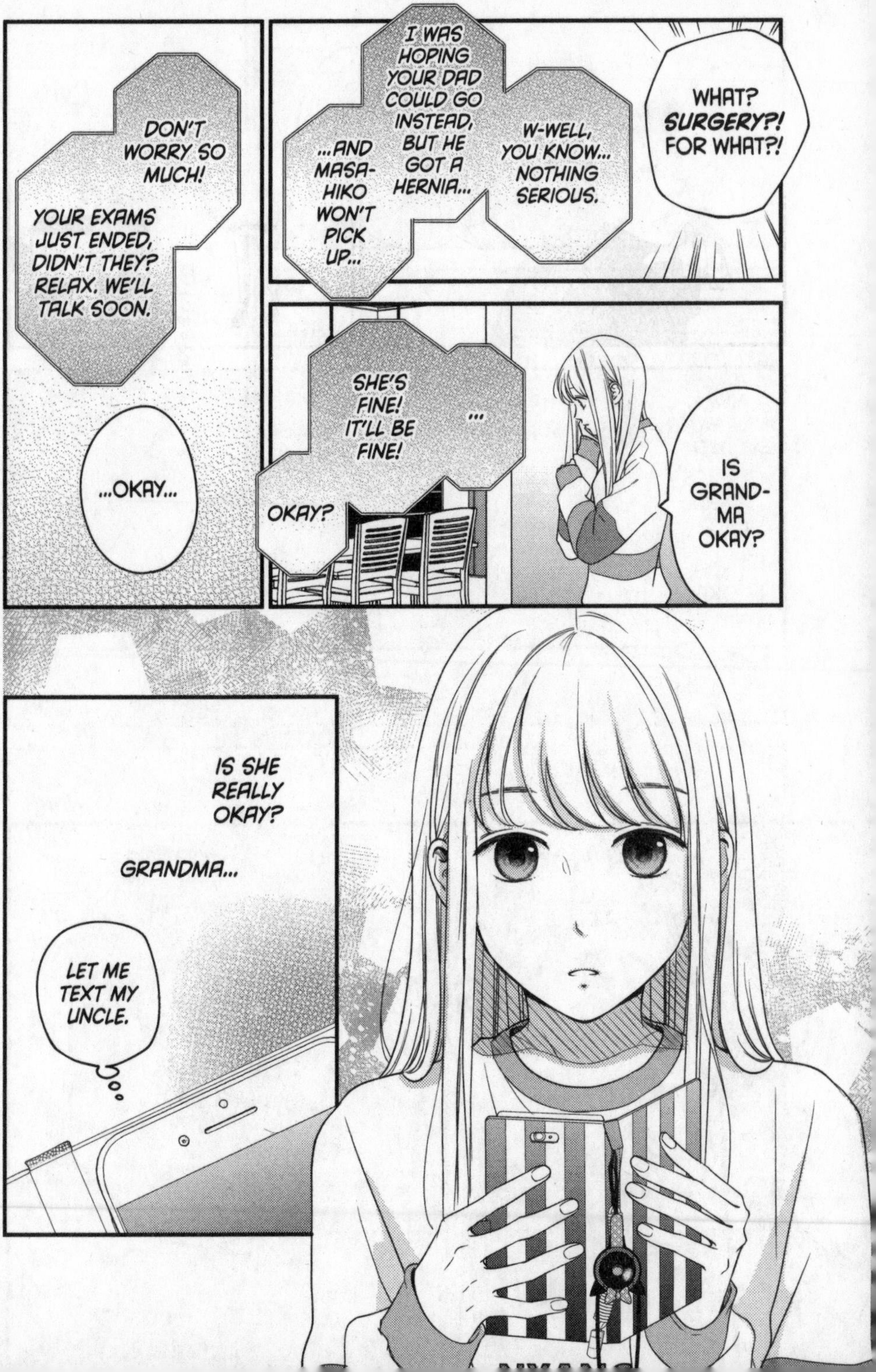
WHAT? SURGERY?! FOR WHAT?!
W-WELL, YOU KNOW... NOTHING SERIOUS.
I WAS HOPING YOUR DAD COULD GO INSTEAD, BUT HE GOT A HERNIA...
...AND MASA-HIKO WON'T PICK UP...
IS GRAND-MA OKAY?
...
SHE'S FINE! IT'LL BE FINE!
OKAY?
DON'T WORRY SO MUCH!
YOUR EXAMS JUST ENDED, DIDN'T THEY? RELAX. WE'LL TALK SOON.
...OKAY...
IS SHE REALLY OKAY?
GRANDMA...
LET ME TEXT MY UNCLE.

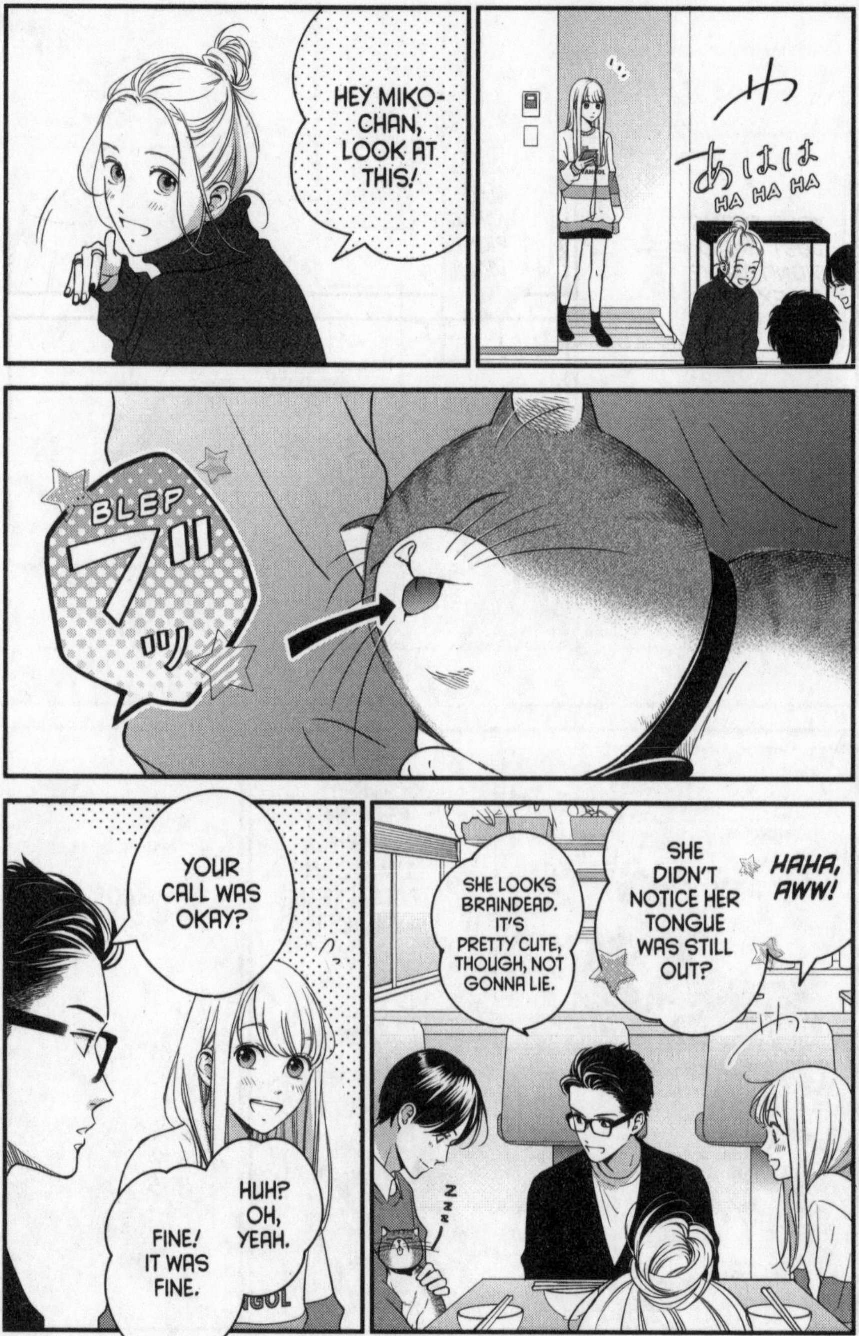
あはは
HA HA HA
HEY MIKO-CHAN, LOOK AT THIS!
BLEP
HAHA, AWW!
SHE DIDN'T NOTICE HER TONGUE WAS STILL OUT?
SHE LOOKS BRAINDEAD. IT'S PRETTY CUTE, THOUGH, NOT GONNA LIE.
YOUR CALL WAS OKAY?
HUH? OH, YEAH.
FINE! IT WAS FINE.

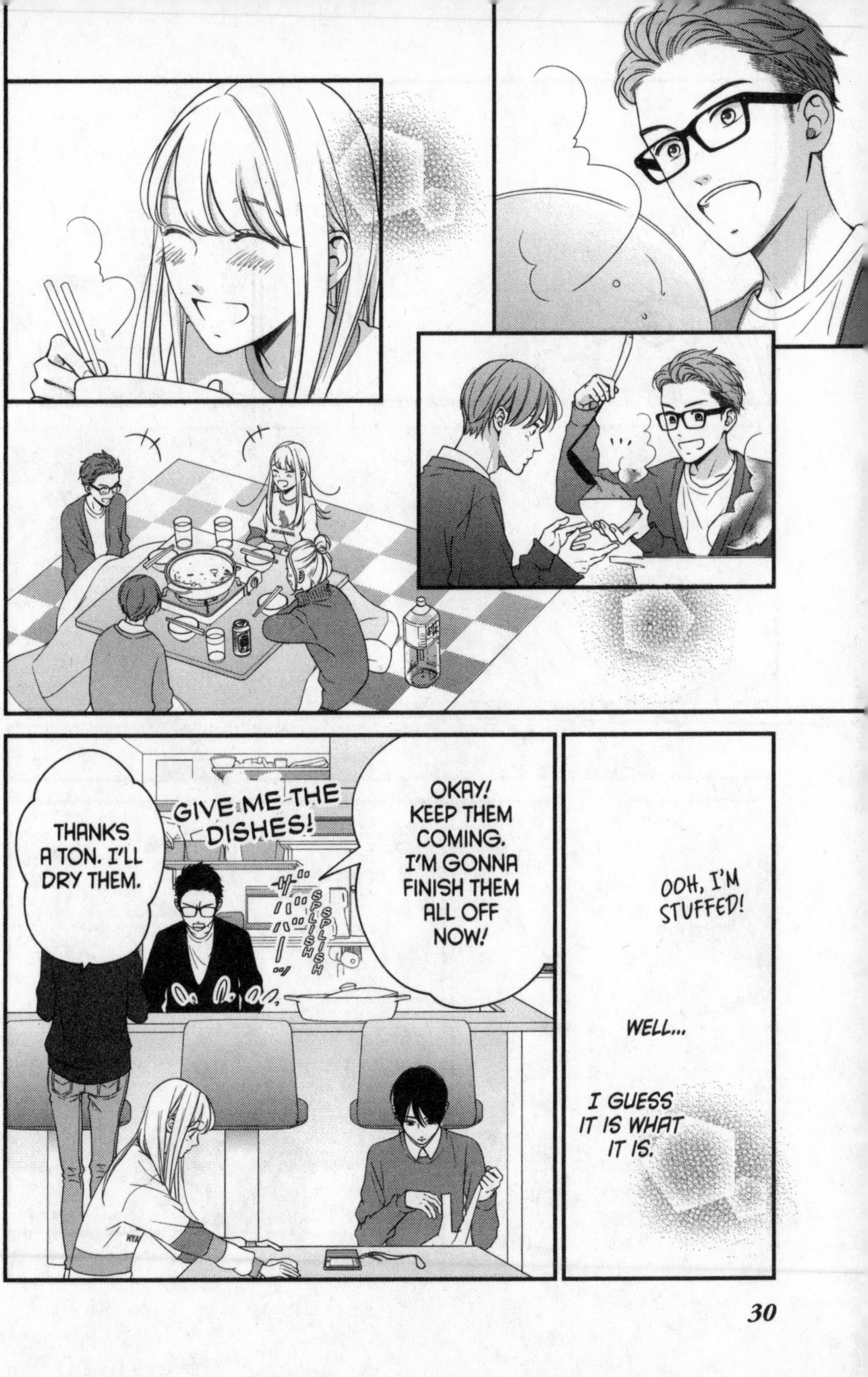
OOH, I'M STUFFED!
WELL...
I GUESS IT IS WHAT IT IS.
OKAY! KEEP THEM COMING. I'M GONNA FINISH THEM ALL OFF NOW!
GIVE ME THE DISHES!
SPLISH SPLISH
THANKS A TON. I'LL DRY THEM.

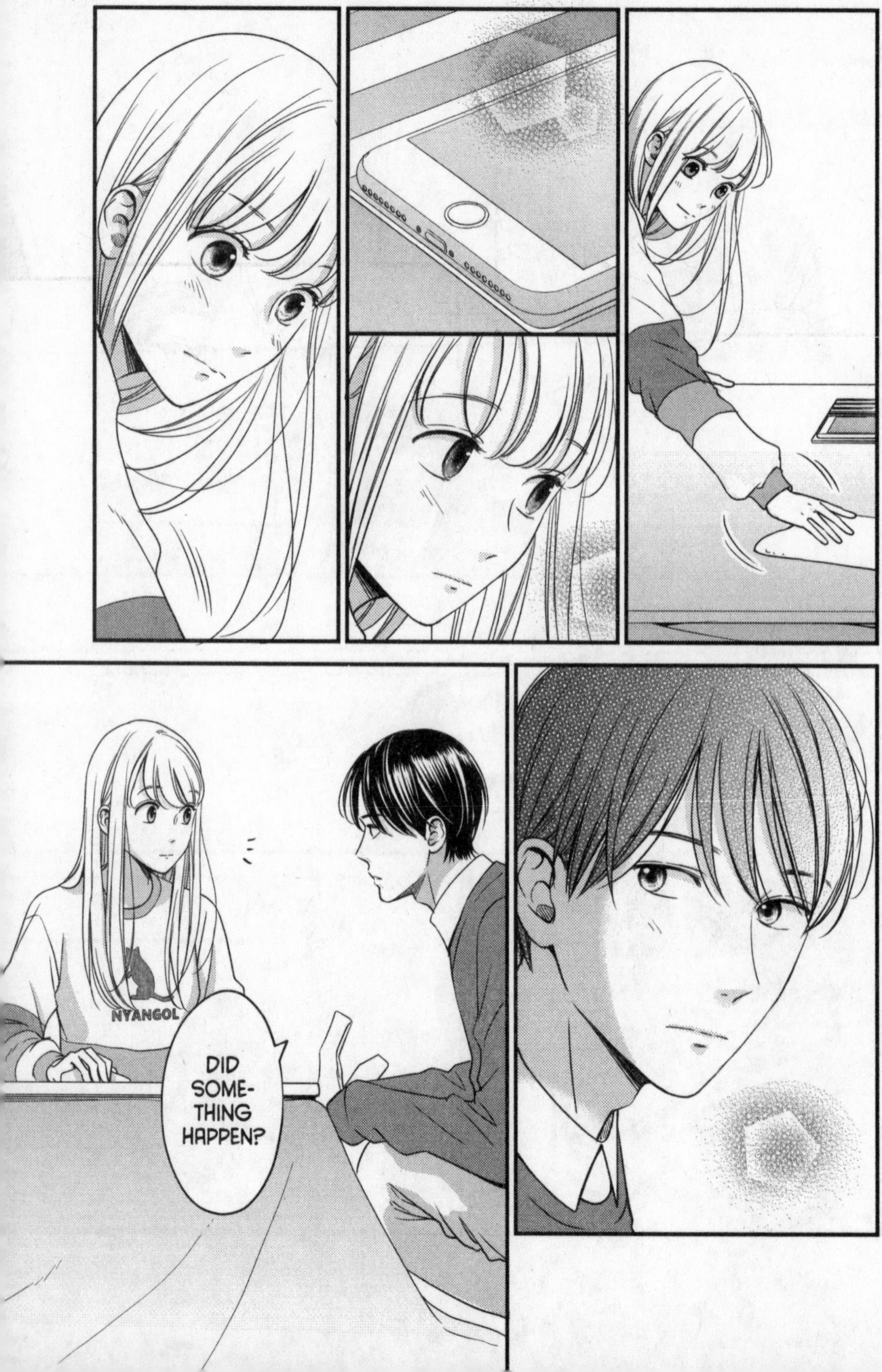
NYANGOL
DID SOME-THING HAPPEN?

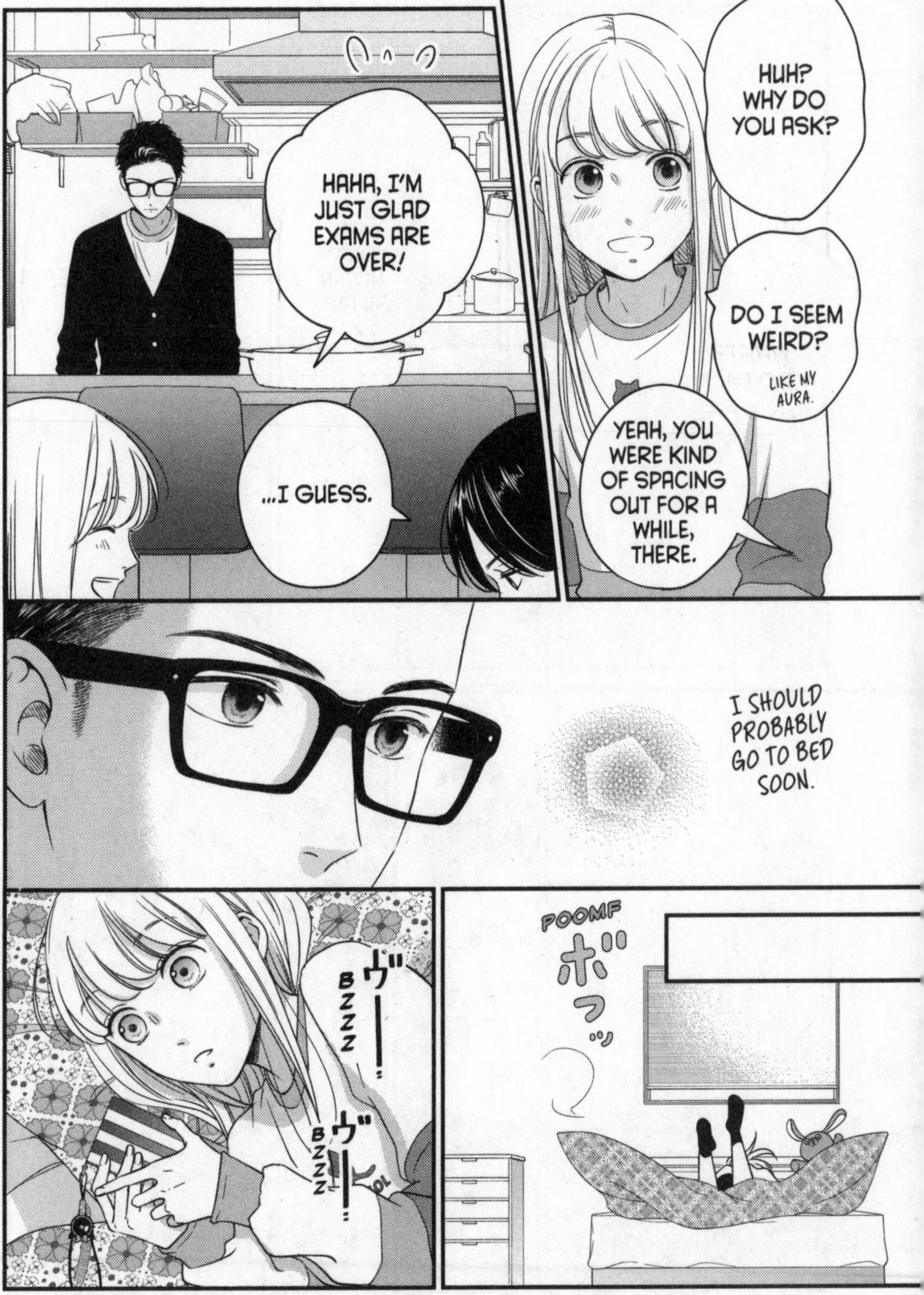
HUH? WHY DO YOU ASK?
DO I SEEM WEIRD?
LIKE MY AURA.
YEAH, YOU WERE KIND OF SPACING OUT FOR A WHILE, THERE.
HAHA, I'M JUST GLAD EXAMS ARE OVER!
...I GUESS.
I SHOULD PROBABLY GO TO BED SOON.
POOMF
ボフッ
BZZZ
ヴー!!
BZZZ
ヴー!!

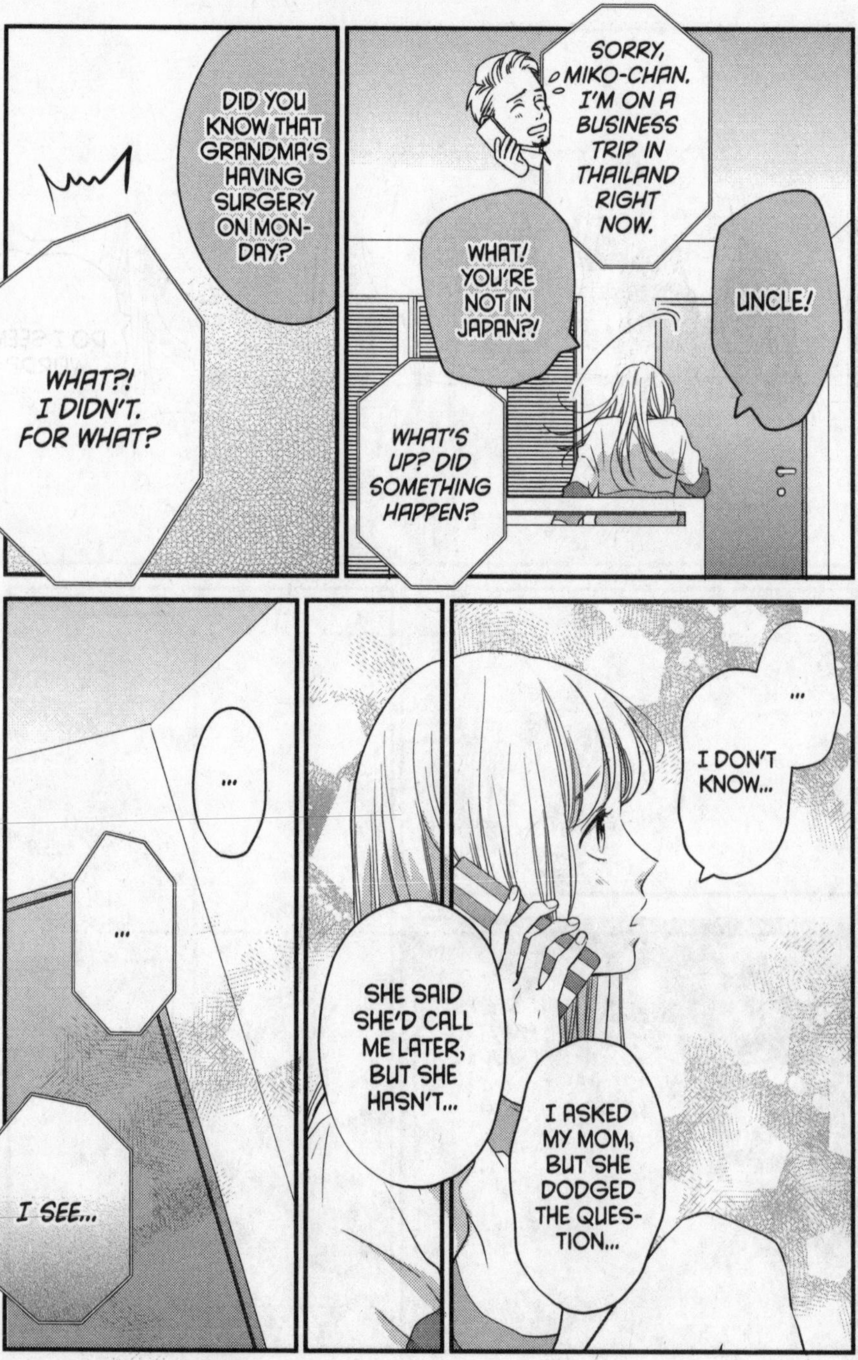
UNCLE!
SORRY, MIKO-CHAN. I'M ON A BUSINESS TRIP IN THAILAND RIGHT NOW.
WHAT! YOU'RE NOT IN JAPAN?!
WHAT'S UP? DID SOMETHING HAPPEN?
DID YOU KNOW THAT GRANDMA'S HAVING SURGERY ON MON-DAY?
WHAT?! I DIDN'T. FOR WHAT?
...
I DON'T KNOW...
I ASKED MY MOM, BUT SHE DODGED THE QUES-TION...
SHE SAID SHE'D CALL ME LATER, BUT SHE HASN'T...
...
...
I SEE...

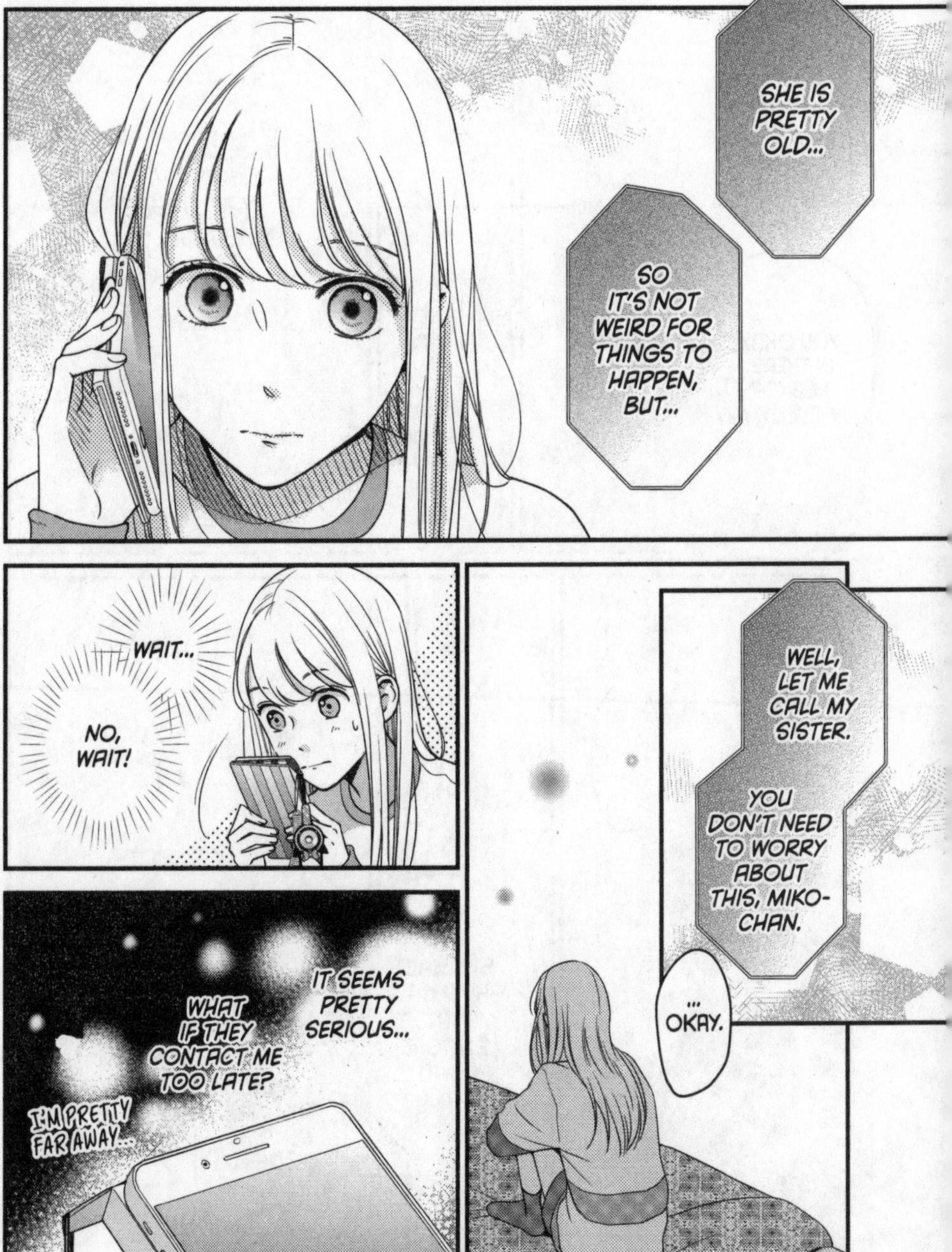
SHE IS PRETTY OLD...
SO IT'S NOT WEIRD FOR THINGS TO HAPPEN, BUT...
WELL, LET ME CALL MY SISTER.
YOU DON'T NEED TO WORRY ABOUT THIS, MIKO-CHAN.
...OKAY.
WAIT...
NO, WAIT!
IT SEEMS PRETTY SERIOUS...
WHAT IF THEY CONTACT ME TOO LATE?
I'M PRETTY FAR AWAY...

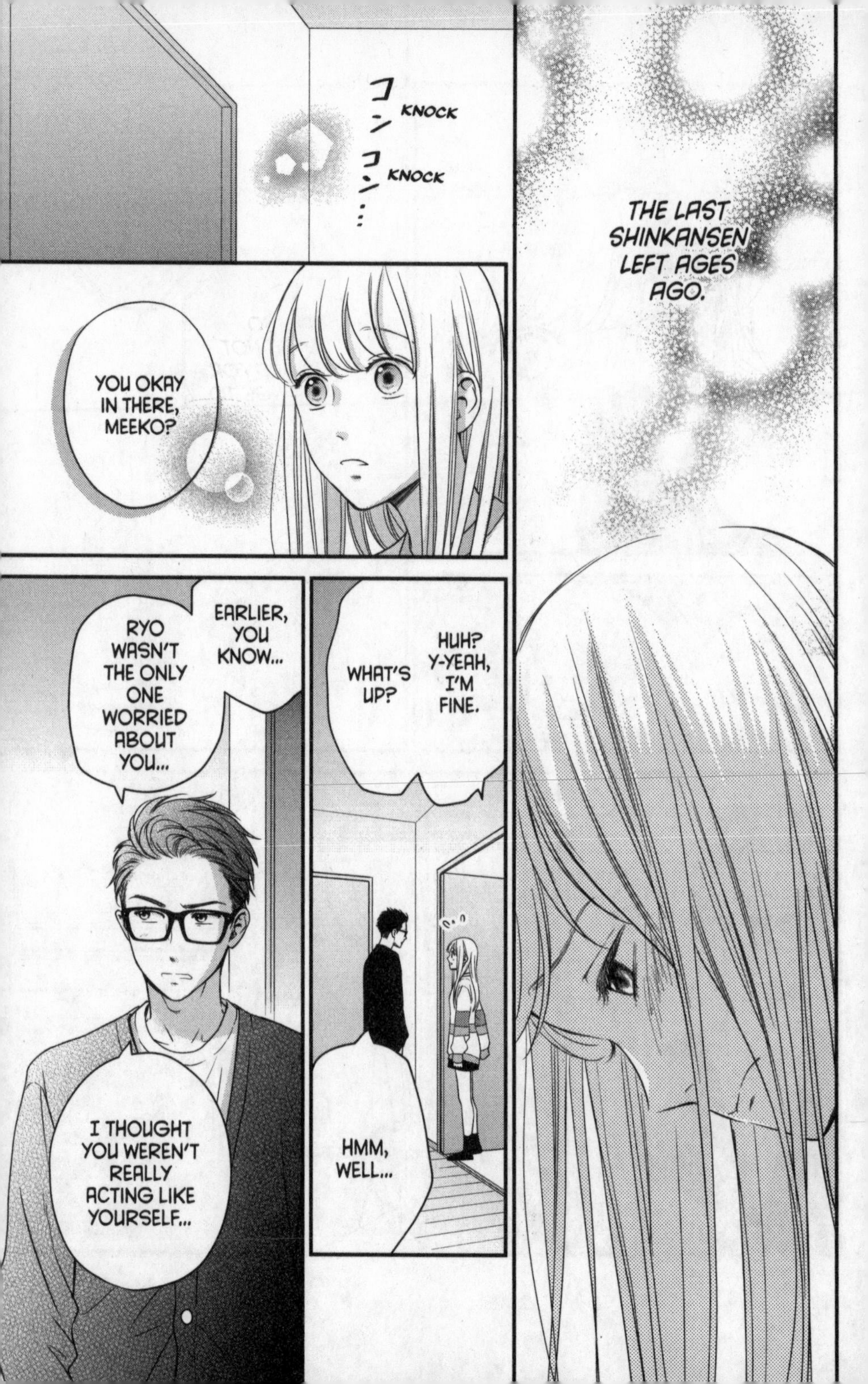
THE LAST SHINKANSEN LEFT AGES AGO.
コン KNOCK
コン… KNOCK
YOU OKAY IN THERE, MEEKO?
HUH? Y-YEAH, I'M FINE.
WHAT'S UP?
HMM, WELL...
EARLIER, YOU KNOW...
RYO WASN'T THE ONLY ONE WORRIED ABOUT YOU...
I THOUGHT YOU WEREN'T REALLY ACTING LIKE YOURSELF...

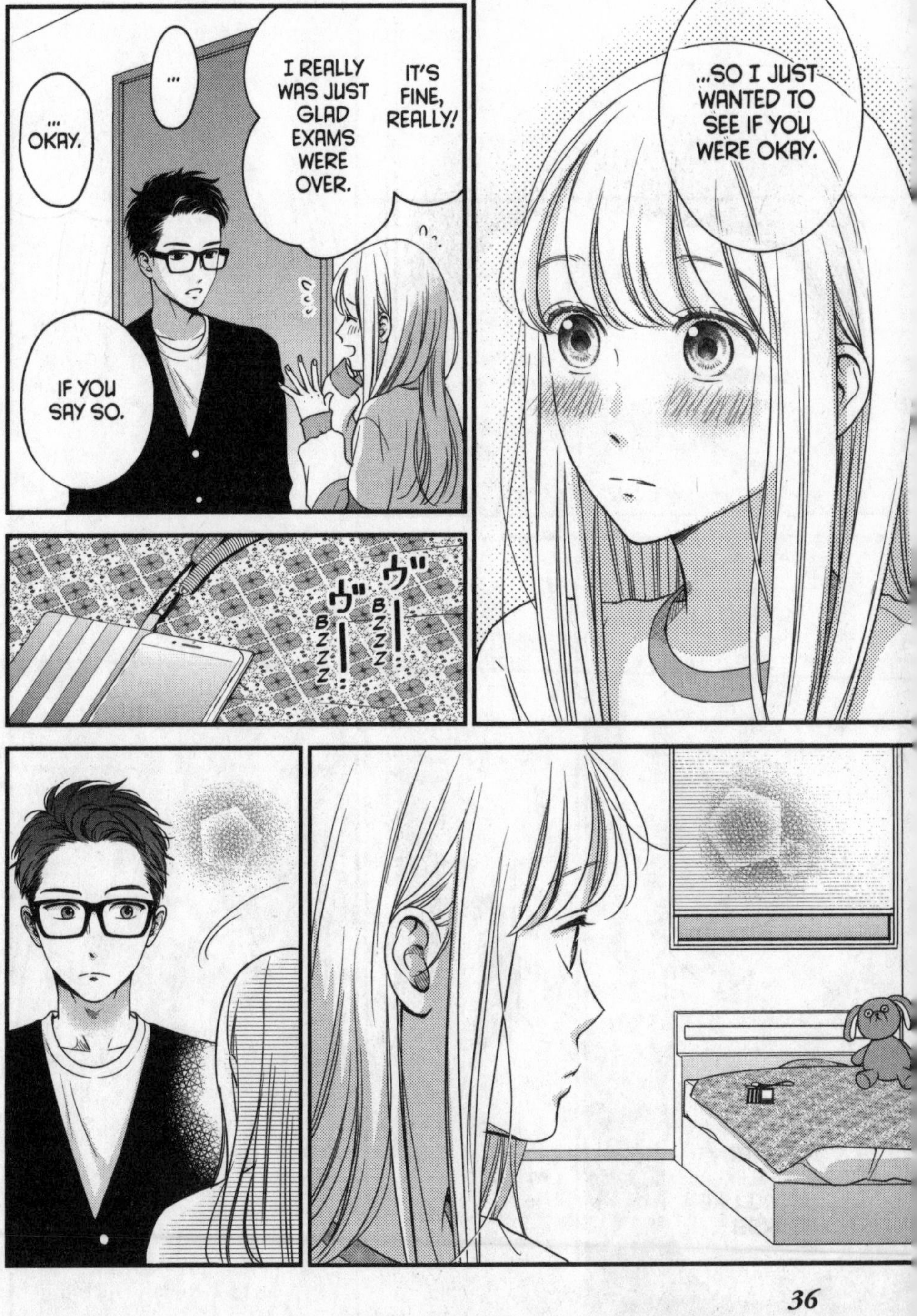
...SO I JUST WANTED TO SEE IF YOU WERE OKAY.
IT'S FINE, REALLY!
I REALLY WAS JUST GLAD EXAMS WERE OVER.
...
... OKAY.
IF YOU SAY SO.
ヴー
BZZZ
ヴー
BZZZ

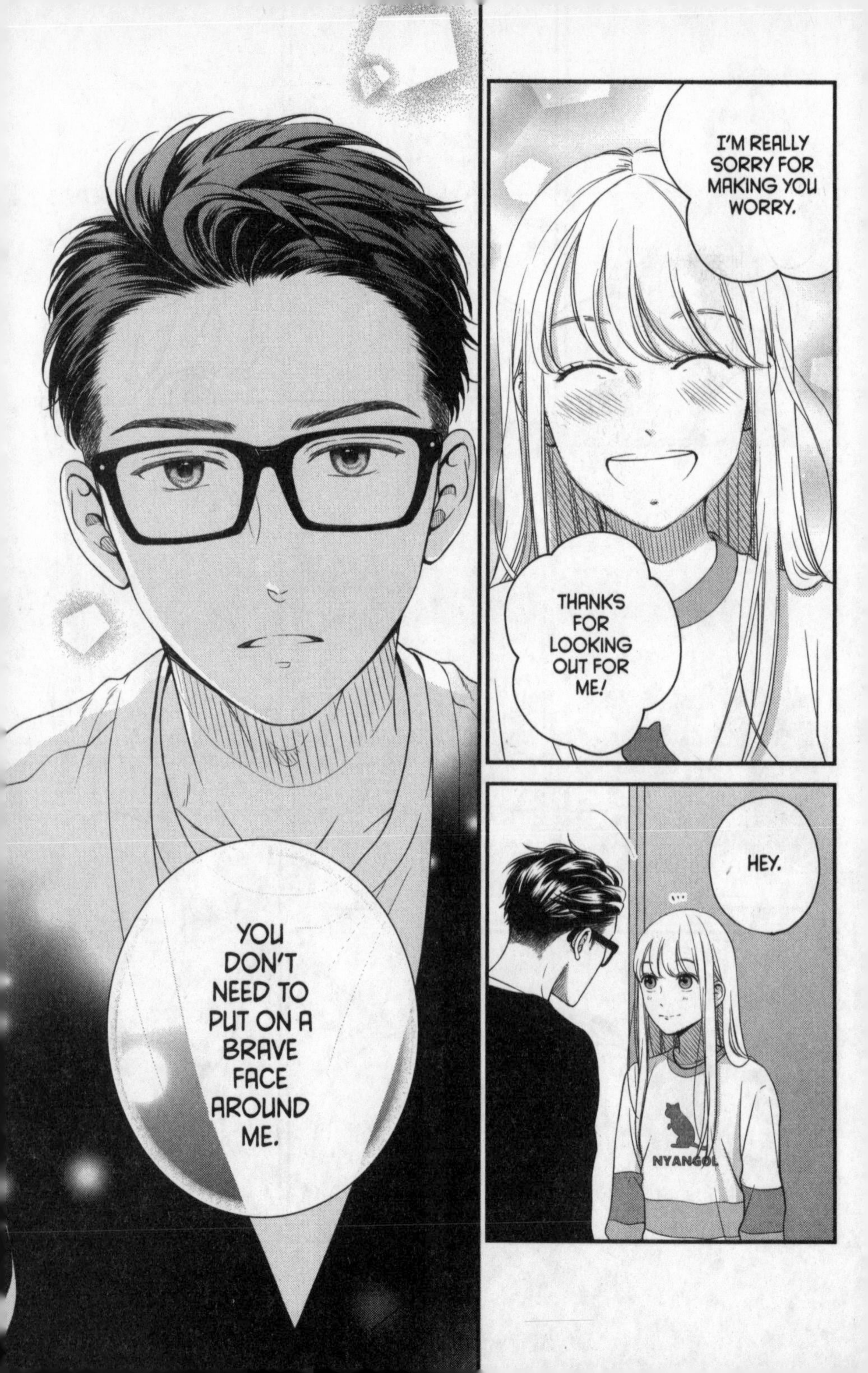
I'M REALLY SORRY FOR MAKING YOU WORRY.
THANKS FOR LOOKING OUT FOR ME!
HEY.
NYANGOL
YOU DON'T NEED TO PUT ON A BRAVE FACE AROUND ME.

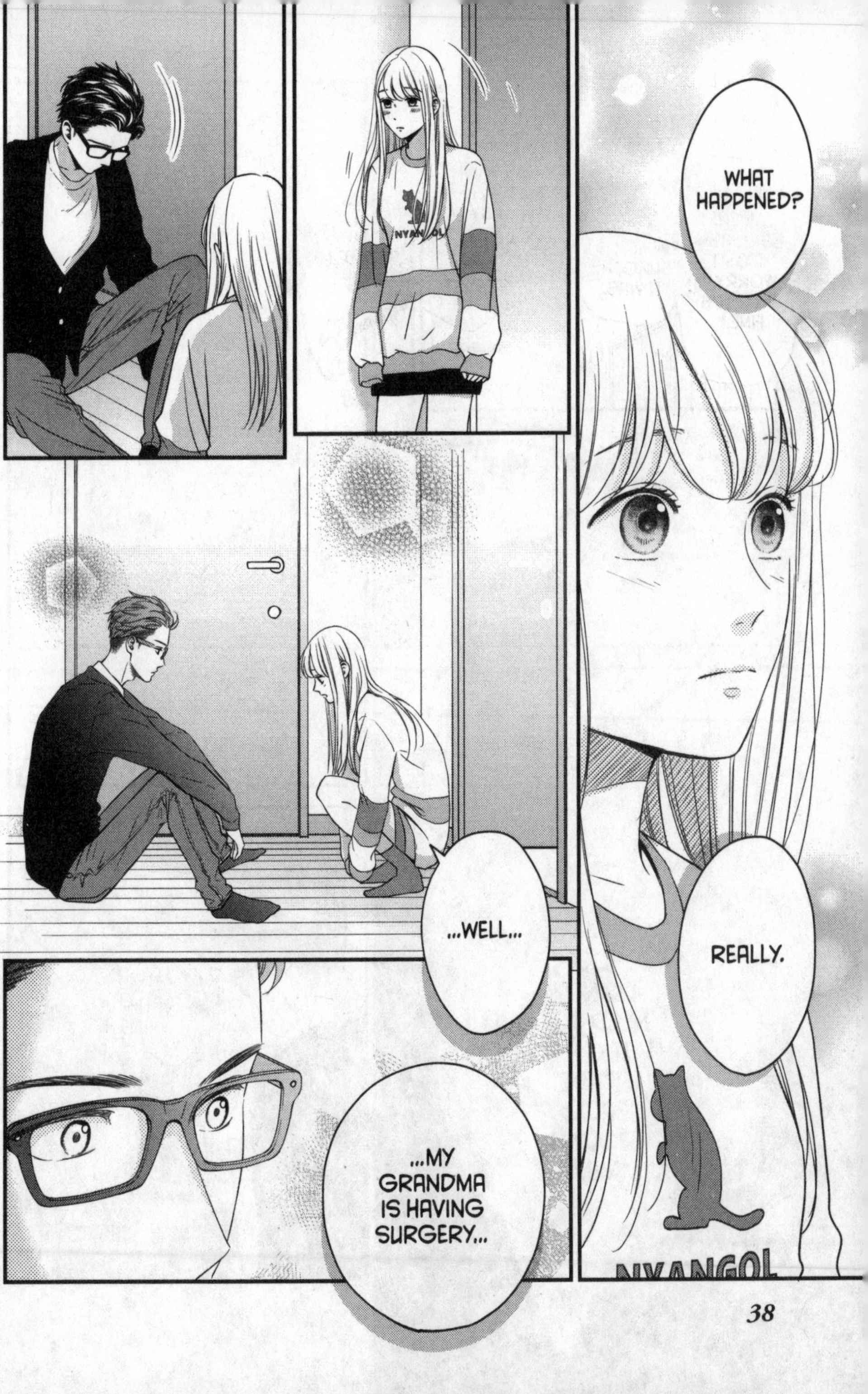
WHAT HAPPENED?
REALLY.
NYANGOL
...WELL...
...MY GRANDMA IS HAVING SURGERY...

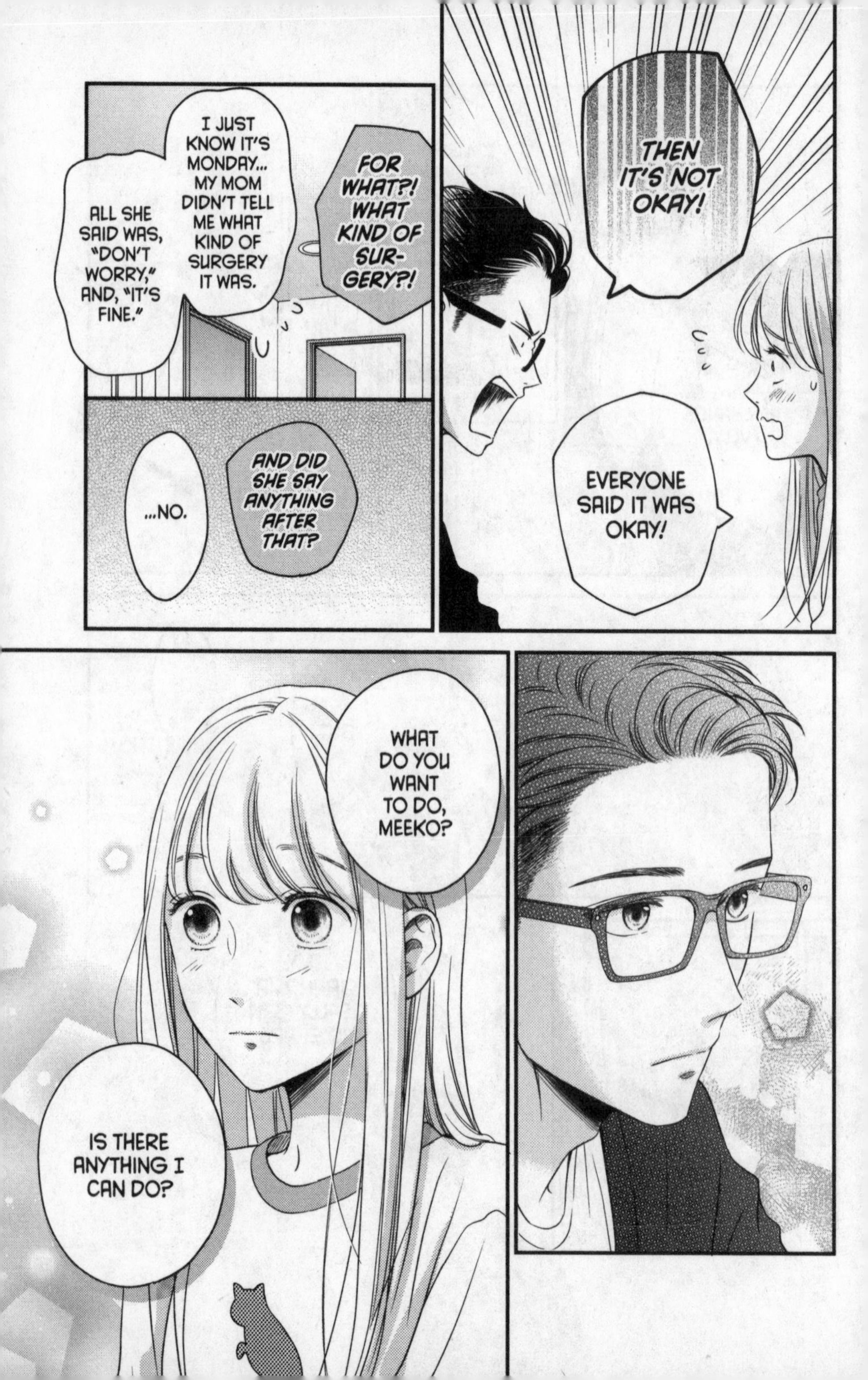
THEN IT'S NOT OKAY!
EVERYONE SAID IT WAS OKAY!
FOR WHAT?! WHAT KIND OF SUR-GERY?!
I JUST KNOW IT'S MONDAY... MY MOM DIDN'T TELL ME WHAT KIND OF SURGERY IT WAS.
ALL SHE SAID WAS, "DON'T WORRY," AND, "IT'S FINE."
AND DID SHE SAY ANYTHING AFTER THAT?
...NO.
WHAT DO YOU WANT TO DO, MEEKO?
IS THERE ANYTHING I CAN DO?

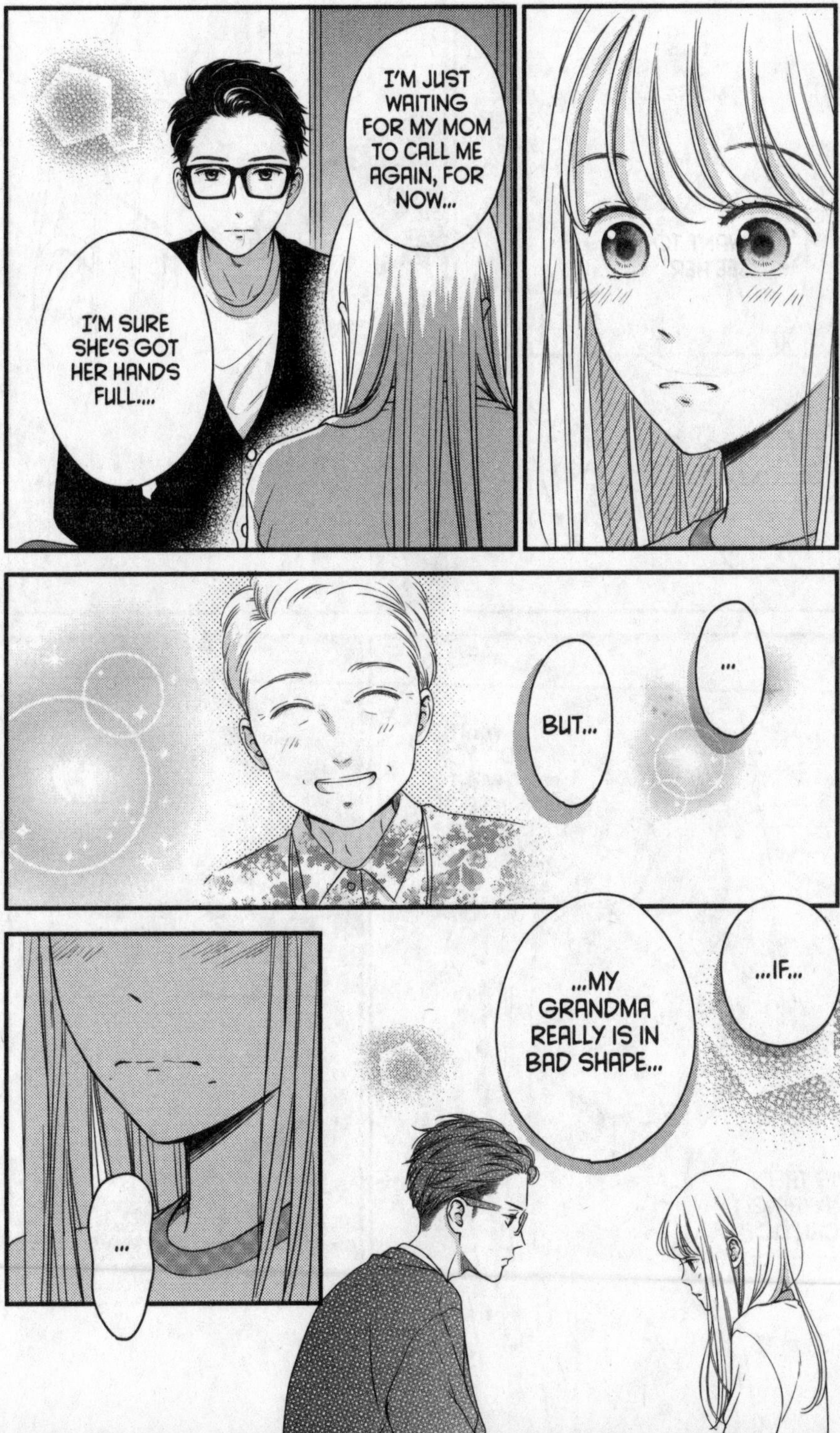
I'M JUST WAITING FOR MY MOM TO CALL ME AGAIN, FOR NOW...
I'M SURE SHE'S GOT HER HANDS FULL....
...
BUT...
...IF...
...MY GRANDMA REALLY IS IN BAD SHAPE...
...

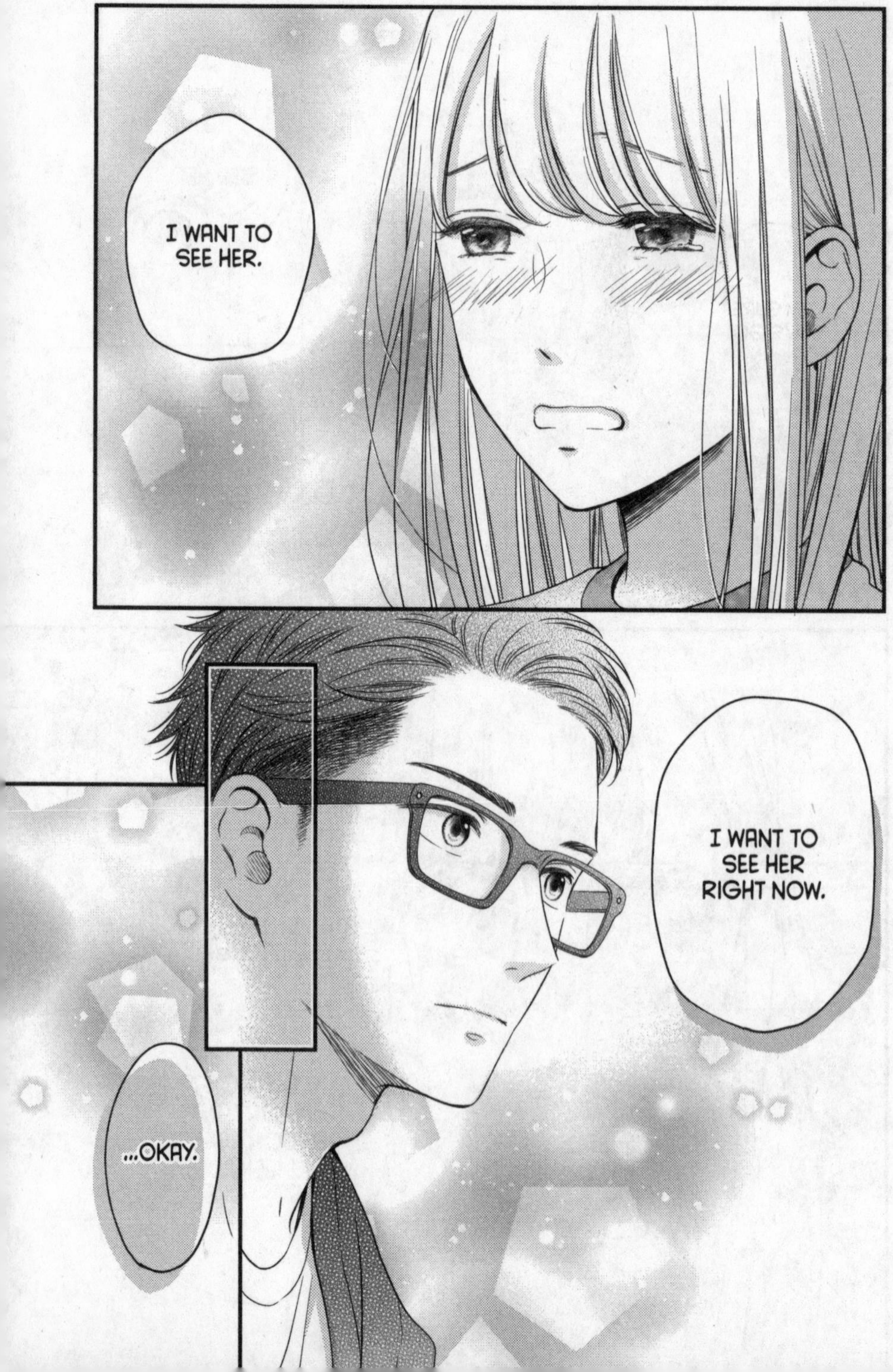
I WANT TO SEE HER.
I WANT TO SEE HER RIGHT NOW.
...OKAY.

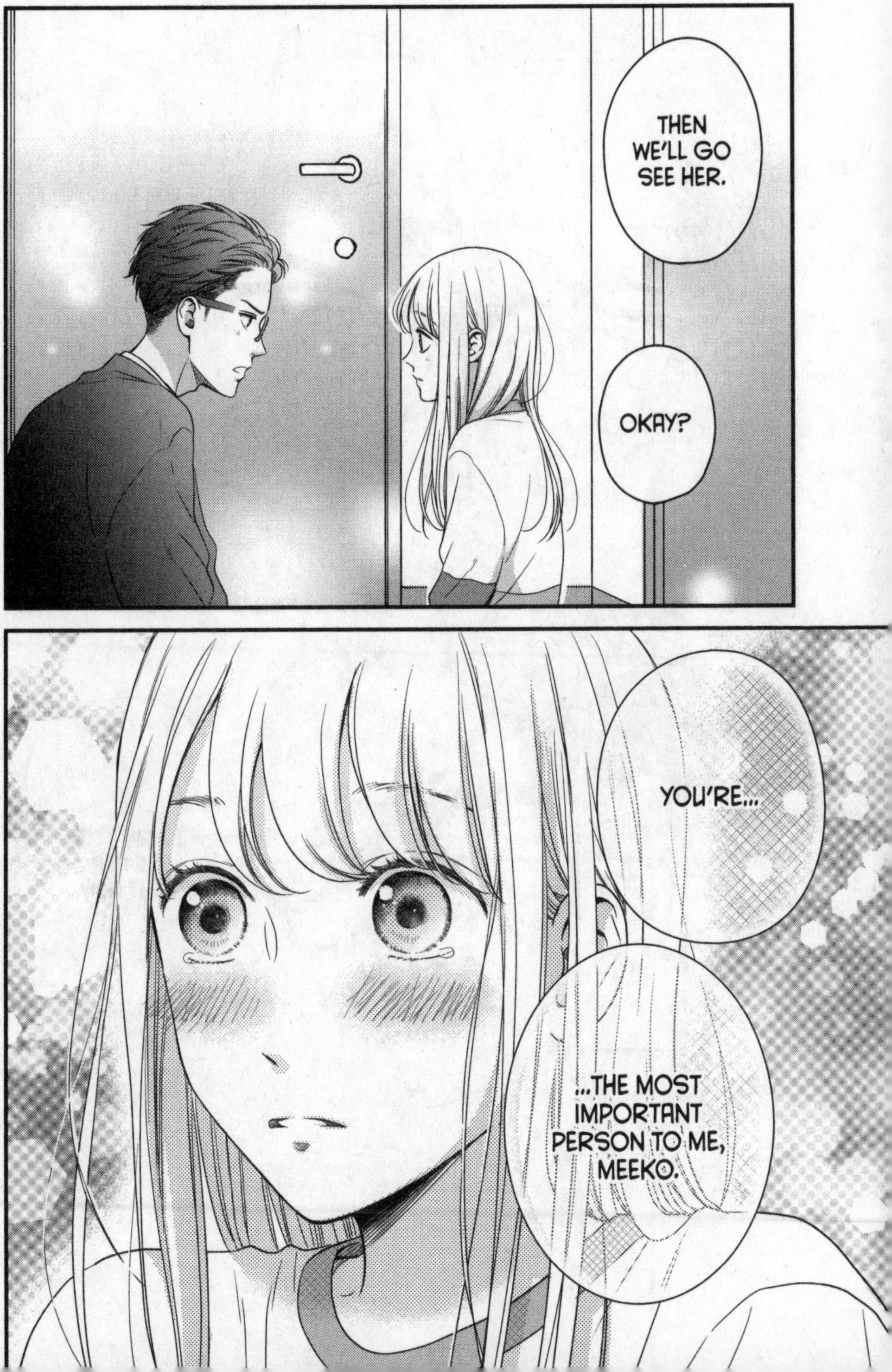
THEN WE'LL GO SEE HER.
OKAY?
YOU'RE...
...THE MOST IMPORTANT PERSON TO ME, MEEKO.

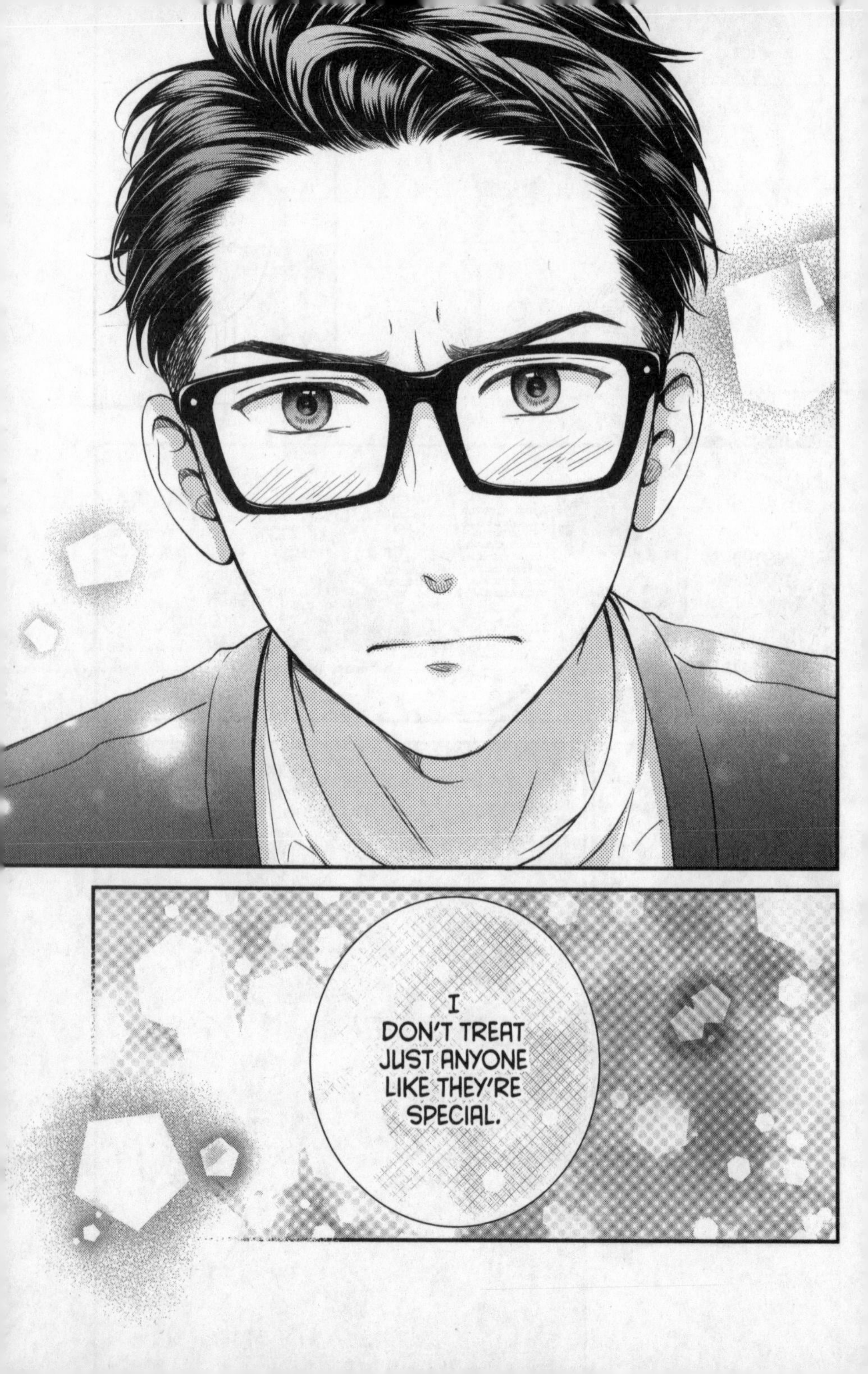
I DON'T TREAT JUST ANYONE LIKE THEY'RE SPECIAL.

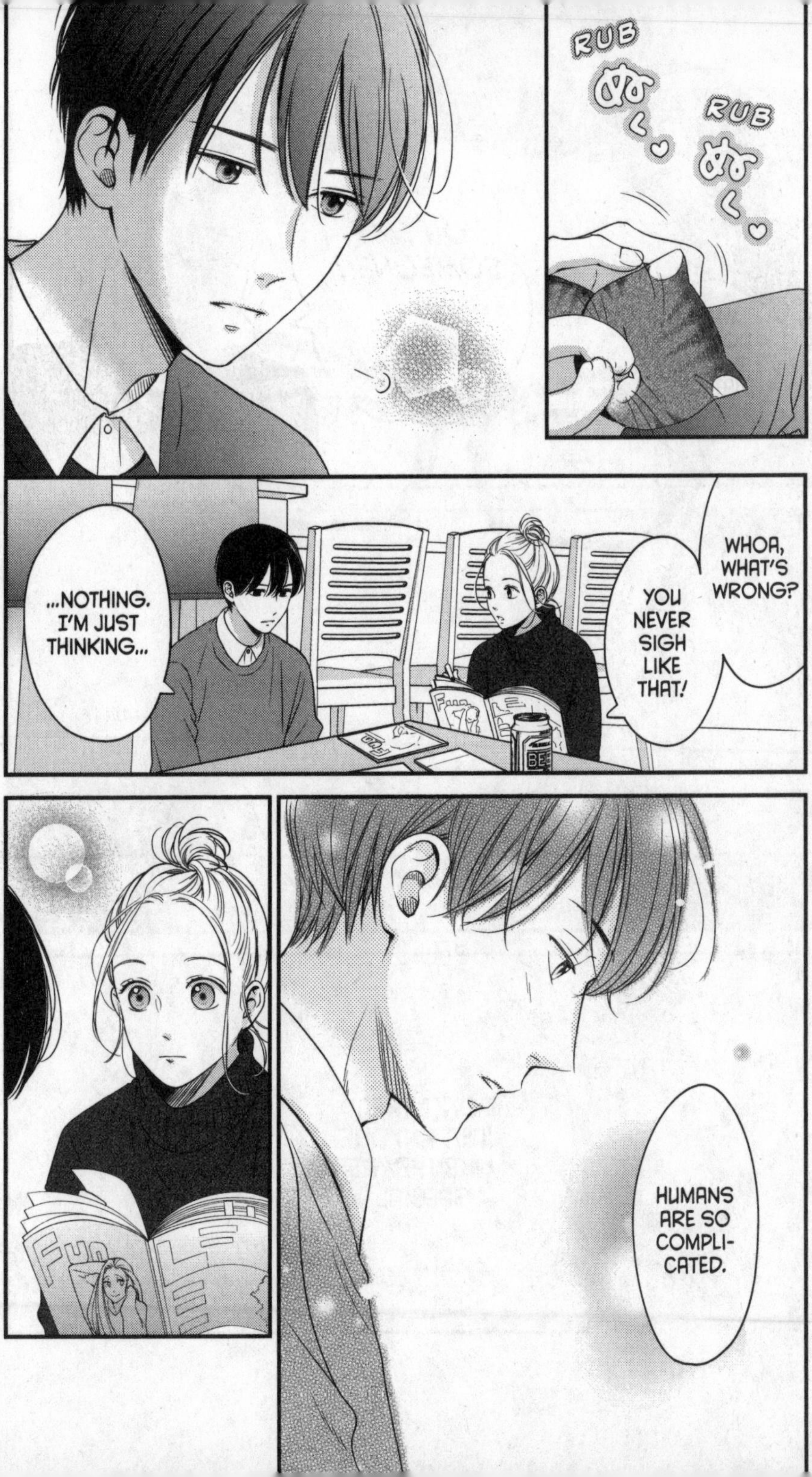
RUB
ぬく
RUB
ぬく
WHOA, WHAT'S WRONG?
YOU NEVER SIGH LIKE THAT!
...NOTHING. I'M JUST THINKING...
HUMANS ARE SO COMPLI-CATED.

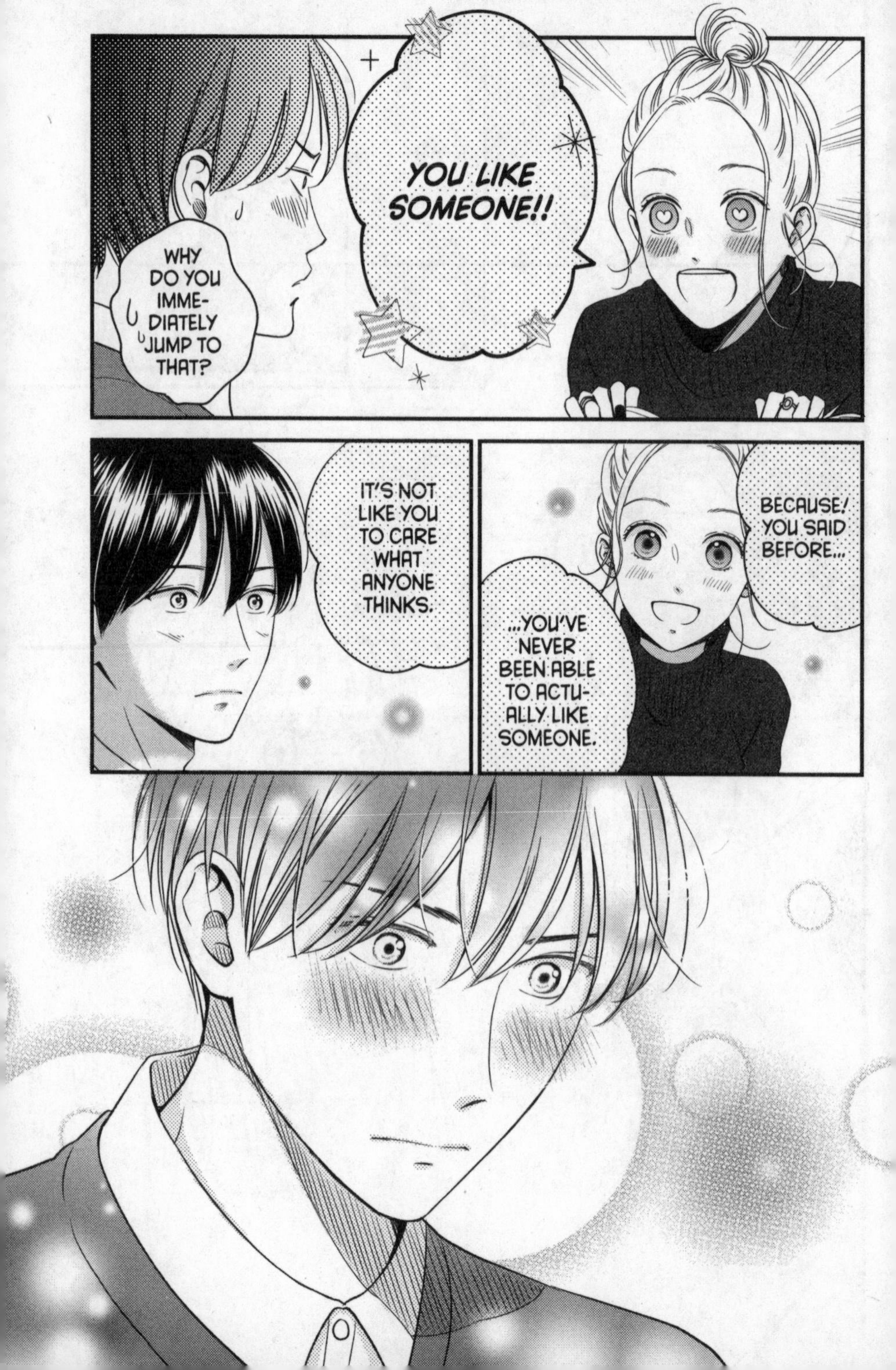
YOU LIKE SOMEONE!!
WHY DO YOU IMME-DIATELY JUMP TO THAT?
BECAUSE! YOU SAID BEFORE...
...YOU'VE NEVER BEEN ABLE TO ACTU-ALLY LIKE SOMEONE.
IT'S NOT LIKE YOU TO CARE WHAT ANYONE THINKS.

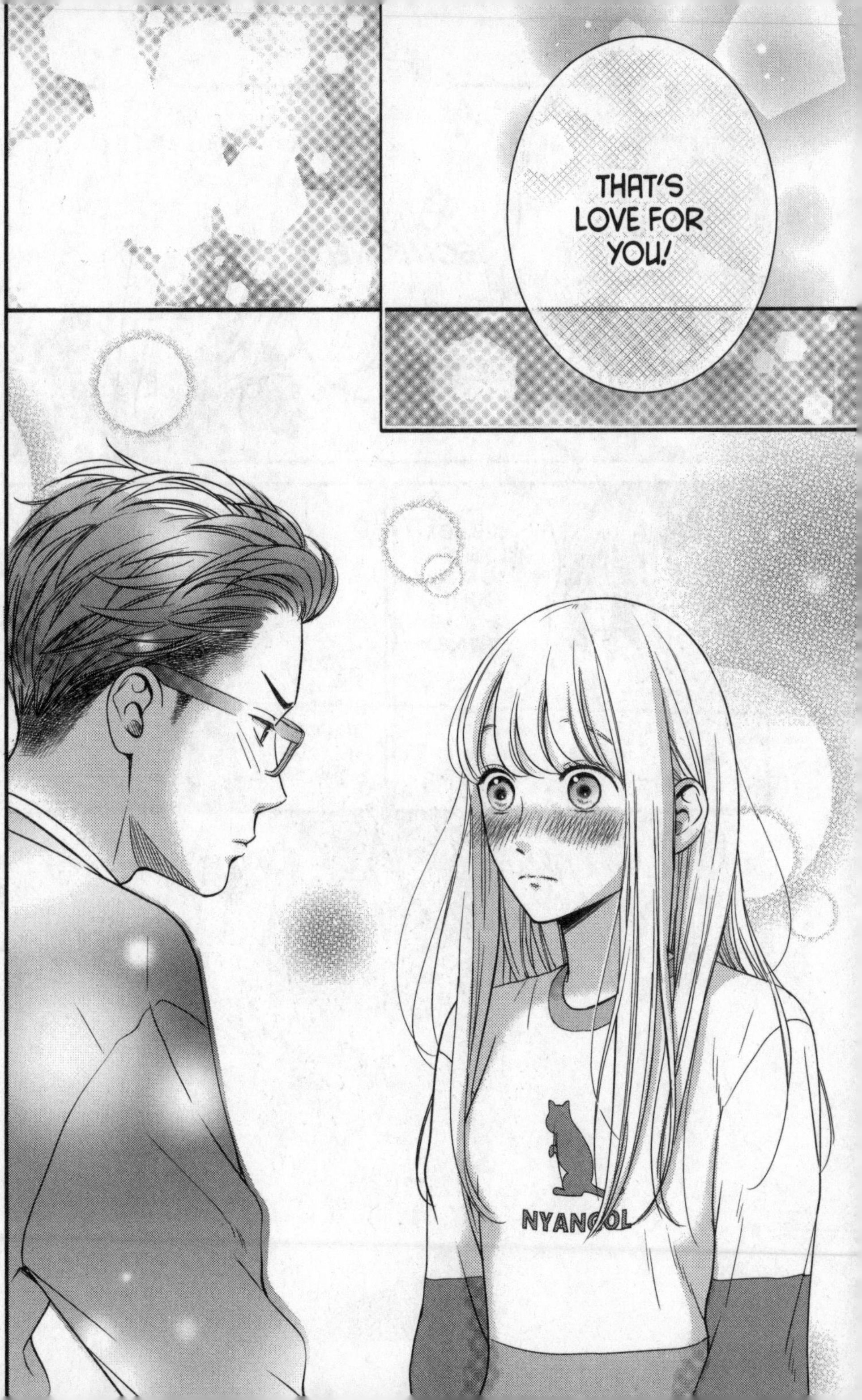
THAT'S LOVE FOR YOU!
NYANCOL

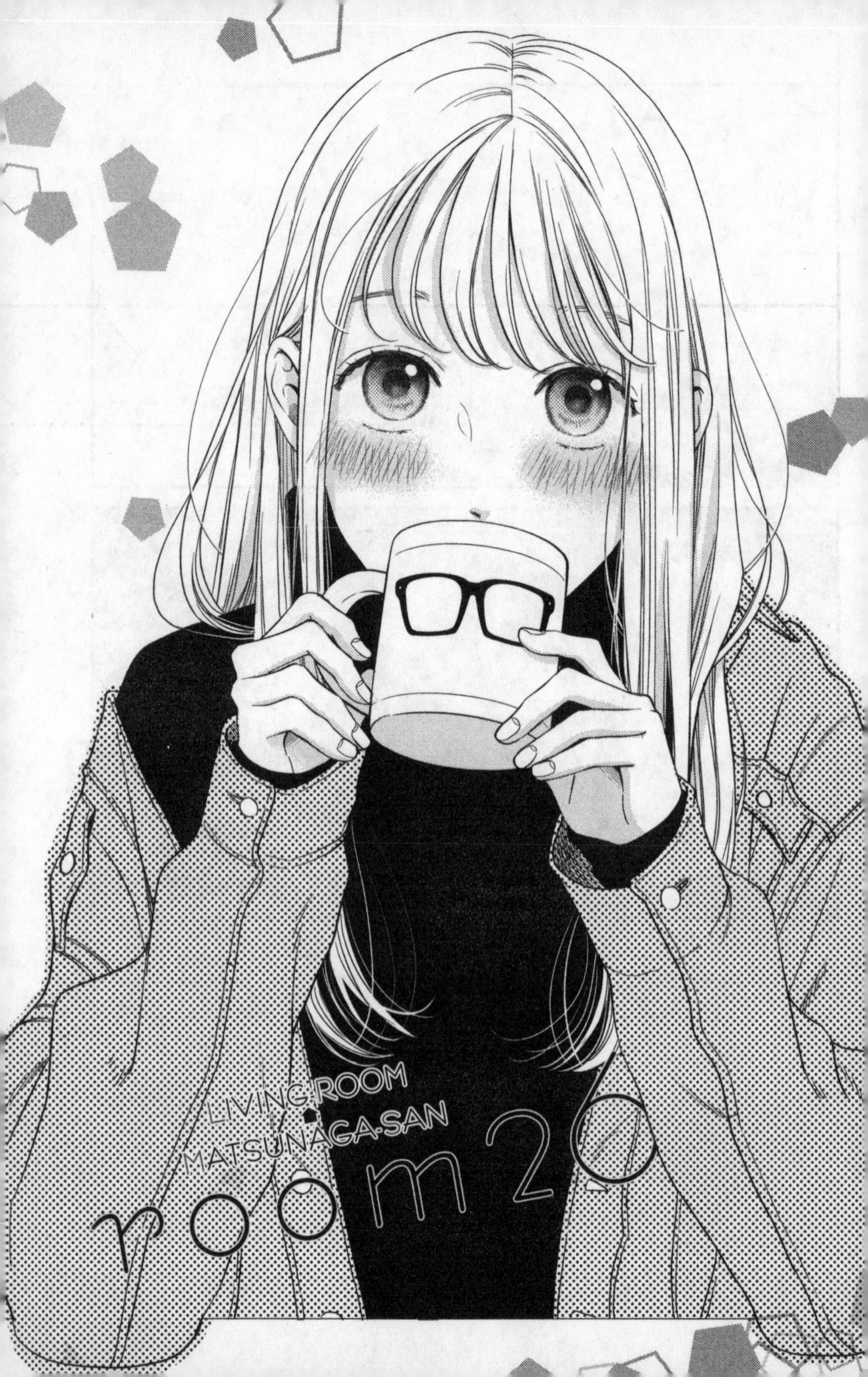

LIVING ROOM
MATSUNAGA-SAN
room 20

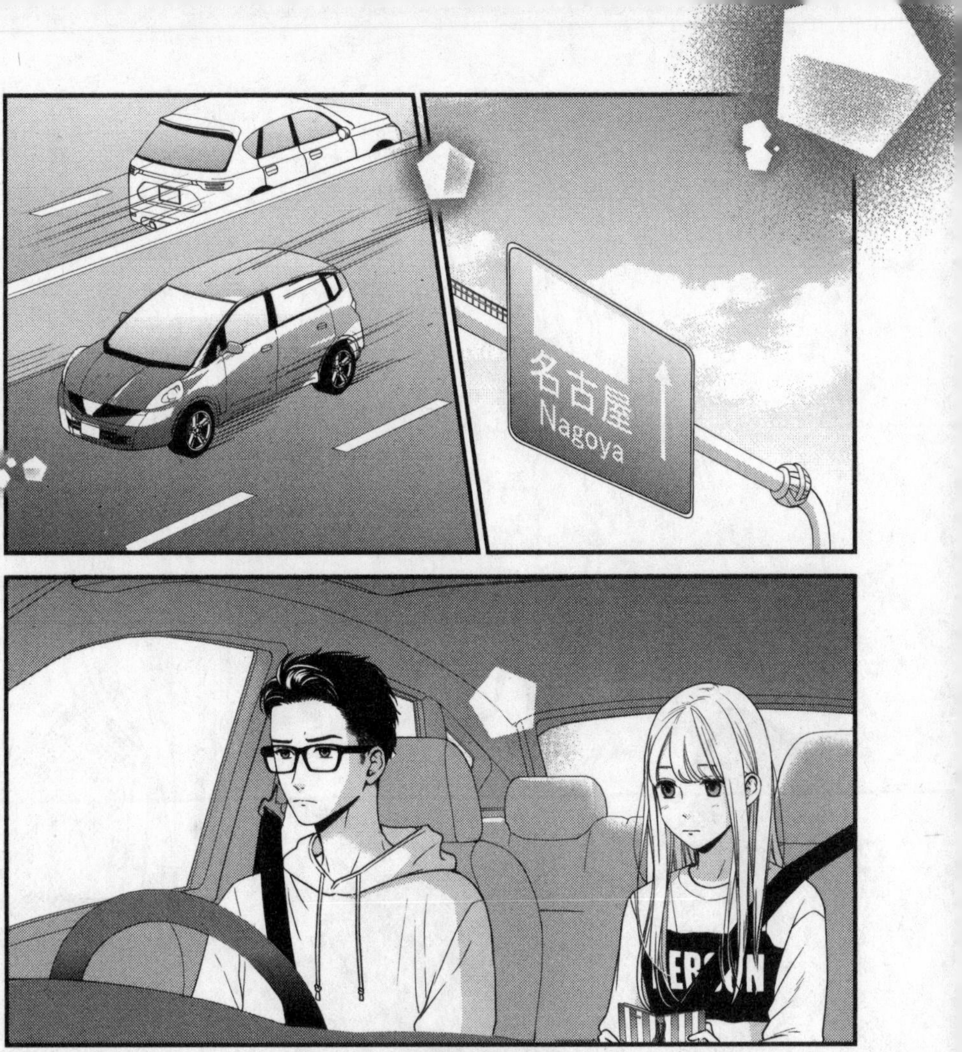
名古屋
Nagoya

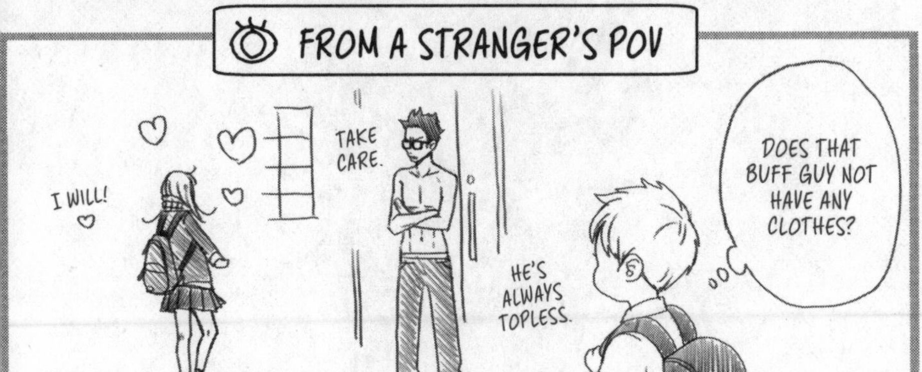
FROM A STRANGER'S POV
DOES THAT BUFF GUY NOT HAVE ANY CLOTHES?
HE'S ALWAYS TOPLESS.
TAKE CARE.
I WILL!

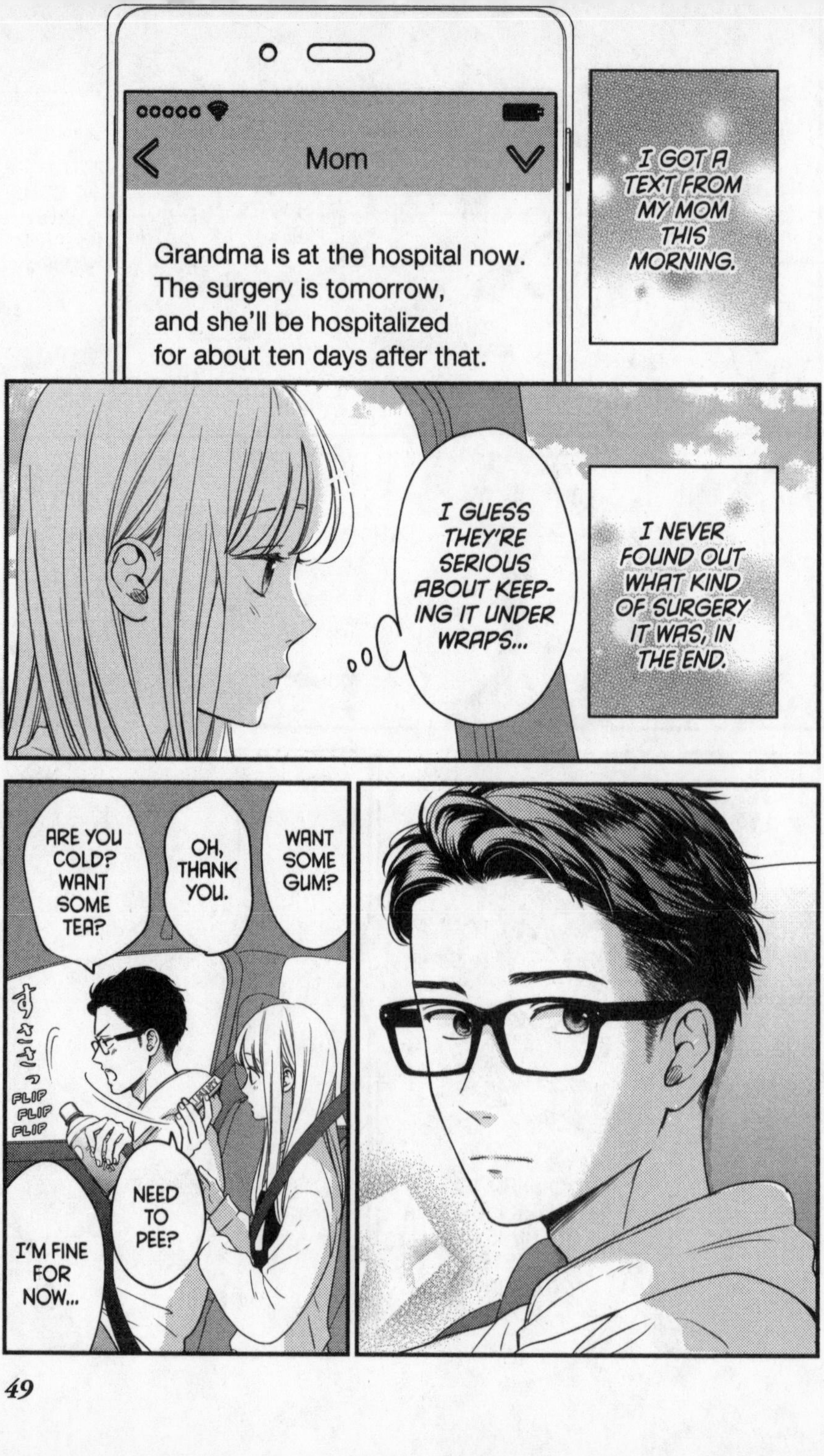
I GOT A TEXT FROM MY MOM THIS MORNING.
Mom
Grandma is at the hospital now. The surgery is tomorrow, and she'll be hospitalized for about ten days after that.
I NEVER FOUND OUT WHAT KIND OF SURGERY IT WAS, IN THE END.
I GUESS THEY'RE SERIOUS ABOUT KEEP-ING IT UNDER WRAPS...
WANT SOME GUM?
OH, THANK YOU.
ARE YOU COLD? WANT SOME TEA?
FLIP FLIP FLIP
NEED TO PEE?
I'M FINE FOR NOW...

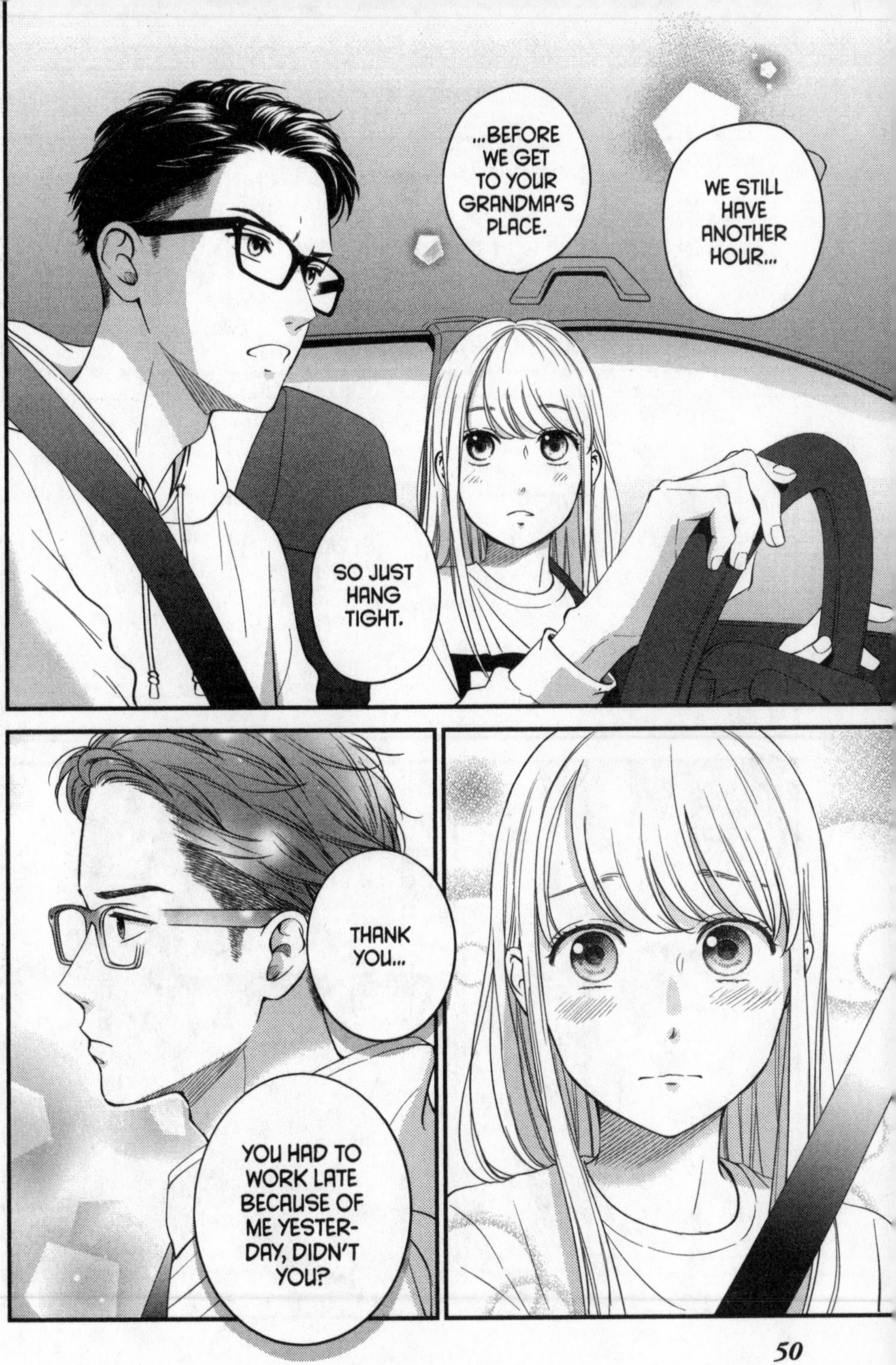
WE STILL HAVE ANOTHER HOUR...
...BEFORE WE GET TO YOUR GRANDMA'S PLACE.
SO JUST HANG TIGHT.
THANK YOU...
YOU HAD TO WORK LATE BECAUSE OF ME YESTER-DAY, DIDN'T YOU?

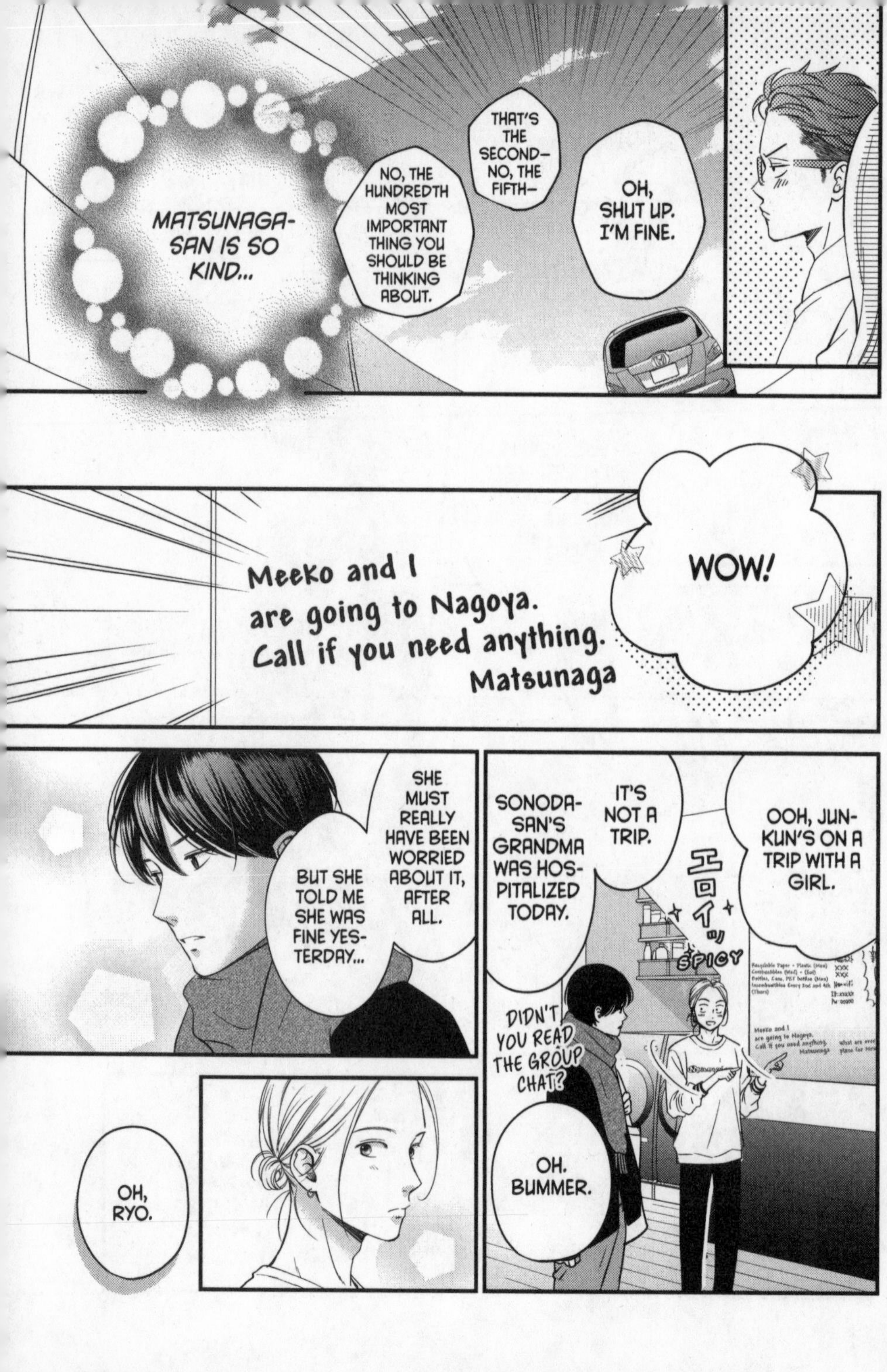
OH, SHUT UP. I'M FINE.
THAT'S THE SECOND— NO, THE FIFTH—
NO, THE HUNDREDTH MOST IMPORTANT THING YOU SHOULD BE THINKING ABOUT.
MATSUNAGA-SAN IS SO KIND...
WOW!
Meeko and I
are going to Nagoya.
Call if you need anything.
Matsunaga
OOH, JUN-KUN'S ON A TRIP WITH A GIRL.
エロイッ
SPICY
IT'S NOT A TRIP.
SONODA-SAN'S GRANDMA WAS HOSPITALIZED TODAY.
DIDN'T YOU READ THE GROUP CHAT?
OH. BUMMER.
SHE MUST REALLY HAVE BEEN WORRIED ABOUT IT, AFTER ALL.
BUT SHE TOLD ME SHE WAS FINE YESTERDAY...
OH, RYO.

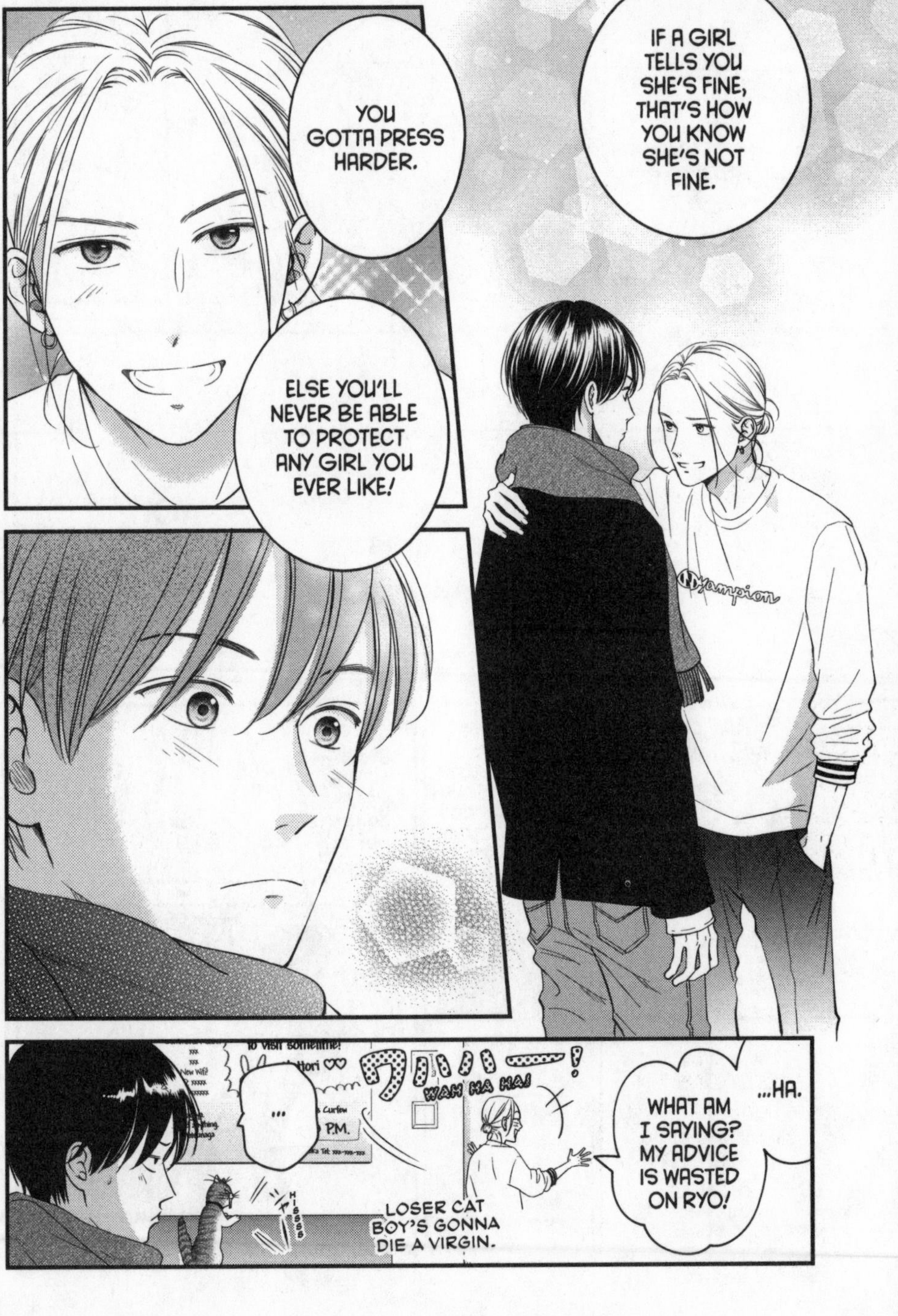
IF A GIRL TELLS YOU SHE'S FINE, THAT'S HOW YOU KNOW SHE'S NOT FINE.
YOU GOTTA PRESS HARDER.
ELSE YOU'LL NEVER BE ABLE TO PROTECT ANY GIRL YOU EVER LIKE!
...HA.
WHAT AM I SAYING? MY ADVICE IS WASTED ON RYO!
WAH HA HA!
LOSER CAT BOY'S GONNA DIE A VIRGIN.
...
HISSSS

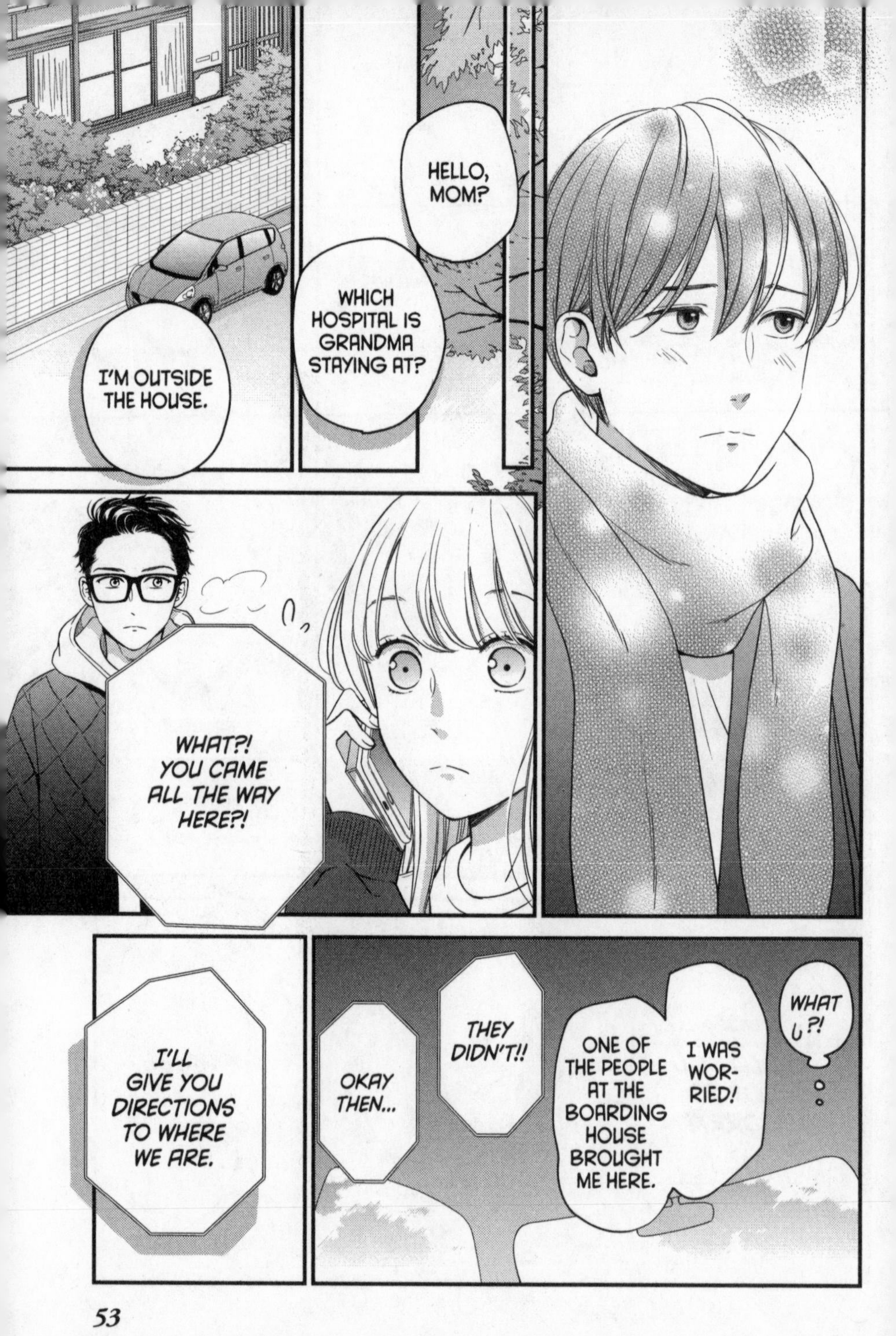

HELLO, MOM?
WHICH HOSPITAL IS GRANDMA STAYING AT?
I'M OUTSIDE THE HOUSE.
WHAT?! YOU CAME ALL THE WAY HERE?!
WHAT?!
I WAS WOR-RIED!
ONE OF THE PEOPLE AT THE BOARDING HOUSE BROUGHT ME HERE.
THEY DIDN'T!!
OKAY THEN...
I'LL GIVE YOU DIRECTIONS TO WHERE WE ARE.

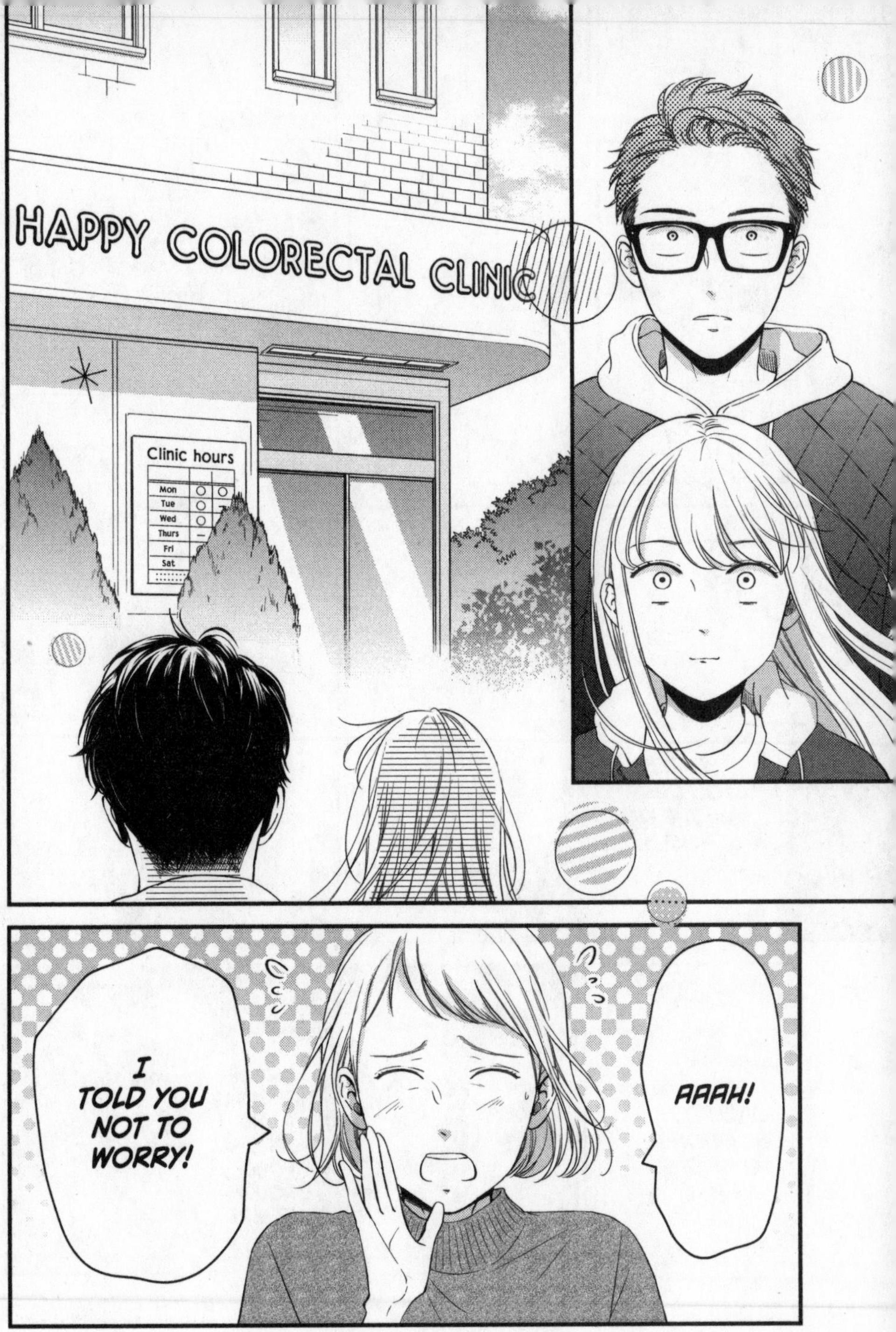
HAPPY COLORECTAL CLINIC
Clinic hours
Mon
Tue
Wed
Thurs
Fri
Sat
AAAH!
I TOLD YOU NOT TO WORRY!

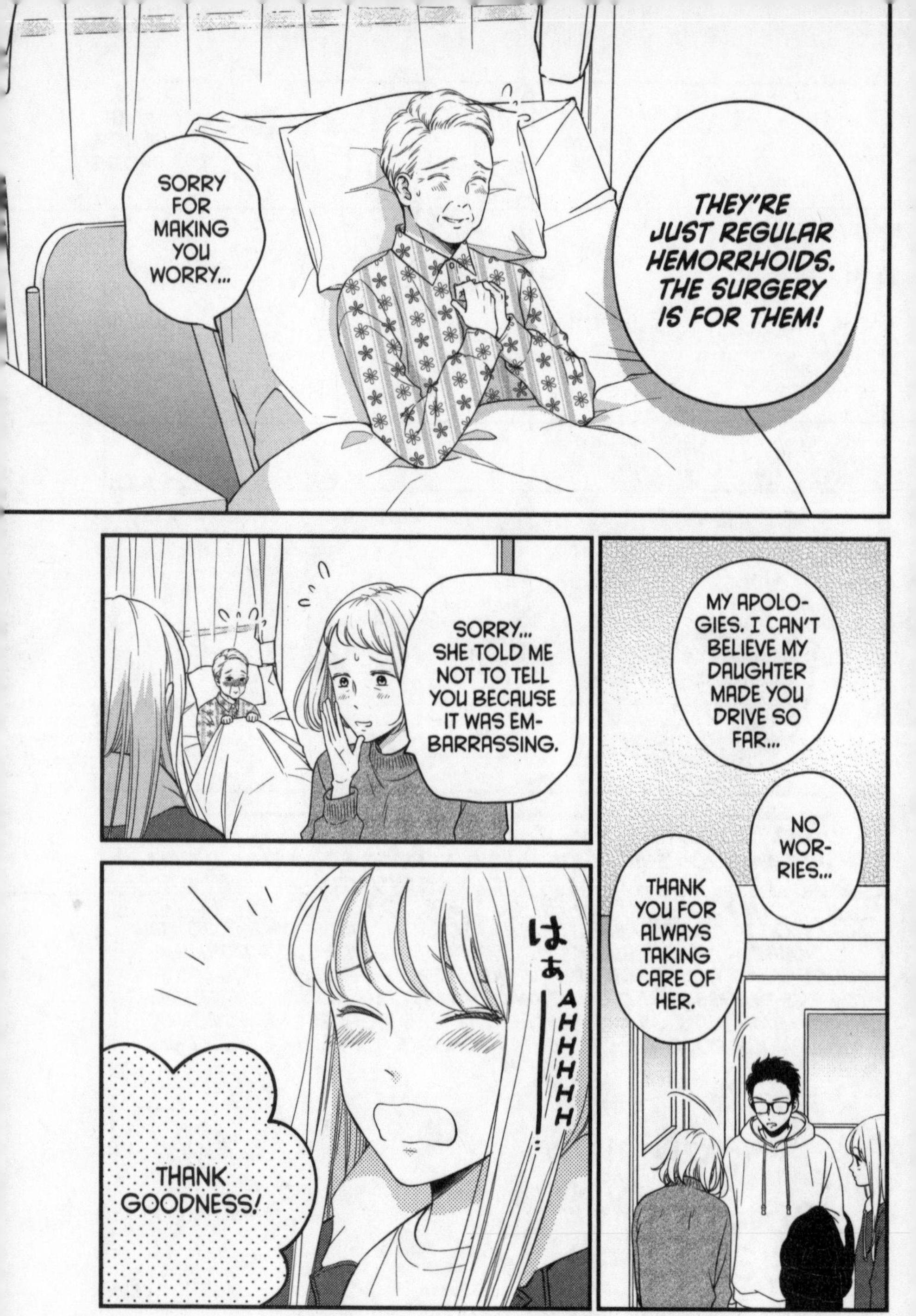
THEY'RE JUST REGULAR HEMORRHOIDS. THE SURGERY IS FOR THEM!
SORRY FOR MAKING YOU WORRY...
MY APOLOGIES. I CAN'T BELIEVE MY DAUGHTER MADE YOU DRIVE SO FAR...
NO WORRIES...
THANK YOU FOR ALWAYS TAKING CARE OF HER.
SORRY... SHE TOLD ME NOT TO TELL YOU BECAUSE IT WAS EMBARRASSING.
はぁ AHHHHH
THANK GOODNESS!

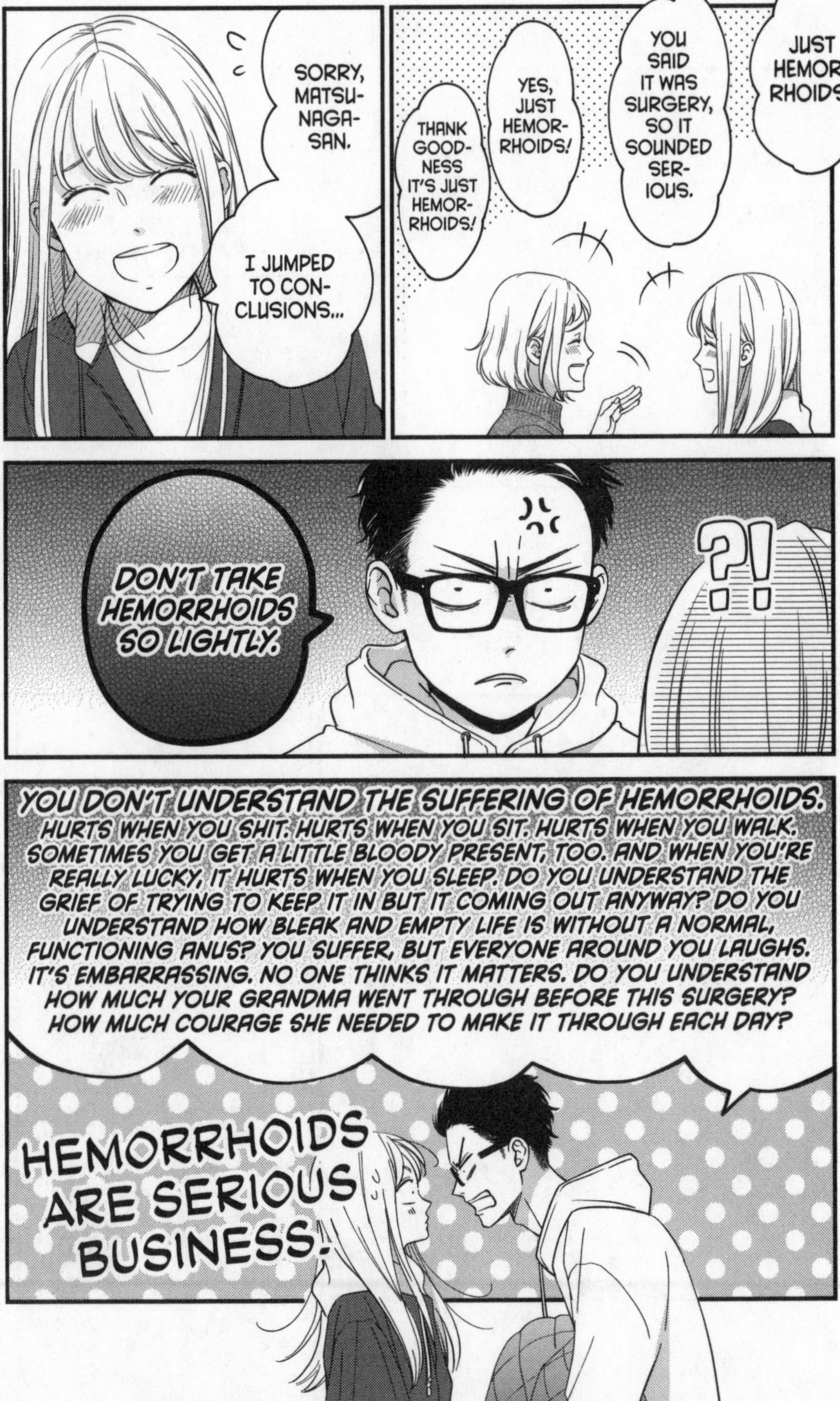
JUST HEMORRHOIDS!
YOU SAID IT WAS SURGERY, SO IT SOUNDED SERIOUS.
YES, JUST HEMORRHOIDS!
THANK GOODNESS IT'S JUST HEMORRHOIDS!
SORRY, MATSUNAGA-SAN.
I JUMPED TO CONCLUSIONS...
?!
DON'T TAKE HEMORRHOIDS SO LIGHTLY.
YOU DON'T UNDERSTAND THE SUFFERING OF HEMORRHOIDS. HURTS WHEN YOU SHIT. HURTS WHEN YOU SIT. HURTS WHEN YOU WALK. SOMETIMES YOU GET A LITTLE BLOODY PRESENT, TOO. AND WHEN YOU'RE REALLY LUCKY, IT HURTS WHEN YOU SLEEP. DO YOU UNDERSTAND THE GRIEF OF TRYING TO KEEP IT IN BUT IT COMING OUT ANYWAY? DO YOU UNDERSTAND HOW BLEAK AND EMPTY LIFE IS WITHOUT A NORMAL, FUNCTIONING ANUS? YOU SUFFER, BUT EVERYONE AROUND YOU LAUGHS. IT'S EMBARRASSING. NO ONE THINKS IT MATTERS. DO YOU UNDERSTAND HOW MUCH YOUR GRANDMA WENT THROUGH BEFORE THIS SURGERY? HOW MUCH COURAGE SHE NEEDED TO MAKE IT THROUGH EACH DAY?
HEMORRHOIDS ARE SERIOUS BUSINESS!

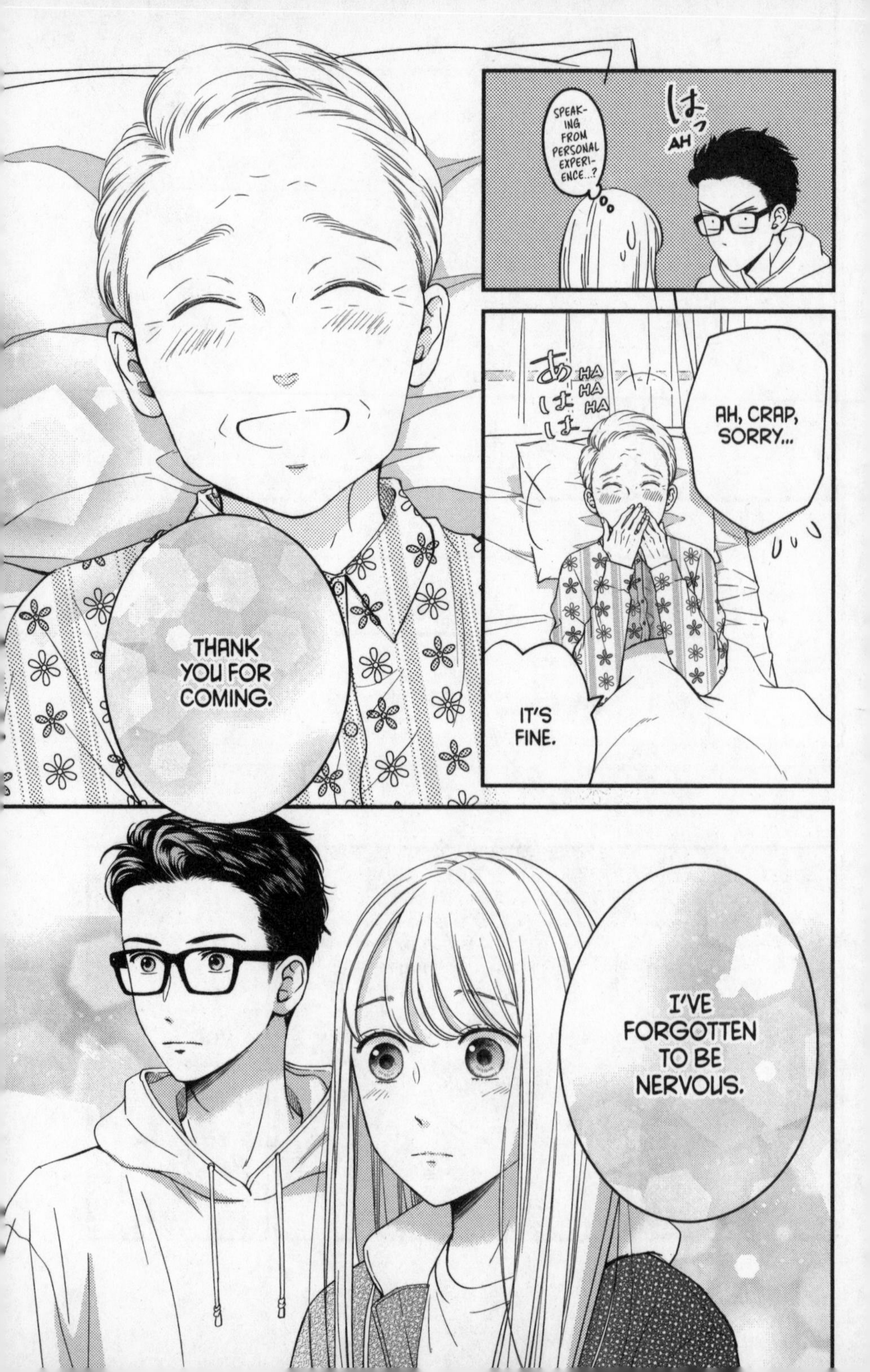
はっ AH
SPEAKING FROM PERSONAL EXPERIENCE...?
AH, CRAP, SORRY...
あははは HA HA HA
IT'S FINE.
THANK YOU FOR COMING.
I'VE FORGOTTEN TO BE NERVOUS.

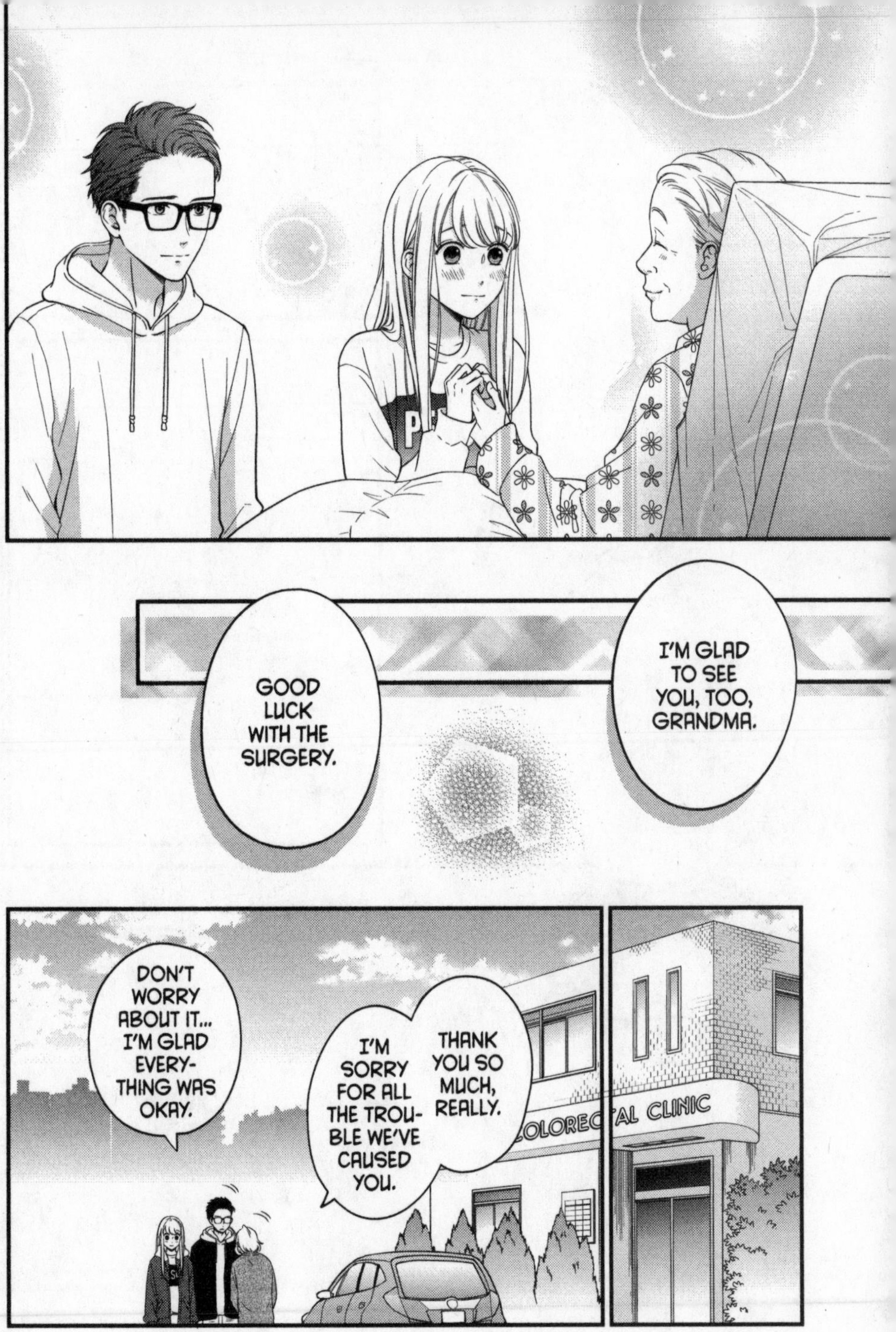
I'M GLAD TO SEE YOU, TOO, GRANDMA.
GOOD LUCK WITH THE SURGERY.
THANK YOU SO MUCH, REALLY.
I'M SORRY FOR ALL THE TROUBLE WE'VE CAUSED YOU.
DON'T WORRY ABOUT IT... I'M GLAD EVERYTHING WAS OKAY.

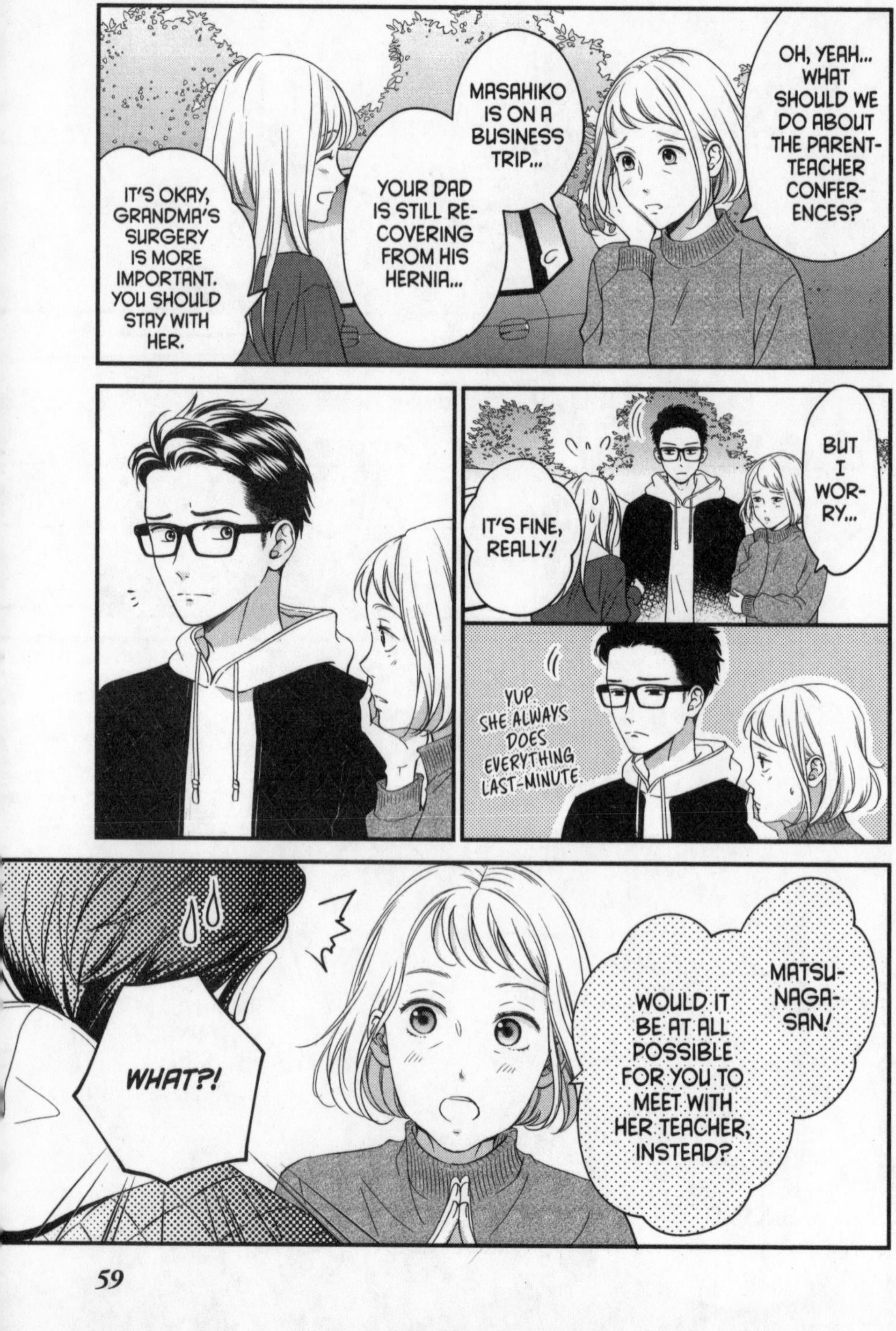
OH, YEAH... WHAT SHOULD WE DO ABOUT THE PARENT-TEACHER CONFERENCES?
MASAHIKO IS ON A BUSINESS TRIP...
YOUR DAD IS STILL RE-COVERING FROM HIS HERNIA...
IT'S OKAY, GRANDMA'S SURGERY IS MORE IMPORTANT. YOU SHOULD STAY WITH HER.
BUT I WOR-RY...
IT'S FINE, REALLY!
YUP. SHE ALWAYS DOES EVERYTHING LAST-MINUTE.
MATSU-NAGA-SAN!
WOULD IT BE AT ALL POSSIBLE FOR YOU TO MEET WITH HER TEACHER, INSTEAD?
WHAT?!

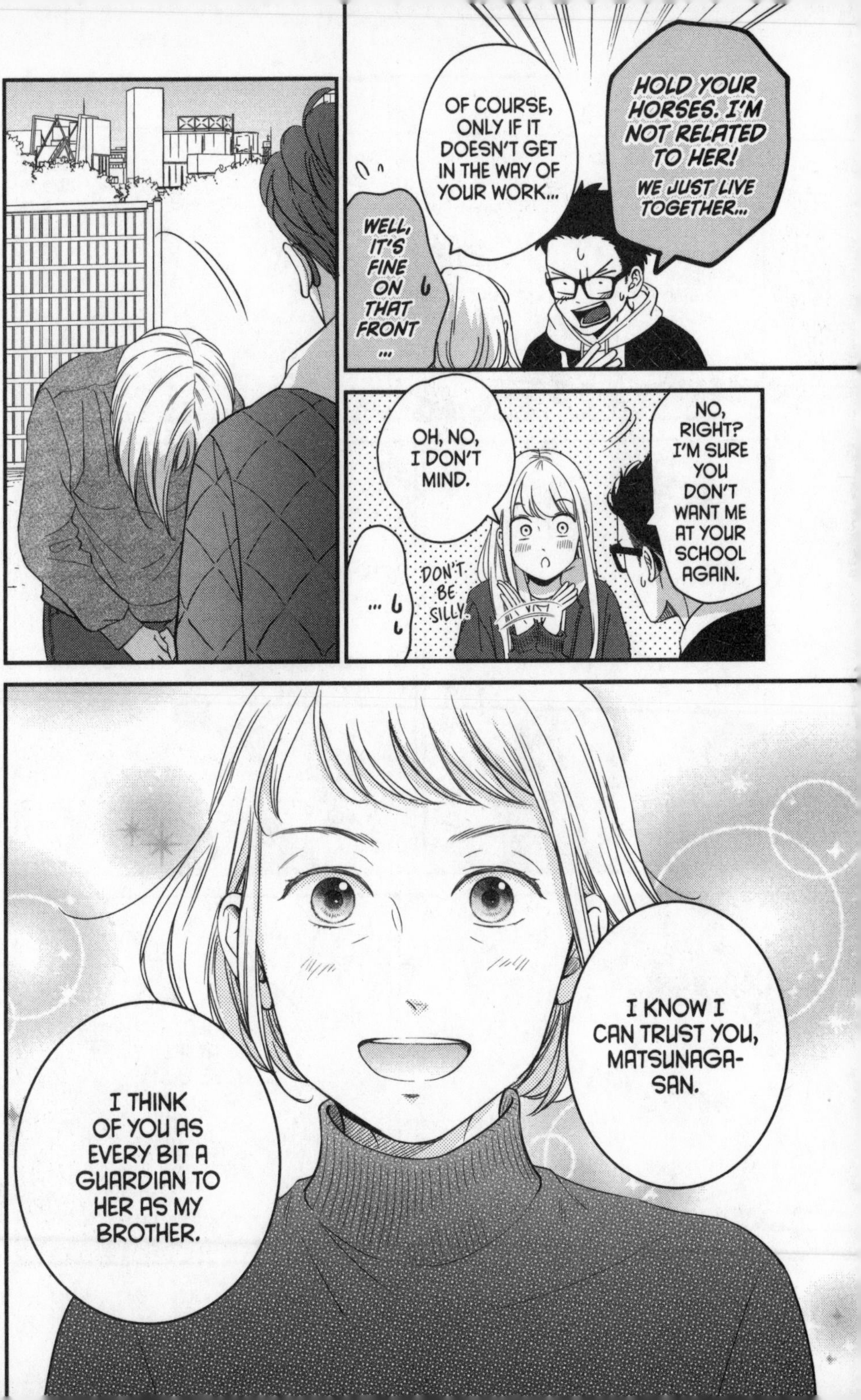
HOLD YOUR HORSES. I'M NOT RELATED TO HER!
WE JUST LIVE TOGETHER...
OF COURSE, ONLY IF IT DOESN'T GET IN THE WAY OF YOUR WORK...
WELL, IT'S FINE ON THAT FRONT...
NO, RIGHT? I'M SURE YOU DON'T WANT ME AT YOUR SCHOOL AGAIN.
OH, NO, I DON'T MIND.
DON'T BE SILLY.
...
I KNOW I CAN TRUST YOU, MATSUNAGA-SAN.
I THINK OF YOU AS EVERY BIT A GUARDIAN TO HER AS MY BROTHER.

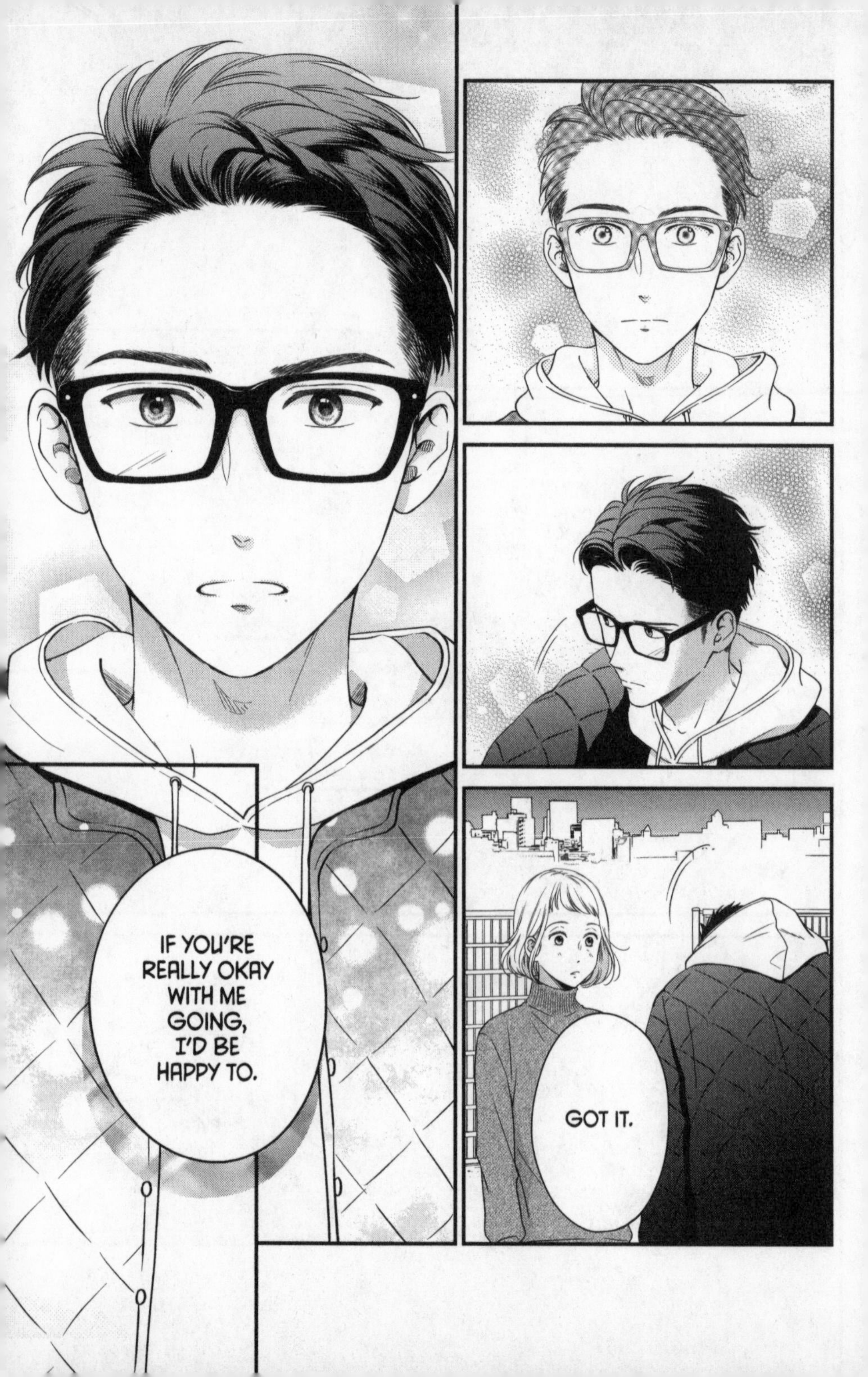
GOT IT.
IF YOU'RE REALLY OKAY WITH ME GOING, I'D BE HAPPY TO.

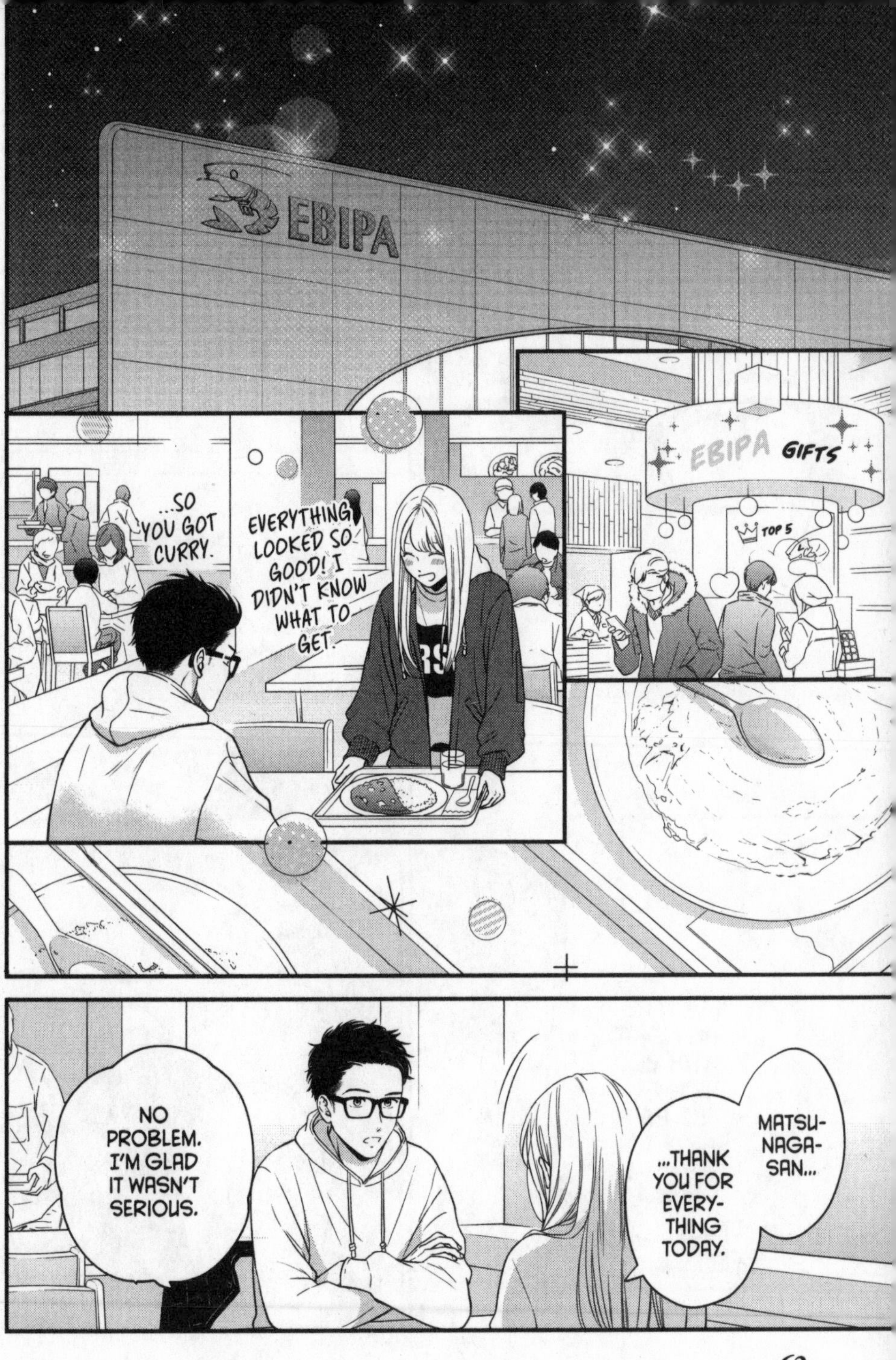
EBIPA
EBIPA GIFTS
TOP 5
EVERYTHING LOOKED SO GOOD! I DIDN'T KNOW WHAT TO GET.
...SO YOU GOT CURRY.
MATSU-NAGA-SAN...
...THANK YOU FOR EVERY-THING TODAY.
NO PROBLEM. I'M GLAD IT WASN'T SERIOUS.

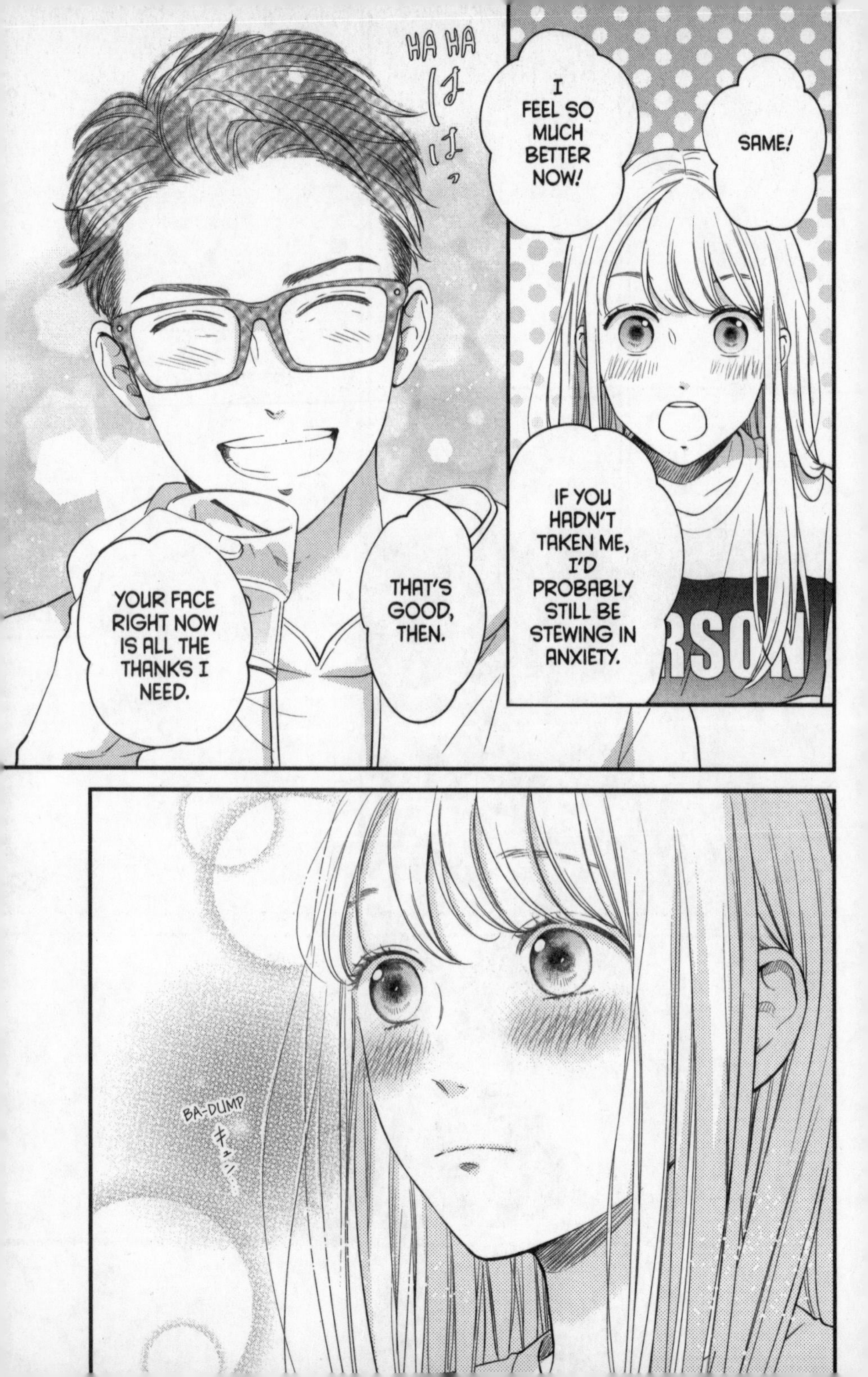
SAME!
I FEEL SO MUCH BETTER NOW!
IF YOU HADN'T TAKEN ME, I'D PROBABLY STILL BE STEWING IN ANXIETY.
HA HA
ははっ
THAT'S GOOD, THEN.
YOUR FACE RIGHT NOW IS ALL THE THANKS I NEED.
BA-DUMP

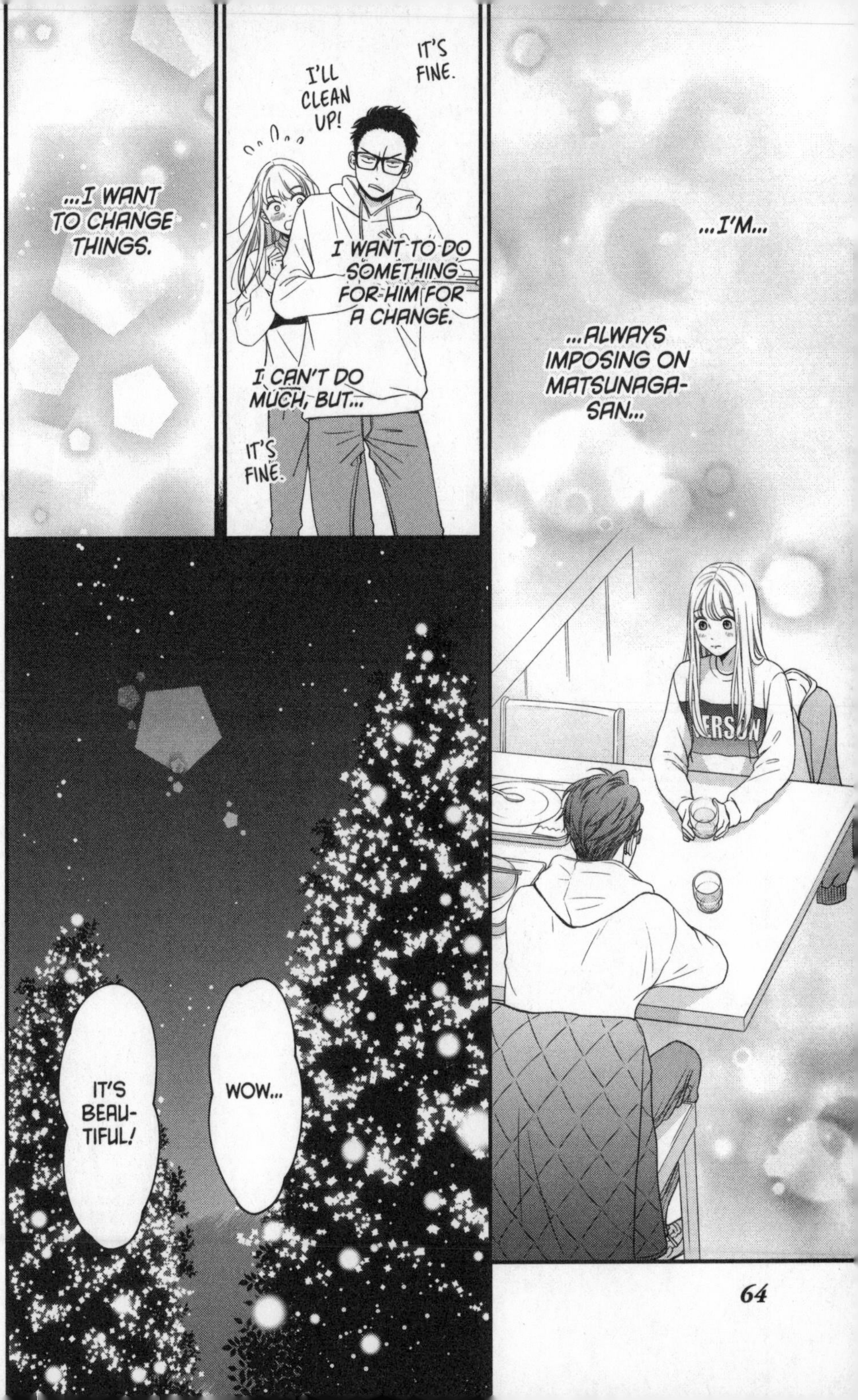
...I'M...
...ALWAYS IMPOSING ON MATSUNAGA-SAN...
IT'S FINE.
I'LL CLEAN UP!
I WANT TO DO SOMETHING FOR HIM FOR A CHANGE.
I CAN'T DO MUCH, BUT...
IT'S FINE.
...I WANT TO CHANGE THINGS.
WOW...
IT'S BEAU-TIFUL!

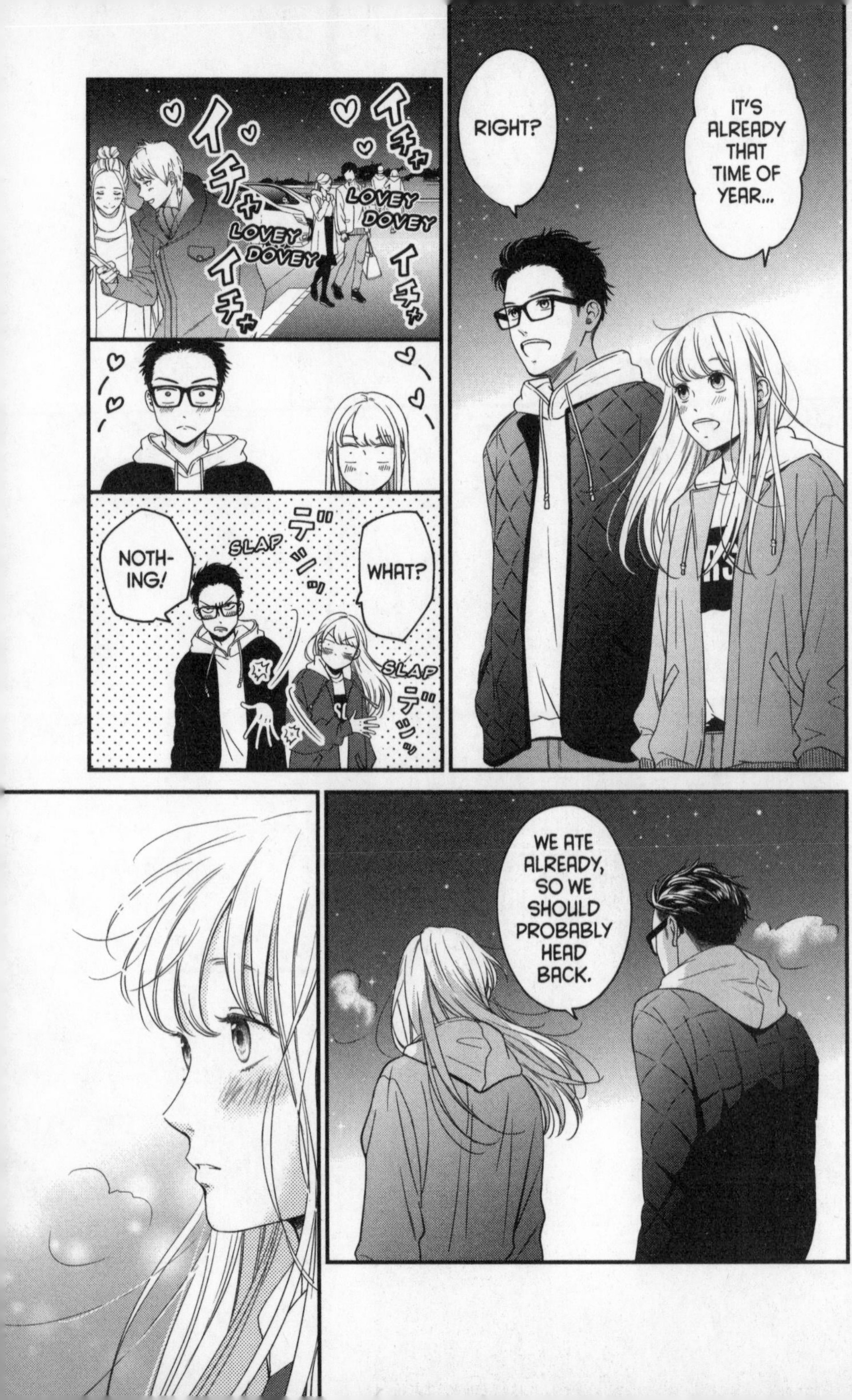
IT'S ALREADY THAT TIME OF YEAR...
RIGHT?
イチャ イチャ
LOVEY DOVEY
イチャ イチャ
LOVEY DOVEY
WHAT?
SLAP
NOTH-ING!
SLAP
WE ATE ALREADY, SO WE SHOULD PROBABLY HEAD BACK.

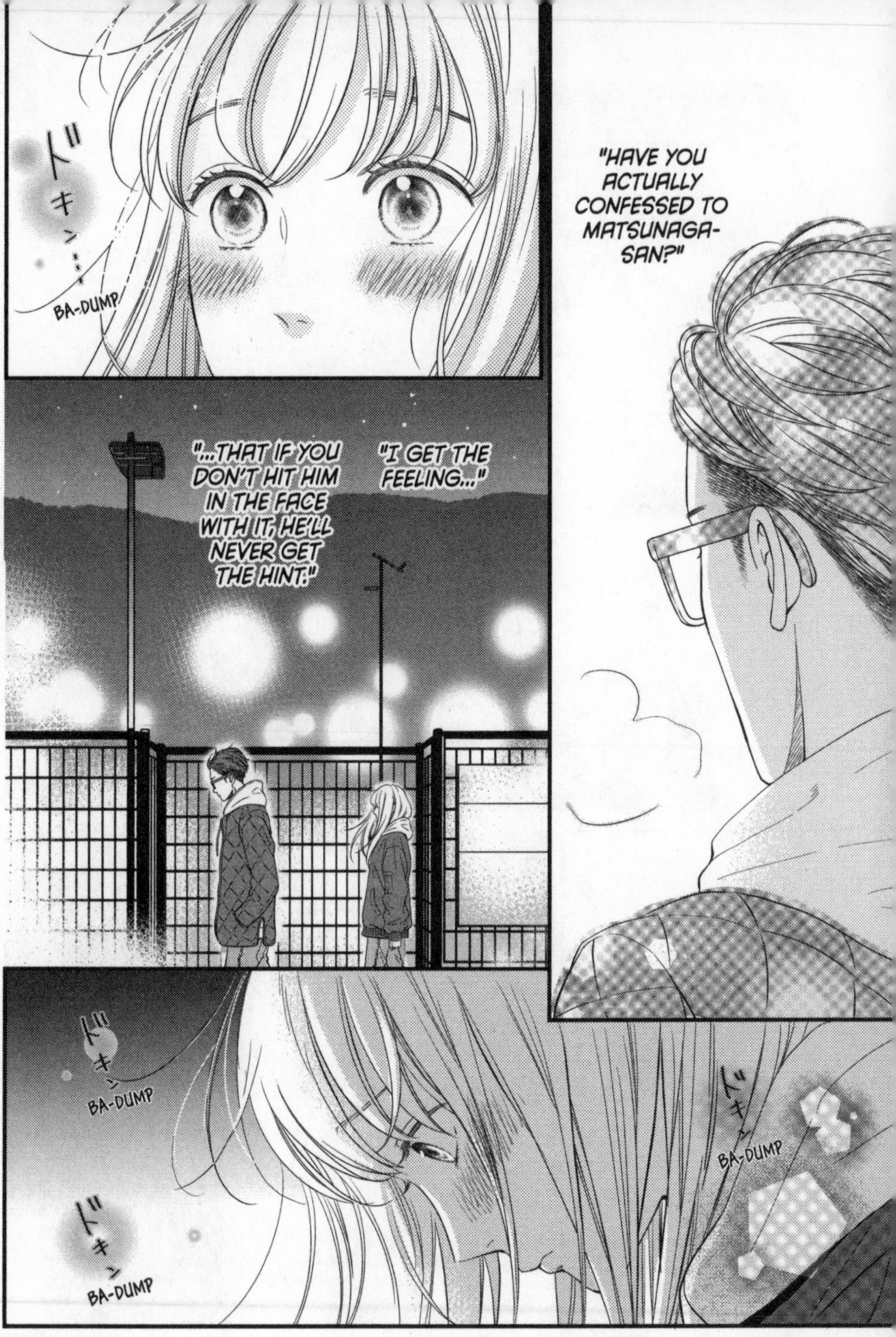
"HAVE YOU ACTUALLY CONFESSED TO MATSUNAGA-SAN?"
ドキン…
BA-DUMP
"I GET THE FEELING..."
"...THAT IF YOU DON'T HIT HIM IN THE FACE WITH IT, HE'LL NEVER GET THE HINT."
ドキン
BA-DUMP
ドキン
BA-DUMP
ドキン
BA-DUMP

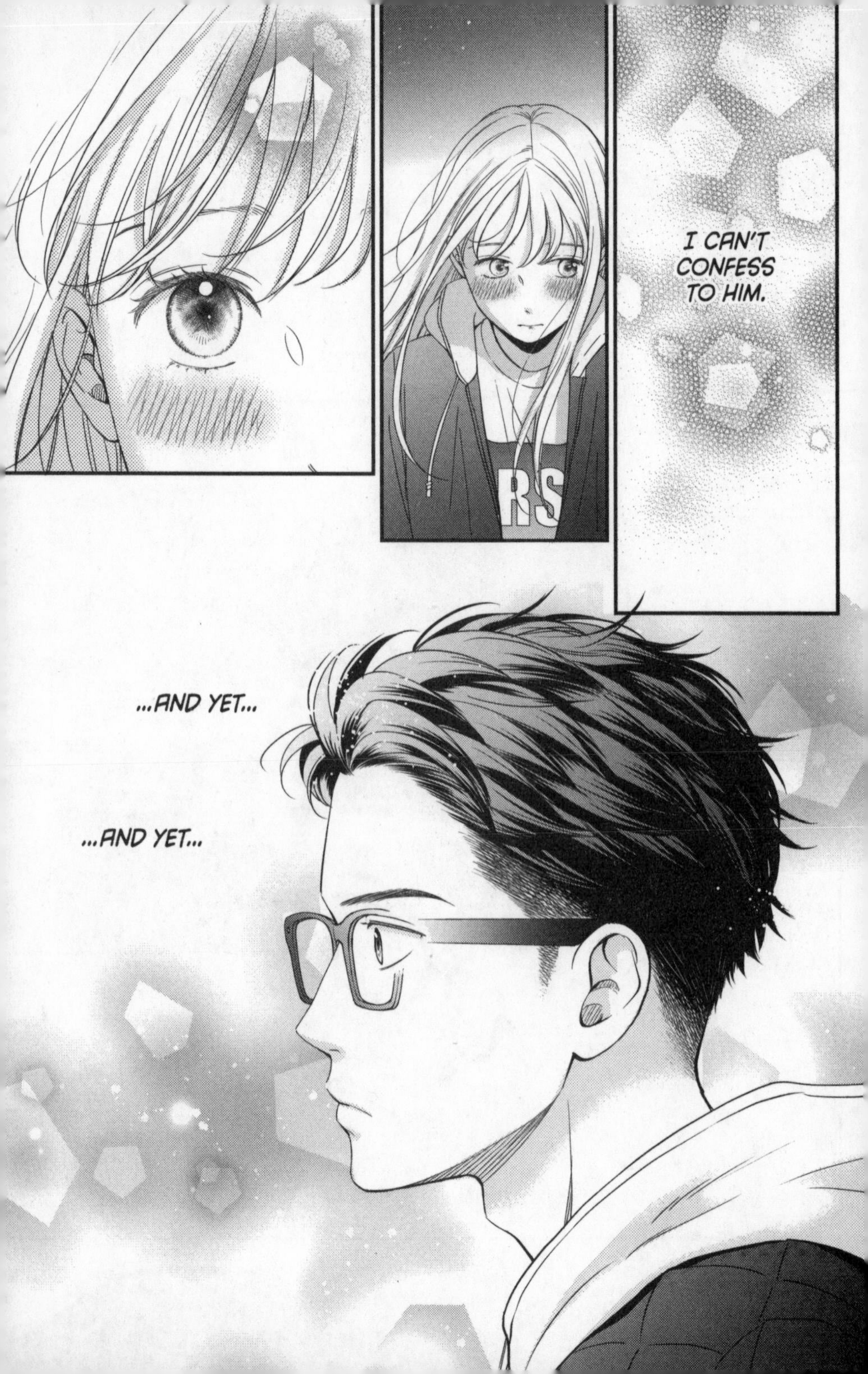
I CAN'T CONFESS TO HIM.
...AND YET...
...AND YET...

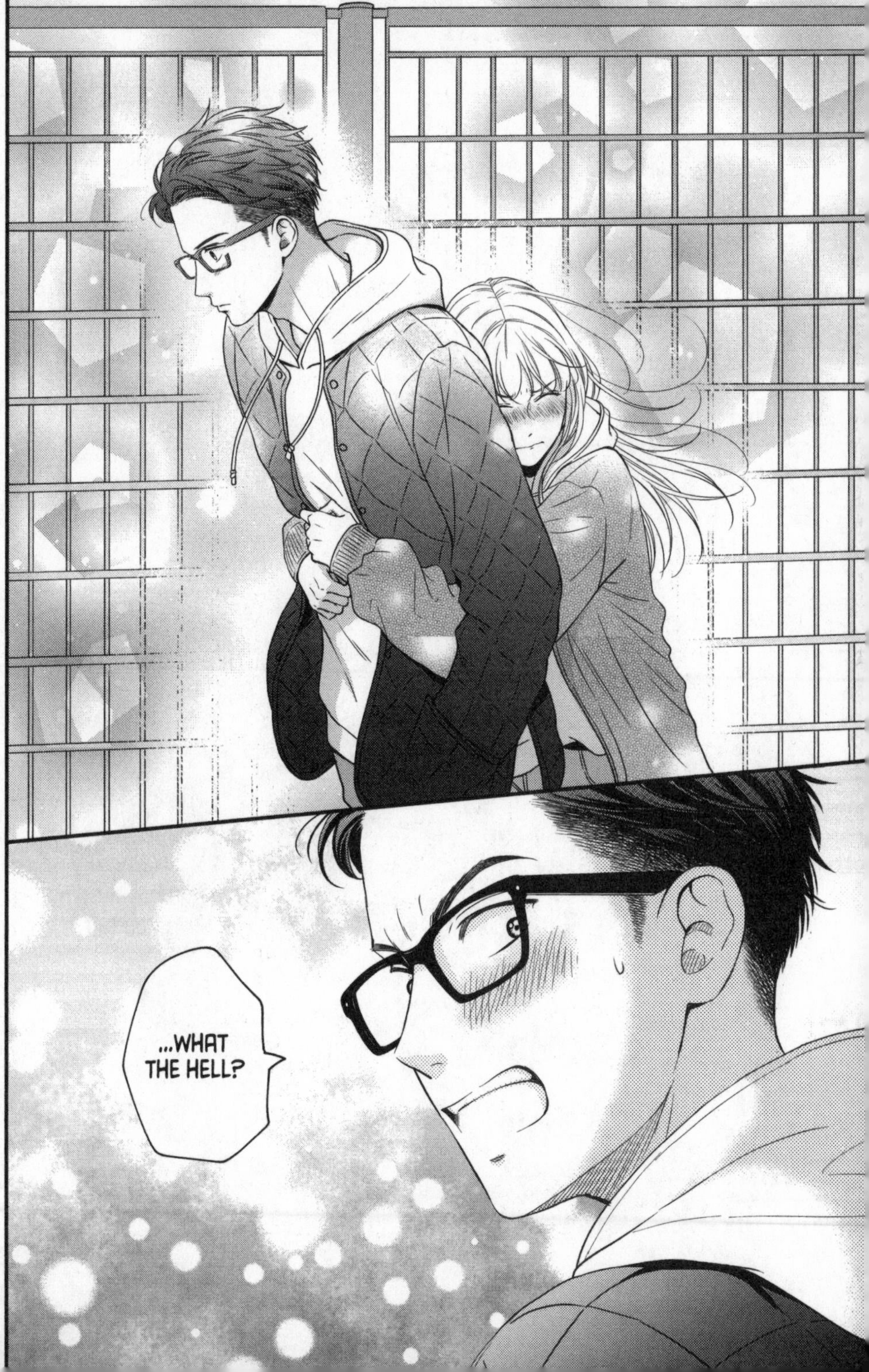
...WHAT THE HELL?

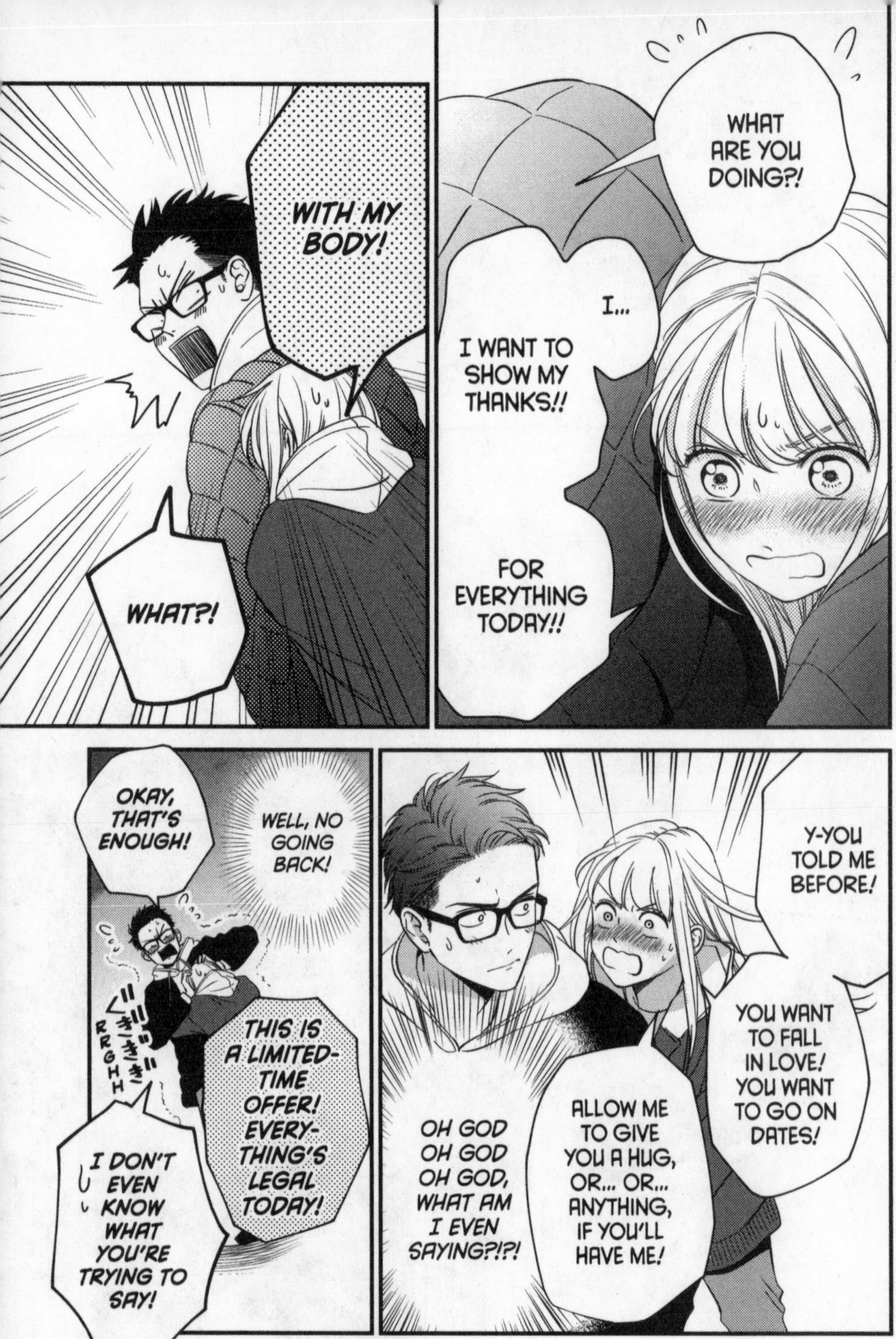
WHAT ARE YOU DOING?!
I...
I WANT TO SHOW MY THANKS!!
FOR EVERYTHING TODAY!!
WITH MY BODY!
WHAT?!
Y-YOU TOLD ME BEFORE!
YOU WANT TO FALL IN LOVE! YOU WANT TO GO ON DATES!
ALLOW ME TO GIVE YOU A HUG, OR... OR... ANYTHING, IF YOU'LL HAVE ME!
OH GOD OH GOD OH GOD, WHAT AM I EVEN SAYING?!?!
WELL, NO GOING BACK!
OKAY, THAT'S ENOUGH!
RRGHH
THIS IS A LIMITED-TIME OFFER! EVERYTHING'S LEGAL TODAY!
I DON'T EVEN KNOW WHAT YOU'RE TRYING TO SAY!

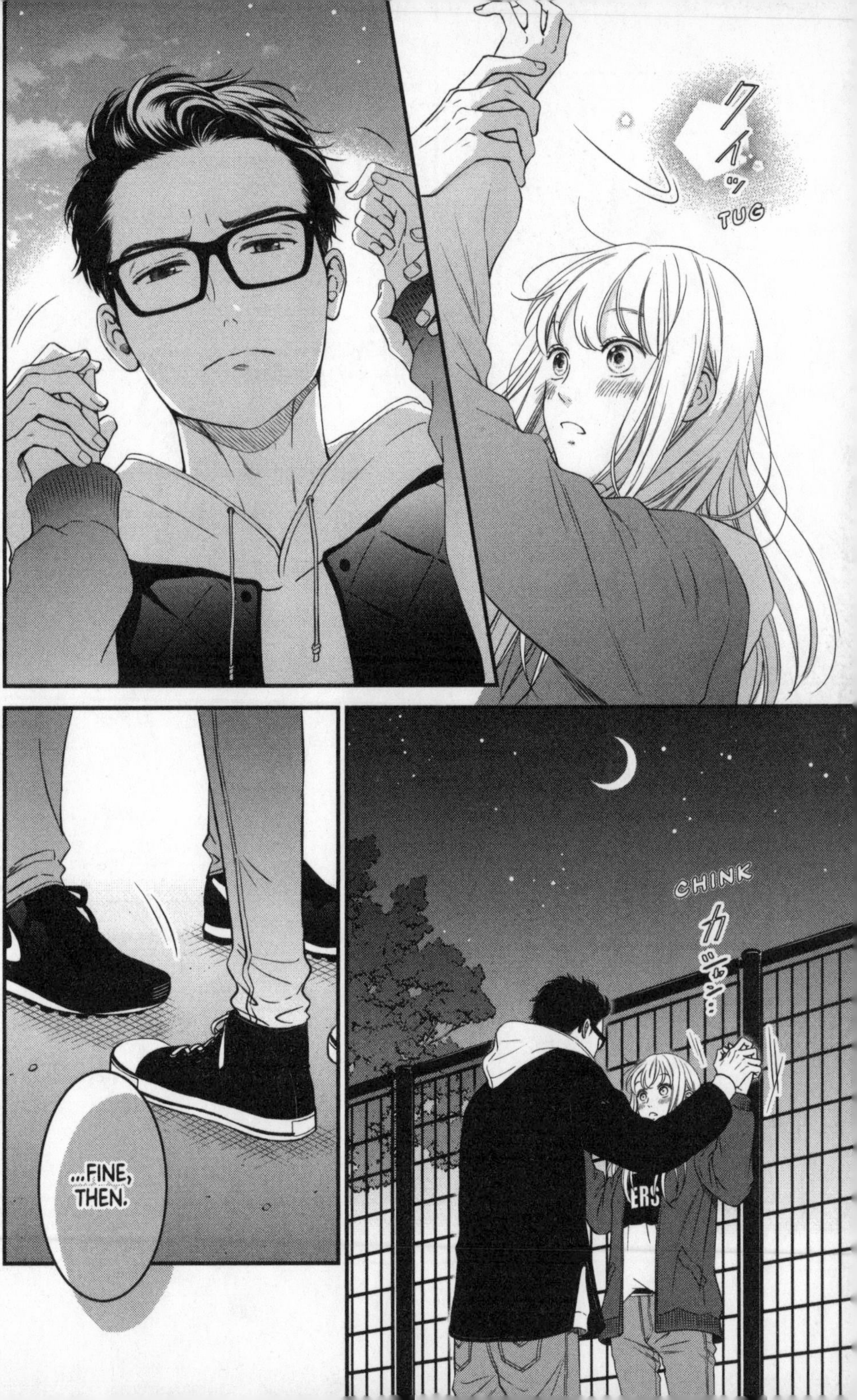

クイッ
TUG
CHINK
...FINE, THEN.

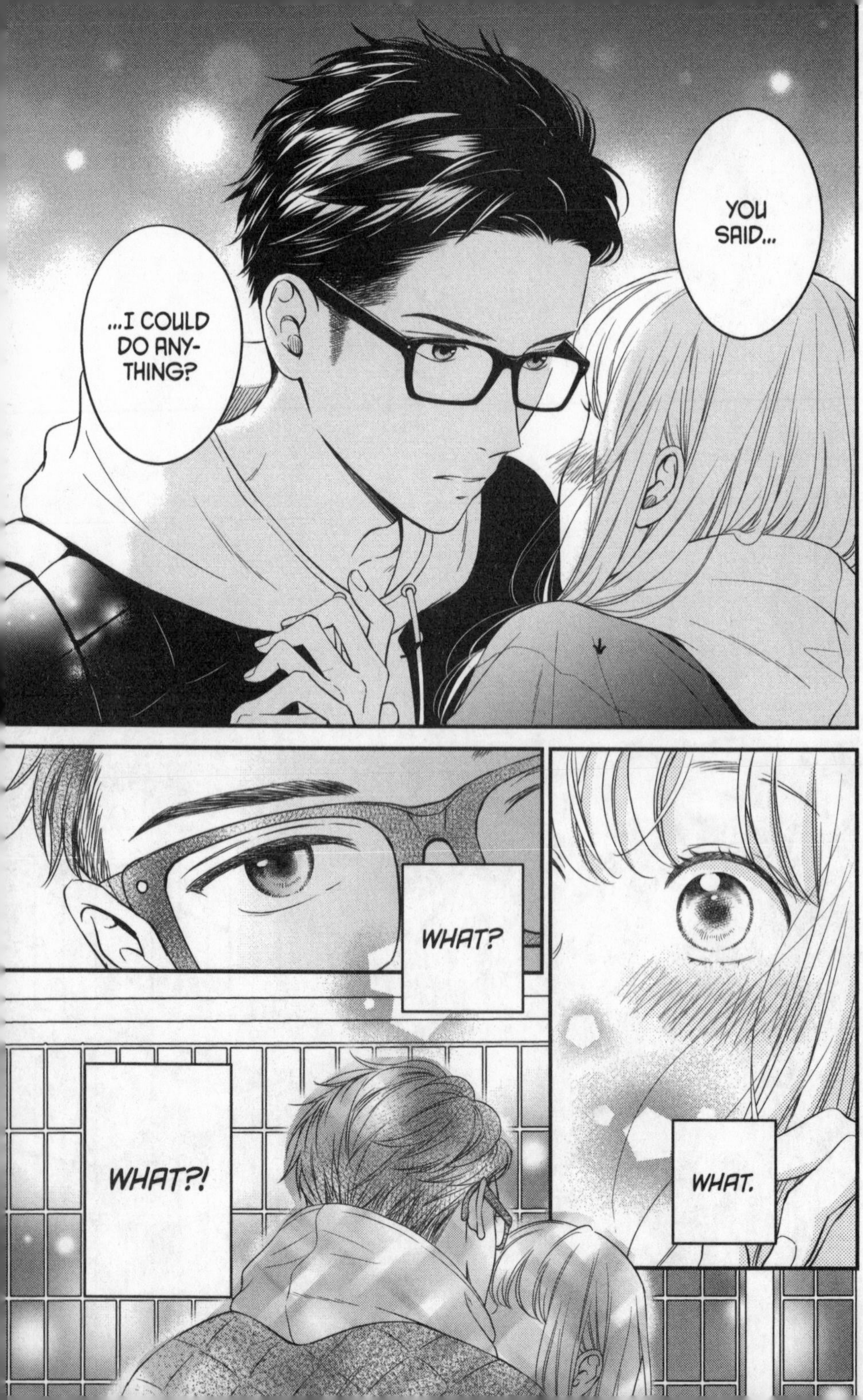
YOU SAID...
...I COULD DO ANYTHING?
WHAT.
WHAT?
WHAT?!

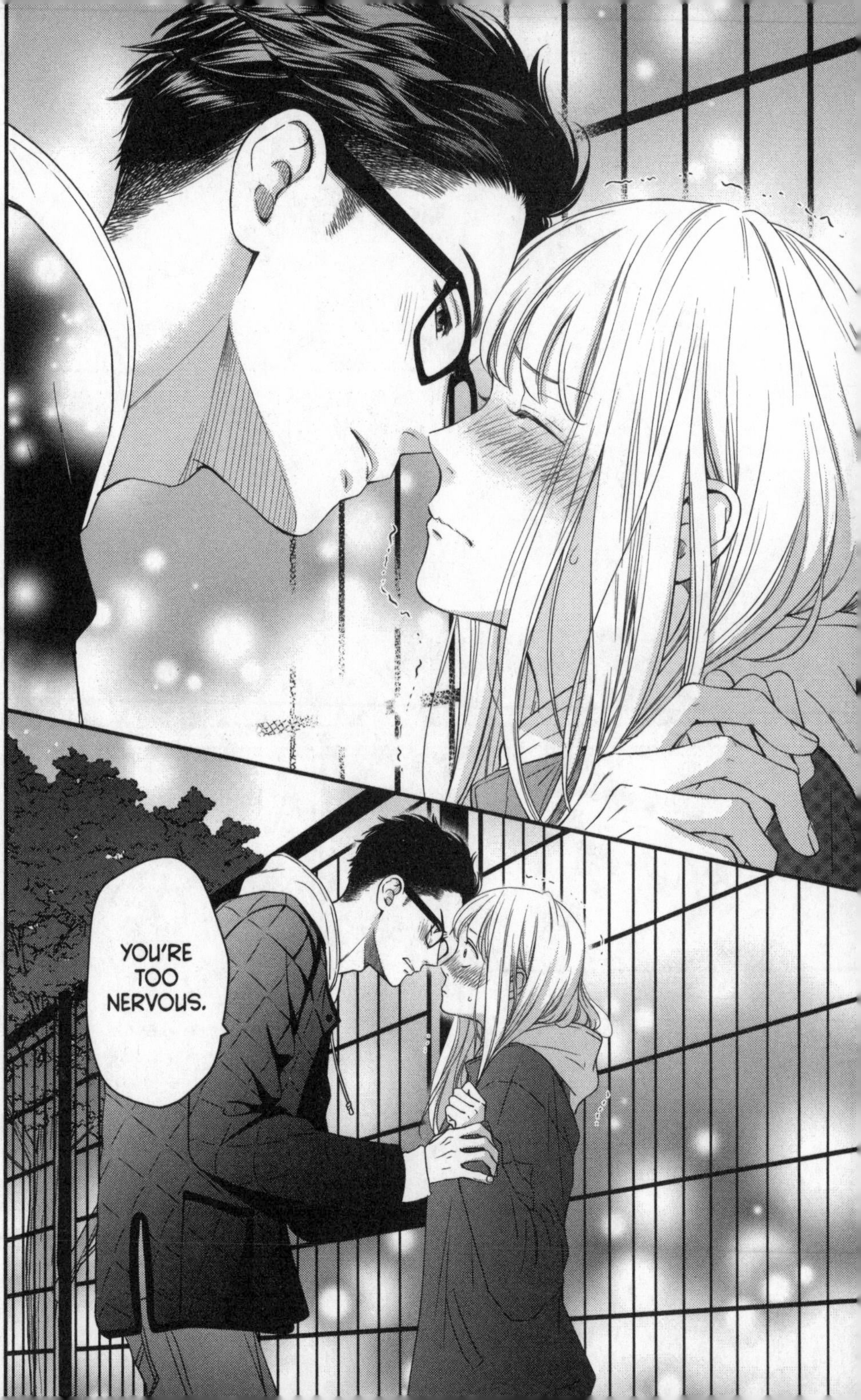
YOU'RE TOO NERVOUS.

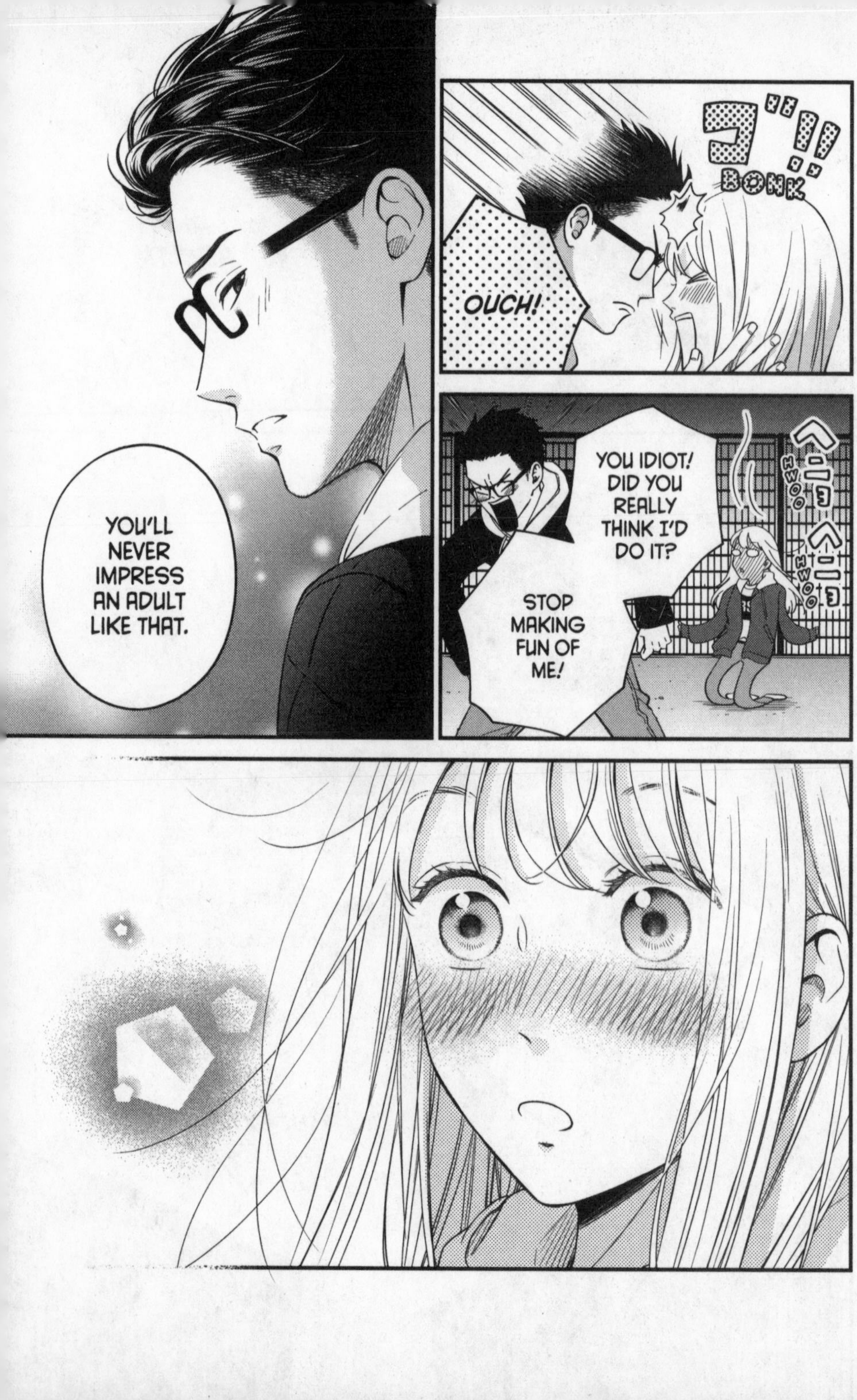
DONK
OUCH!
HWOO
HWOO
YOU IDIOT! DID YOU REALLY THINK I'D DO IT?
STOP MAKING FUN OF ME!
YOU'LL NEVER IMPRESS AN ADULT LIKE THAT.

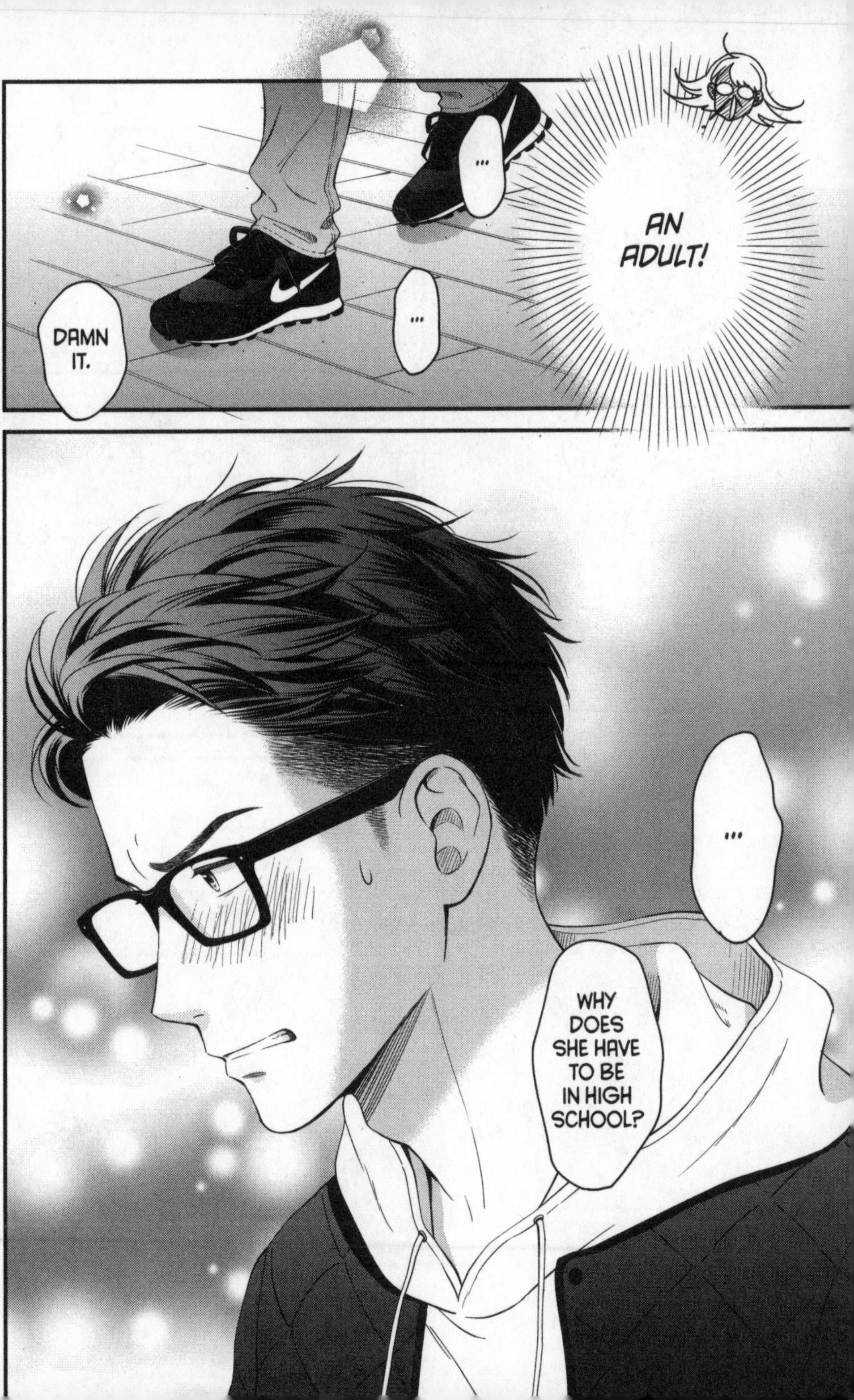
AN ADULT!
...
...
DAMN IT.
...
WHY DOES SHE HAVE TO BE IN HIGH SCHOOL?

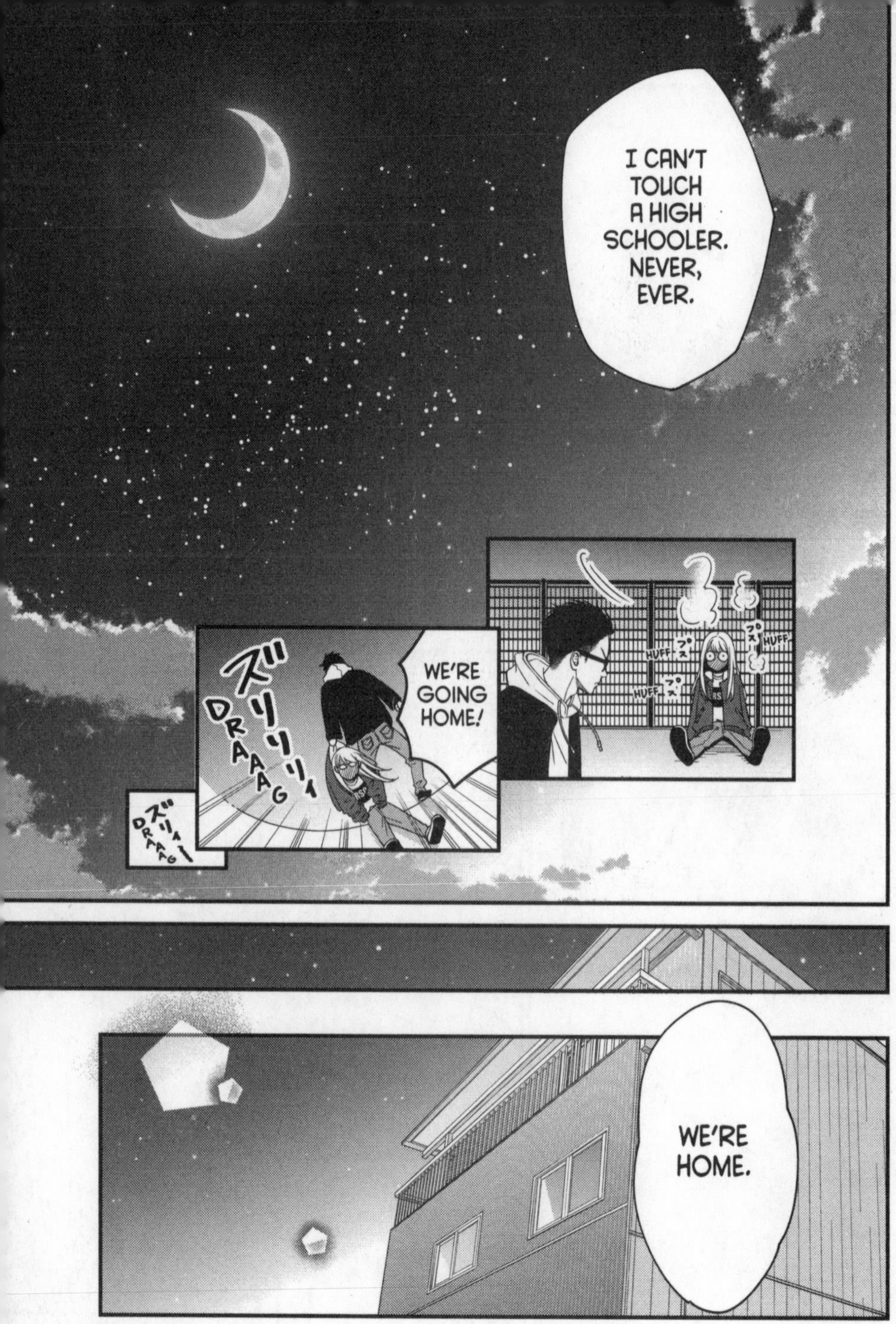
I CAN'T TOUCH A HIGH SCHOOLER. NEVER, EVER.
HUFF
HUFF
HUFF
WE'RE GOING HOME!
ズリリリィ
DRAAAG
DRAAAG
WE'RE HOME.

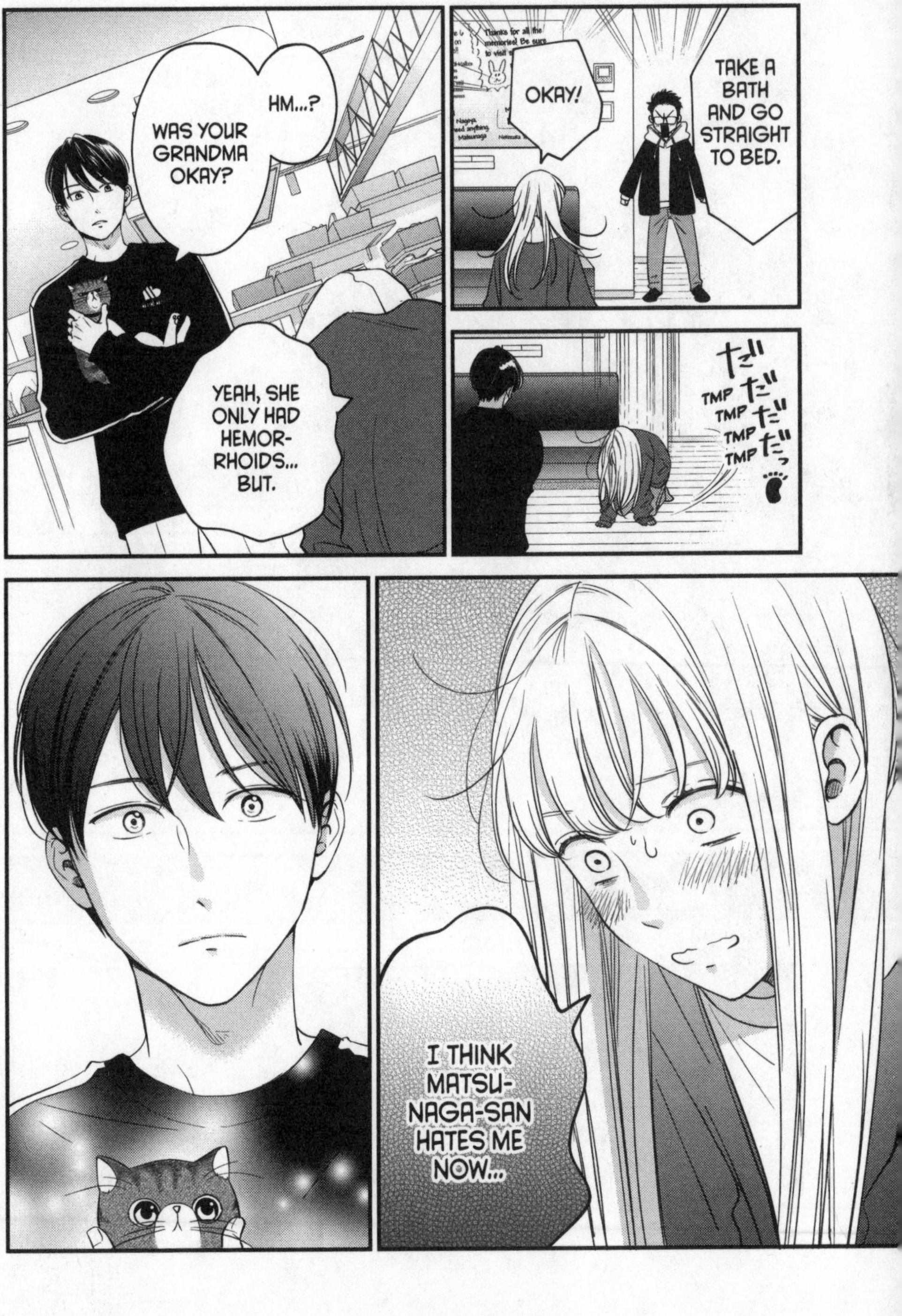
TAKE A BATH AND GO STRAIGHT TO BED.
OKAY!
だ
TMP だ
TMP だ
TMP だっ
TMP
HM...?
WAS YOUR GRANDMA OKAY?
YEAH, SHE ONLY HAD HEMOR-RHOIDS... BUT.
I THINK MATSU-NAGA-SAN HATES ME NOW...

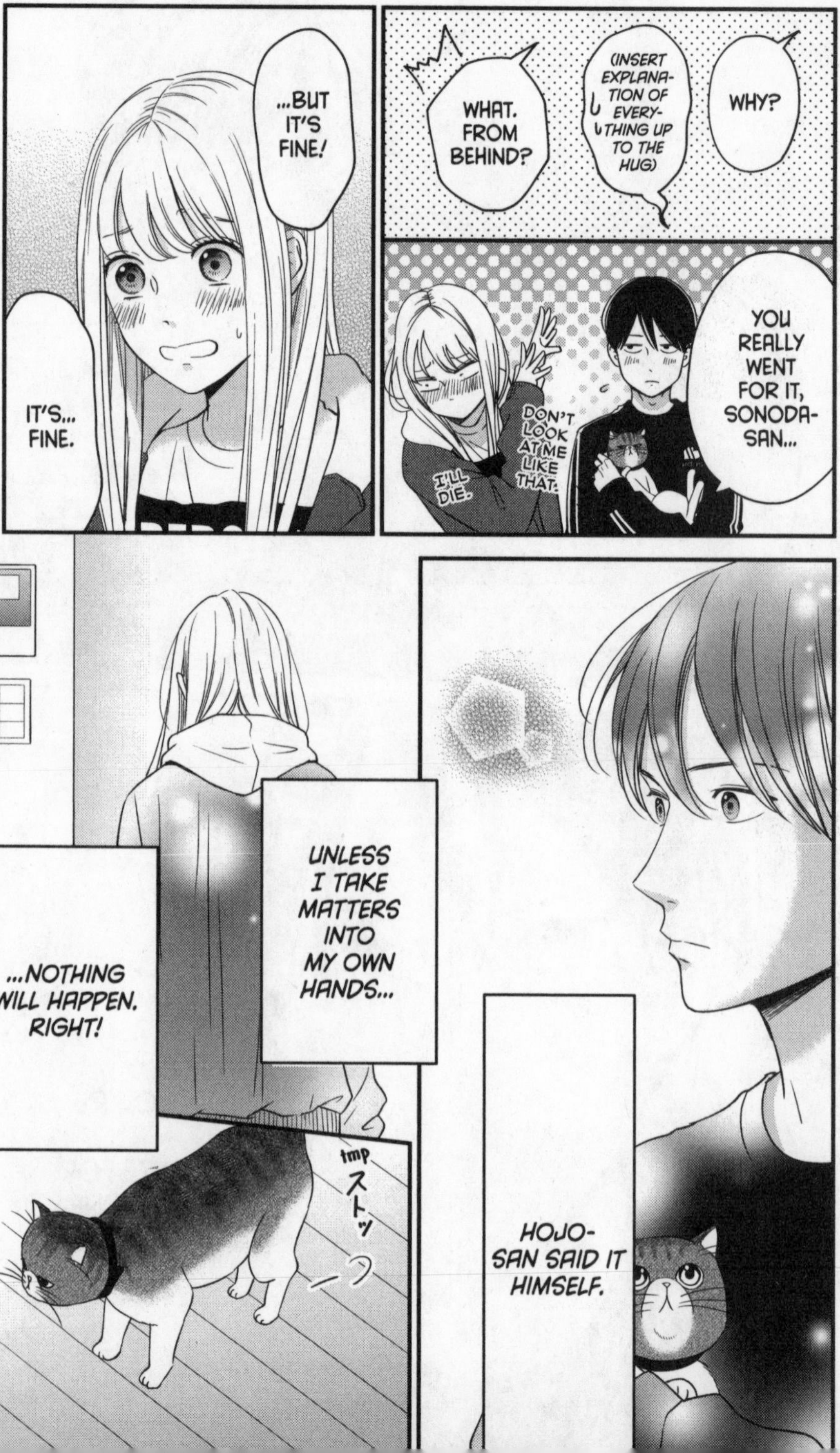
WHY?
(INSERT EXPLANATION OF EVERYTHING UP TO THE HUG)
WHAT. FROM BEHIND?
YOU REALLY WENT FOR IT, SONODA-SAN...
DON'T LOOK AT ME LIKE THAT.
I'LL DIE.
...BUT IT'S FINE!
IT'S... FINE.
HOJO-SAN SAID IT HIMSELF.
UNLESS I TAKE MATTERS INTO MY OWN HANDS...
...NOTHING WILL HAPPEN. RIGHT!
tmp
ストッ

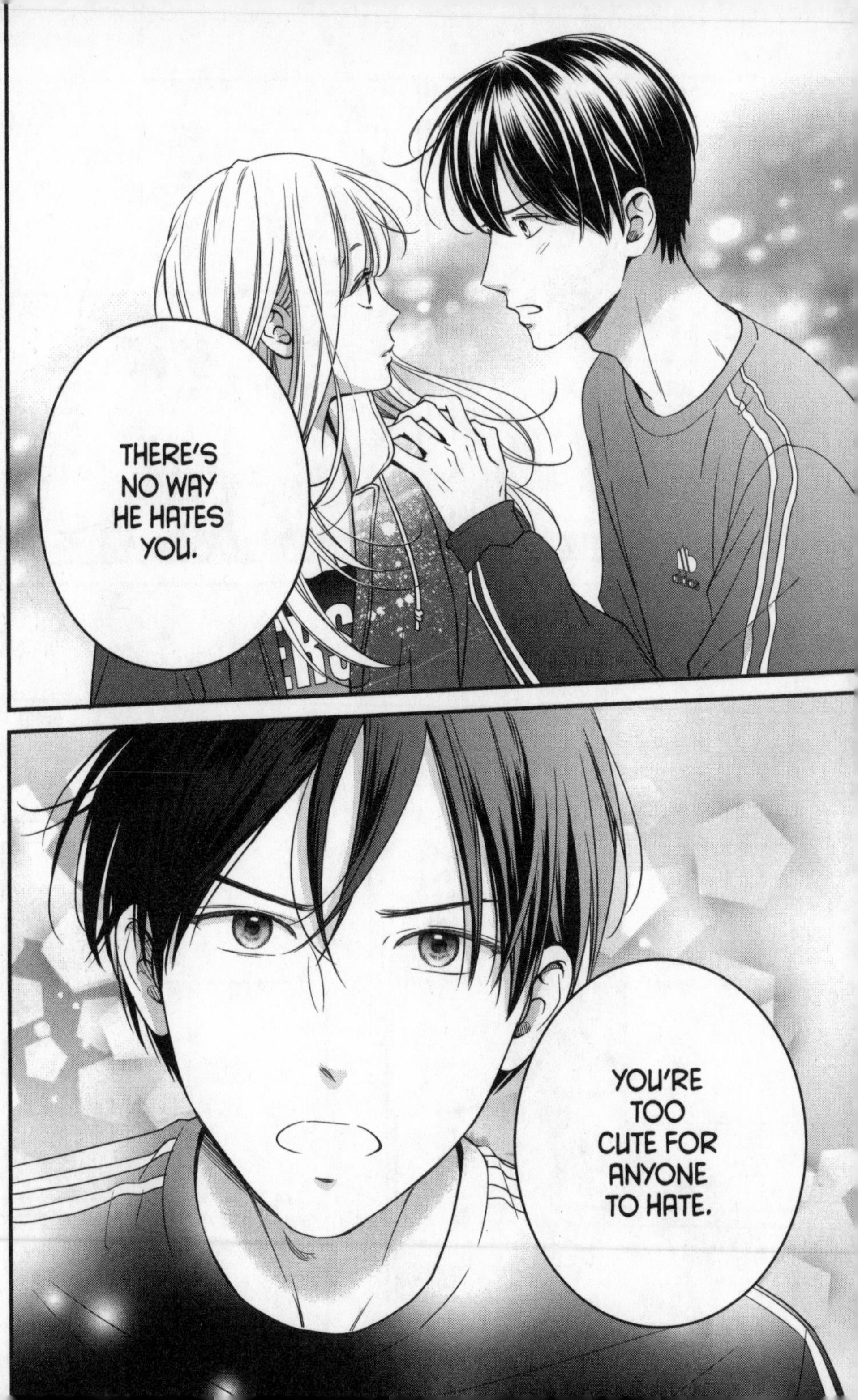
THERE'S NO WAY HE HATES YOU.
YOU'RE TOO CUTE FOR ANYONE TO HATE.

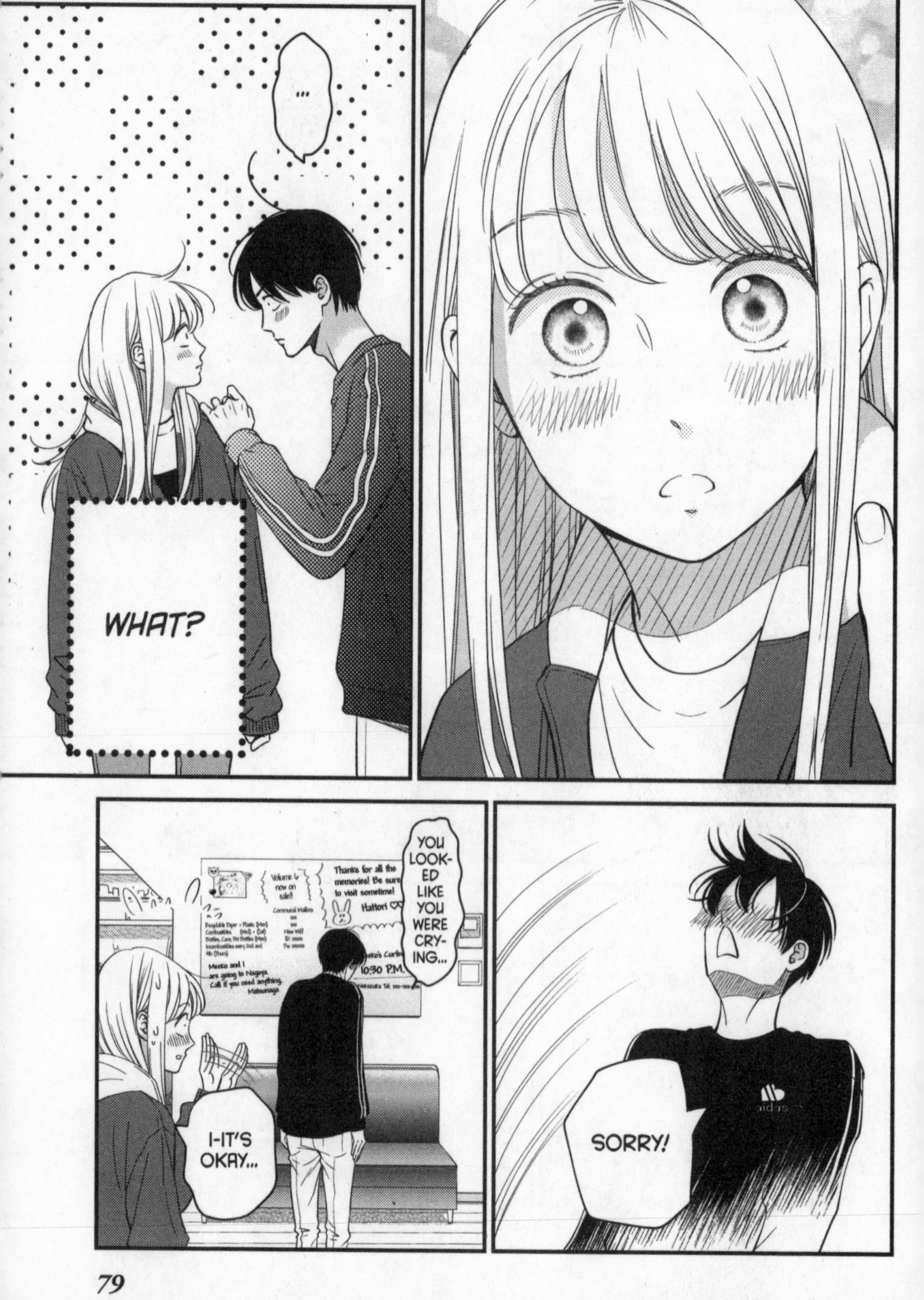

...
WHAT?
SORRY!
YOU LOOKED-ED LIKE YOU WERE CRY-ING...
Thanks for all the memories! Be sure to visit sometime! Hattori
Volume 6 now on sale!!
10:30 P.M.
Meeko and I are going to Nagoya. Call if you need anything. Matsunaga
I-IT'S OKAY...

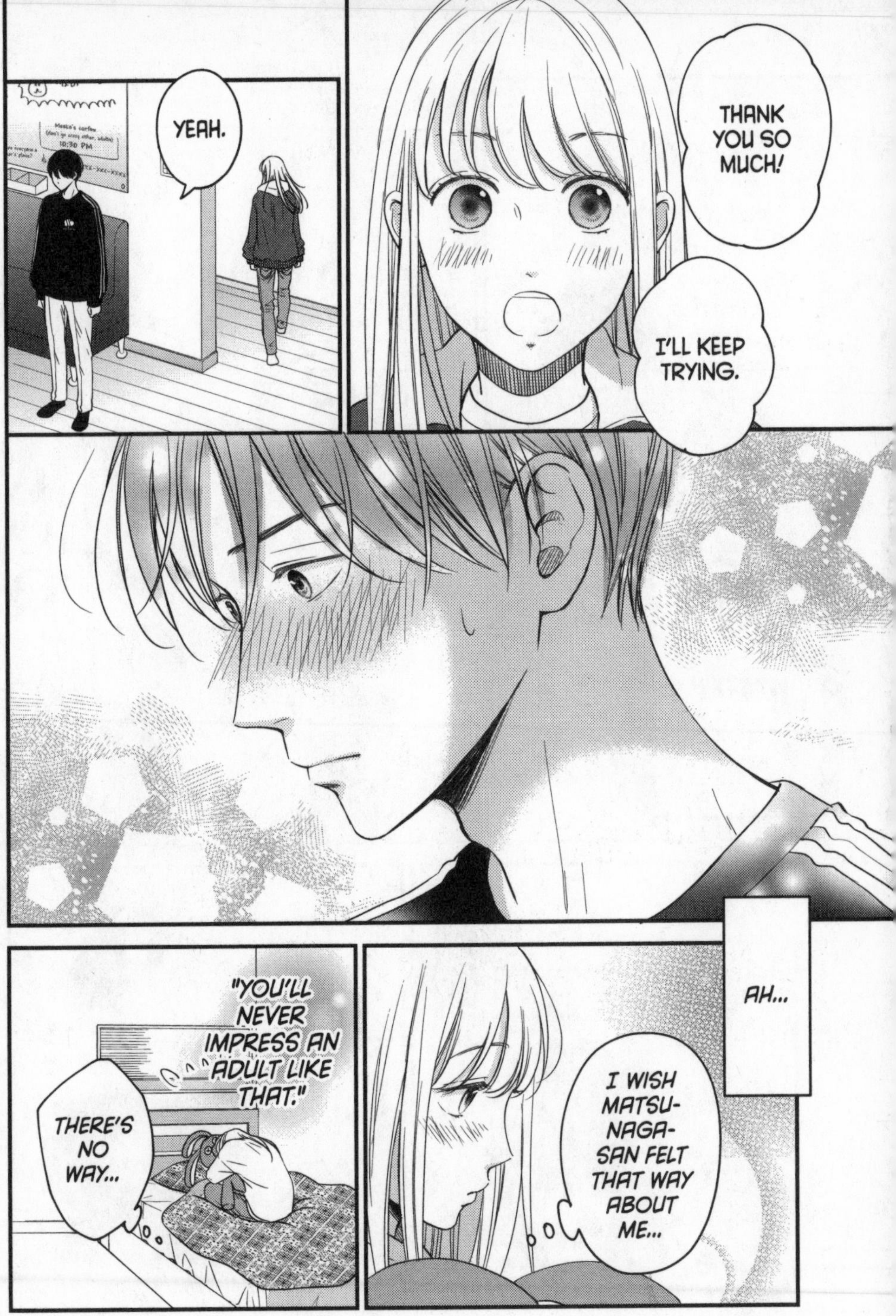
THANK YOU SO MUCH!
I'LL KEEP TRYING.
YEAH.
AH...
I WISH MATSUNAGA-SAN FELT THAT WAY ABOUT ME...
"YOU'LL NEVER IMPRESS AN ADULT LIKE THAT."
THERE'S NO WAY...

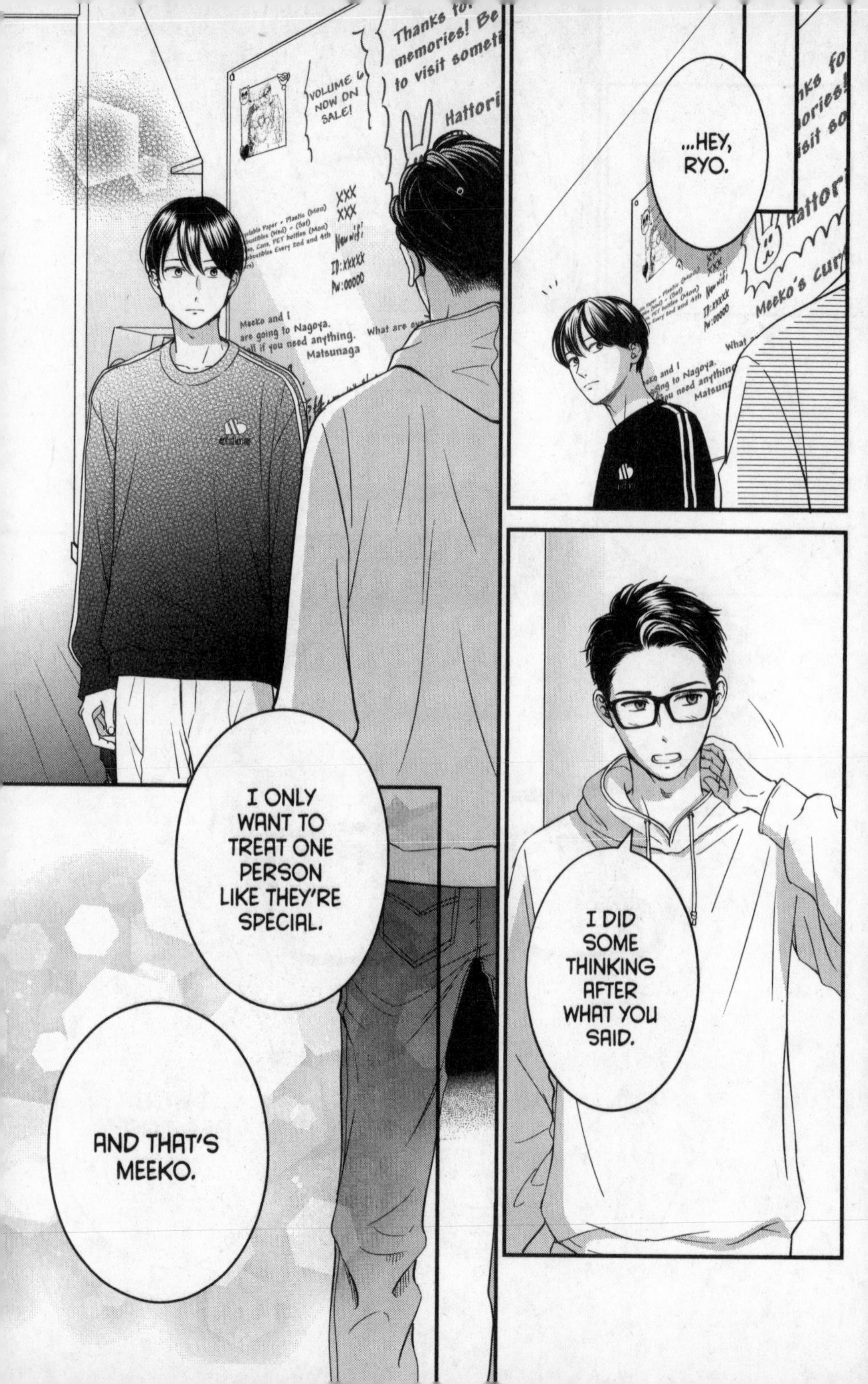
...HEY, RYO.
VOLUME 6 NOW DN SALE!
Hattori
Meeko and I are going to Nagoya.
Matsunaga
I DID SOME THINKING AFTER WHAT YOU SAID.
I ONLY WANT TO TREAT ONE PERSON LIKE THEY'RE SPECIAL.
AND THAT'S MEEKO.

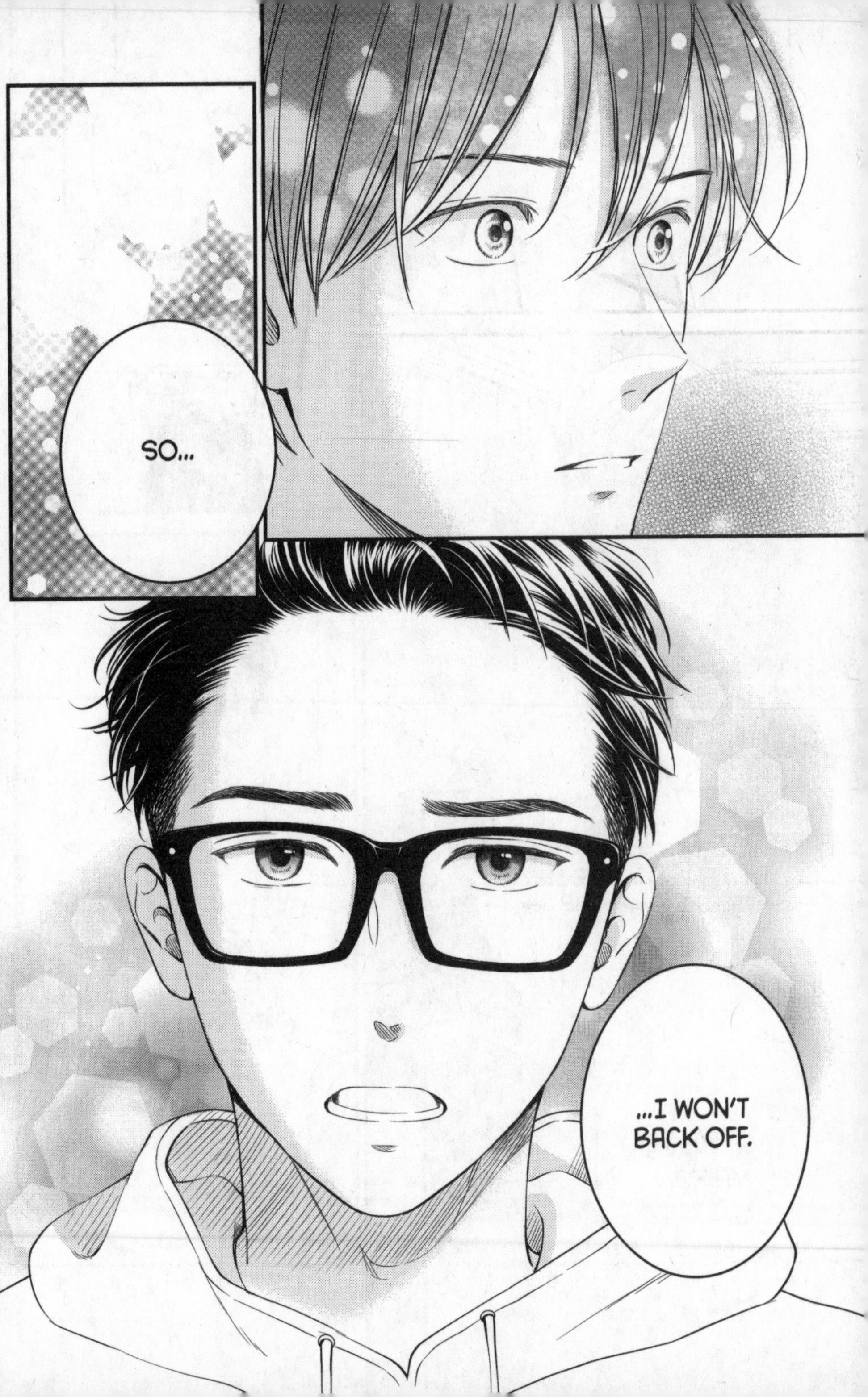
SO...
...I WON'T BACK OFF.

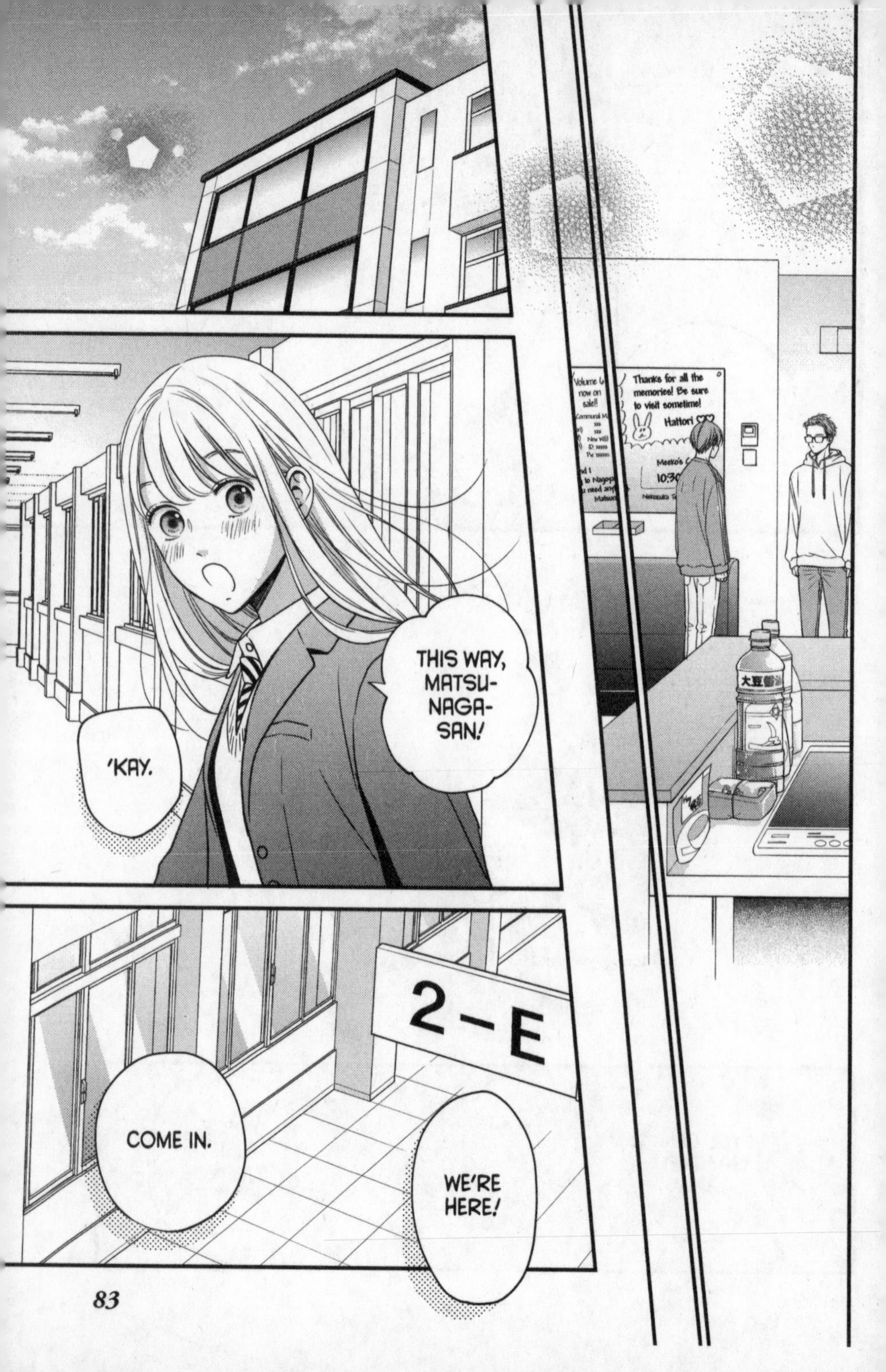
Thanks for all the memories! Be sure to visit sometime!
Hattori
Volume 6 now on sale!!
THIS WAY, MATSUNAGA-SAN!
'KAY.
2-E
WE'RE HERE!
COME IN.

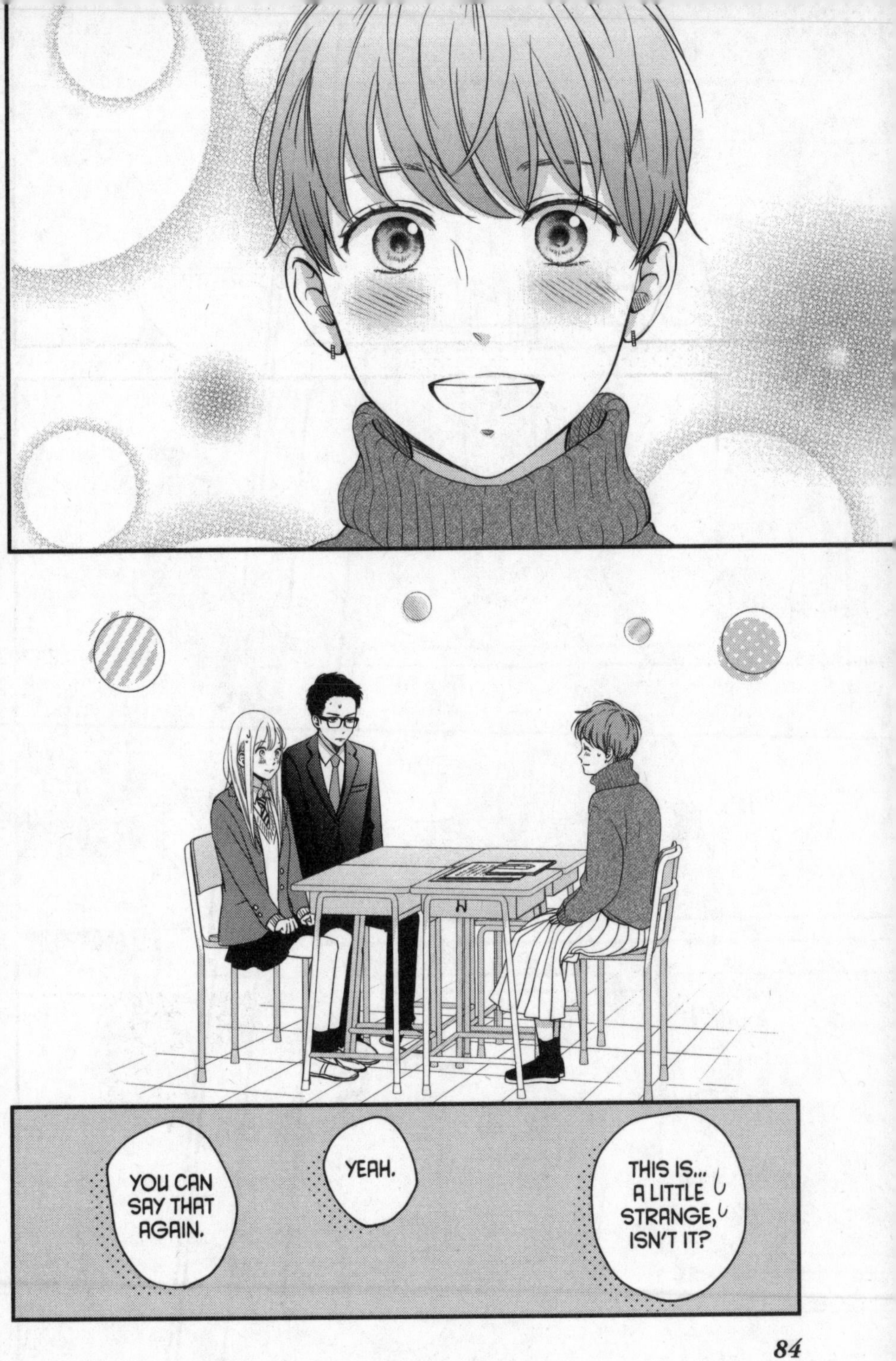
THIS IS... A LITTLE STRANGE, ISN'T IT?
YEAH.
YOU CAN SAY THAT AGAIN.

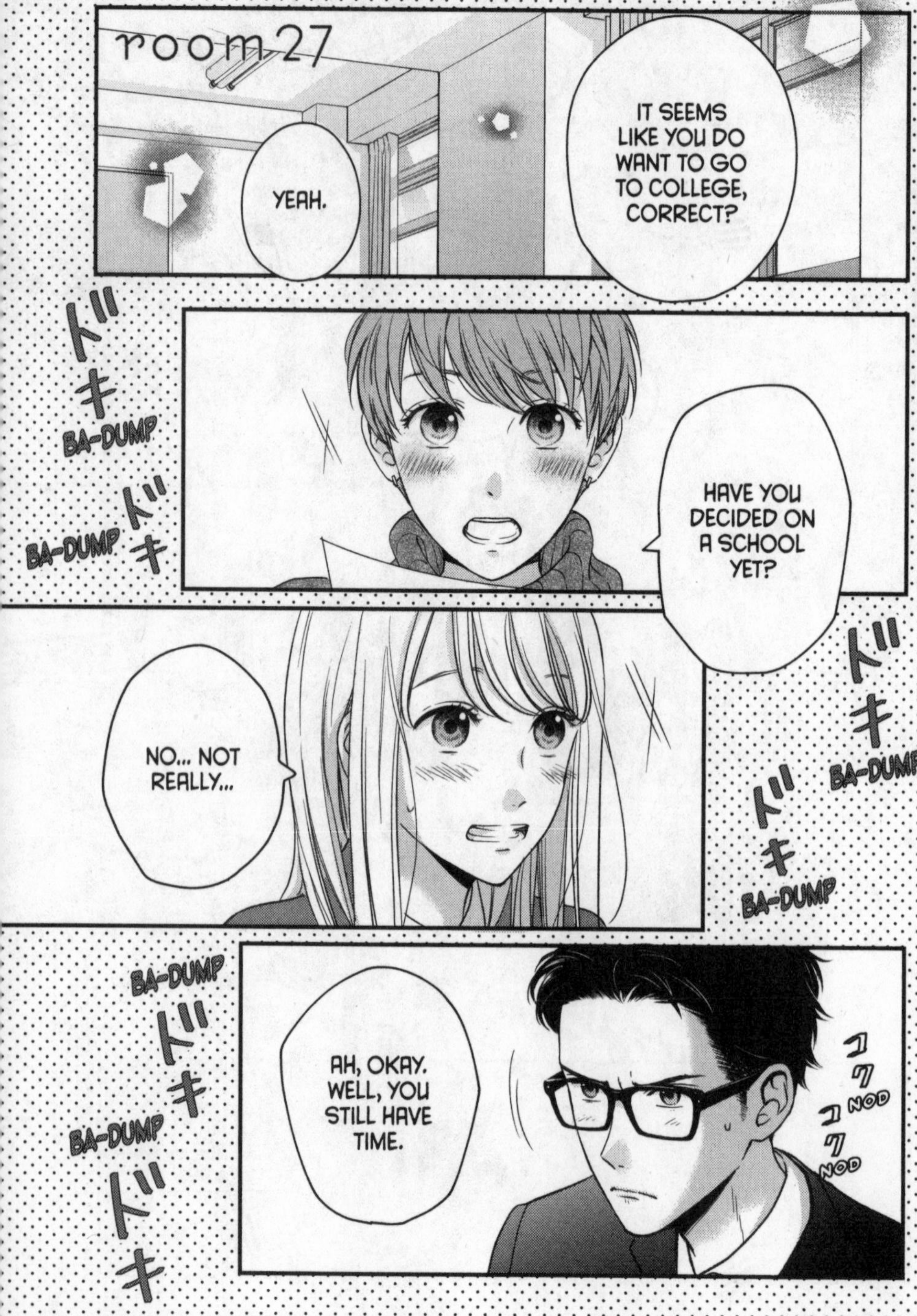
room 27
IT SEEMS LIKE YOU DO WANT TO GO TO COLLEGE, CORRECT?
YEAH.
HAVE YOU DECIDED ON A SCHOOL YET?
ドキ
BA-DUMP
ドキ
BA-DUMP
ドキ
BA-DUMP
ドキ
BA-DUMP
NO... NOT REALLY...
コク
NOD
コク
NOD
AH, OKAY. WELL, YOU STILL HAVE TIME.
BA-DUMP
ドキ
BA-DUMP
ドキ

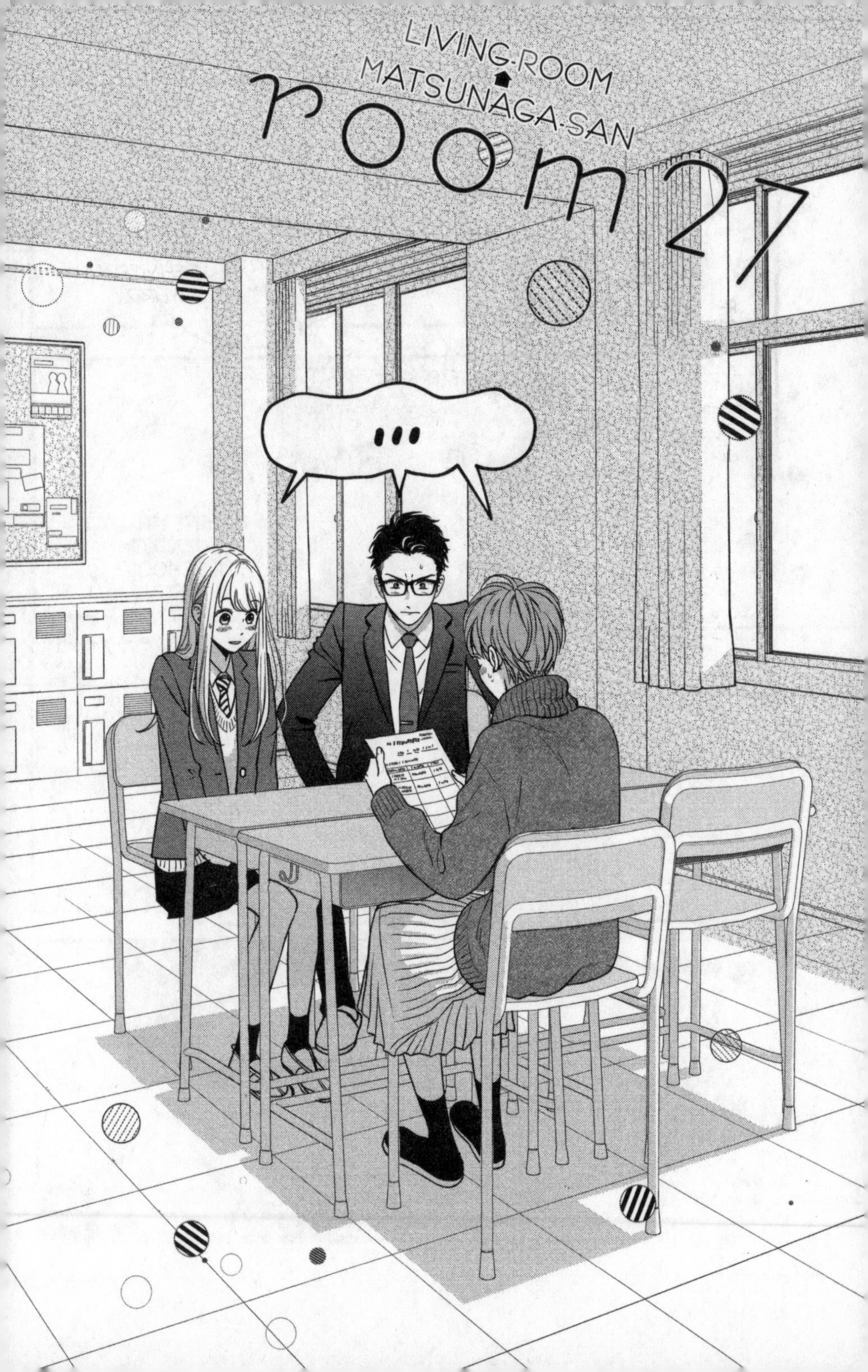
LIVING-ROOM
MATSUNAGA-SAN
room 27
...

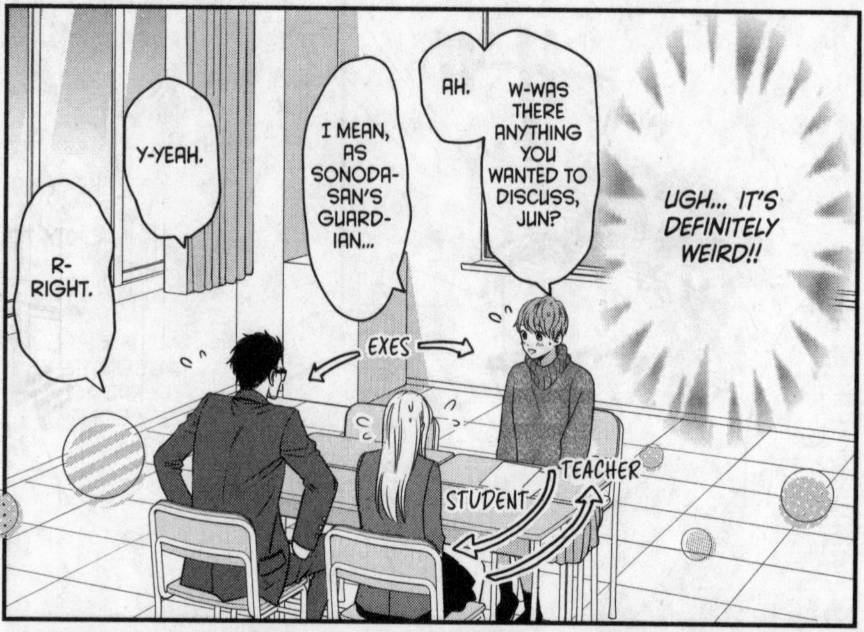
UGH... IT'S DEFINITELY WEIRD!!
AH.
W-WAS THERE ANYTHING YOU WANTED TO DISCUSS, JUN?
I MEAN, AS SONODA-SAN'S GUARDIAN...
Y-YEAH.
R-RIGHT.
EXES
TEACHER
STUDENT

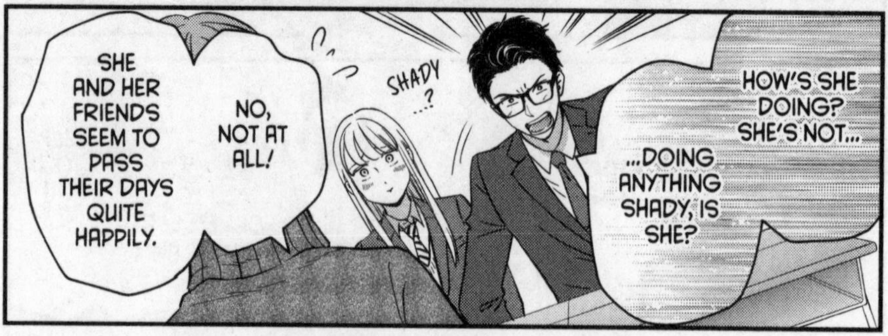
HOW'S SHE DOING? SHE'S NOT...
...DOING ANYTHING SHADY, IS SHE?
SHADY...?
NO, NOT AT ALL!
SHE AND HER FRIENDS SEEM TO PASS THEIR DAYS QUITE HAPPILY.

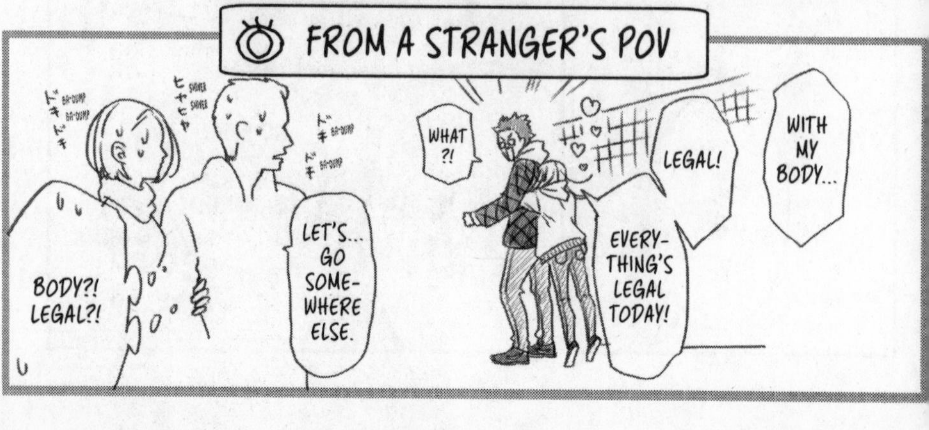
FROM A STRANGER'S POV
WITH MY BODY...
LEGAL!
EVERYTHING'S LEGAL TODAY!
WHAT?!
BA-DUMP BA-DUMP
SHIVER SHIVER
LET'S... GO SOMEWHERE ELSE.
BODY?! LEGAL?!

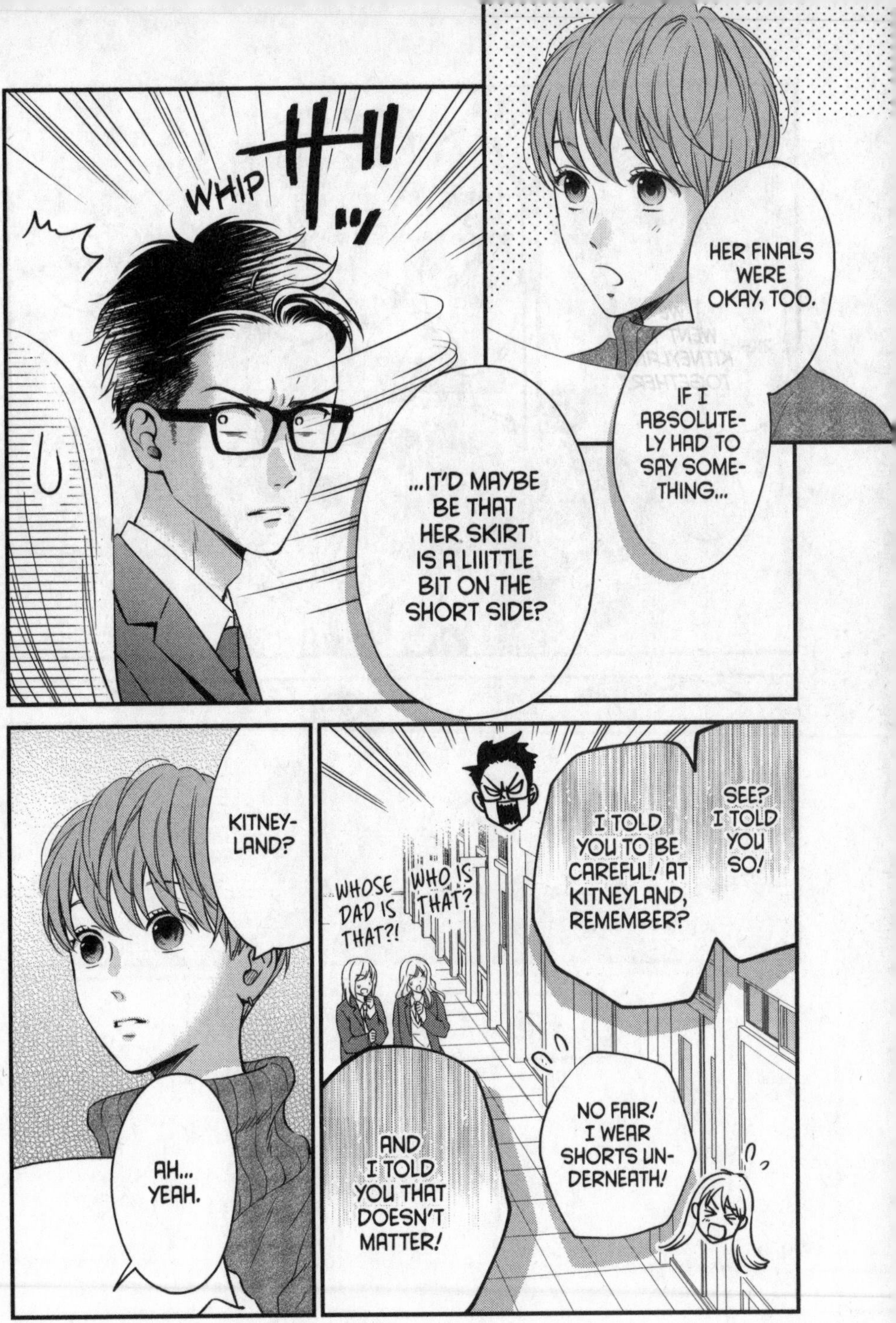
HER FINALS WERE OKAY, TOO.
IF I ABSOLUTE-LY HAD TO SAY SOME-THING...
WHIP
ザッ
...IT'D MAYBE BE THAT HER SKIRT IS A LIIITTLE BIT ON THE SHORT SIDE?
SEE? I TOLD YOU SO!
I TOLD YOU TO BE CAREFUL! AT KITNEYLAND, REMEMBER?
WHO IS THAT?
WHOSE DAD IS THAT?!
NO FAIR! I WEAR SHORTS UN-DERNEATH!
AND I TOLD YOU THAT DOESN'T MATTER!
KITNEY-LAND?
AH... YEAH.

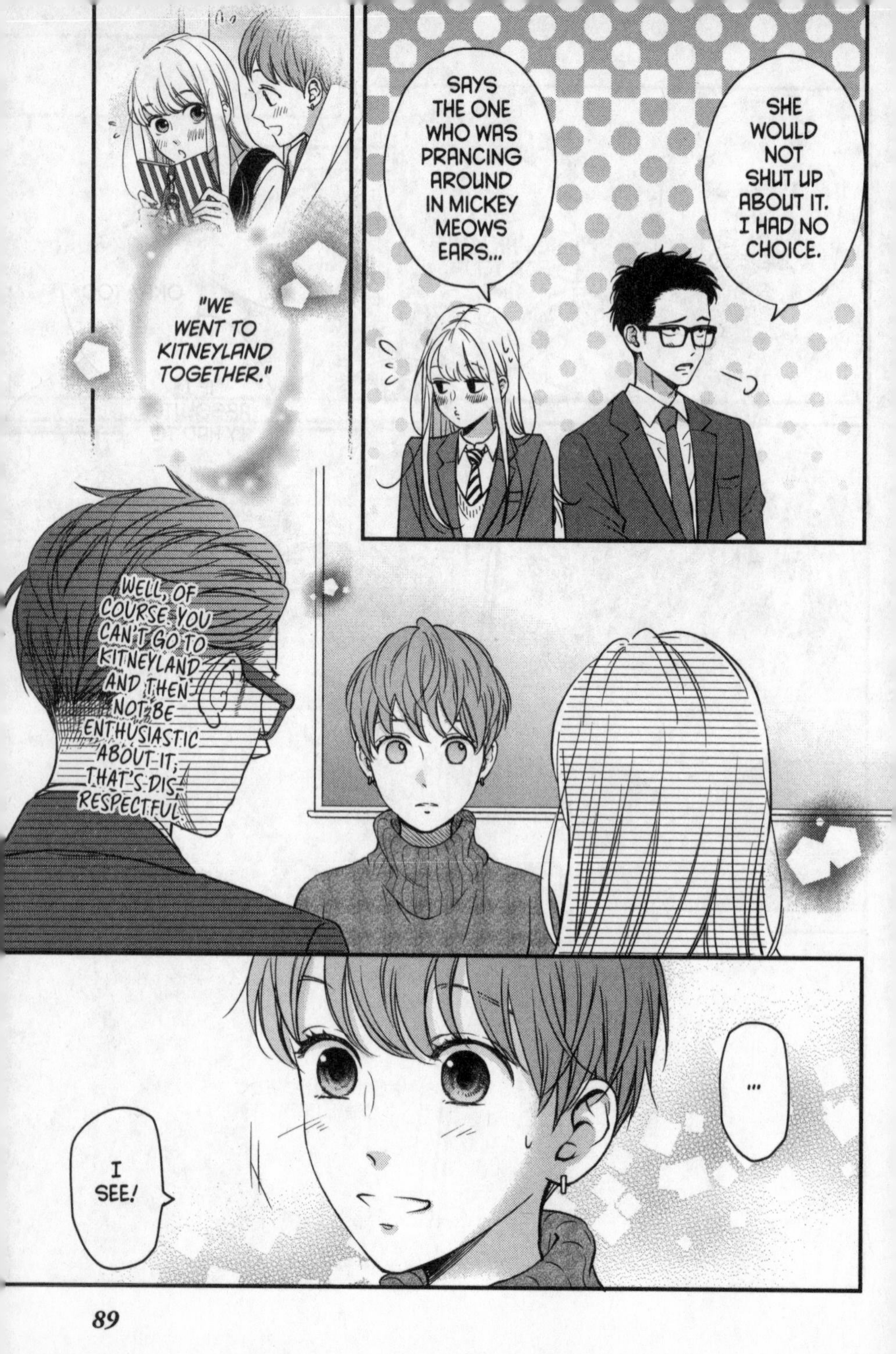
SHE WOULD NOT SHUT UP ABOUT IT. I HAD NO CHOICE.
SAYS THE ONE WHO WAS PRANCING AROUND IN MICKEY MEOWS EARS...
"WE WENT TO KITNEYLAND TOGETHER."
WELL, OF COURSE YOU CAN'T GO TO KITNEYLAND AND THEN NOT BE ENTHUSIASTIC ABOUT IT, THAT'S DISRESPECTFUL
...
I SEE!

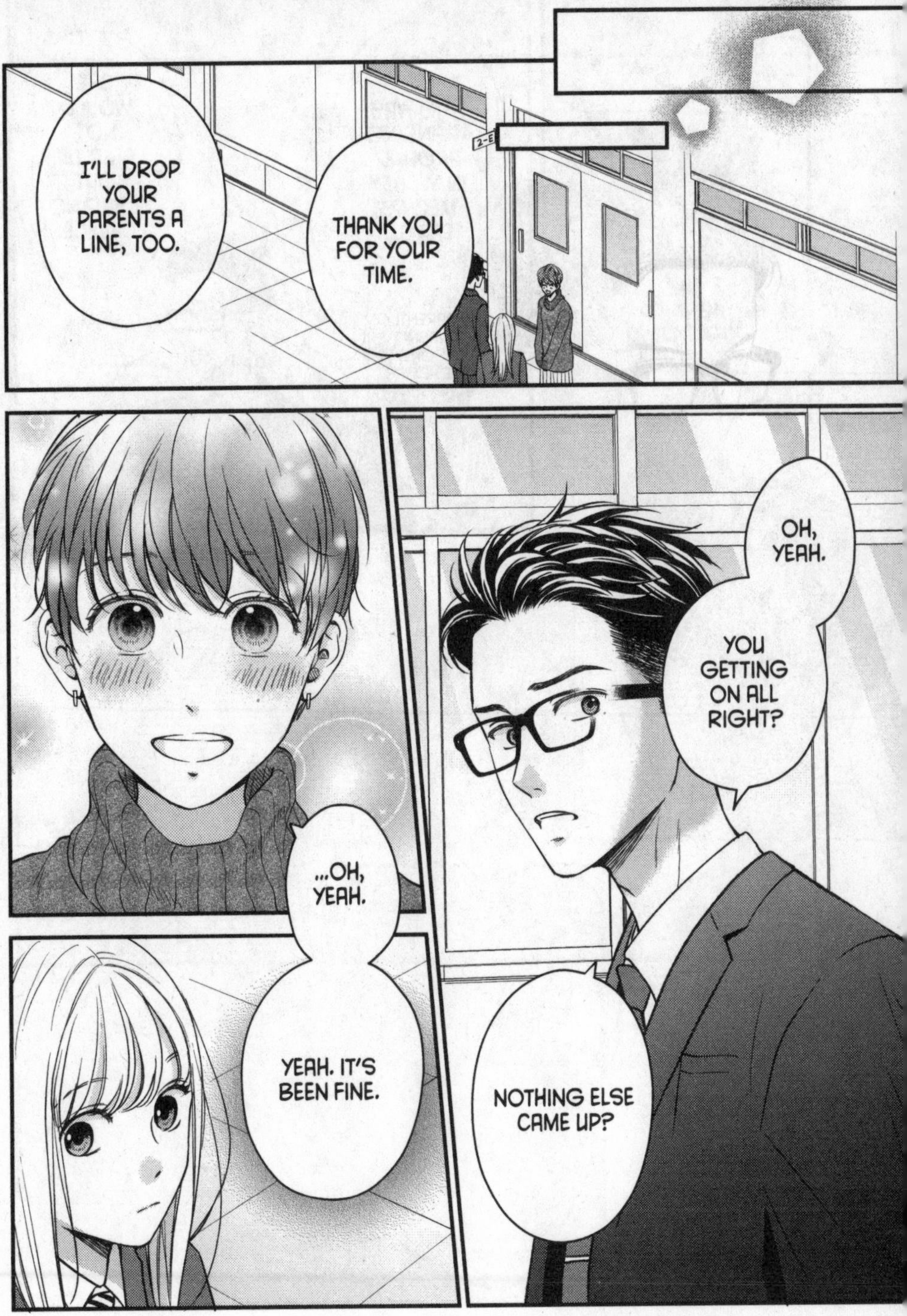
THANK YOU FOR YOUR TIME.
I'LL DROP YOUR PARENTS A LINE, TOO.
OH, YEAH.
YOU GETTING ON ALL RIGHT?
NOTHING ELSE CAME UP?
...OH, YEAH.
YEAH. IT'S BEEN FINE.

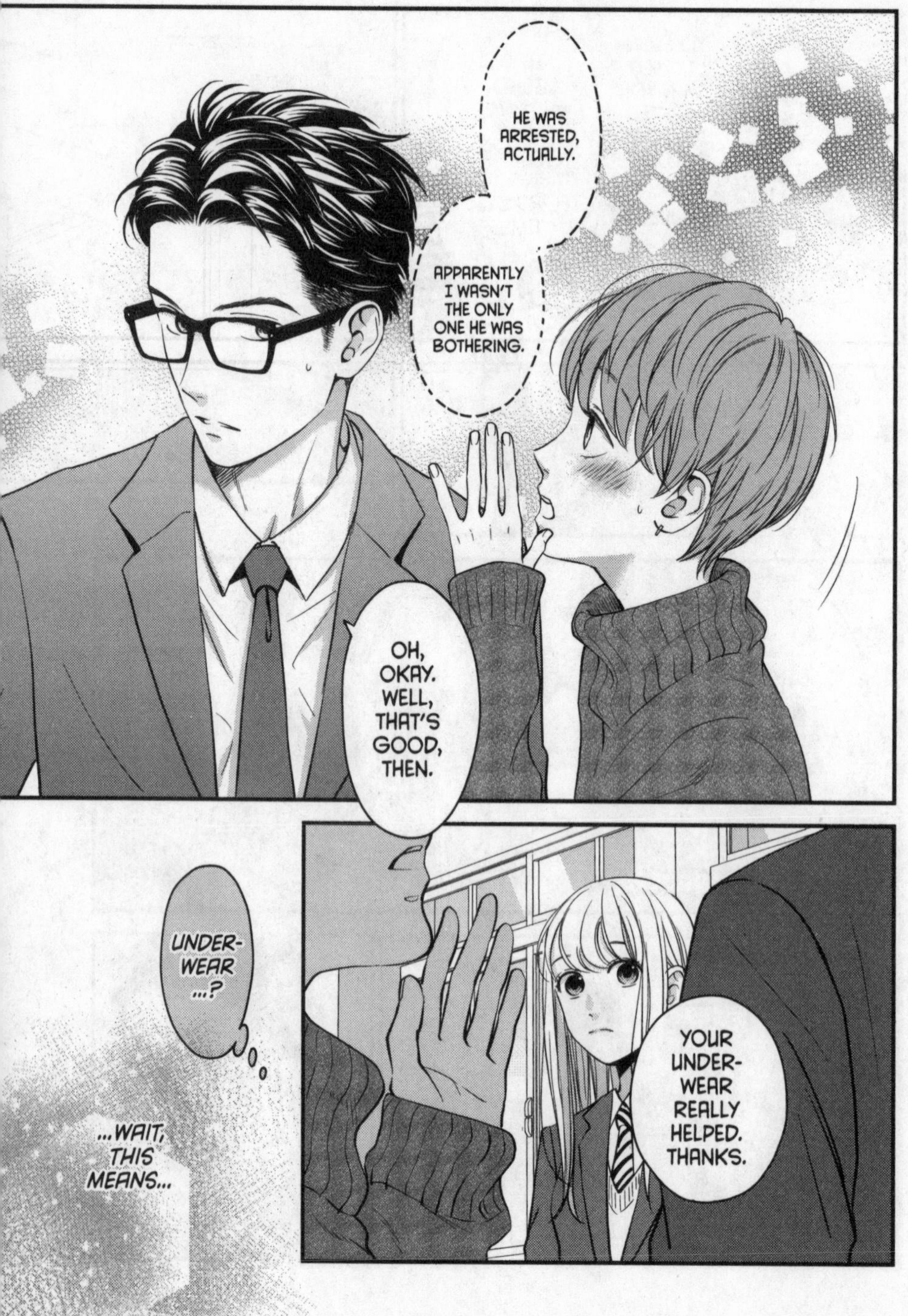
HE WAS ARRESTED, ACTUALLY.
APPARENTLY I WASN'T THE ONLY ONE HE WAS BOTHERING.
OH, OKAY. WELL, THAT'S GOOD, THEN.
YOUR UNDER-WEAR REALLY HELPED. THANKS.
UNDER-WEAR ...?
...WAIT, THIS MEANS...

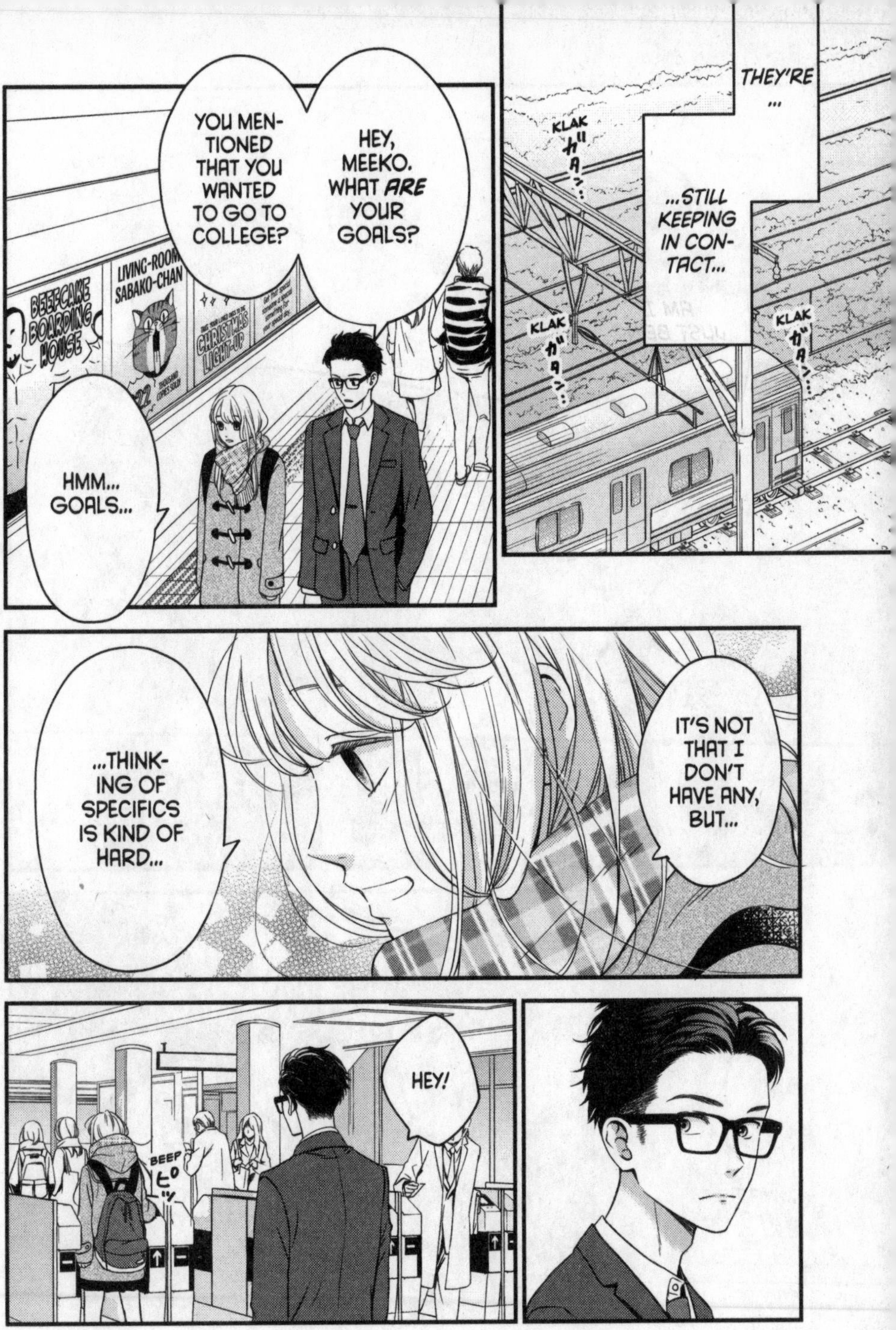
THEY'RE ...
KLAK
KLAK
KLAK
...STILL KEEPING IN CONTACT...
HEY, MEEKO. WHAT ARE YOUR GOALS?
YOU MENTIONED THAT YOU WANTED TO GO TO COLLEGE?
LIVING-ROOM SABAKO-CHAN
BEEFCAKE BOARDING HOUSE
CHRISTMAS LIGHT-UP
HMM... GOALS...
IT'S NOT THAT I DON'T HAVE ANY, BUT...
...THINKING OF SPECIFICS IS KIND OF HARD...
HEY!
BEEP

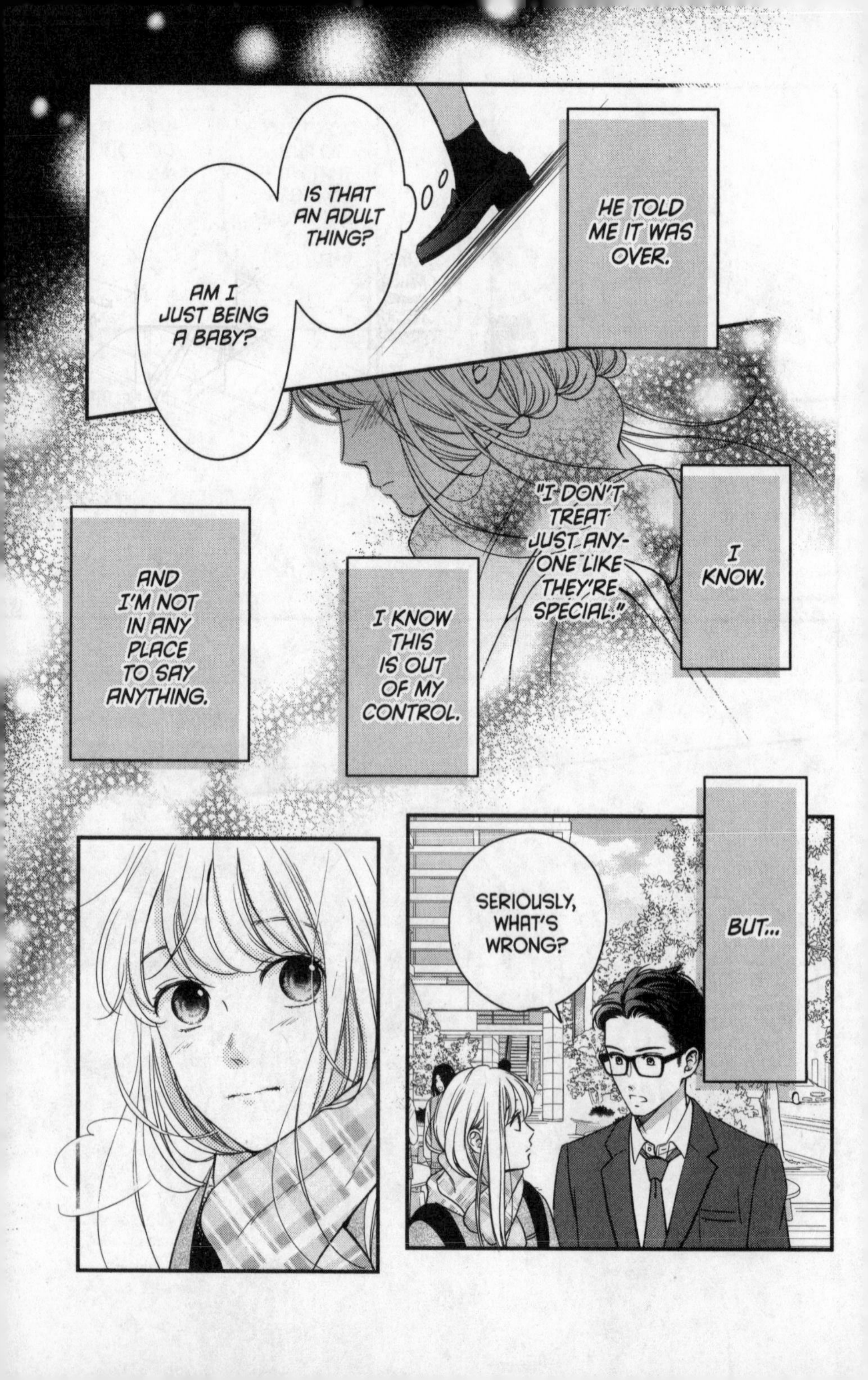
HE TOLD ME IT WAS OVER.
IS THAT AN ADULT THING?
AM I JUST BEING A BABY?
I KNOW.
"I DON'T TREAT JUST ANY-ONE LIKE THEY'RE SPECIAL."
I KNOW THIS IS OUT OF MY CONTROL.
AND I'M NOT IN ANY PLACE TO SAY ANYTHING.
BUT...
SERIOUSLY, WHAT'S WRONG?

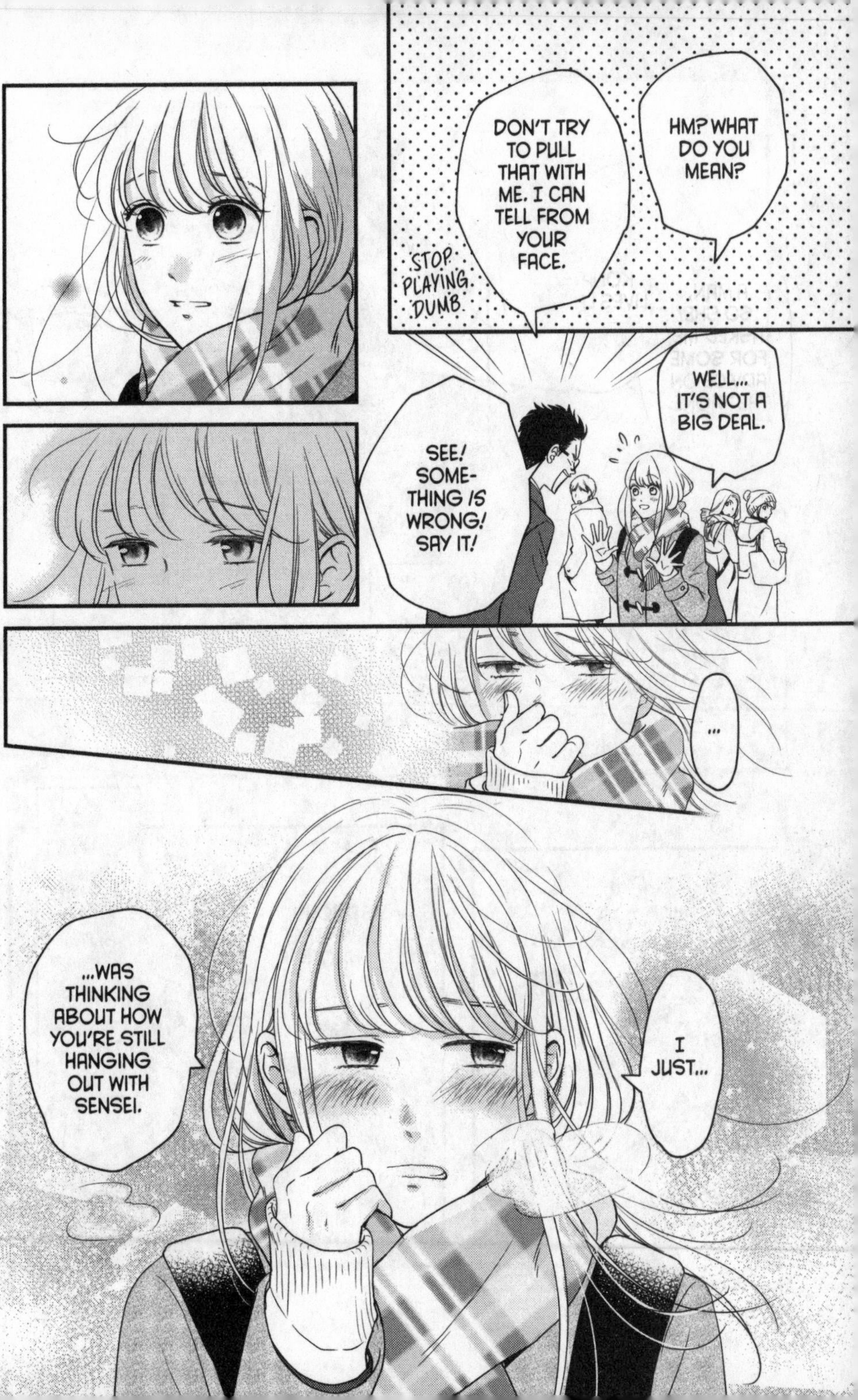
HM? WHAT DO YOU MEAN?
DON'T TRY TO PULL THAT WITH ME. I CAN TELL FROM YOUR FACE.
STOP PLAYING DUMB.
WELL... IT'S NOT A BIG DEAL.
SEE! SOMETHING IS WRONG! SAY IT!
...
I JUST...
...WAS THINKING ABOUT HOW YOU'RE STILL HANGING OUT WITH SENSEI.

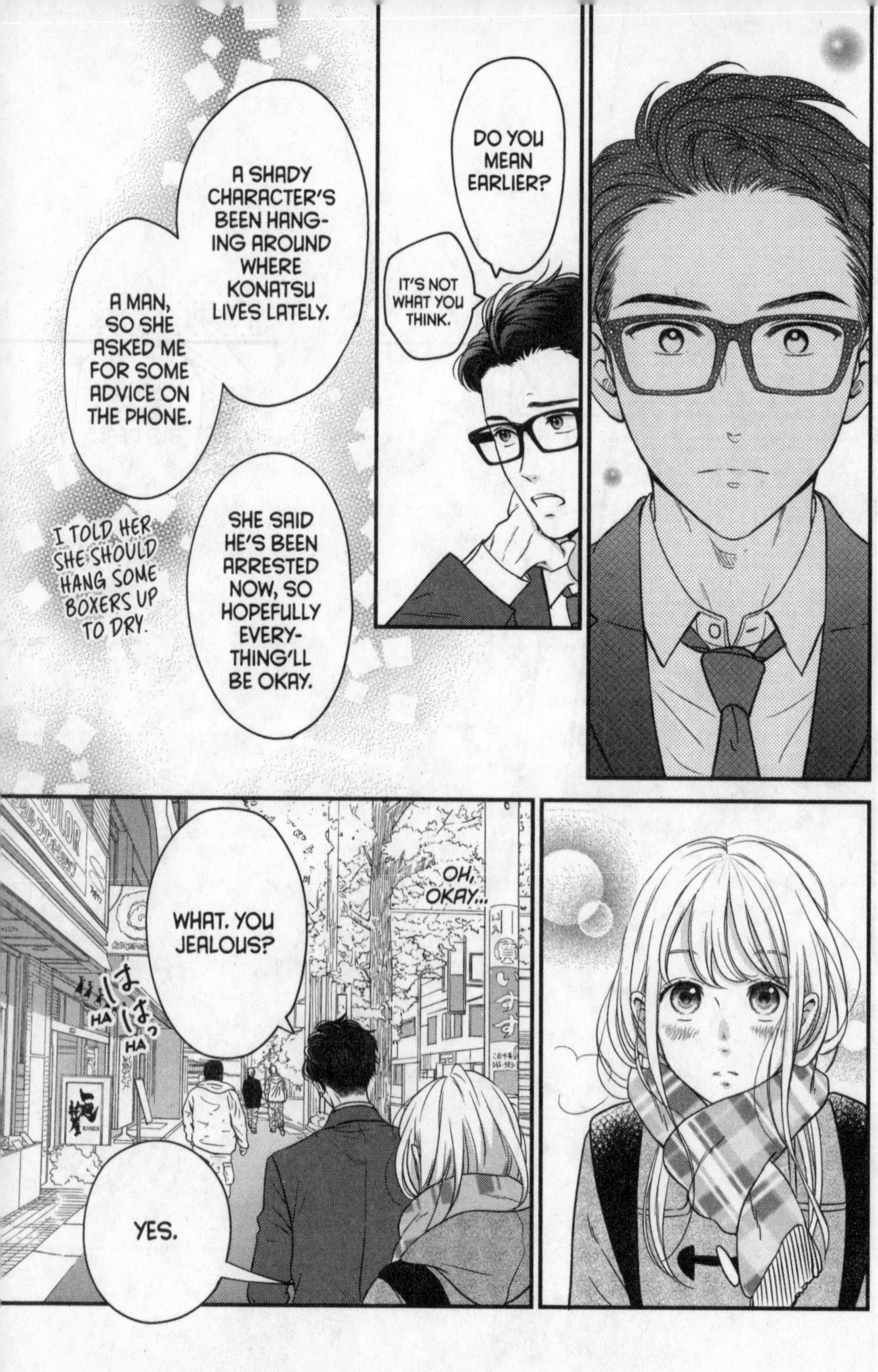
DO YOU MEAN EARLIER?
IT'S NOT WHAT YOU THINK.
A SHADY CHARACTER'S BEEN HANGING AROUND WHERE KONATSU LIVES LATELY.
A MAN, SO SHE ASKED ME FOR SOME ADVICE ON THE PHONE.
SHE SAID HE'S BEEN ARRESTED NOW, SO HOPEFULLY EVERYTHING'LL BE OKAY.
I TOLD HER SHE SHOULD HANG SOME BOXERS UP TO DRY.
OH, OKAY...
WHAT. YOU JEALOUS?
HA HA
YES.

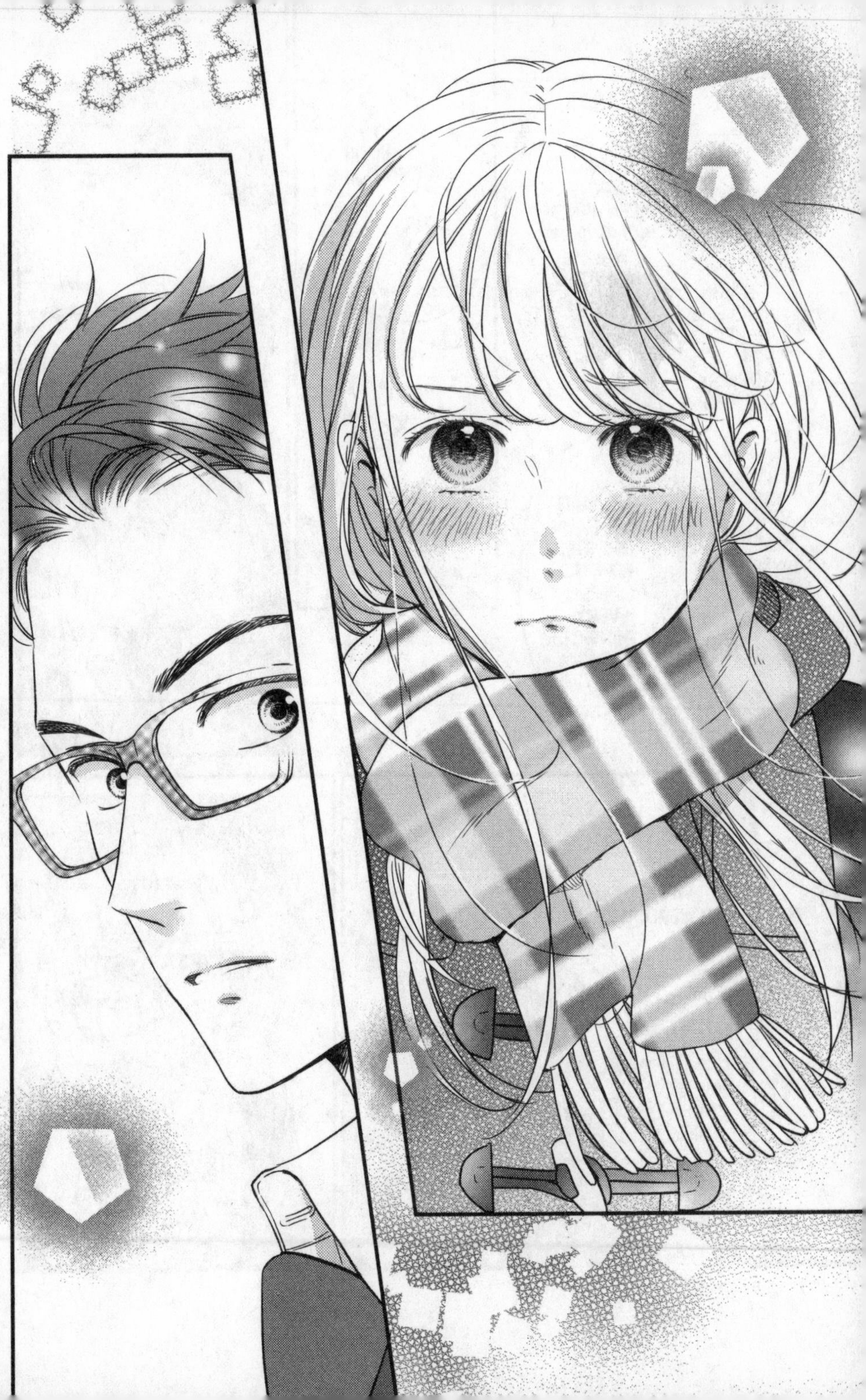

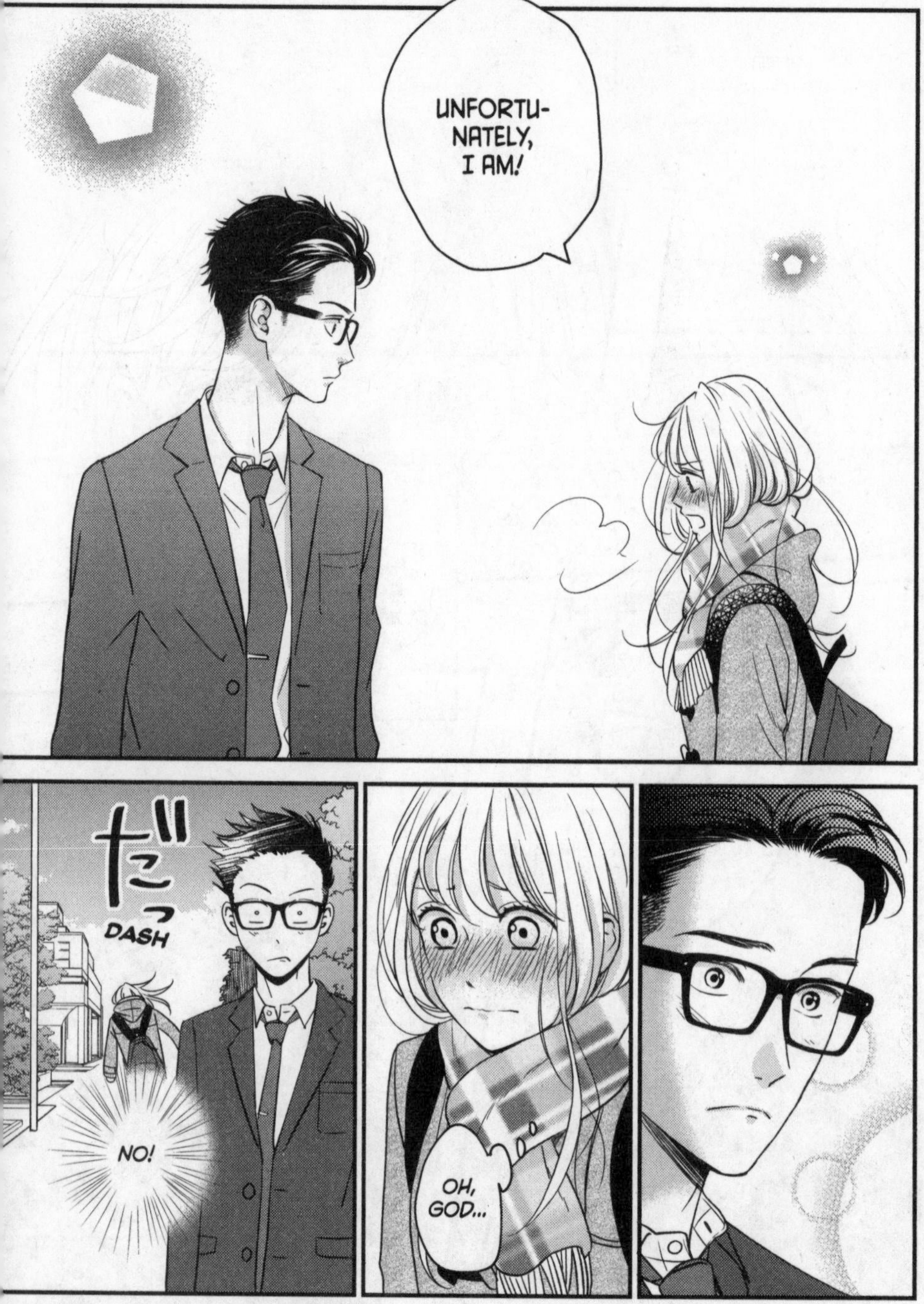
UNFORTU-NATELY, I AM!
OH, GOD...
だっ
DASH
NO!

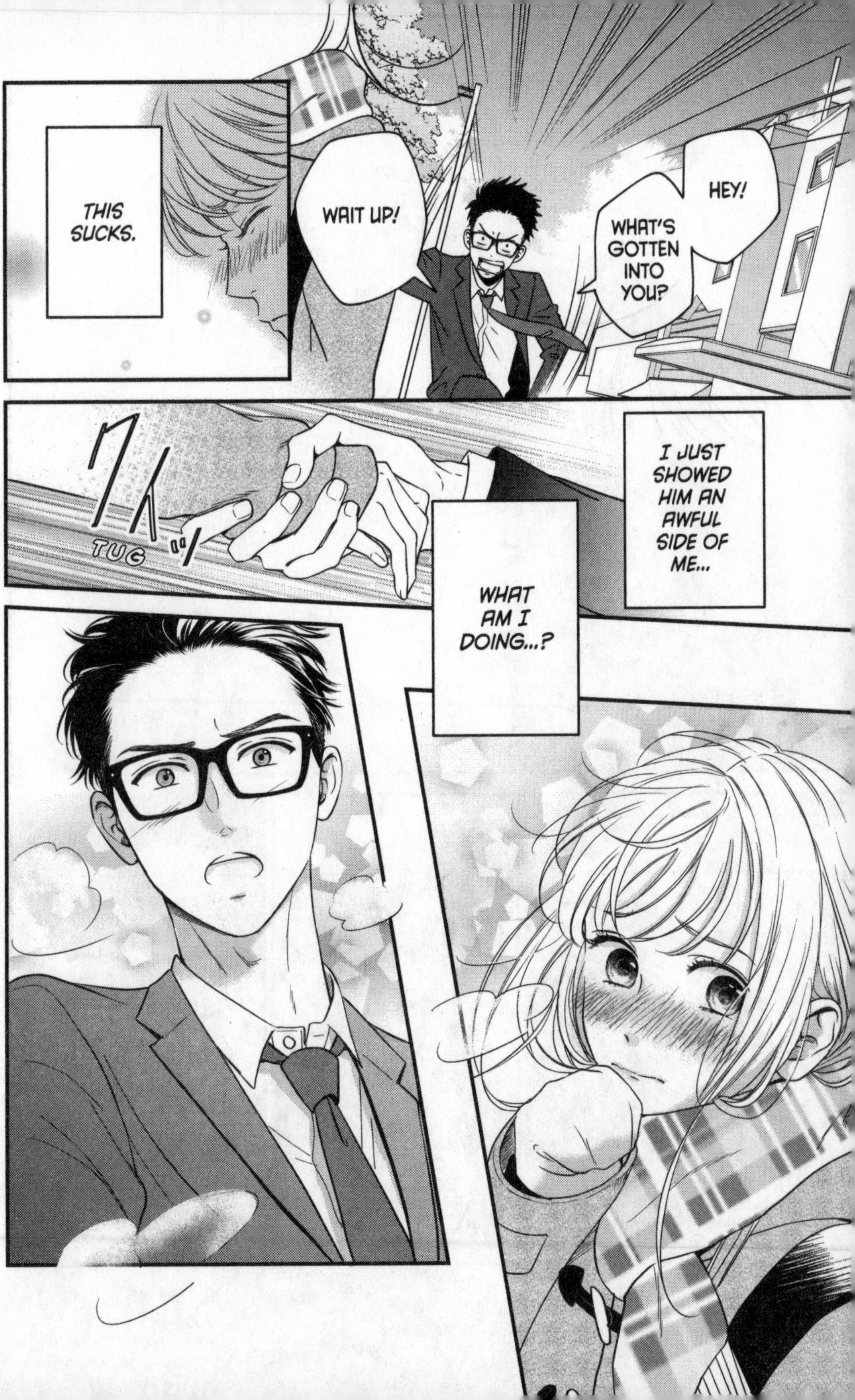
HEY!
WHAT'S GOTTEN INTO YOU?
WAIT UP!
THIS SUCKS.
I JUST SHOWED HIM AN AWFUL SIDE OF ME...
TUG
WHAT AM I DOING...?

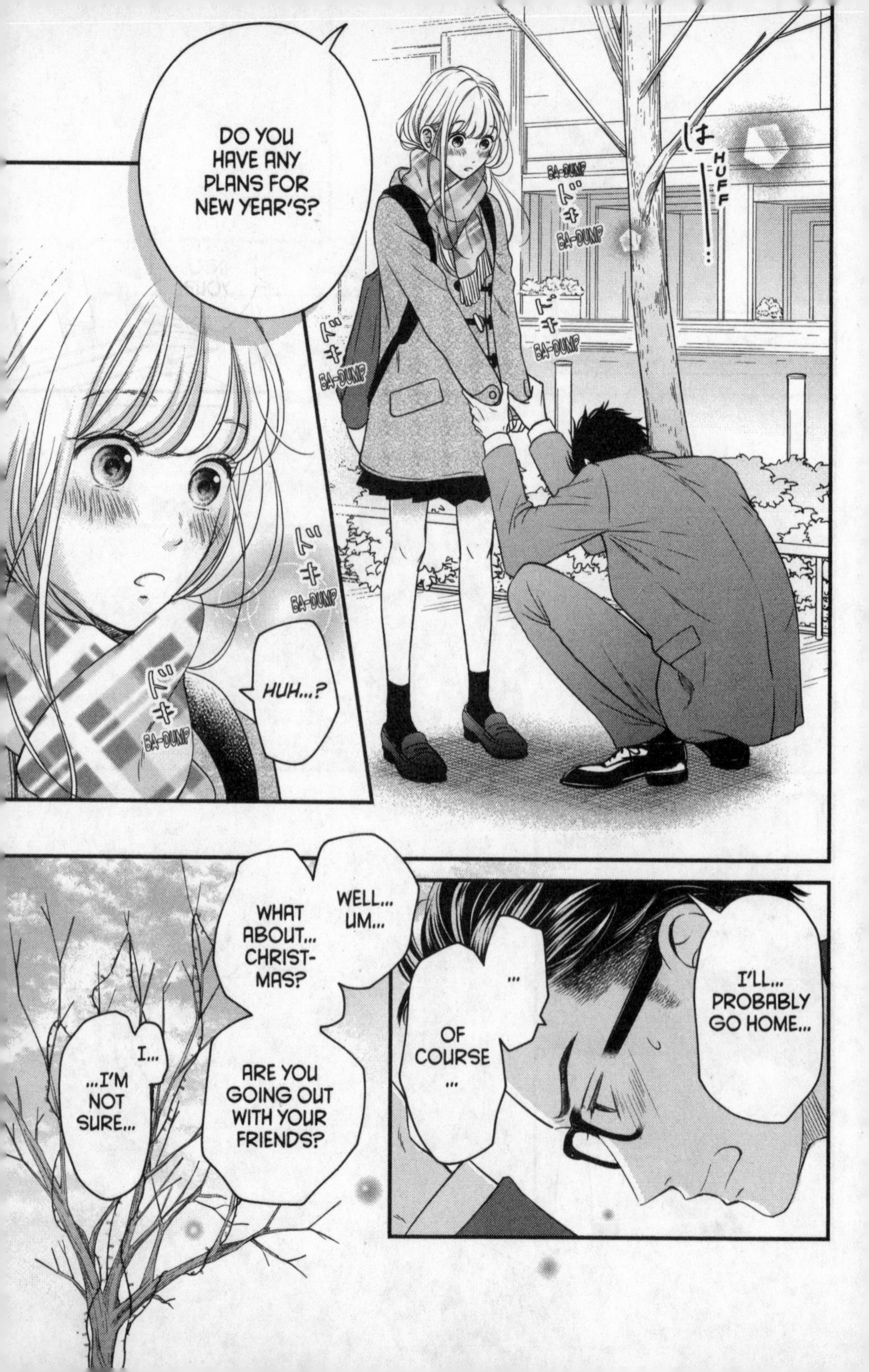
は
HUFF
ドキ
BA-DUMP
ドキ
BA-DUMP
ドキ
BA-DUMP
DO YOU HAVE ANY PLANS FOR NEW YEAR'S?
ドキ
BA-DUMP
ドキ
BA-DUMP
HUH...?
I'LL... PROBABLY GO HOME...
OF COURSE ...
...
WELL... UM...
WHAT ABOUT... CHRIST-MAS?
ARE YOU GOING OUT WITH YOUR FRIENDS?
I...
...I'M NOT SURE...

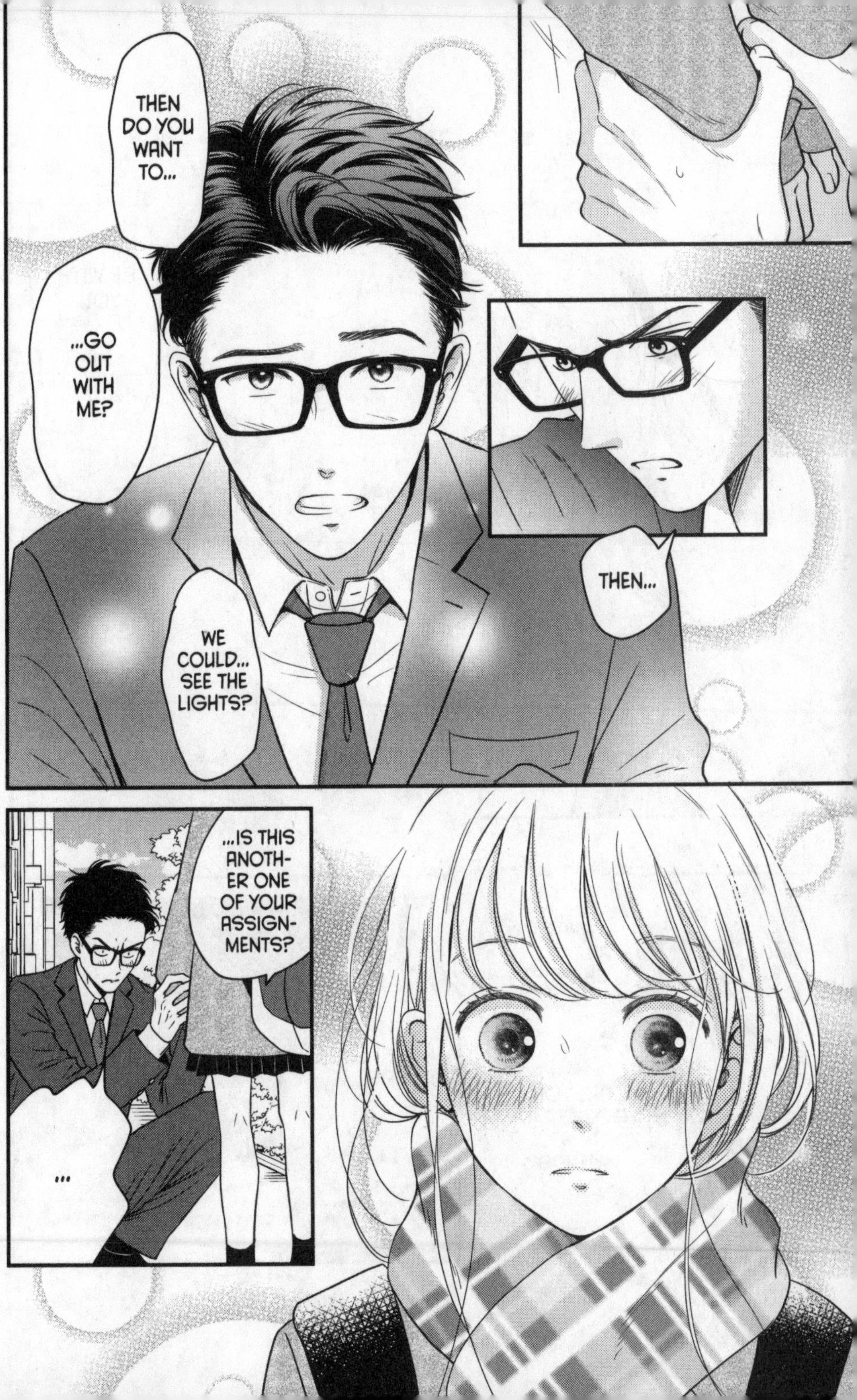
THEN...
THEN DO YOU WANT TO...
...GO OUT WITH ME?
WE COULD... SEE THE LIGHTS?
...IS THIS ANOTHER ONE OF YOUR ASSIGNMENTS?
...

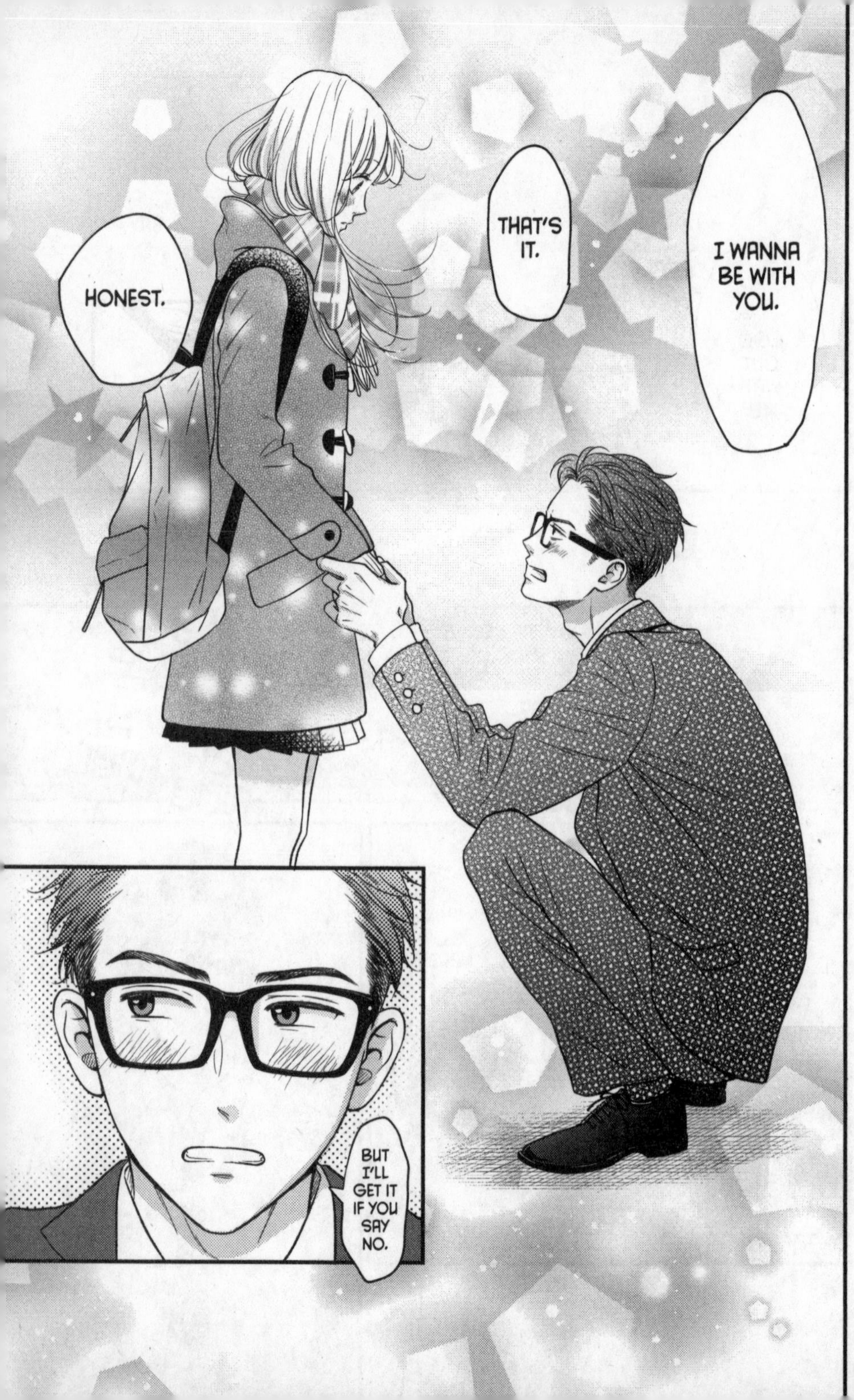
I WANNA BE WITH YOU.
THAT'S IT.
HONEST.
BUT I'LL GET IT IF YOU SAY NO.

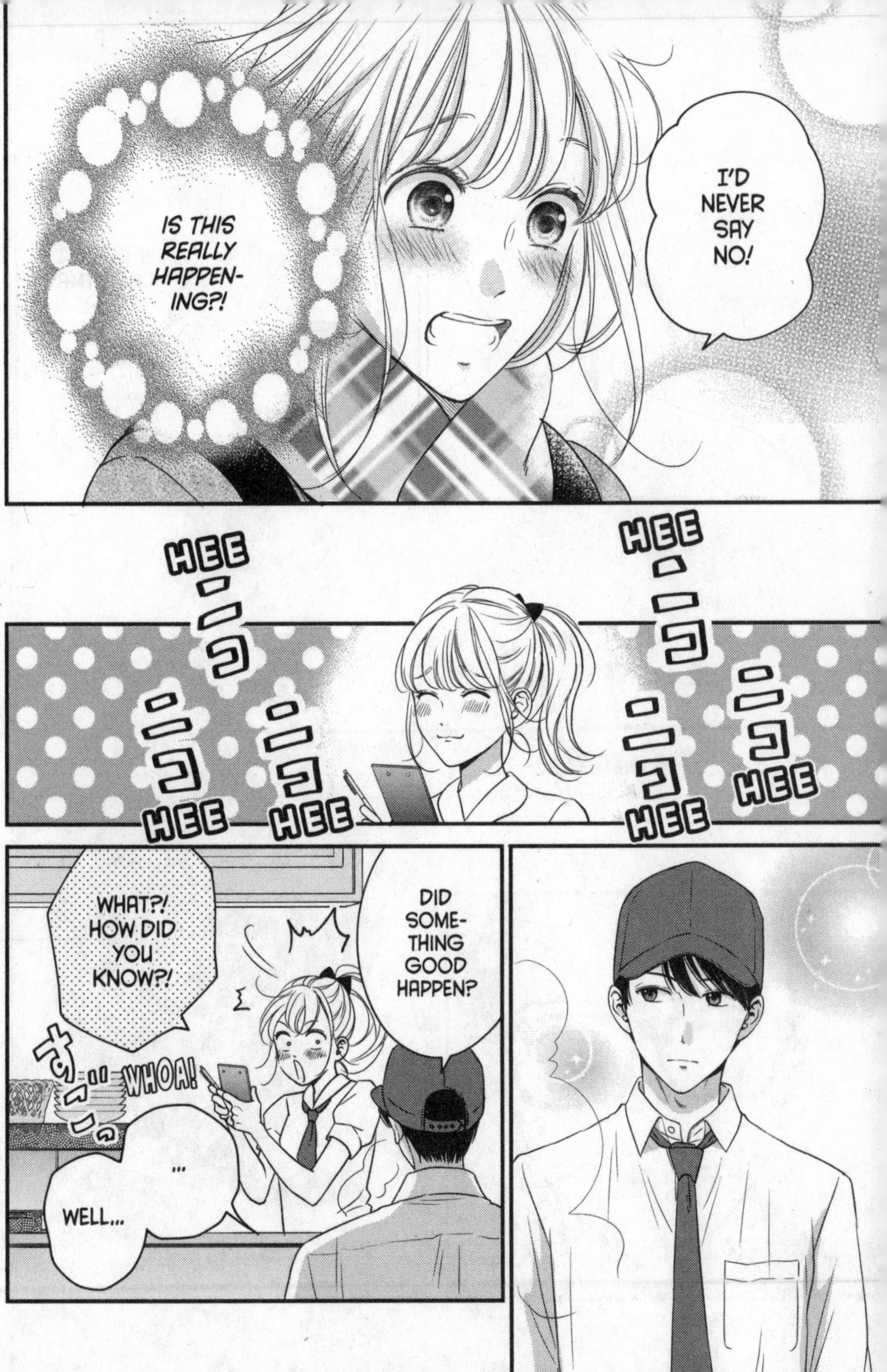
I'D NEVER SAY NO!
IS THIS REALLY HAPPEN-ING?!
HEE
HEE
HEE
HEE
HEE
HEE
DID SOME-THING GOOD HAPPEN?
WHAT?! HOW DID YOU KNOW?!
WHOA!
...
WELL...

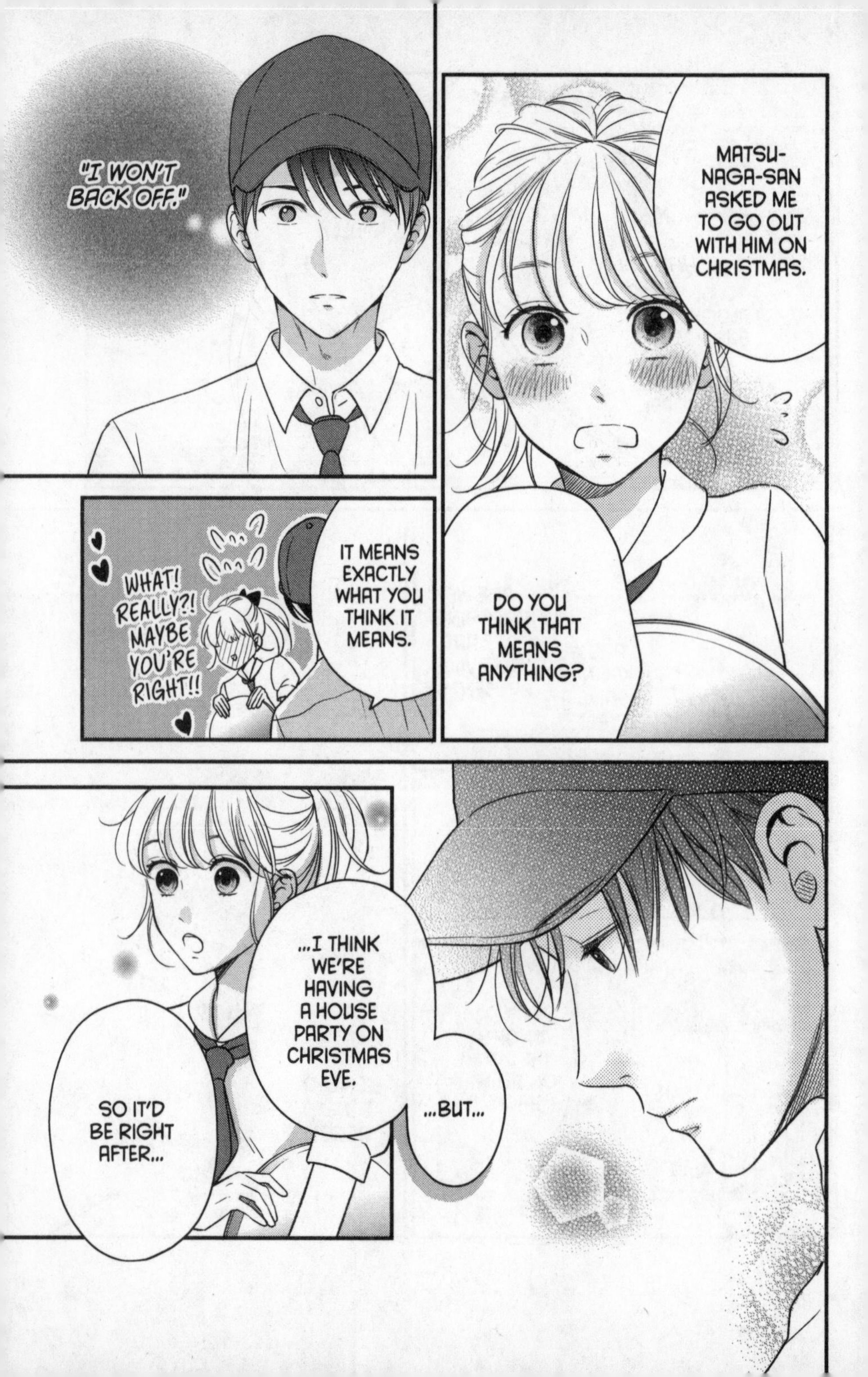
MATSU-NAGA-SAN ASKED ME TO GO OUT WITH HIM ON CHRISTMAS.
DO YOU THINK THAT MEANS ANYTHING?
"I WON'T BACK OFF."
IT MEANS EXACTLY WHAT YOU THINK IT MEANS.
WHAT! REALLY?! MAYBE YOU'RE RIGHT!!
...I THINK WE'RE HAVING A HOUSE PARTY ON CHRISTMAS EVE.
...BUT...
SO IT'D BE RIGHT AFTER...

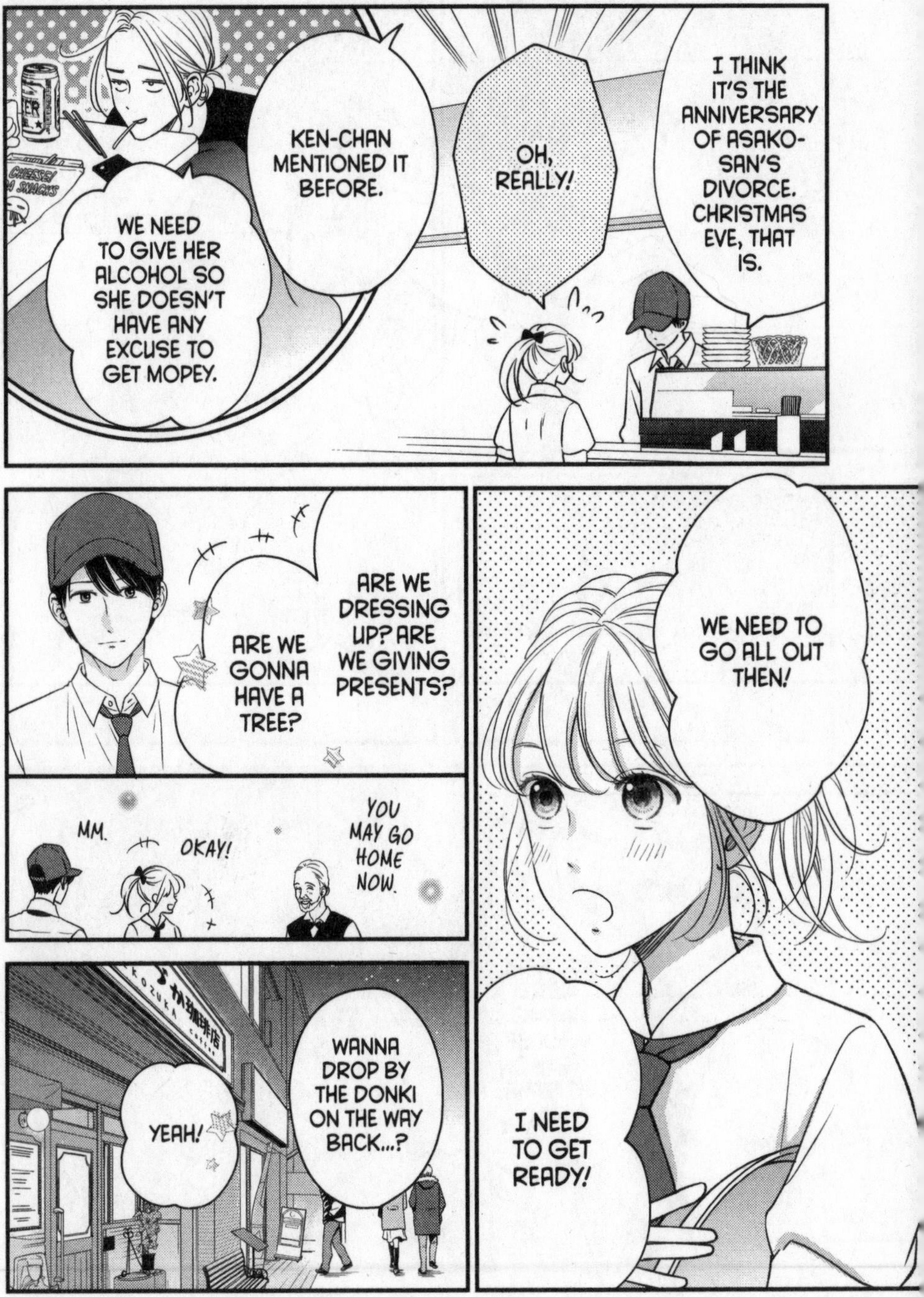
I THINK IT'S THE ANNIVERSARY OF ASAKO-SAN'S DIVORCE. CHRISTMAS EVE, THAT IS.
OH, REALLY!
KEN-CHAN MENTIONED IT BEFORE.
WE NEED TO GIVE HER ALCOHOL SO SHE DOESN'T HAVE ANY EXCUSE TO GET MOPEY.
WE NEED TO GO ALL OUT THEN!
I NEED TO GET READY!
ARE WE DRESSING UP? ARE WE GIVING PRESENTS?
ARE WE GONNA HAVE A TREE?
YOU MAY GO HOME NOW.
OKAY!
MM.
WANNA DROP BY THE DONKI ON THE WAY BACK...?
YEAH!

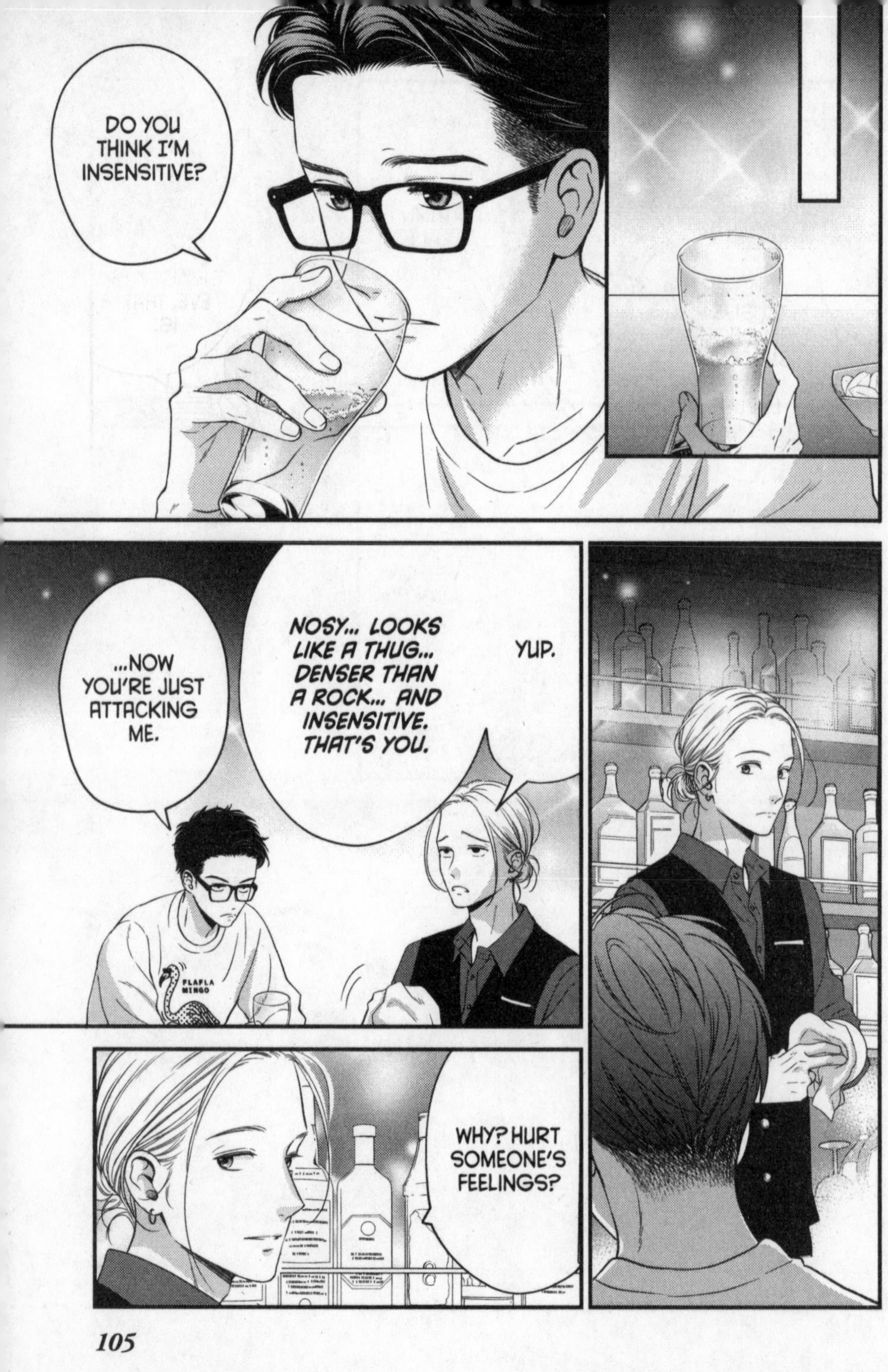
DO YOU THINK I'M INSENSITIVE?
YUP.
NOSY... LOOKS LIKE A THUG... DENSER THAN A ROCK... AND INSENSITIVE. THAT'S YOU.
...NOW YOU'RE JUST ATTACKING ME.
FLAFLA MINGO
WHY? HURT SOMEONE'S FEELINGS?

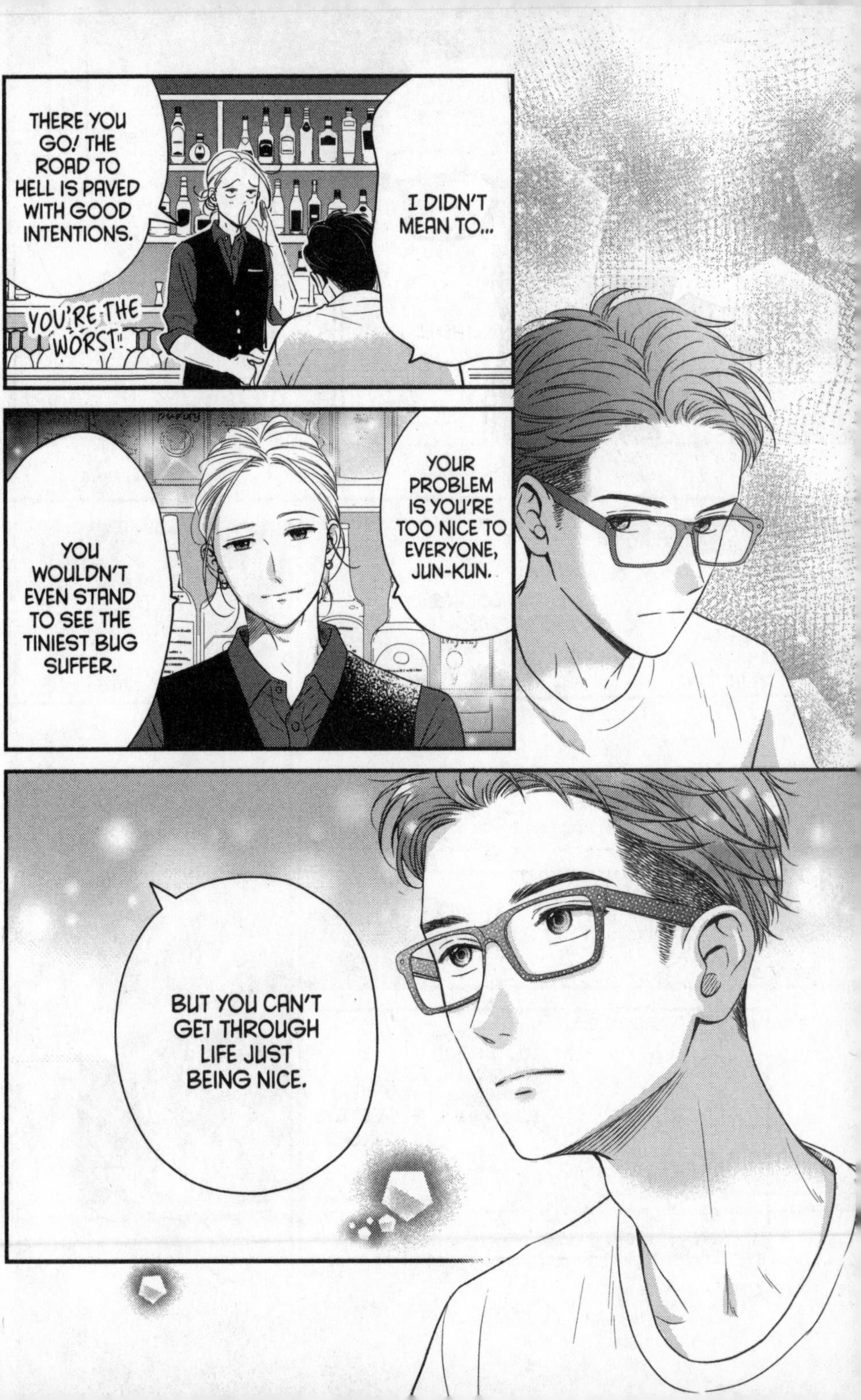
I DIDN'T MEAN TO...
THERE YOU GO! THE ROAD TO HELL IS PAVED WITH GOOD INTENTIONS.
YOU'RE THE WORST!
YOUR PROBLEM IS YOU'RE TOO NICE TO EVERYONE, JUN-KUN.
YOU WOULDN'T EVEN STAND TO SEE THE TINIEST BUG SUFFER.
BUT YOU CAN'T GET THROUGH LIFE JUST BEING NICE.

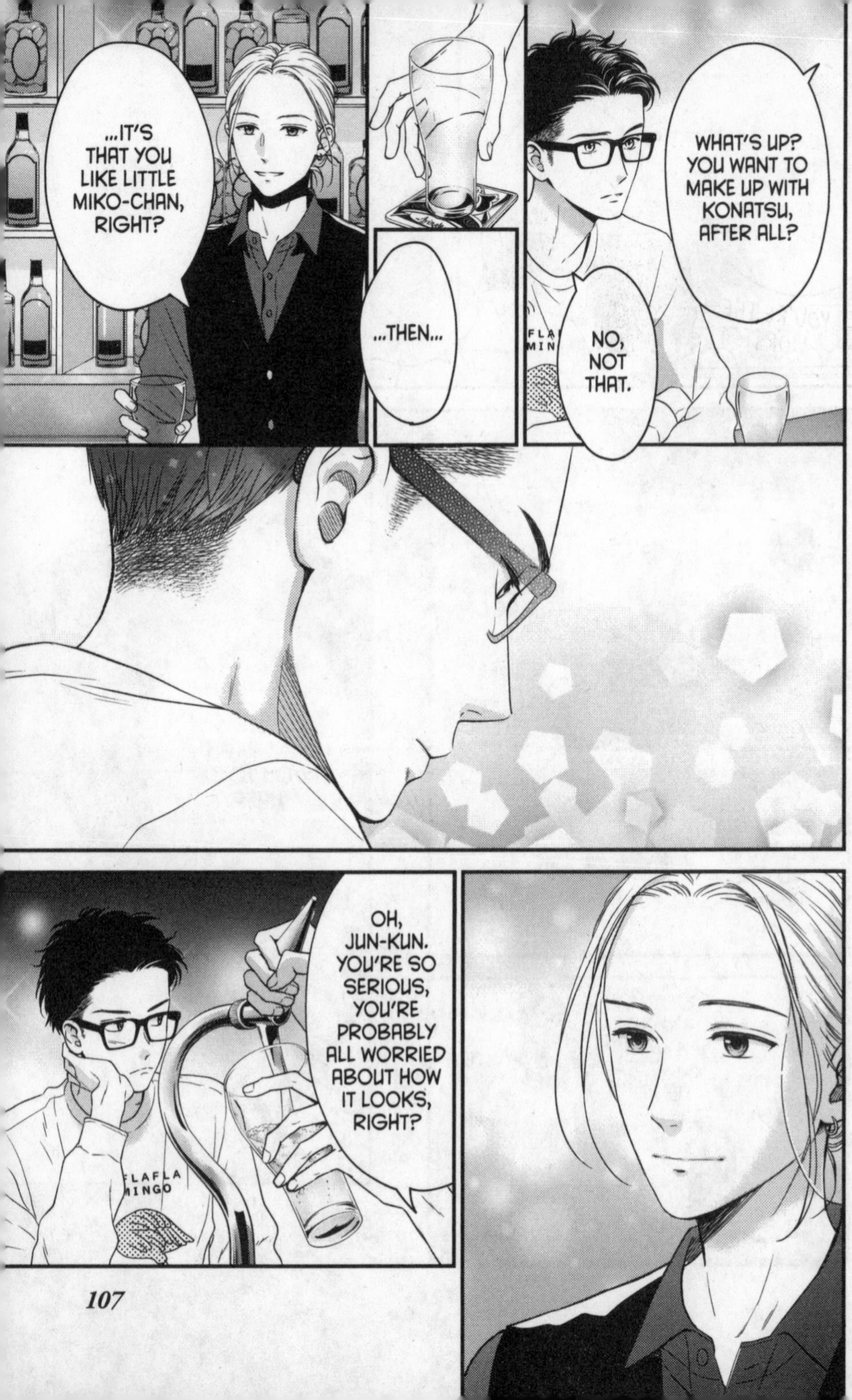
WHAT'S UP? YOU WANT TO MAKE UP WITH KONATSU, AFTER ALL?
NO, NOT THAT.
...THEN...
...IT'S THAT YOU LIKE LITTLE MIKO-CHAN, RIGHT?
OH, JUN-KUN. YOU'RE SO SERIOUS, YOU'RE PROBABLY ALL WORRIED ABOUT HOW IT LOOKS, RIGHT?
FLAFLA MINGO

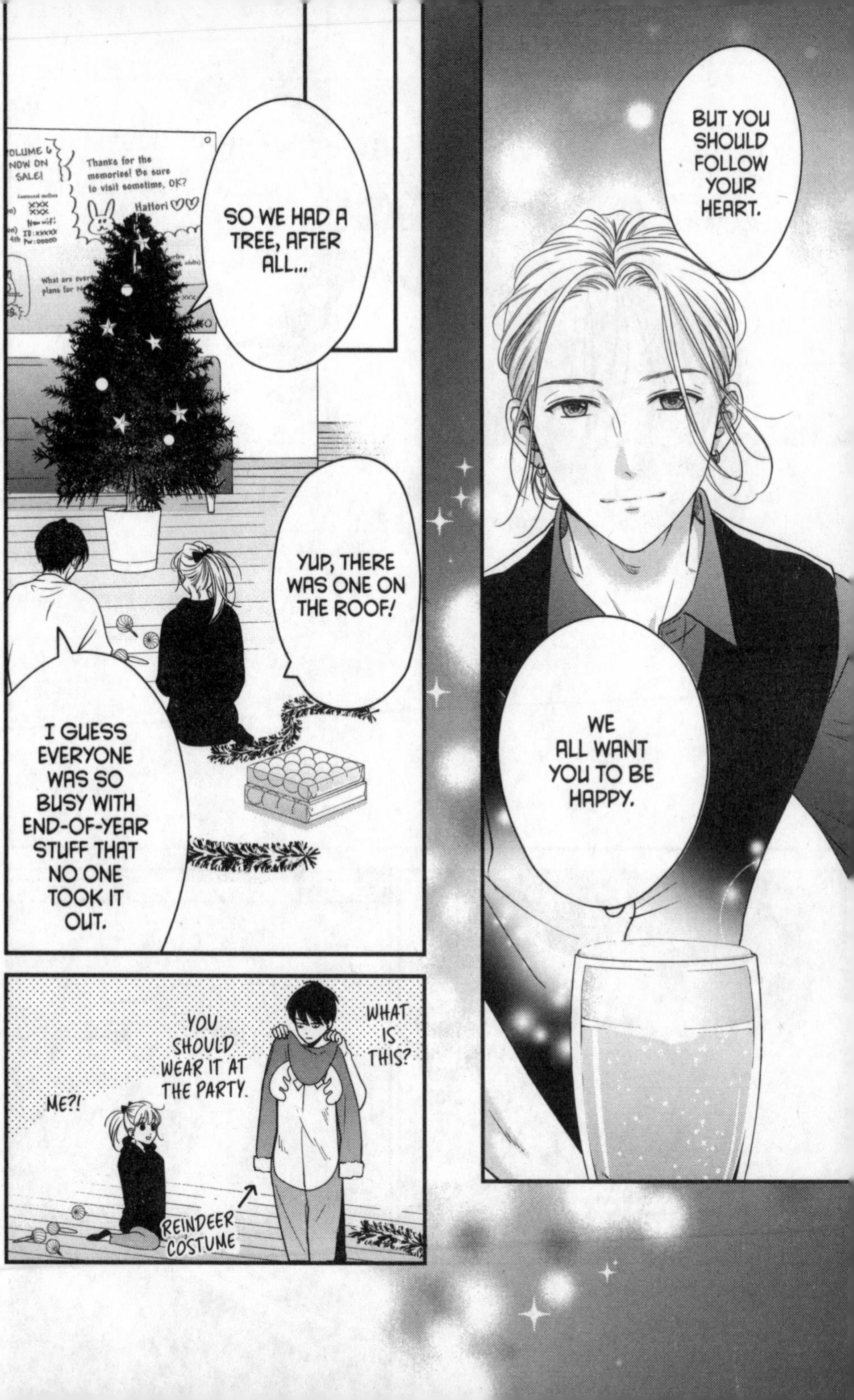
BUT YOU SHOULD FOLLOW YOUR HEART.
WE ALL WANT YOU TO BE HAPPY.
OLUME 6 NOW ON SALE!
Thanks for the memories! Be sure to visit sometime, OK?
Hattori
SO WE HAD A TREE, AFTER ALL...
YUP, THERE WAS ONE ON THE ROOF!
I GUESS EVERYONE WAS SO BUSY WITH END-OF-YEAR STUFF THAT NO ONE TOOK IT OUT.
WHAT IS THIS?
YOU SHOULD WEAR IT AT THE PARTY.
ME?!
REINDEER COSTUME

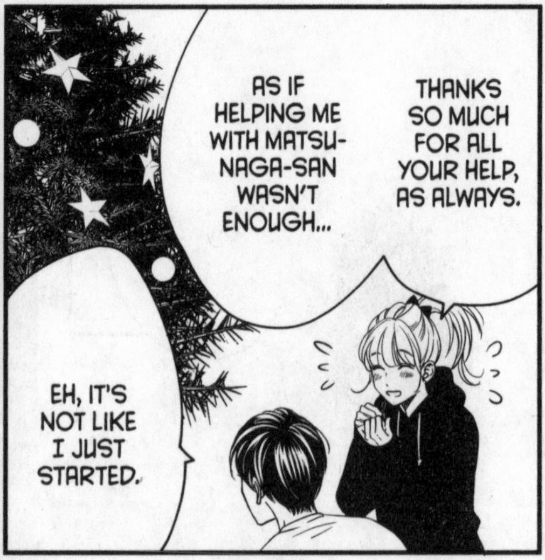
THANKS SO MUCH FOR ALL YOUR HELP, AS ALWAYS.
AS IF HELPING ME WITH MATSU-NAGA-SAN WASN'T ENOUGH...
EH, IT'S NOT LIKE I JUST STARTED.

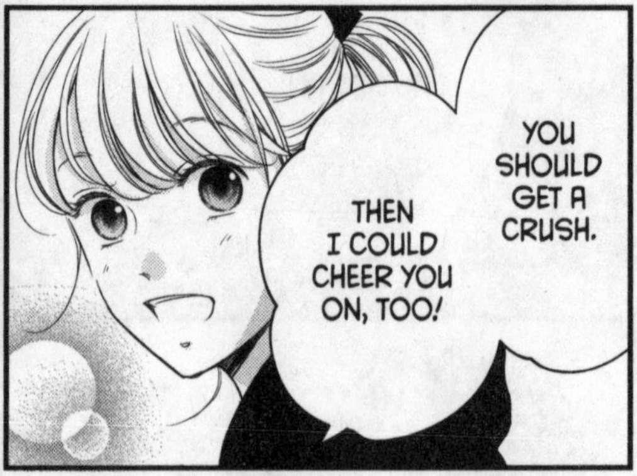
YOU SHOULD GET A CRUSH.
THEN I COULD CHEER YOU ON, TOO!

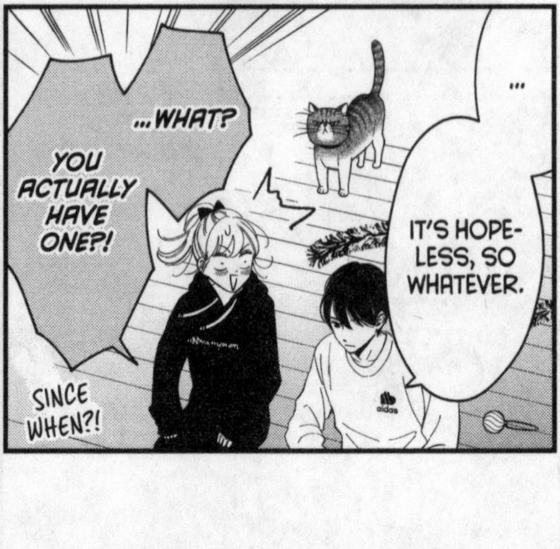
...
IT'S HOPE-LESS, SO WHATEVER.
...WHAT?
YOU ACTUALLY HAVE ONE?!
SINCE WHEN?!

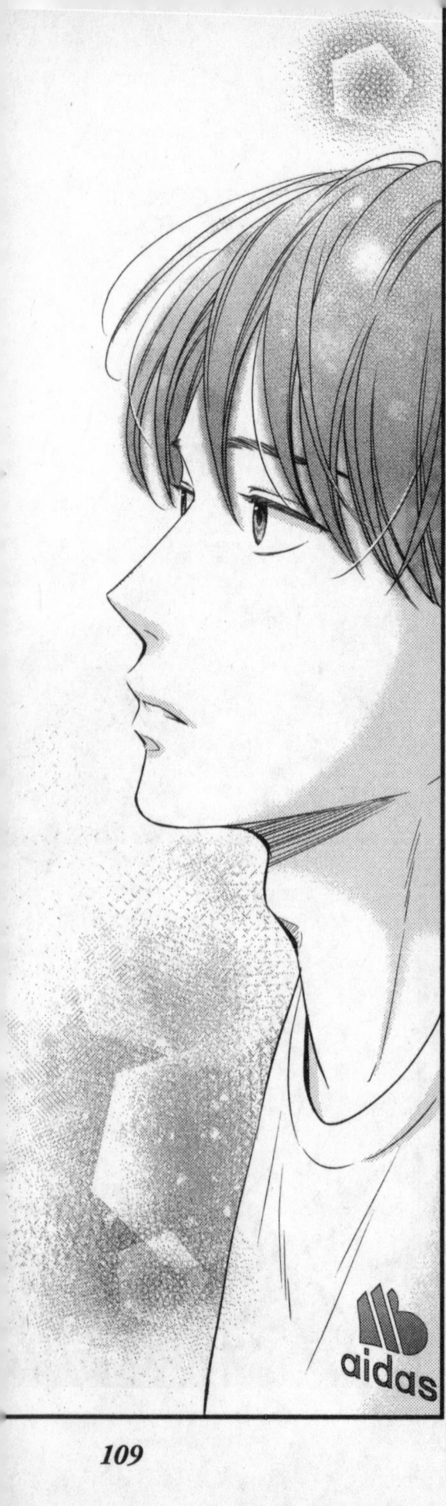
aidas

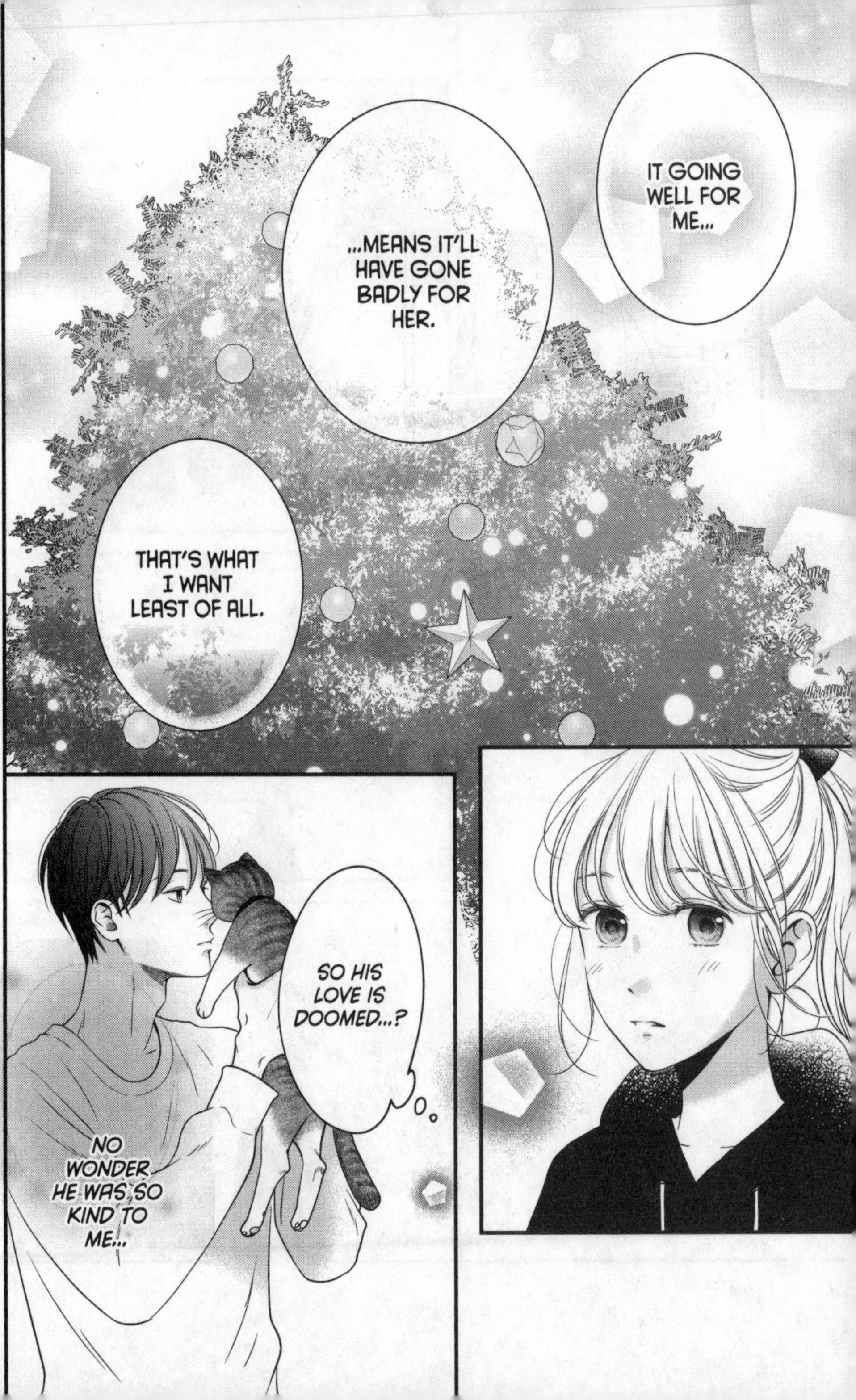
IT GOING WELL FOR ME...
...MEANS IT'LL HAVE GONE BADLY FOR HER.
THAT'S WHAT I WANT LEAST OF ALL.
SO HIS LOVE IS DOOMED...?
NO WONDER HE WAS SO KIND TO ME...

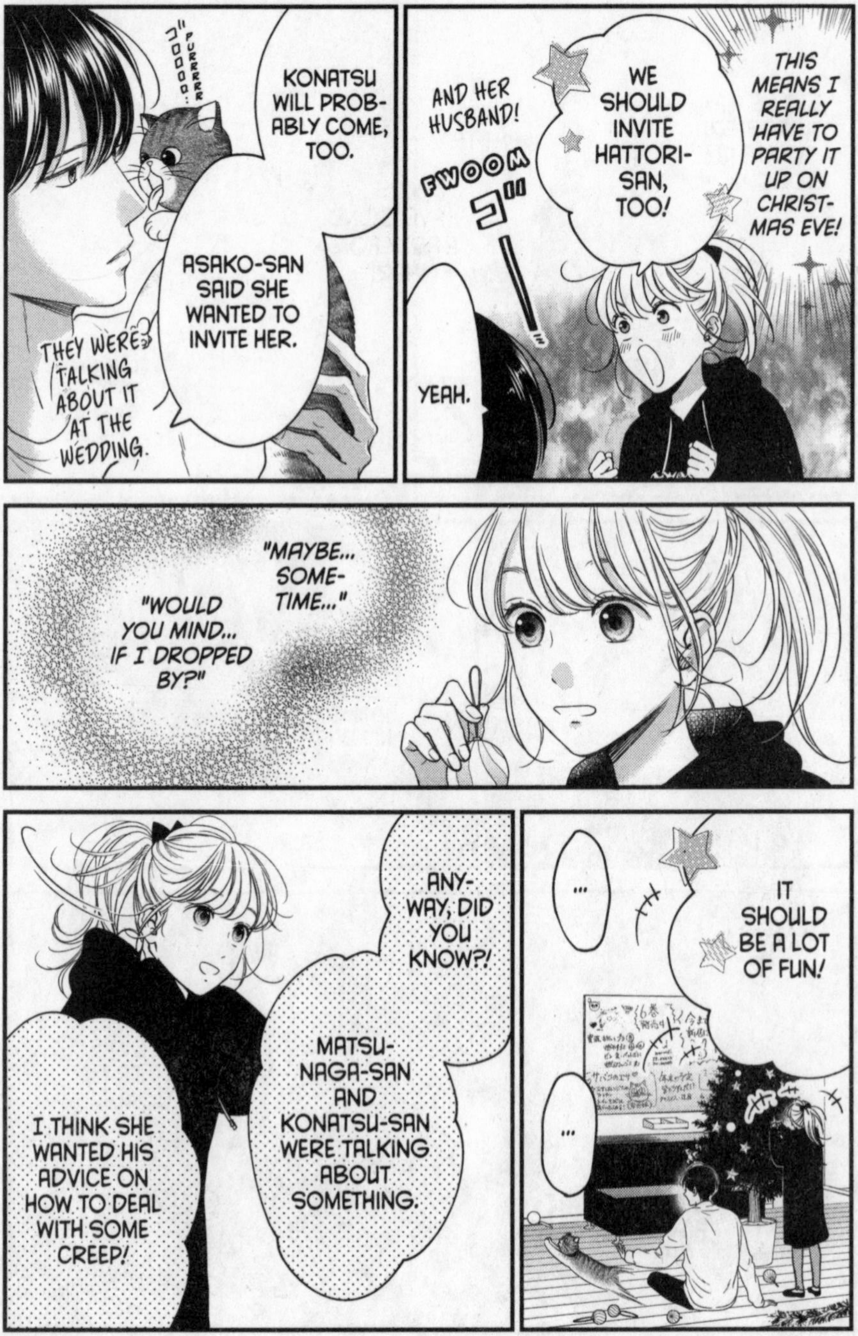
THIS MEANS I REALLY HAVE TO PARTY IT UP ON CHRISTMAS EVE!
WE SHOULD INVITE HATTORI-SAN, TOO!
AND HER HUSBAND!
FWOOM
YEAH.
KONATSU WILL PROBABLY COME, TOO.
PURRRR
ASAKO-SAN SAID SHE WANTED TO INVITE HER.
THEY WERE TALKING ABOUT IT AT THE WEDDING.
"MAYBE... SOMETIME..."
"WOULD YOU MIND... IF I DROPPED BY?"
IT SHOULD BE A LOT OF FUN!
...
...
ANYWAY, DID YOU KNOW?!
MATSUNAGA-SAN AND KONATSU-SAN WERE TALKING ABOUT SOMETHING.
I THINK SHE WANTED HIS ADVICE ON HOW TO DEAL WITH SOME CREEP!

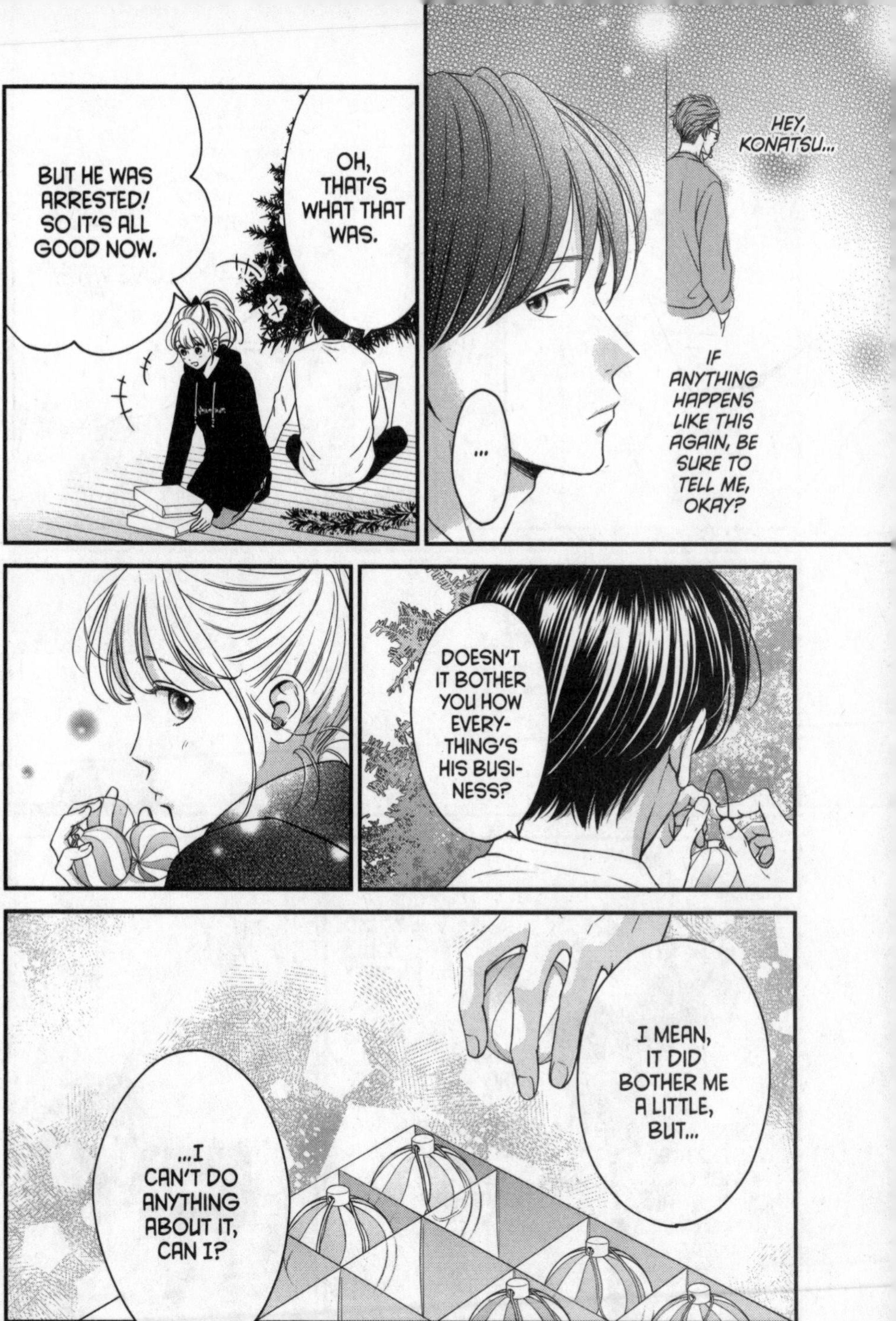
HEY, KONATSU...
IF ANYTHING HAPPENS LIKE THIS AGAIN, BE SURE TO TELL ME, OKAY?
...
OH, THAT'S WHAT THAT WAS.
BUT HE WAS ARRESTED! SO IT'S ALL GOOD NOW.
DOESN'T IT BOTHER YOU HOW EVERYTHING'S HIS BUSINESS?
I MEAN, IT DID BOTHER ME A LITTLE, BUT...
...I CAN'T DO ANYTHING ABOUT IT, CAN I?

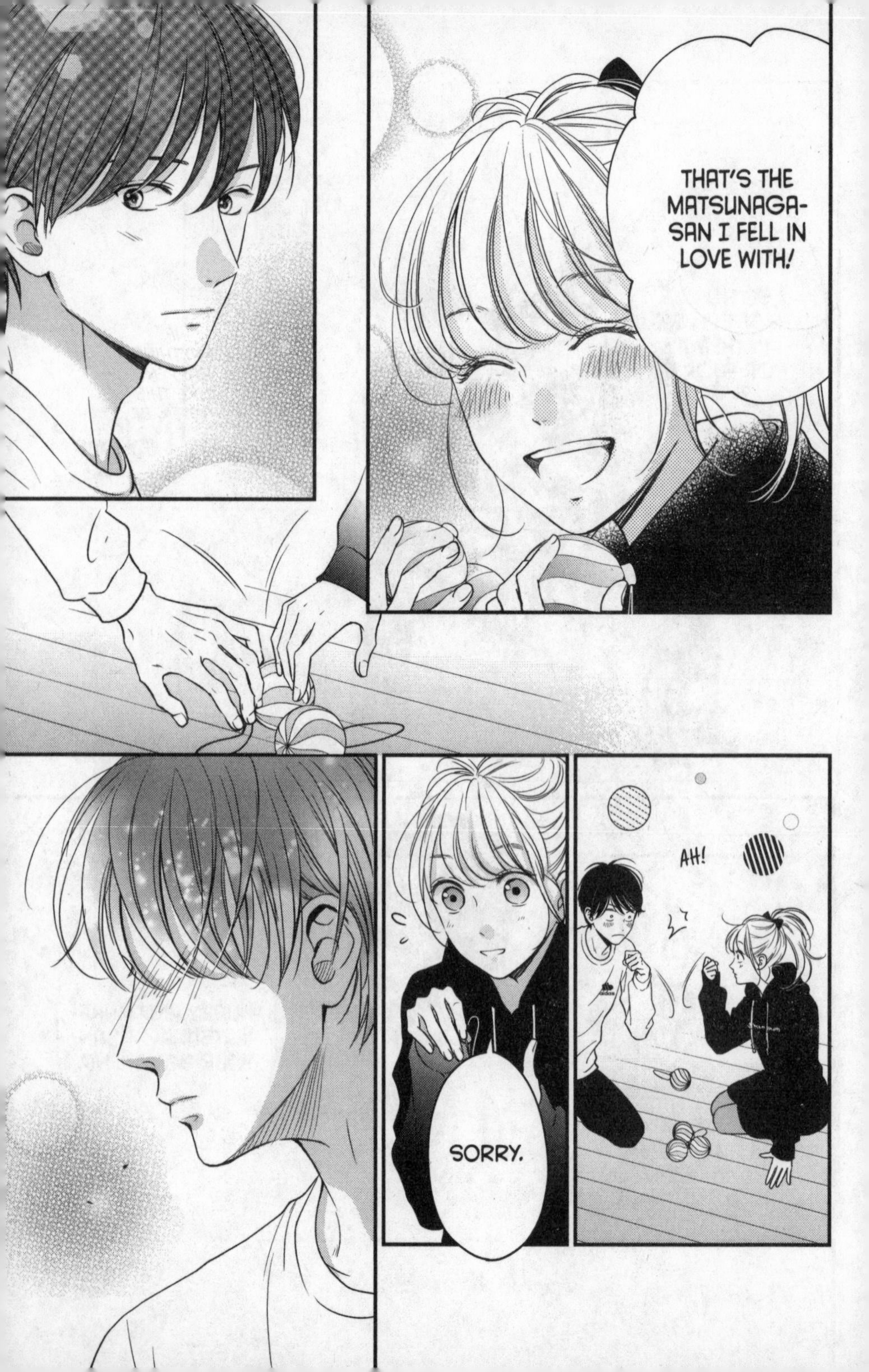
THAT'S THE MATSUNAGA-SAN I FELL IN LOVE WITH!
AH!
SORRY.

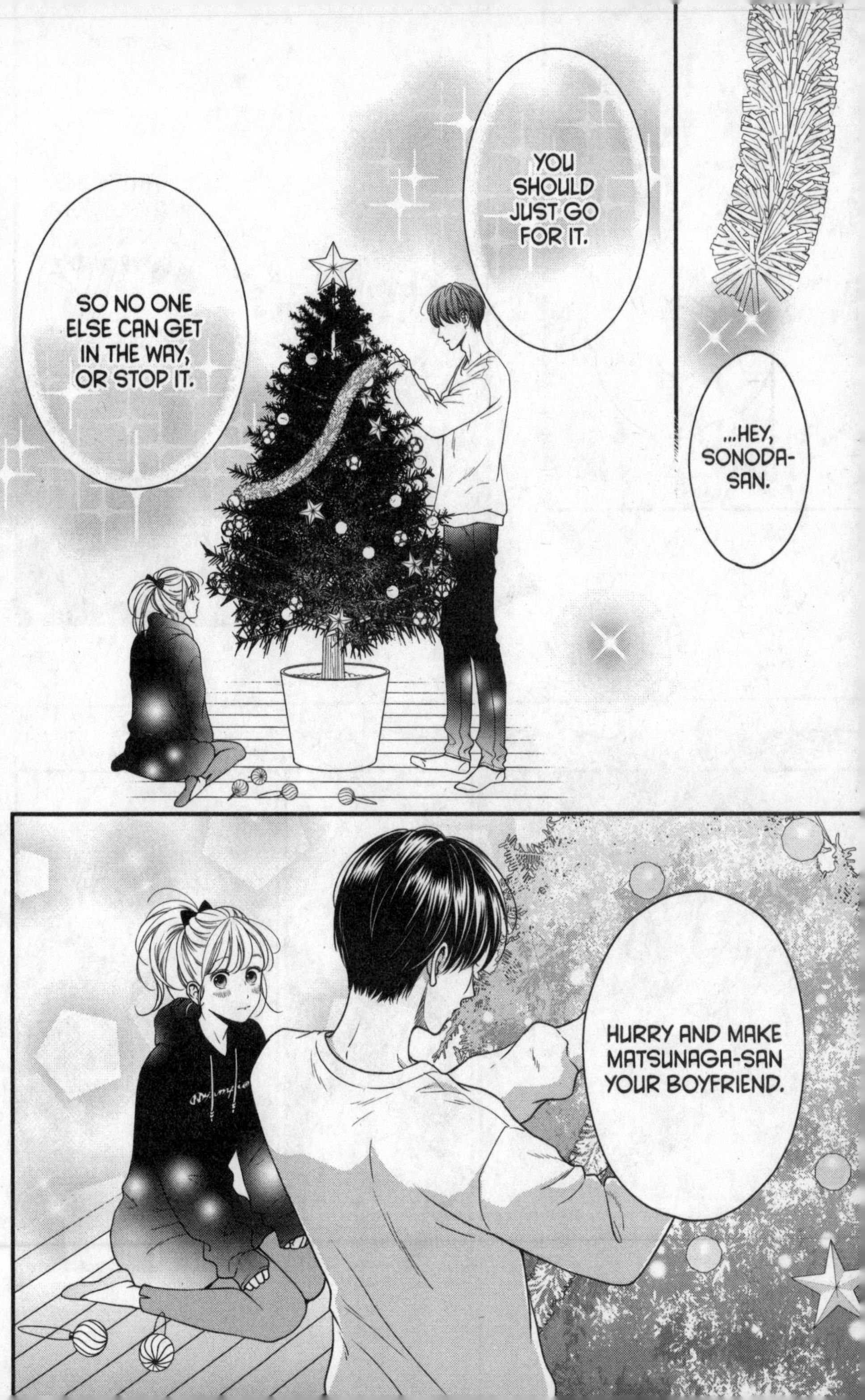
...HEY, SONODA-SAN.
YOU SHOULD JUST GO FOR IT.
SO NO ONE ELSE CAN GET IN THE WAY, OR STOP IT.
HURRY AND MAKE MATSUNAGA-SAN YOUR BOYFRIEND.

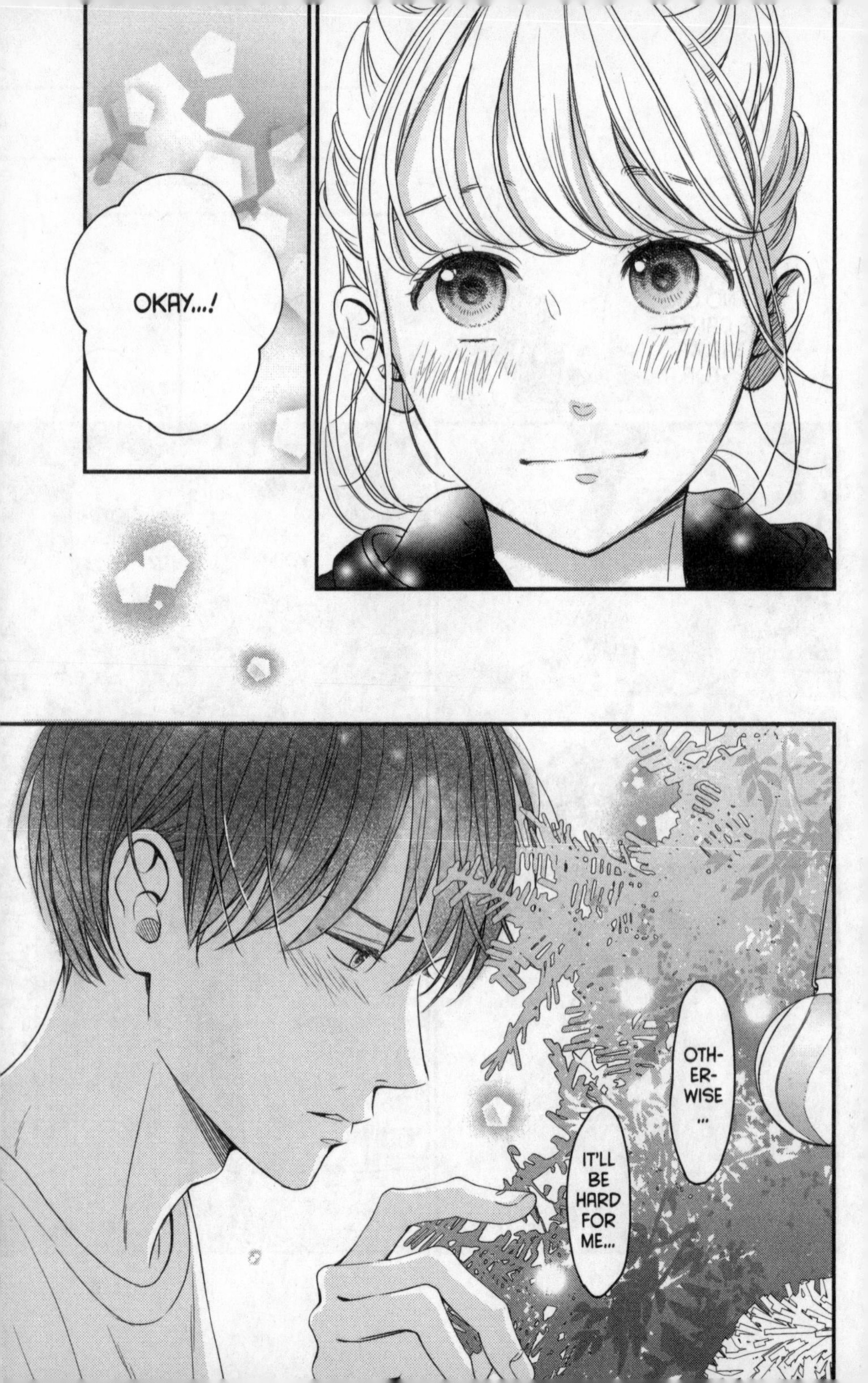
OKAY...!
OTH-ER-WISE...
IT'LL BE HARD FOR ME...

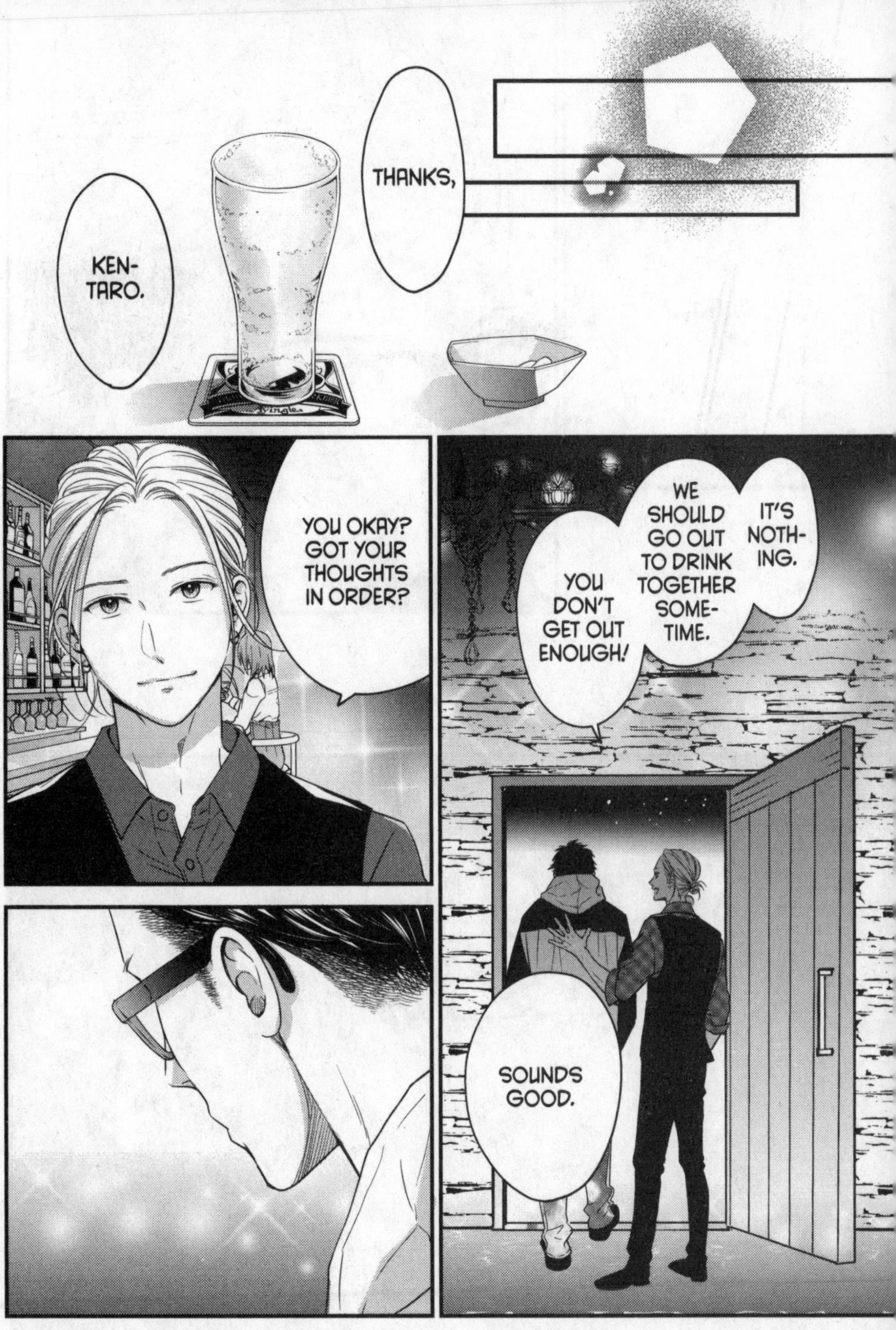
THANKS,
KEN-TARO.
IT'S NOTH-ING.
WE SHOULD GO OUT TO DRINK TOGETHER SOME-TIME.
YOU DON'T GET OUT ENOUGH!
SOUNDS GOOD.
YOU OKAY? GOT YOUR THOUGHTS IN ORDER?

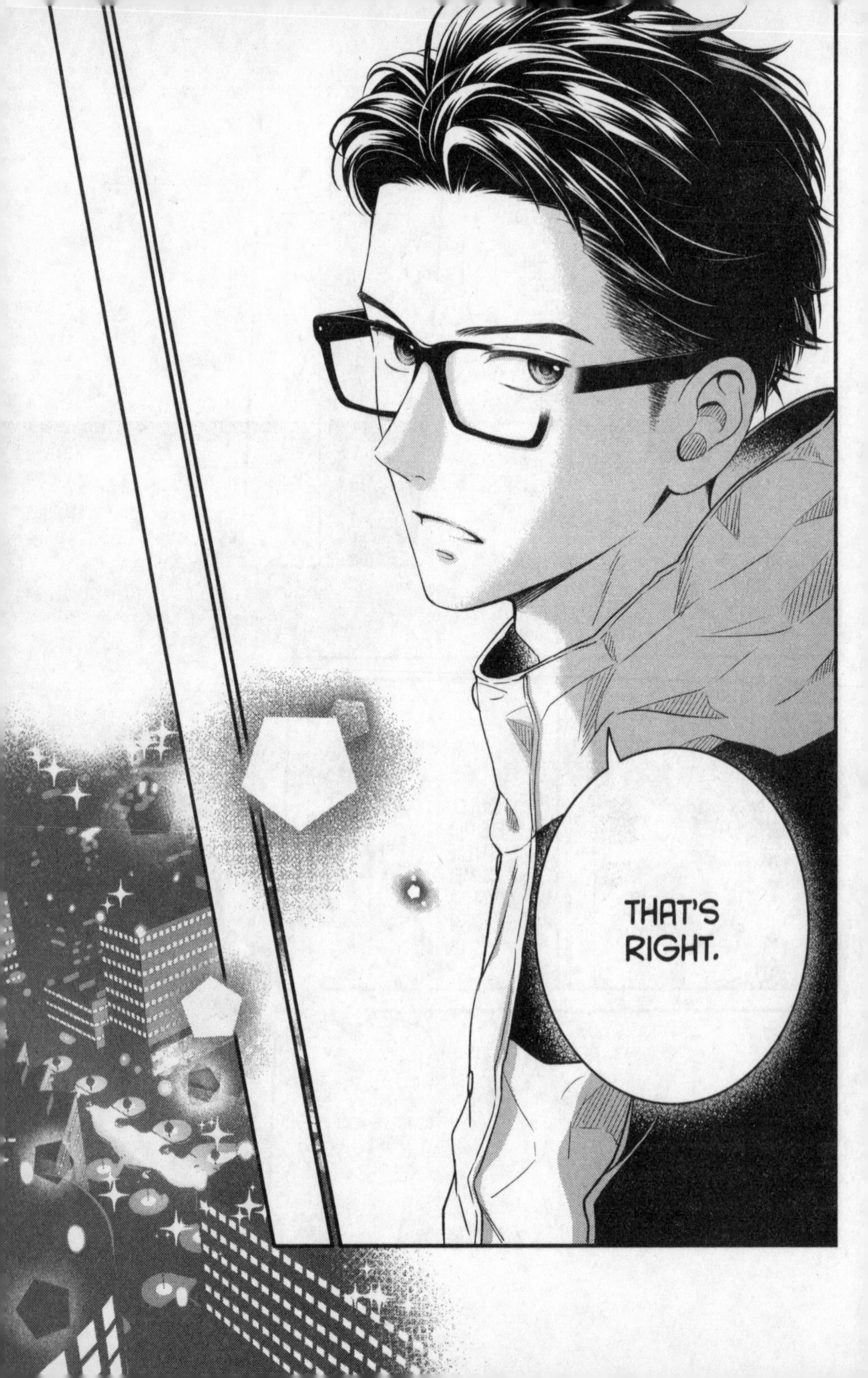
THAT'S RIGHT.

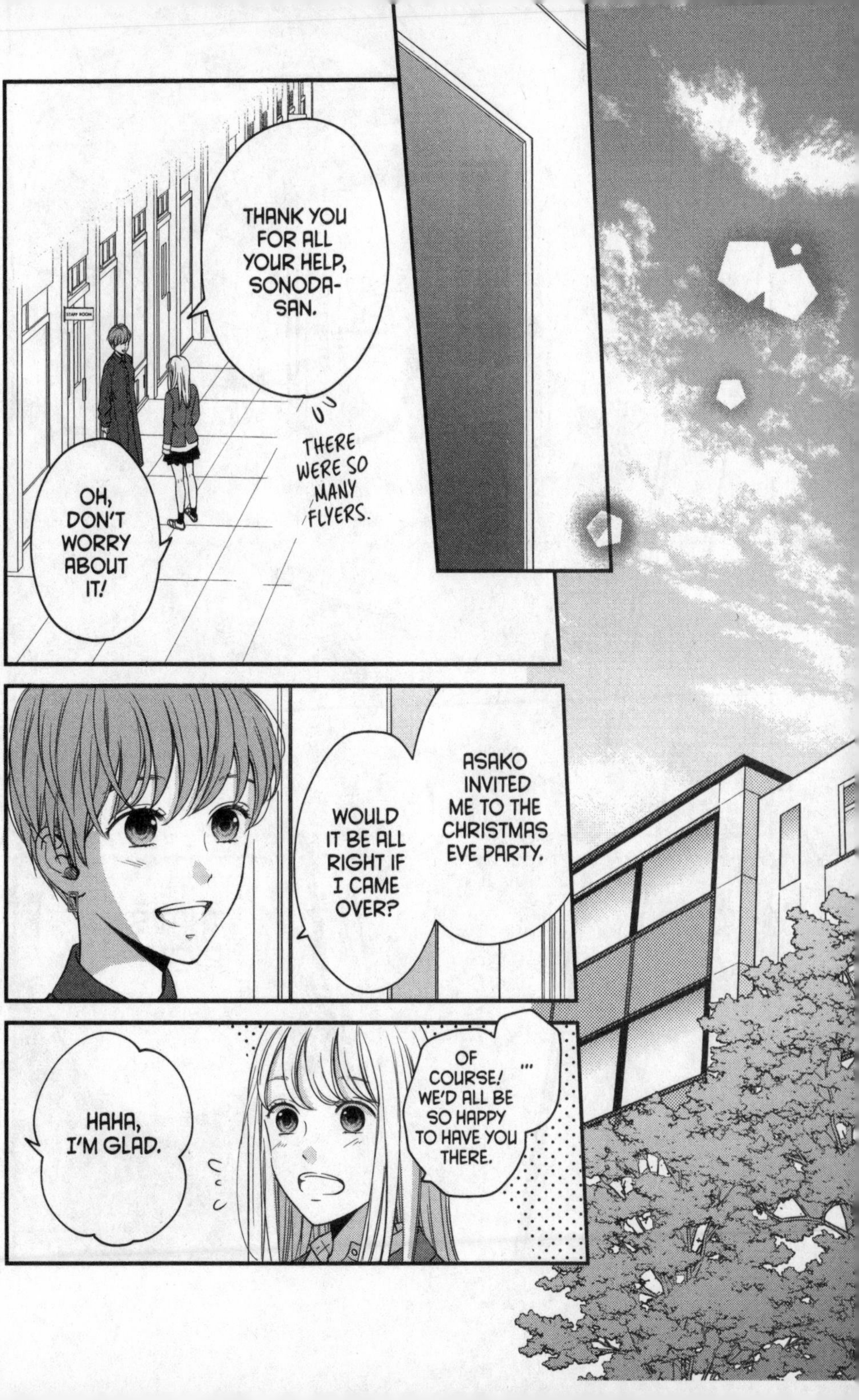
THANK YOU FOR ALL YOUR HELP, SONODA-SAN.
THERE WERE SO MANY FLYERS.
OH, DON'T WORRY ABOUT IT!
ASAKO INVITED ME TO THE CHRISTMAS EVE PARTY.
WOULD IT BE ALL RIGHT IF I CAME OVER?
OF COURSE! WE'D ALL BE SO HAPPY TO HAVE YOU THERE.
HAHA, I'M GLAD.

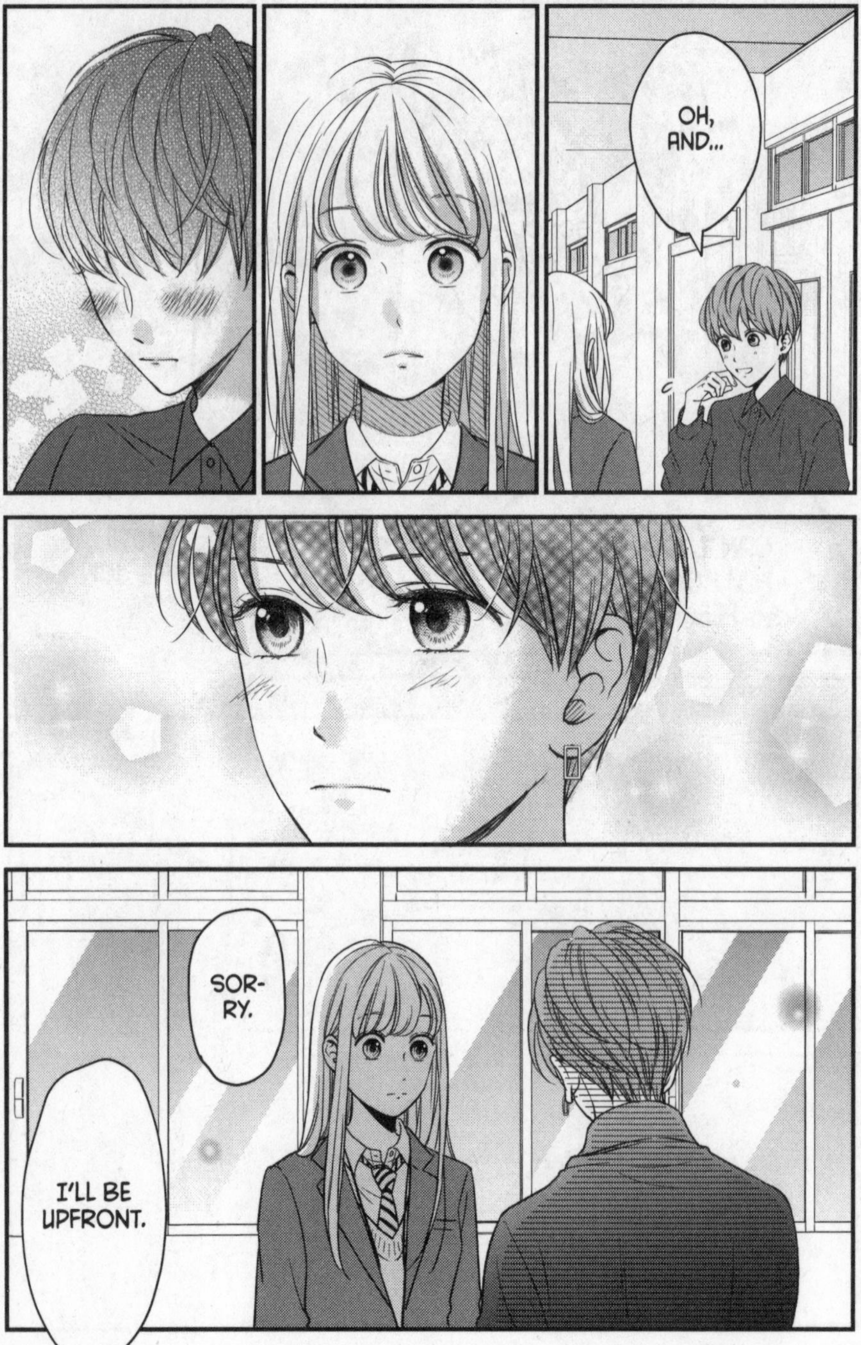
OH, AND...
SORRY.
I'LL BE UPFRONT.

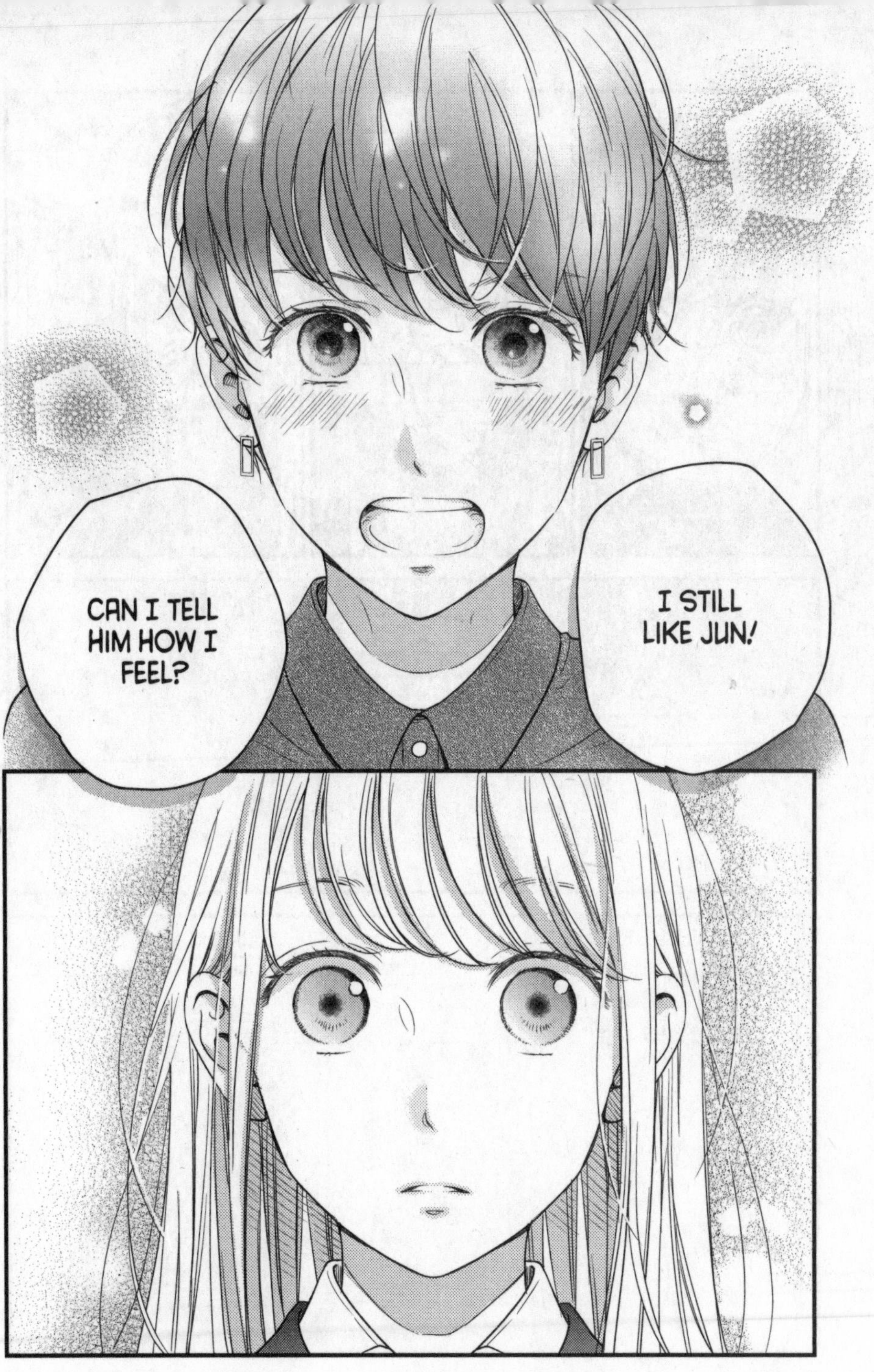
I STILL LIKE JUN!
CAN I TELL HIM HOW I FEEL?

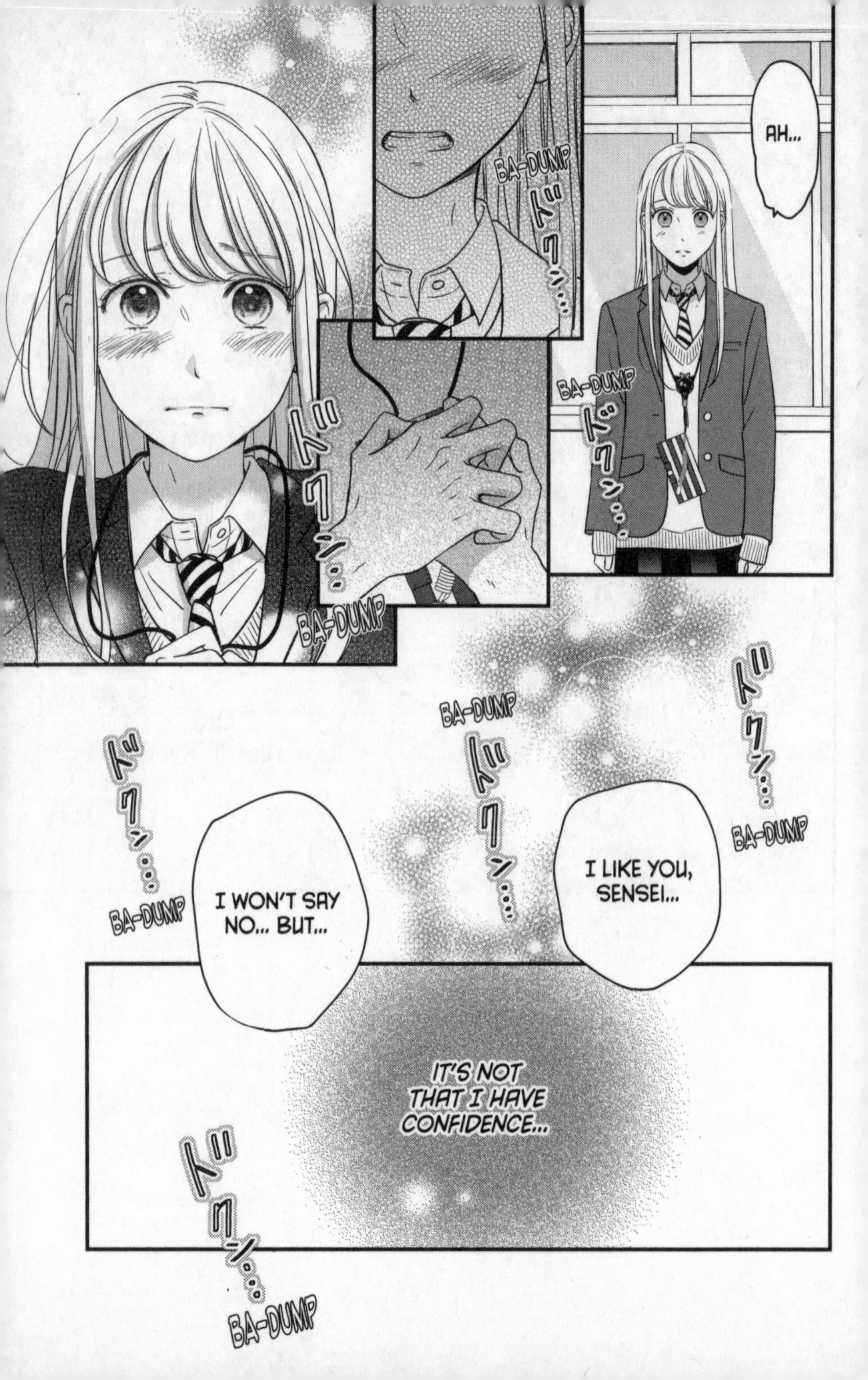
AH...
BA-DUMP
ドクン…
BA-DUMP
ドクン…
BA-DUMP
ドクン…
I LIKE YOU, SENSEI...
ドクン…
BA-DUMP
BA-DUMP
ドクン…
I WON'T SAY NO... BUT...
ドクン…
BA-DUMP
IT'S NOT THAT I HAVE CONFIDENCE...
ドクン…
BA-DUMP

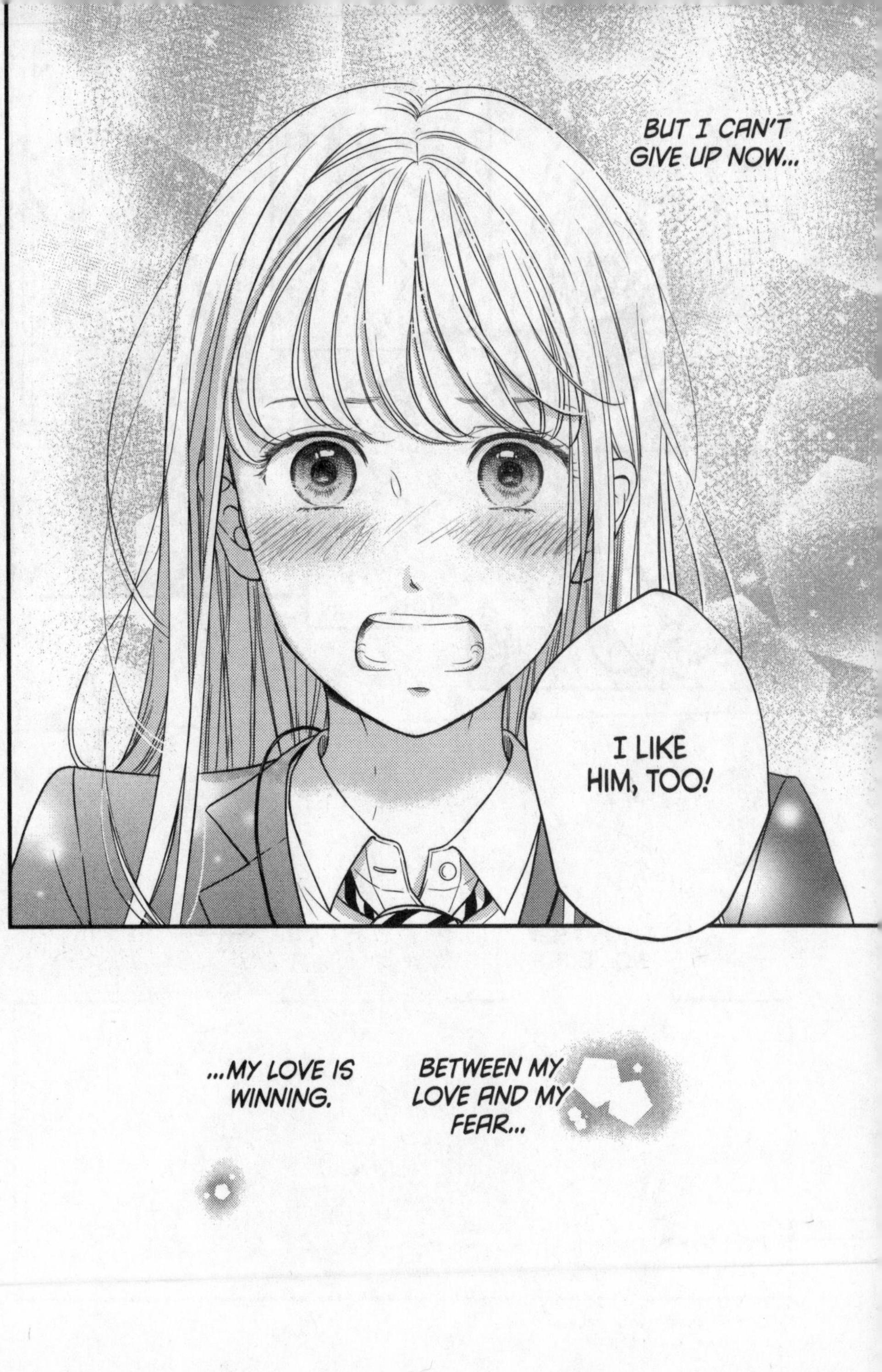
BUT I CAN'T GIVE UP NOW...
I LIKE HIM, TOO!
BETWEEN MY LOVE AND MY FEAR...
...MY LOVE IS WINNING.

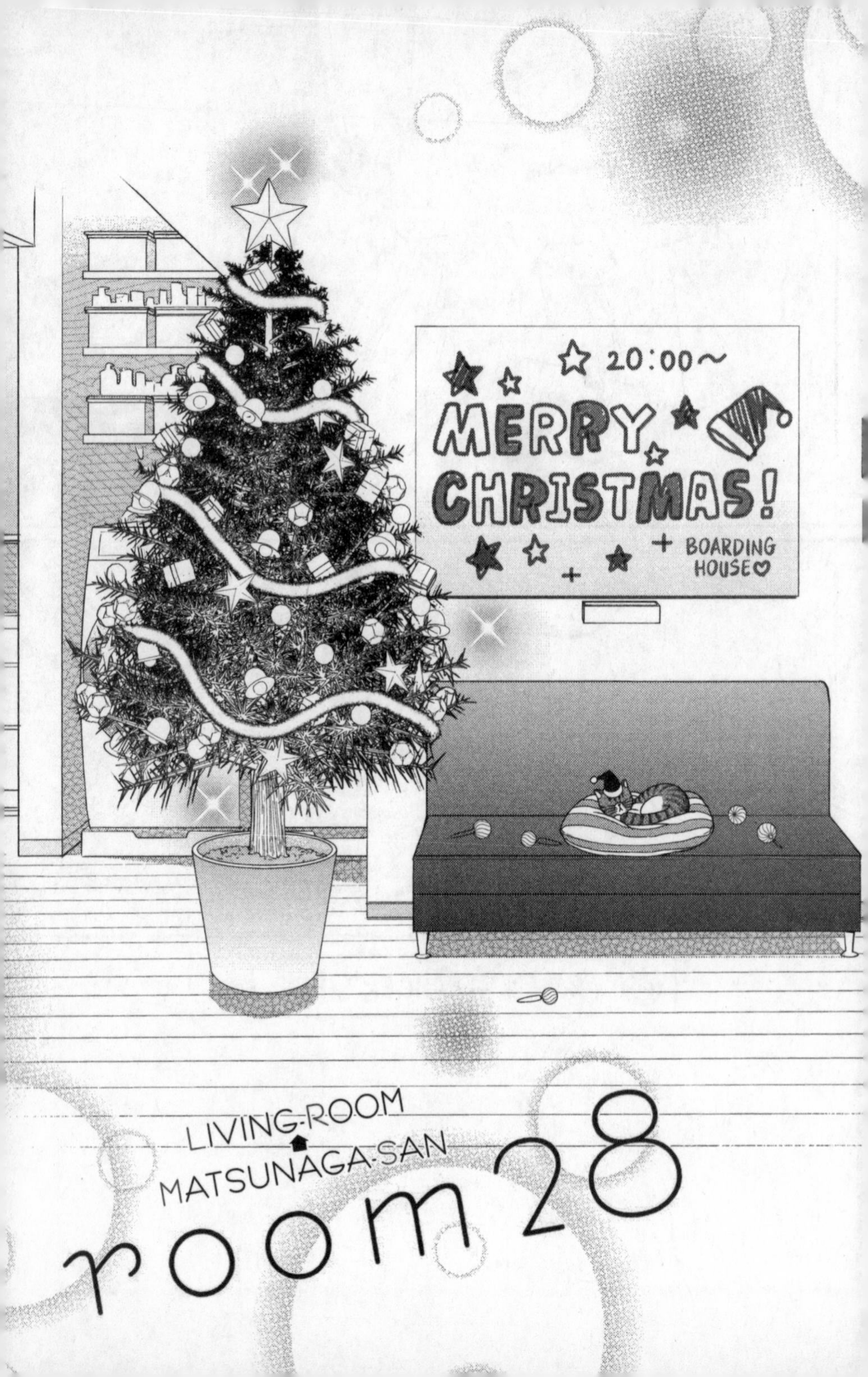
20:00~
MERRY CHRISTMAS!
BOARDING HOUSE♡
LIVING-ROOM MATSUNAGA-SAN
room 28

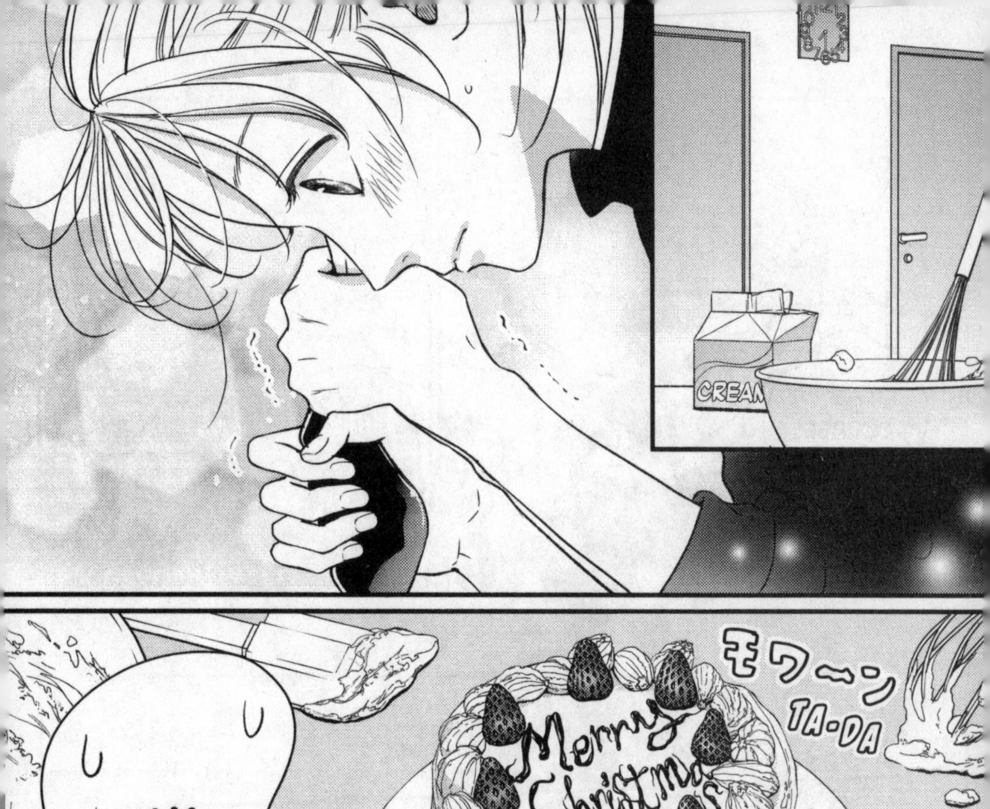
CREAM
モワ～ン
TA-DA
...

FROM A STRANGER'S POV

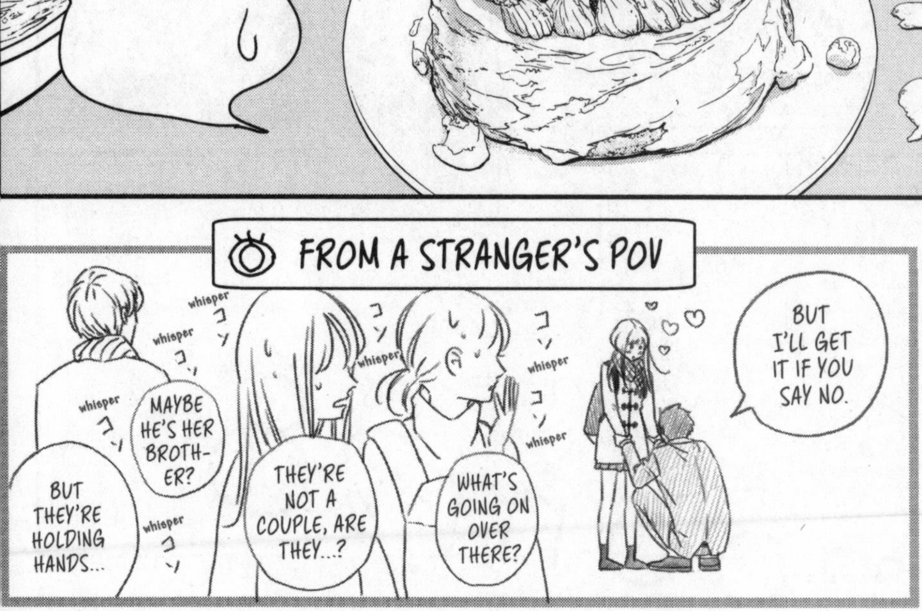
BUT I'LL GET IT IF YOU SAY NO.
whisper
コソ
WHAT'S GOING ON OVER THERE?
THEY'RE NOT A COUPLE, ARE THEY...?
MAYBE HE'S HER BROTHER?
BUT THEY'RE HOLDING HANDS...

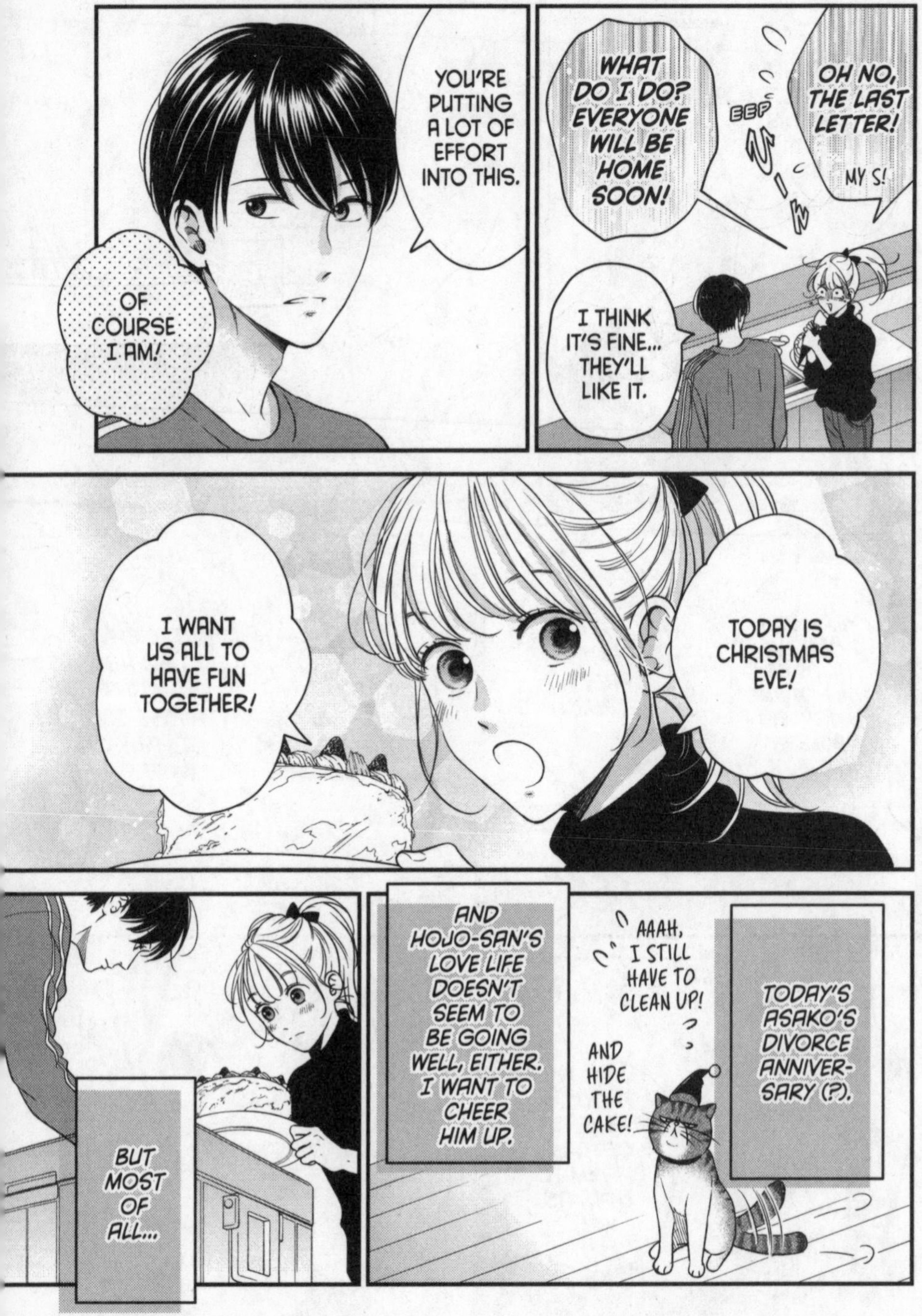
OH NO, THE LAST LETTER!
MY S!
EEP
WHAT DO I DO? EVERYONE WILL BE HOME SOON!
I THINK IT'S FINE... THEY'LL LIKE IT.
YOU'RE PUTTING A LOT OF EFFORT INTO THIS.
OF COURSE I AM!
TODAY IS CHRISTMAS EVE!
I WANT US ALL TO HAVE FUN TOGETHER!
TODAY'S ASAKO'S DIVORCE ANNIVERSARY (?).
AAAH, I STILL HAVE TO CLEAN UP!
AND HIDE THE CAKE!
AND HOJO-SAN'S LOVE LIFE DOESN'T SEEM TO BE GOING WELL, EITHER. I WANT TO CHEER HIM UP.
BUT MOST OF ALL...

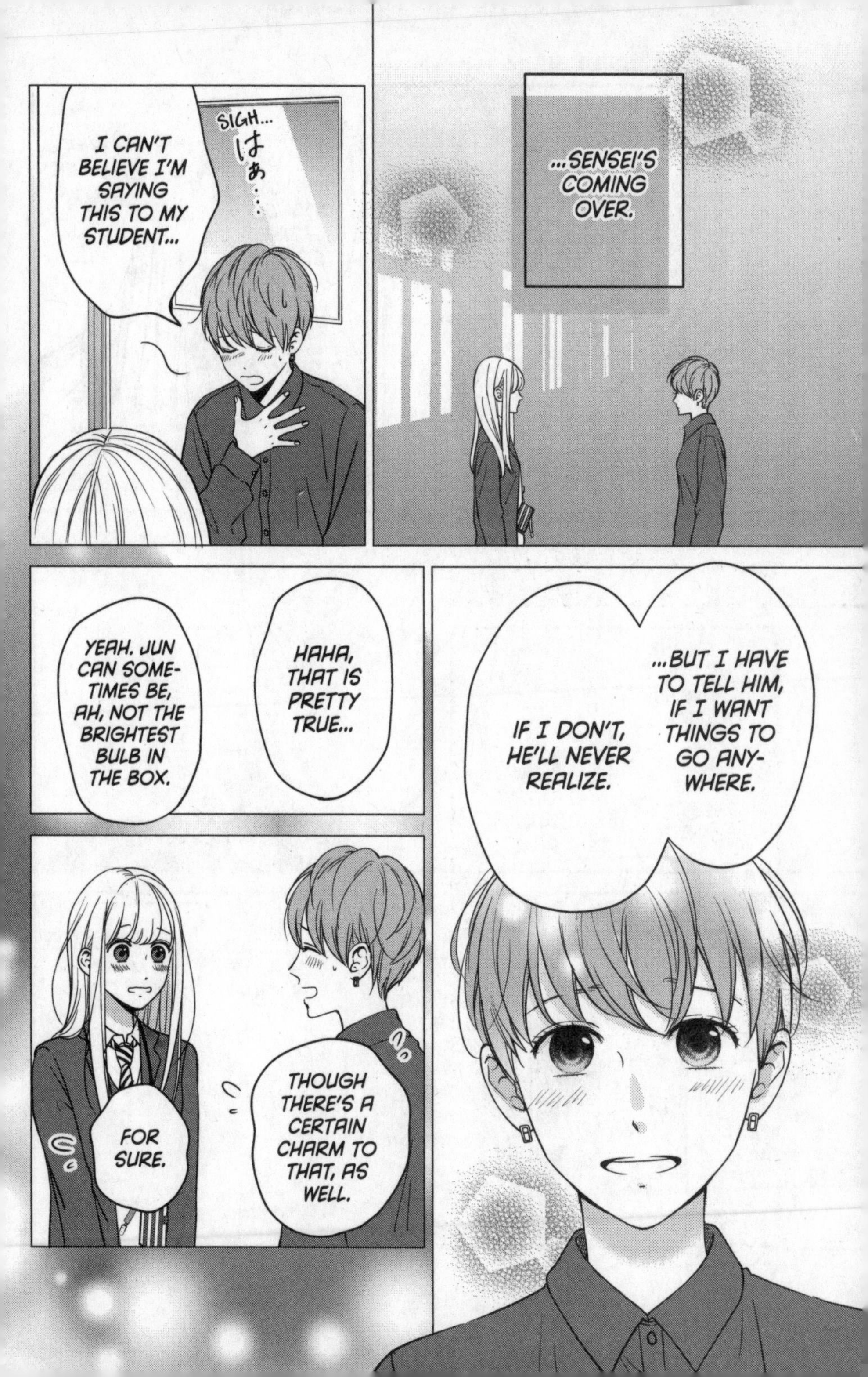
...SENSEI'S COMING OVER.
I CAN'T BELIEVE I'M SAYING THIS TO MY STUDENT...
SIGH...
はぁ…
...BUT I HAVE TO TELL HIM, IF I WANT THINGS TO GO ANY-WHERE.
IF I DON'T, HE'LL NEVER REALIZE.
HAHA, THAT IS PRETTY TRUE...
YEAH. JUN CAN SOME-TIMES BE, AH, NOT THE BRIGHTEST BULB IN THE BOX.
THOUGH THERE'S A CERTAIN CHARM TO THAT, AS WELL.
FOR SURE.

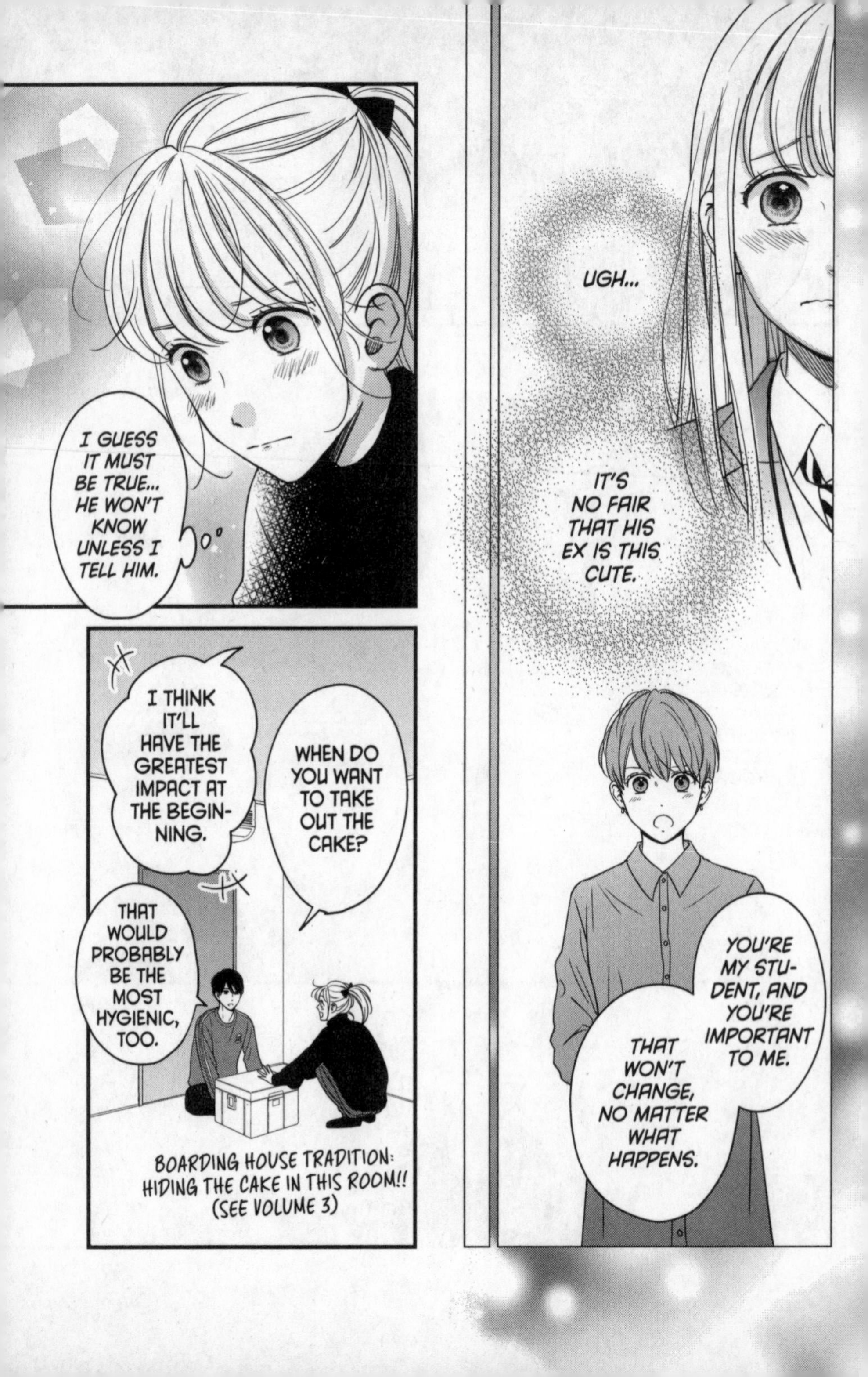
UGH...
IT'S NO FAIR THAT HIS EX IS THIS CUTE.
YOU'RE MY STU-DENT, AND YOU'RE IMPORTANT TO ME.
THAT WON'T CHANGE, NO MATTER WHAT HAPPENS.
I GUESS IT MUST BE TRUE... HE WON'T KNOW UNLESS I TELL HIM.
WHEN DO YOU WANT TO TAKE OUT THE CAKE?
I THINK IT'LL HAVE THE GREATEST IMPACT AT THE BEGIN-NING.
THAT WOULD PROBABLY BE THE MOST HYGIENIC, TOO.
BOARDING HOUSE TRADITION: HIDING THE CAKE IN THIS ROOM!! (SEE VOLUME 3)

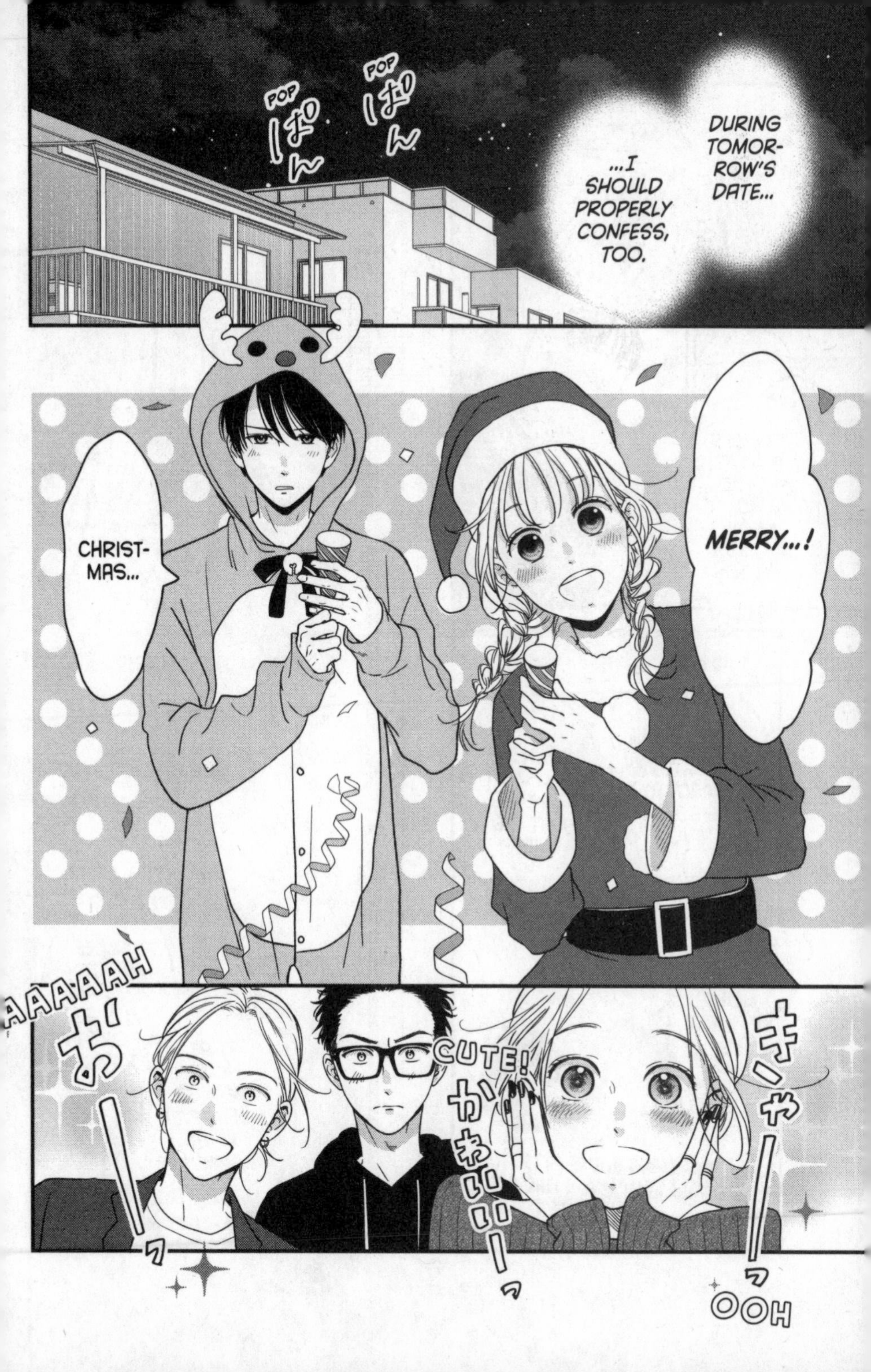
POP ぱん
POP ぱん
DURING TOMOR-ROW'S DATE...
...I SHOULD PROPERLY CONFESS, TOO.
MERRY...!
CHRIST-MAS...
きゃーっ OOH
CUTE! かわいいーっ
おーっ AAAAAAH

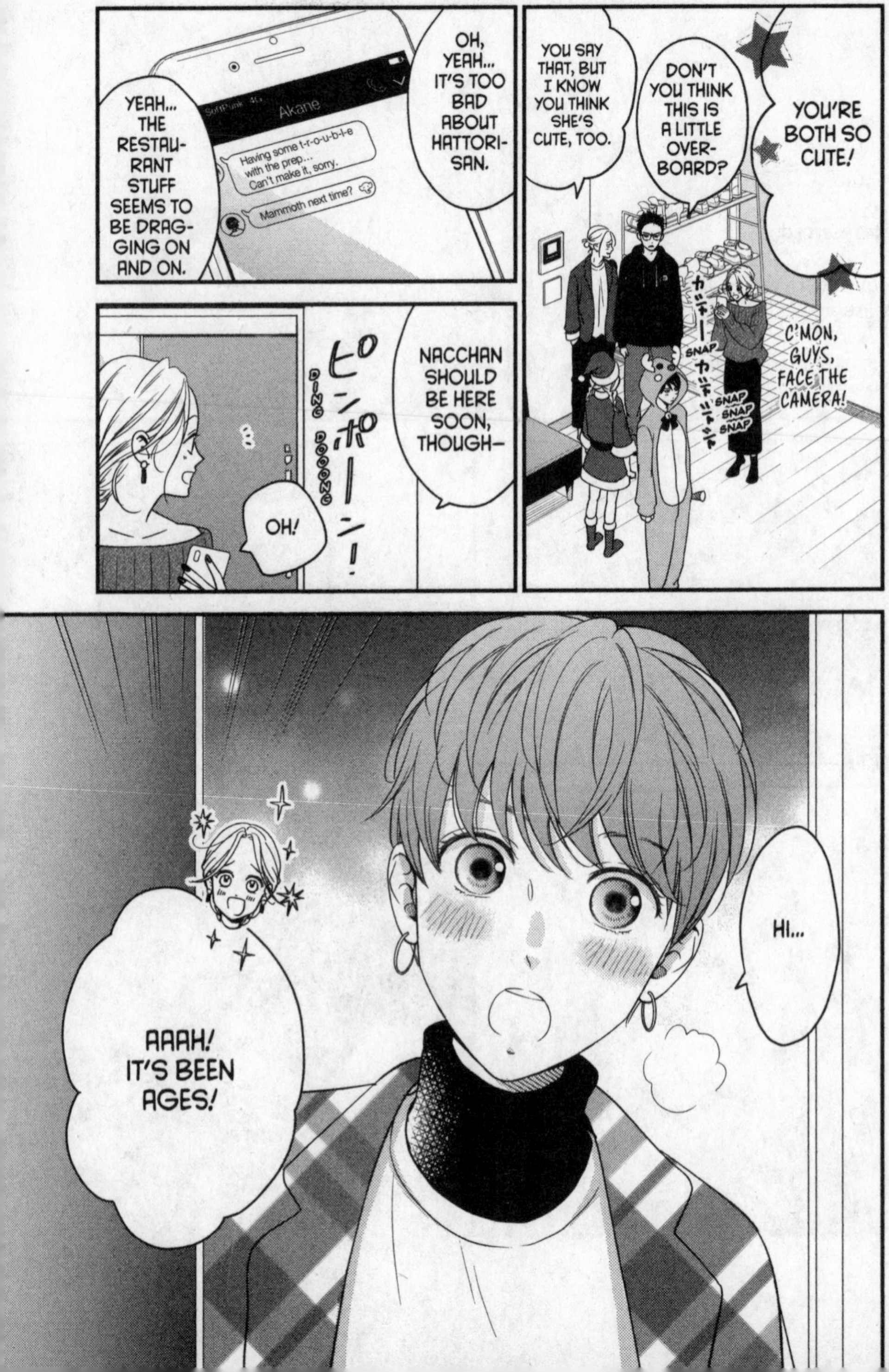
YOU'RE BOTH SO CUTE!
DON'T YOU THINK THIS IS A LITTLE OVER-BOARD?
YOU SAY THAT, BUT I KNOW YOU THINK SHE'S CUTE, TOO.
C'MON, GUYS, FACE THE CAMERA!
SNAP
SNAP
SNAP
SNAP
OH, YEAH... IT'S TOO BAD ABOUT HATTORI-SAN.
Akane
Having some t-r-o-u-b-l-e with the prep... Can't make it, sorry.
Mammoth next time?
YEAH... THE RESTAU-RANT STUFF SEEMS TO BE DRAG-GING ON AND ON.
NACCHAN SHOULD BE HERE SOON, THOUGH—
ピンポーン!
DING DOOONG
OH!
HI...
AAAH! IT'S BEEN AGES!

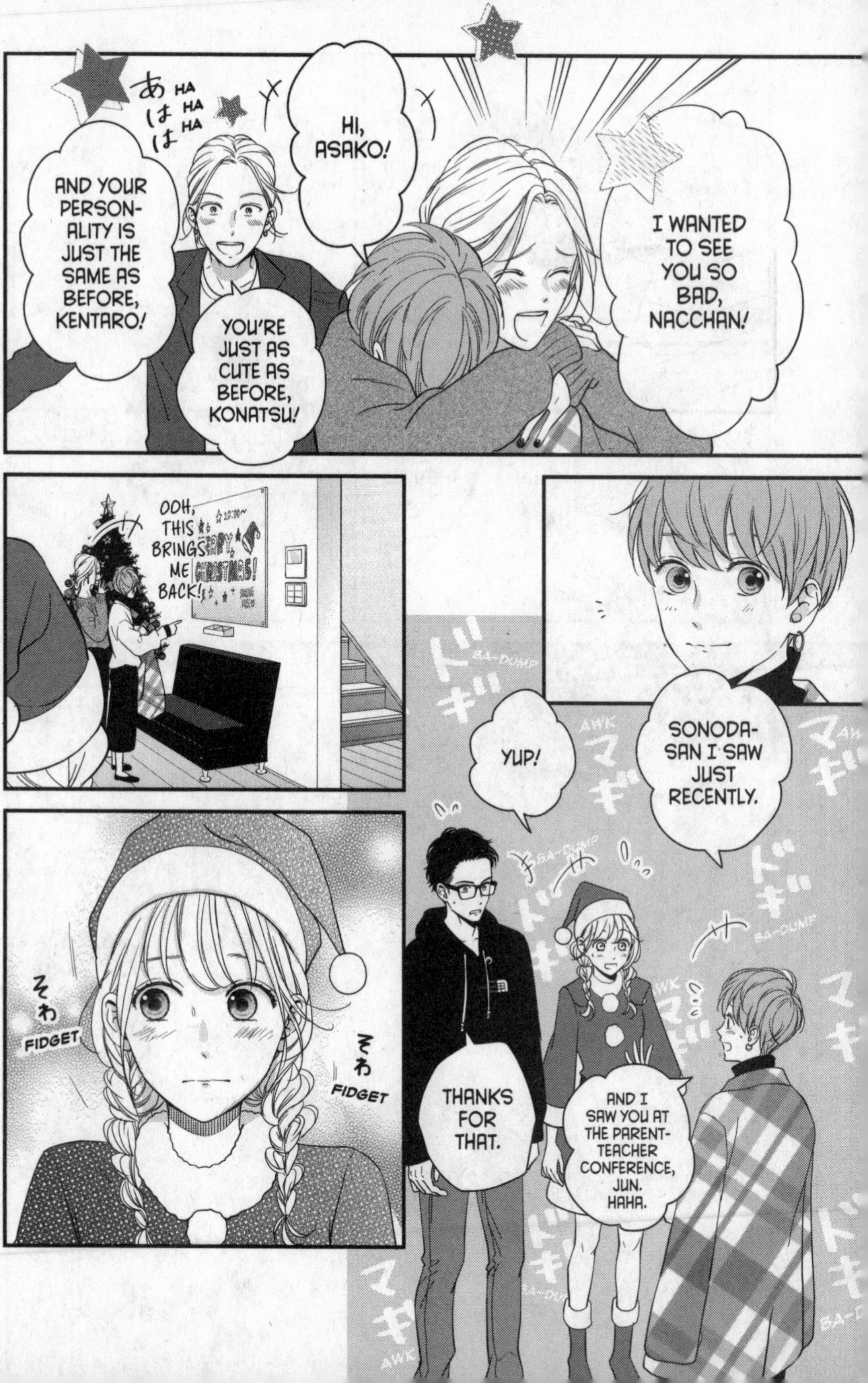
I WANTED TO SEE YOU SO BAD, NACCHAN!
HI, ASAKO!
あはは HA HA HA
AND YOUR PERSONALITY IS JUST THE SAME AS BEFORE, KENTARO!
YOU'RE JUST AS CUTE AS BEFORE, KONATSU!
OOH, THIS BRINGS ME BACK!
ドキ BA-DUMP
マギ AWK
SONODA-SAN I SAW JUST RECENTLY.
YUP!
ドキ BA-DUMP
マギ AWK
AND I SAW YOU AT THE PARENT-TEACHER CONFERENCE, JUN. HAHA.
THANKS FOR THAT.
そわ FIDGET
そわ FIDGET

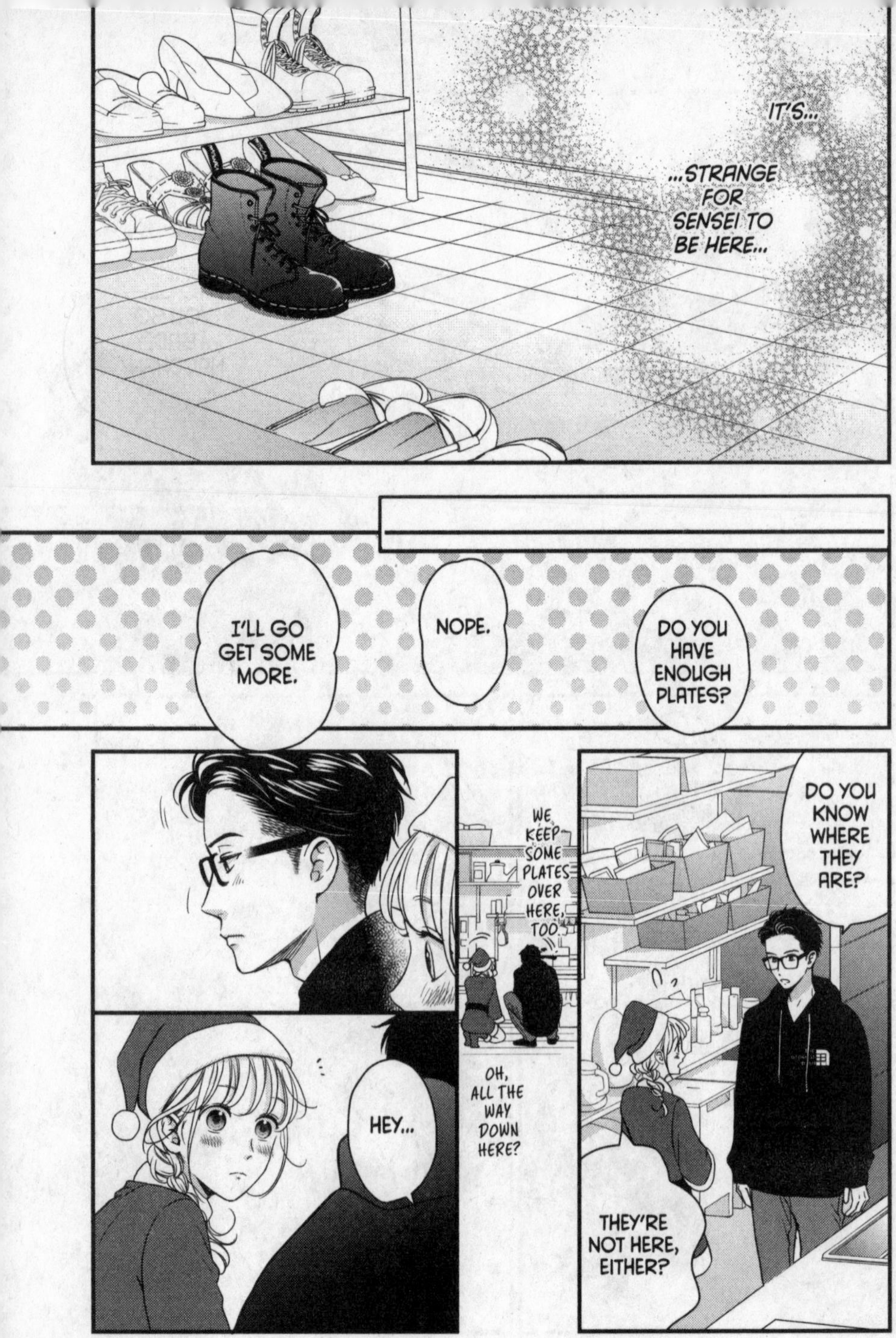
IT'S...
...STRANGE FOR SENSEI TO BE HERE...
DO YOU HAVE ENOUGH PLATES?
NOPE.
I'LL GO GET SOME MORE.
DO YOU KNOW WHERE THEY ARE?
THEY'RE NOT HERE, EITHER?
WE KEEP SOME PLATES OVER HERE, TOO.
OH, ALL THE WAY DOWN HERE?
HEY...

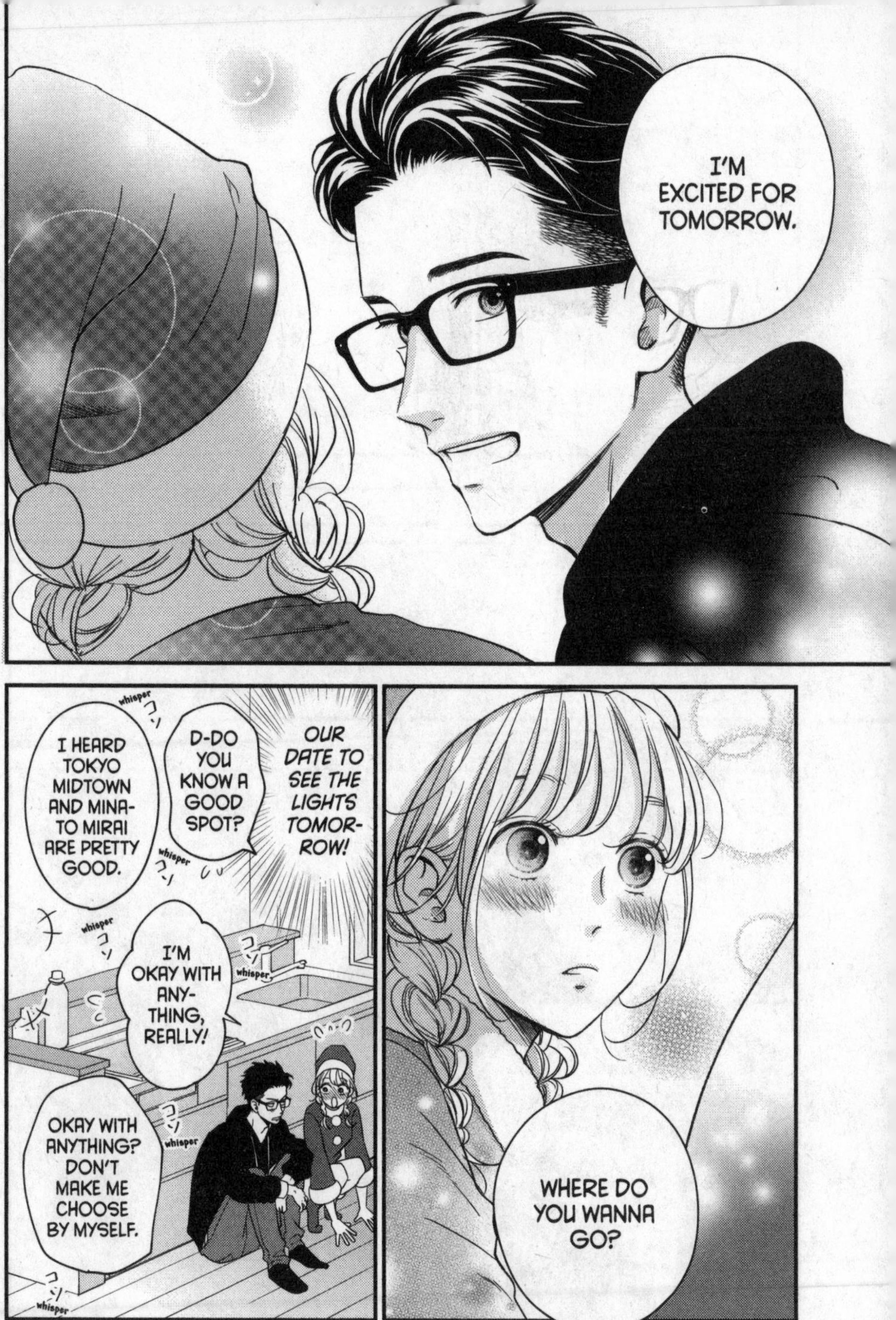
I'M EXCITED FOR TOMORROW.
WHERE DO YOU WANNA GO?
OUR DATE TO SEE THE LIGHTS TOMORROW!
D-DO YOU KNOW A GOOD SPOT?
whisper
I HEARD TOKYO MIDTOWN AND MINATO MIRAI ARE PRETTY GOOD.
whisper
whisper
I'M OKAY WITH ANYTHING, REALLY!
whisper
OKAY WITH ANYTHING? DON'T MAKE ME CHOOSE BY MYSELF.
whisper
whisper

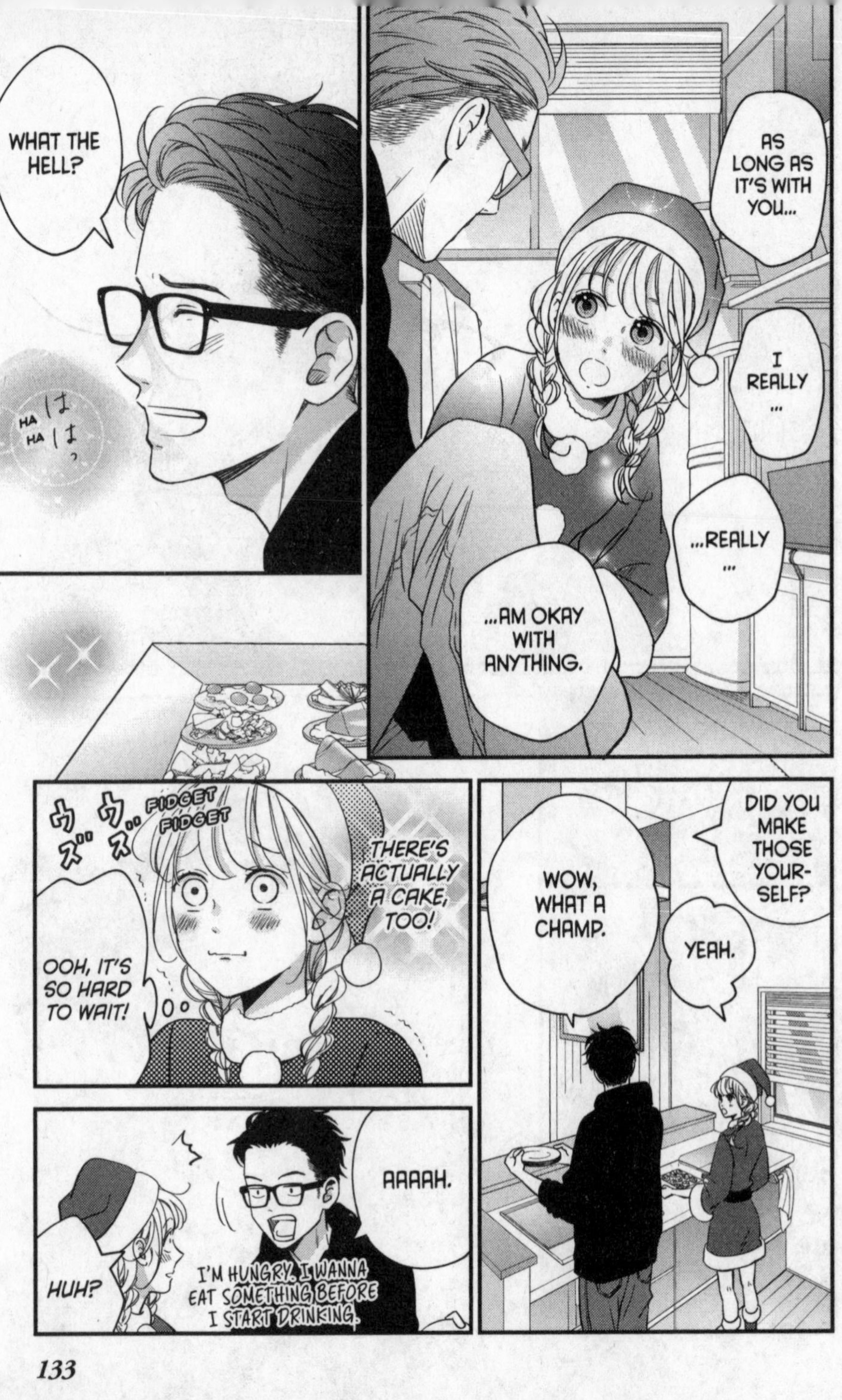
AS LONG AS IT'S WITH YOU...
I REALLY ...
...REALLY ...
...AM OKAY WITH ANYTHING.
WHAT THE HELL?
HA はは HA
DID YOU MAKE THOSE YOUR-SELF?
YEAH.
WOW, WHAT A CHAMP.
ウズウズ FIDGET FIDGET
THERE'S ACTUALLY A CAKE, TOO!
OOH, IT'S SO HARD TO WAIT!
AAAAH.
I'M HUNGRY. I WANNA EAT SOMETHING BEFORE I START DRINKING.
HUH?

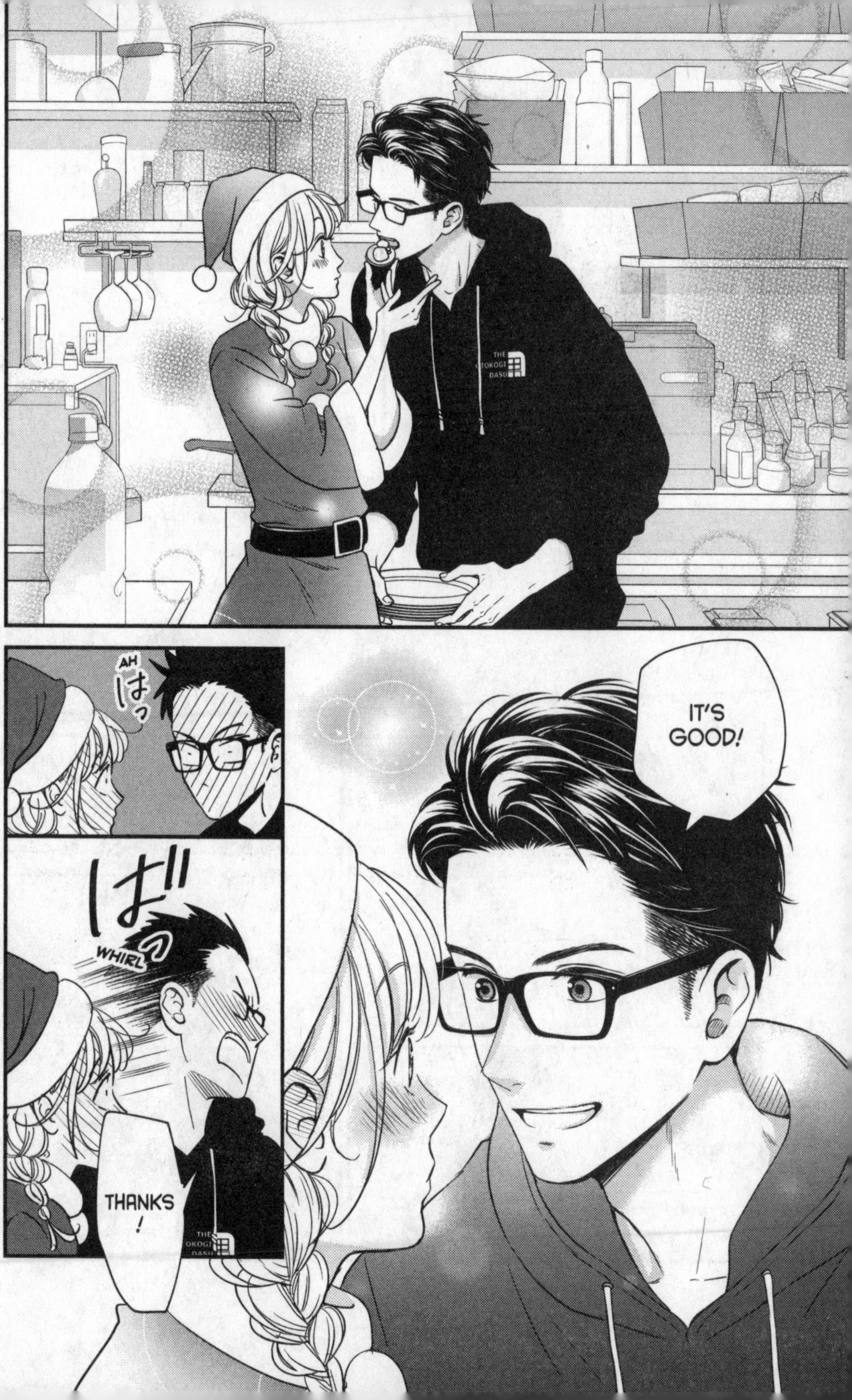
IT'S GOOD!
AH
はっ
ばっ
WHIRL
THANKS!
THE OTOKOGI DASU

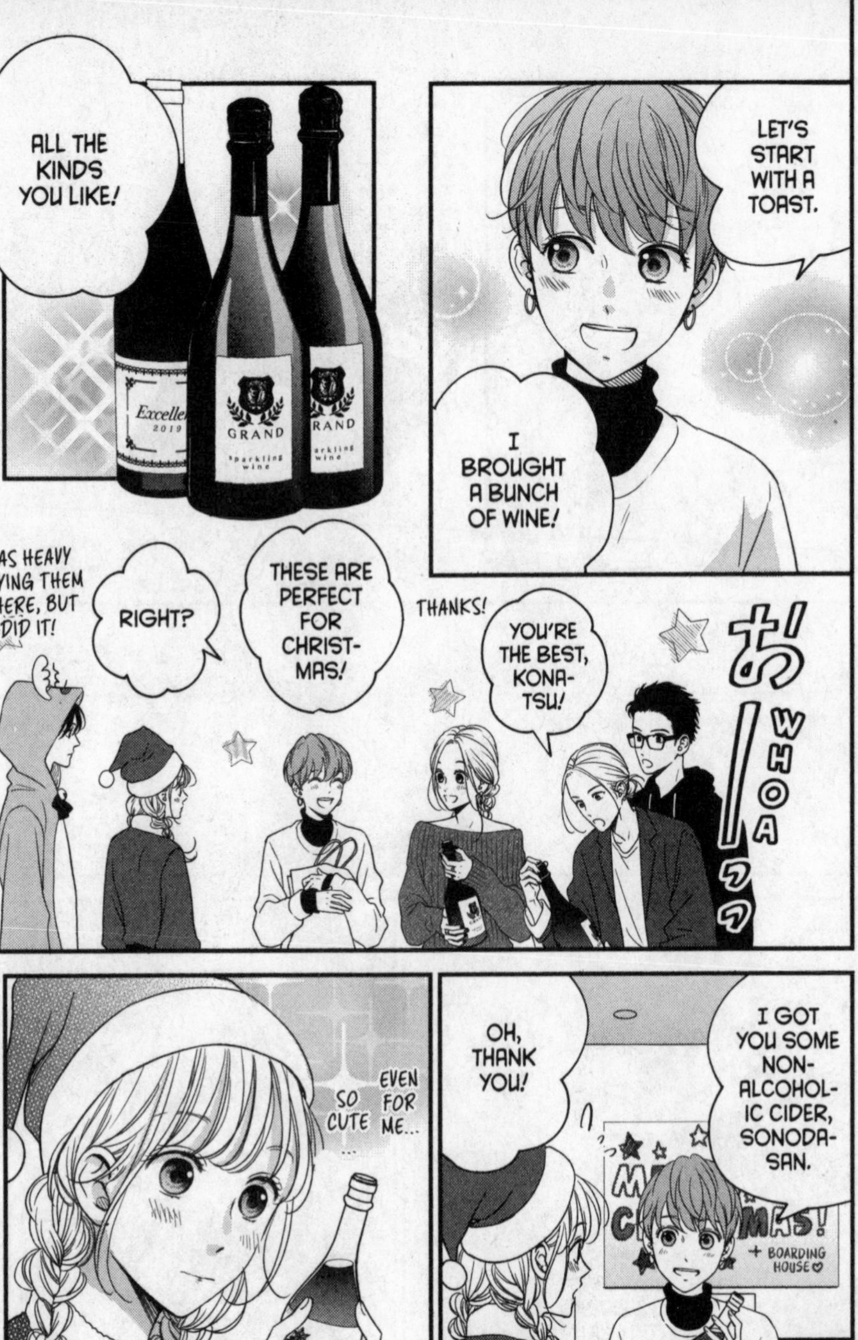
LET'S START WITH A TOAST.
I BROUGHT A BUNCH OF WINE!
ALL THE KINDS YOU LIKE!
Excellen 2019
GRAND sparkling wine
GRAND sparkling wine
おーっっ
WHOA
YOU'RE THE BEST, KONATSU!
THANKS!
THESE ARE PERFECT FOR CHRISTMAS!
RIGHT?
IT WAS HEAVY CARRYING THEM ALL HERE, BUT I DID IT!
I GOT YOU SOME NON-ALCOHOLIC CIDER, SONODA-SAN.
OH, THANK YOU!
+ BOARDING HOUSE♡
EVEN FOR ME...
SO CUTE...

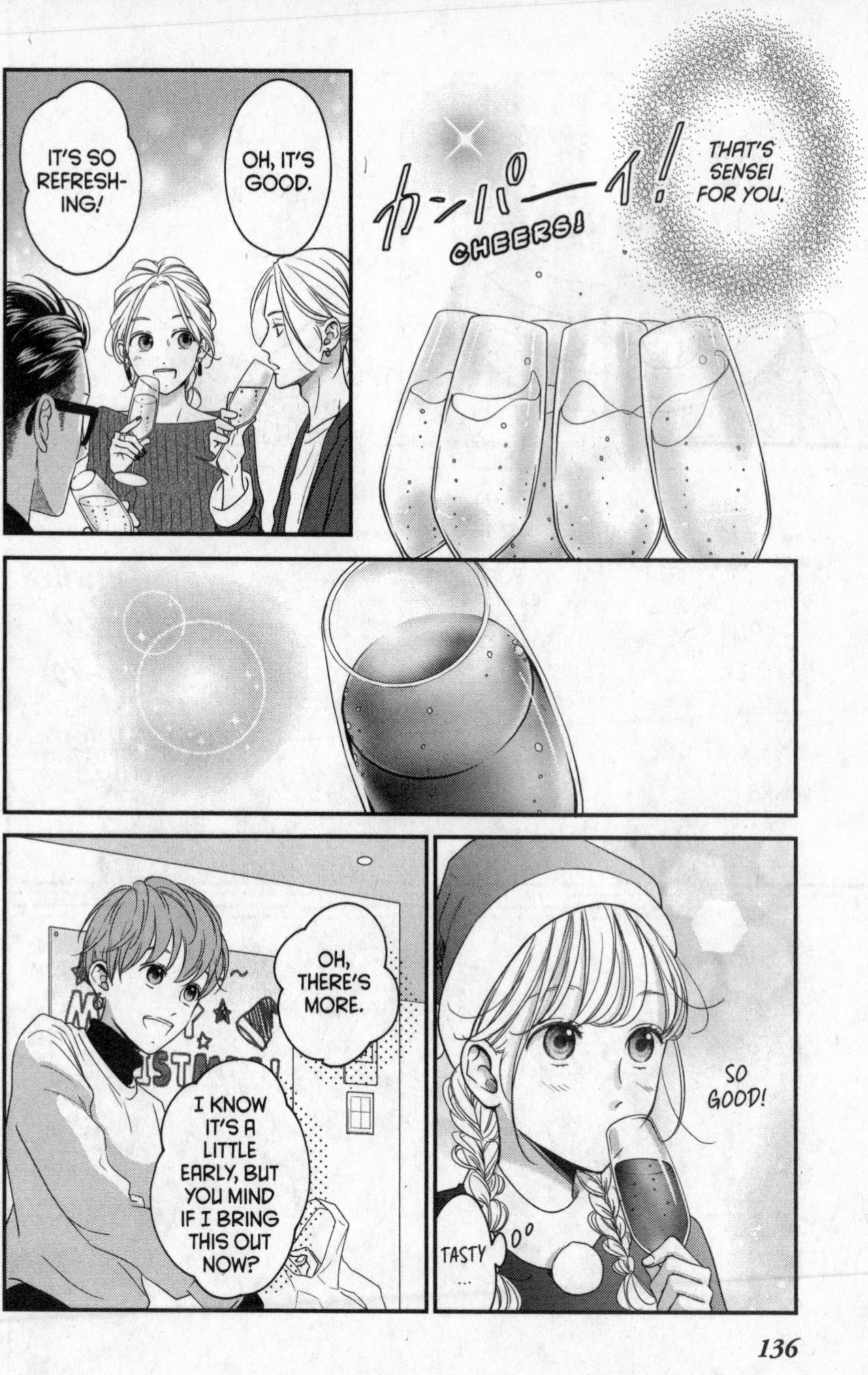
THAT'S SENSEI FOR YOU.
カンパーイ!
CHEERS!
OH, IT'S GOOD.
IT'S SO REFRESHING!
SO GOOD!
TASTY...
OH, THERE'S MORE.
I KNOW IT'S A LITTLE EARLY, BUT YOU MIND IF I BRING THIS OUT NOW?

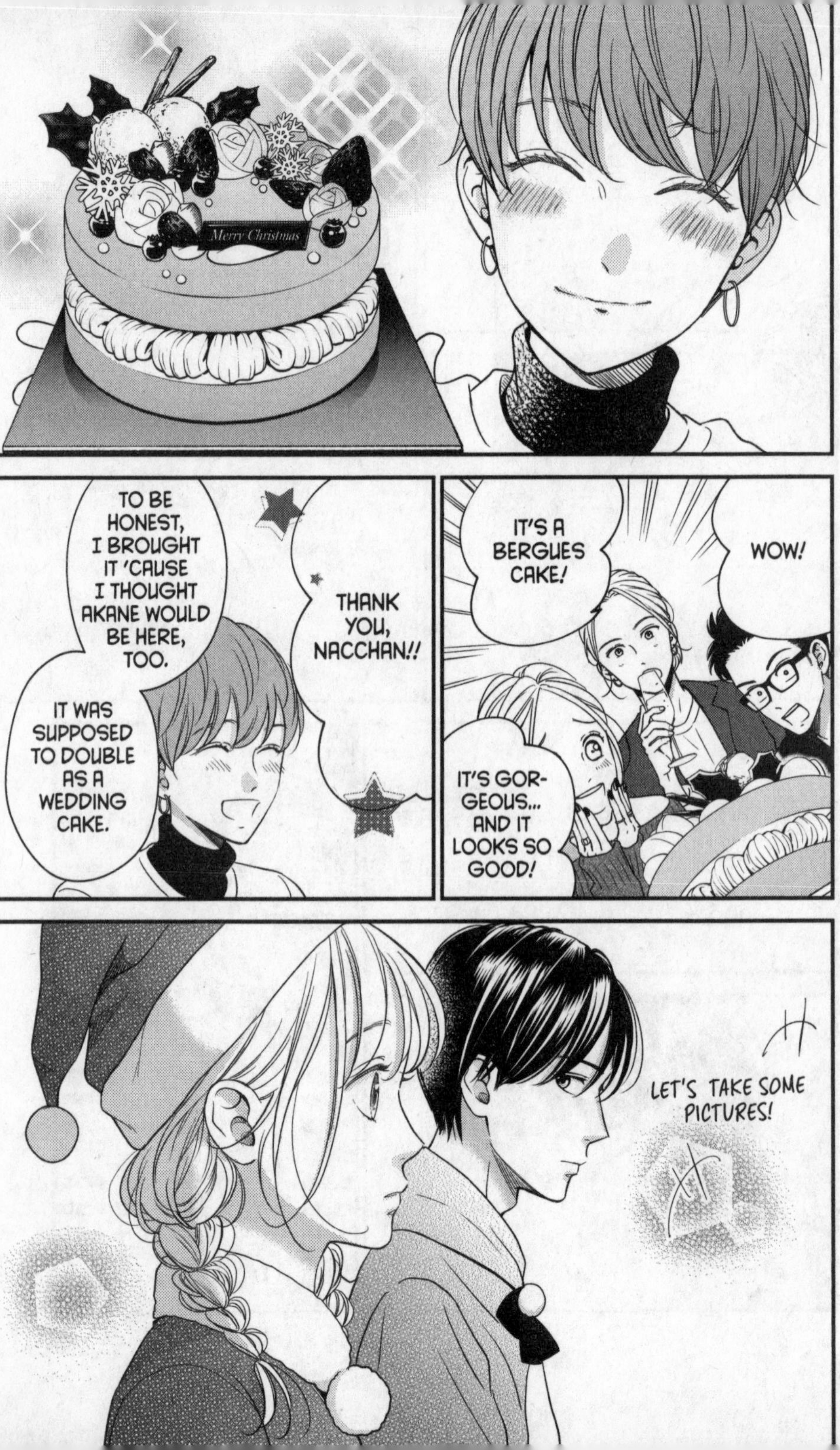
Merry Christmas
WOW!
IT'S A BERGUES CAKE!
IT'S GOR-GEOUS... AND IT LOOKS SO GOOD!
THANK YOU, NACCHAN!!
TO BE HONEST, I BROUGHT IT 'CAUSE I THOUGHT AKANE WOULD BE HERE, TOO.
IT WAS SUPPOSED TO DOUBLE AS A WEDDING CAKE.
LET'S TAKE SOME PICTURES!

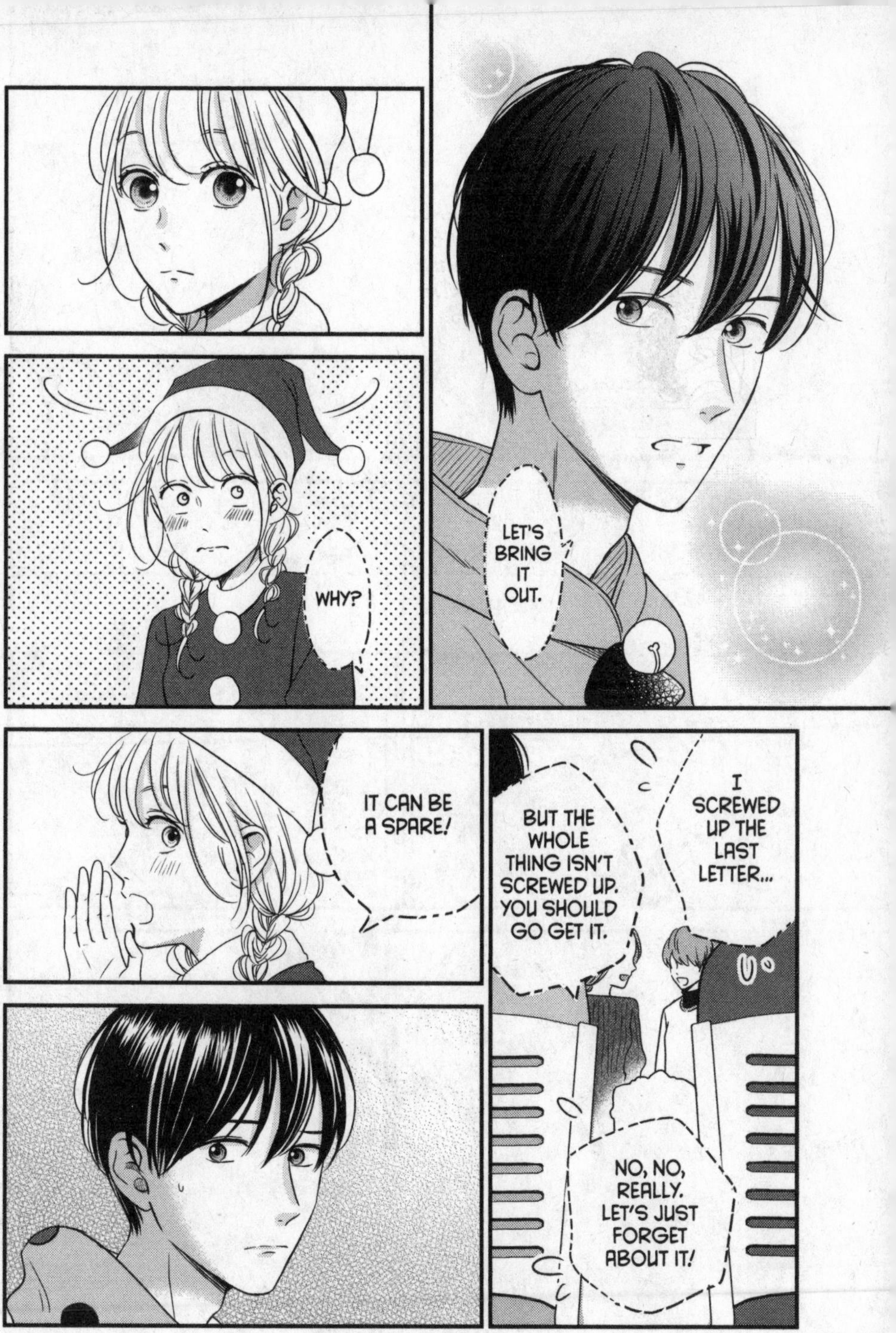
LET'S BRING IT OUT.
WHY?
I SCREWED UP THE LAST LETTER...
BUT THE WHOLE THING ISN'T SCREWED UP. YOU SHOULD GO GET IT.
NO, NO, REALLY. LET'S JUST FORGET ABOUT IT!
IT CAN BE A SPARE!

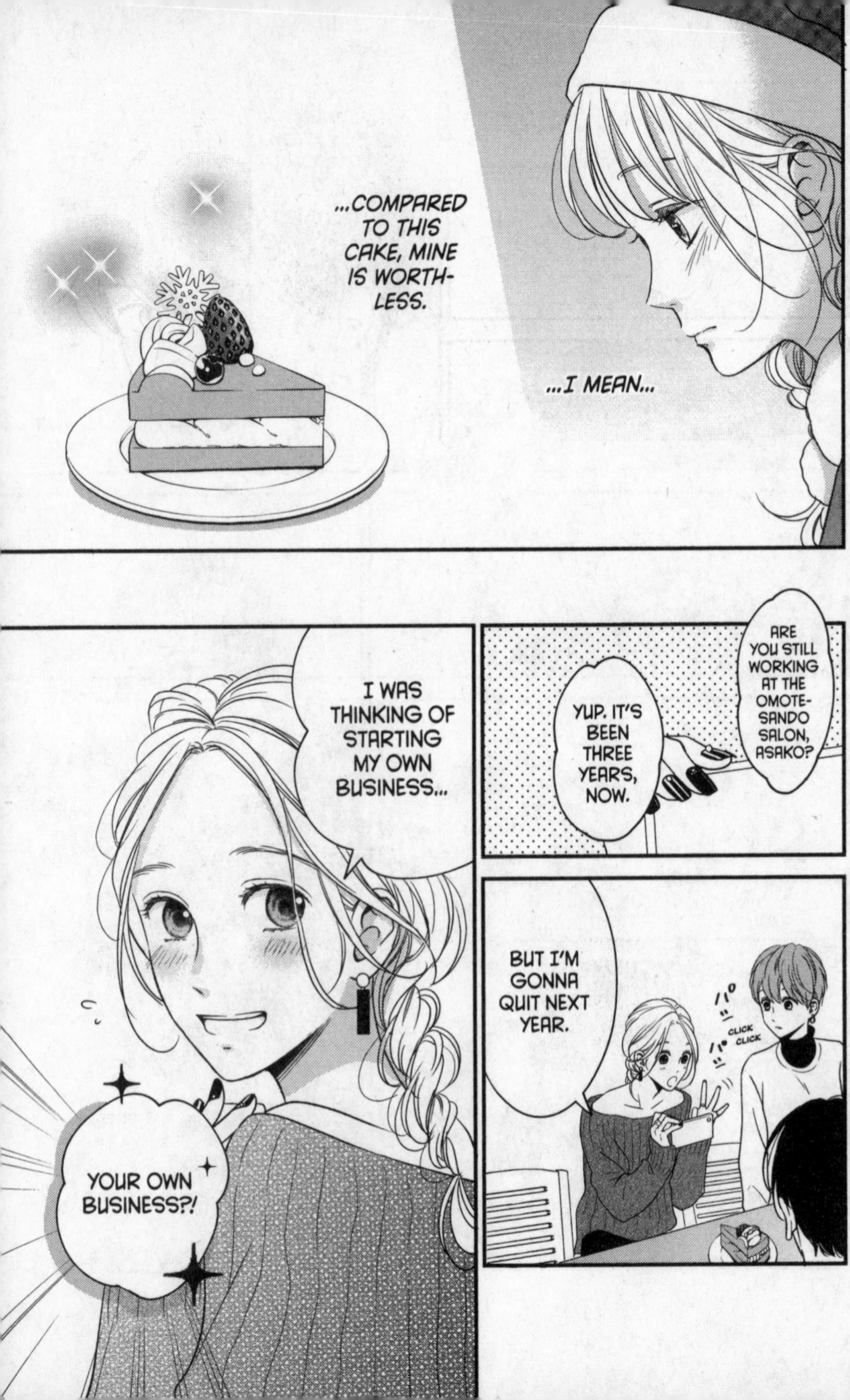
...I MEAN...
...COMPARED TO THIS CAKE, MINE IS WORTH-LESS.
ARE YOU STILL WORKING AT THE OMOTE-SANDO SALON, ASAKO?
YUP. IT'S BEEN THREE YEARS, NOW.
BUT I'M GONNA QUIT NEXT YEAR.
CLICK CLICK
I WAS THINKING OF STARTING MY OWN BUSINESS...
YOUR OWN BUSINESS?!

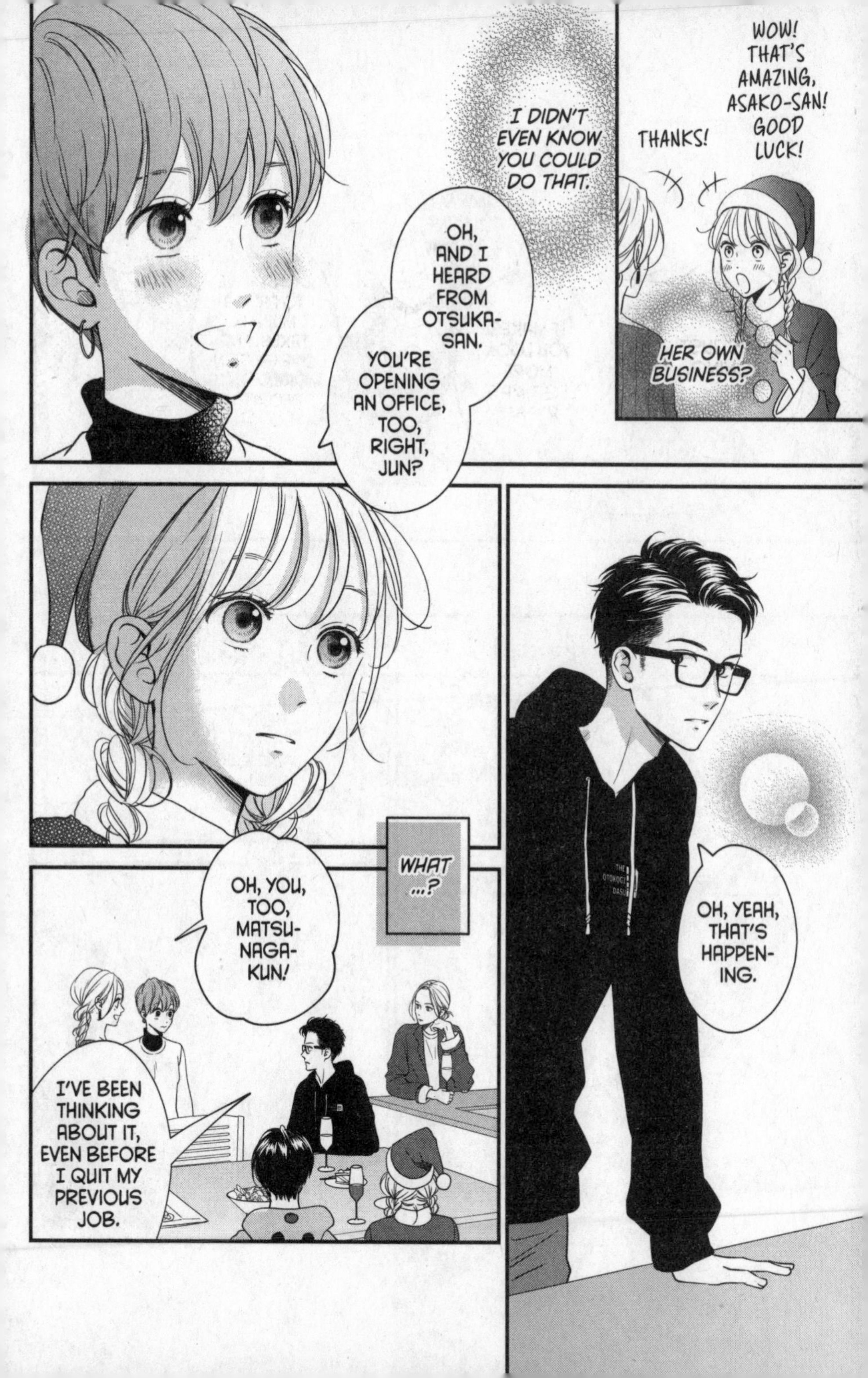
WOW! THAT'S AMAZING, ASAKO-SAN! GOOD LUCK!
THANKS!
HER OWN BUSINESS?
I DIDN'T EVEN KNOW YOU COULD DO THAT.
OH, AND I HEARD FROM OTSUKA-SAN.
YOU'RE OPENING AN OFFICE, TOO, RIGHT, JUN?
OH, YEAH, THAT'S HAPPEN-ING.
WHAT ...?
OH, YOU, TOO, MATSU-NAGA-KUN!
I'VE BEEN THINKING ABOUT IT, EVEN BEFORE I QUIT MY PREVIOUS JOB.

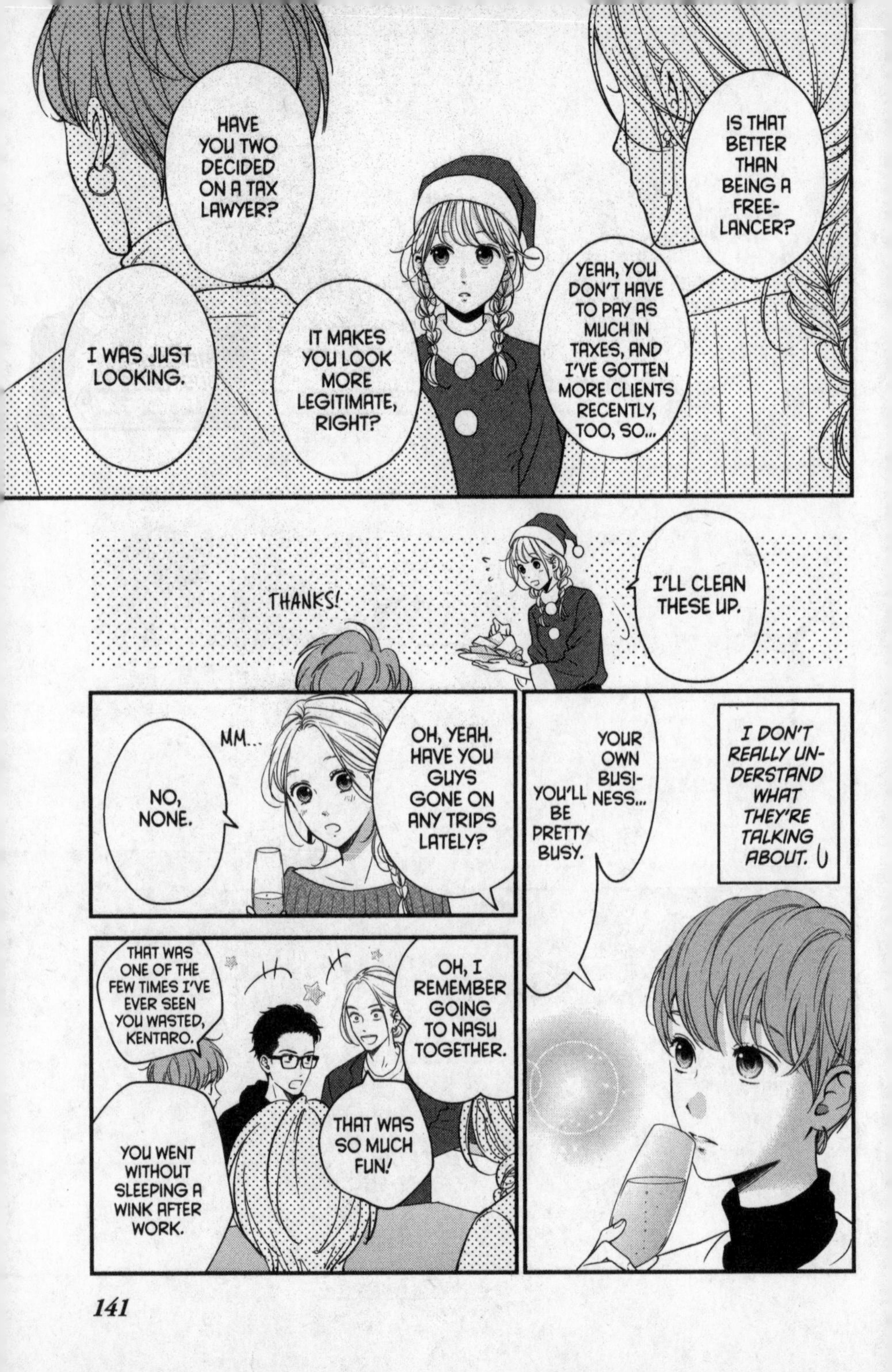
IS THAT BETTER THAN BEING A FREE-LANCER?
YEAH, YOU DON'T HAVE TO PAY AS MUCH IN TAXES, AND I'VE GOTTEN MORE CLIENTS RECENTLY, TOO, SO...
HAVE YOU TWO DECIDED ON A TAX LAWYER?
IT MAKES YOU LOOK MORE LEGITIMATE, RIGHT?
I WAS JUST LOOKING.
I'LL CLEAN THESE UP.
THANKS!
I DON'T REALLY UN-DERSTAND WHAT THEY'RE TALKING ABOUT.
YOUR OWN BUSI-NESS... YOU'LL BE PRETTY BUSY.
OH, YEAH. HAVE YOU GUYS GONE ON ANY TRIPS LATELY?
MM...
NO, NONE.
OH, I REMEMBER GOING TO NASU TOGETHER.
THAT WAS ONE OF THE FEW TIMES I'VE EVER SEEN YOU WASTED, KENTARO.
THAT WAS SO MUCH FUN!
YOU WENT WITHOUT SLEEPING A WINK AFTER WORK.

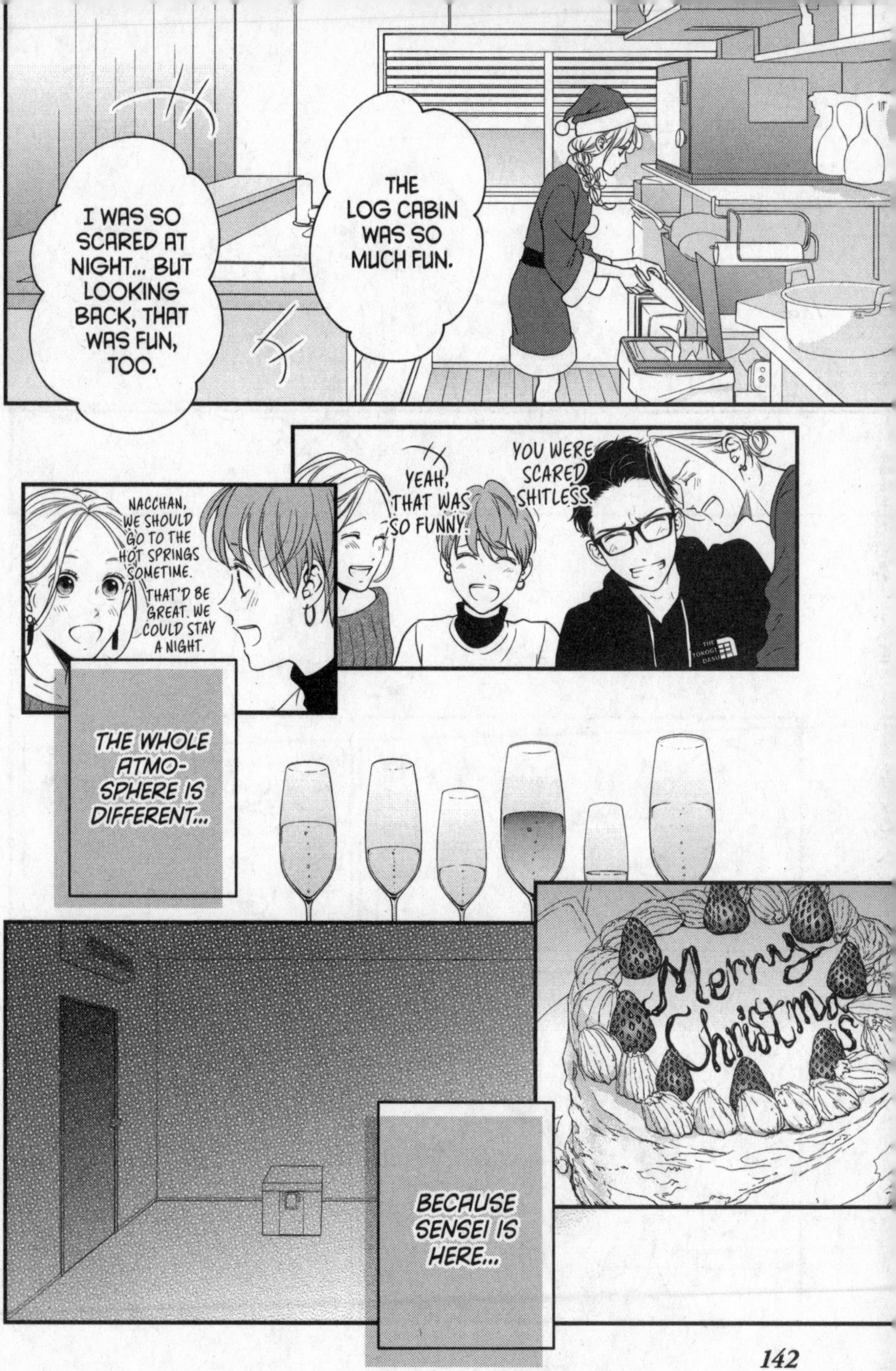
THE LOG CABIN WAS SO MUCH FUN.
I WAS SO SCARED AT NIGHT... BUT LOOKING BACK, THAT WAS FUN, TOO.
YOU WERE SCARED SHITLESS.
YEAH, THAT WAS SO FUNNY.
THE TOKOGI DASU
NACCHAN, WE SHOULD GO TO THE HOT SPRINGS SOMETIME.
THAT'D BE GREAT. WE COULD STAY A NIGHT.
THE WHOLE ATMO-SPHERE IS DIFFERENT...
Merry Christmas
BECAUSE SENSEI IS HERE...

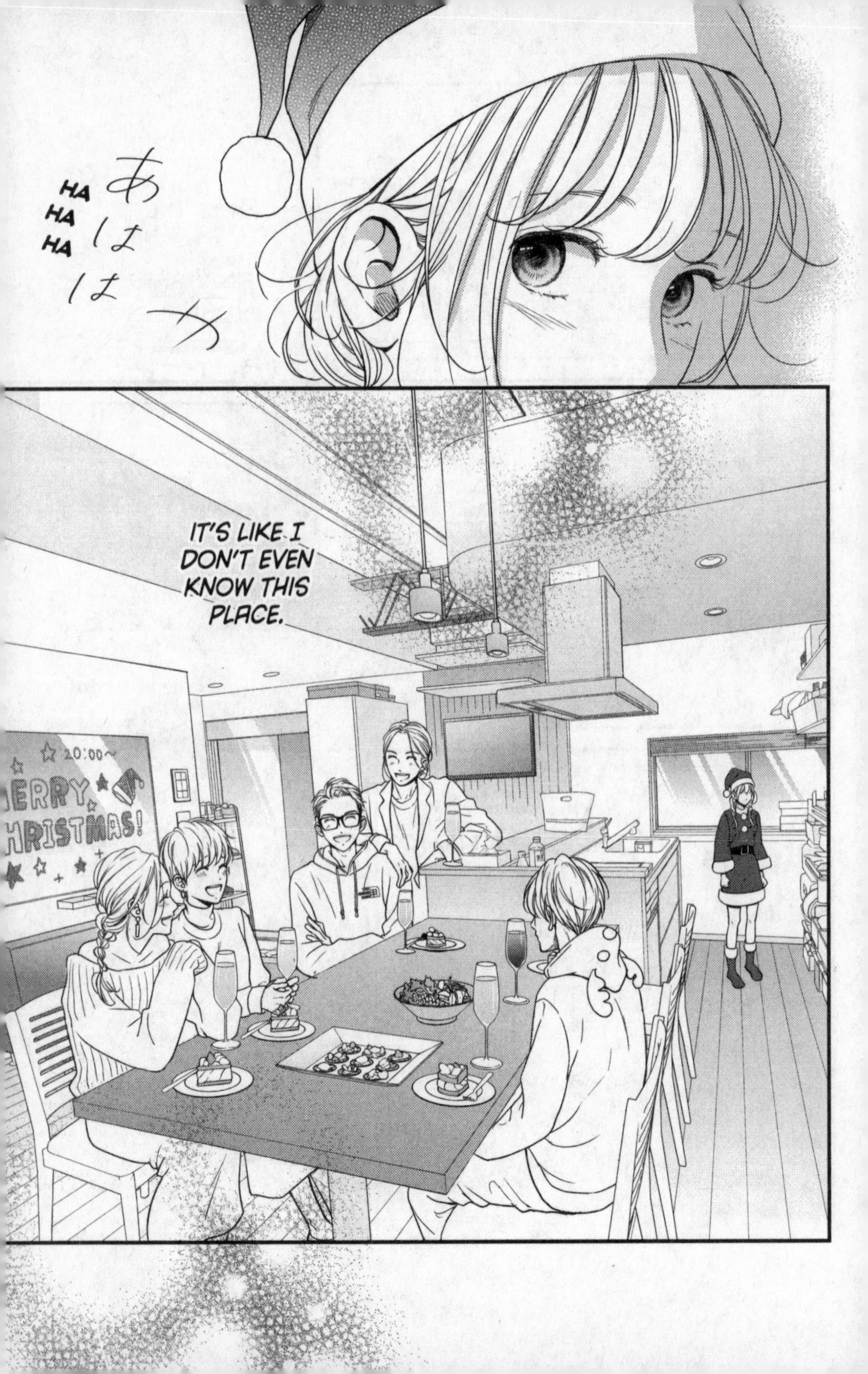
HA HA HA
あははは
IT'S LIKE I DON'T EVEN KNOW THIS PLACE.
20:00~
MERRY CHRISTMAS!

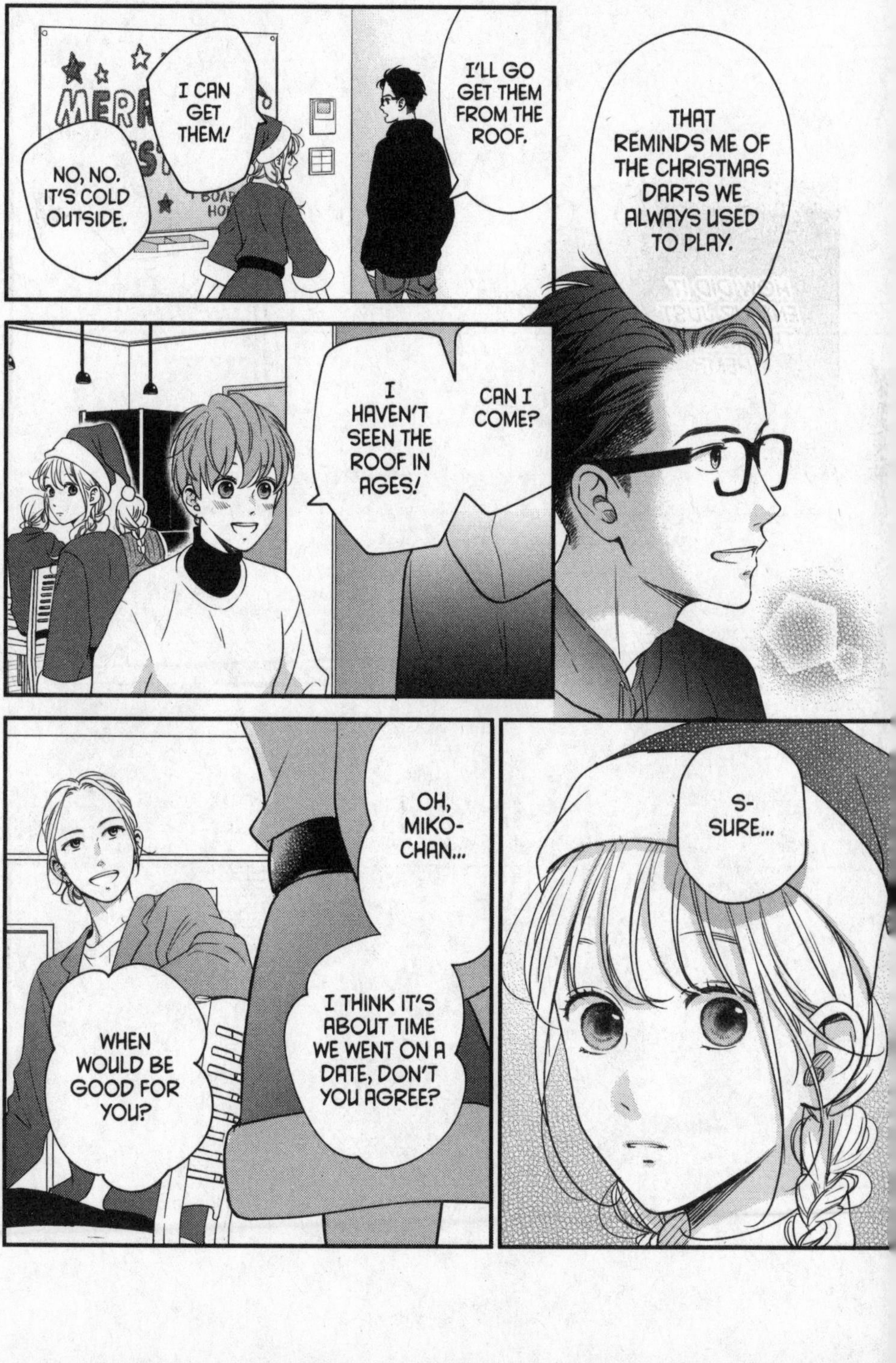
THAT REMINDS ME OF THE CHRISTMAS DARTS WE ALWAYS USED TO PLAY.
I'LL GO GET THEM FROM THE ROOF.
I CAN GET THEM!
NO, NO. IT'S COLD OUTSIDE.
CAN I COME?
I HAVEN'T SEEN THE ROOF IN AGES!
S-SURE...
OH, MIKO-CHAN...
I THINK IT'S ABOUT TIME WE WENT ON A DATE, DON'T YOU AGREE?
WHEN WOULD BE GOOD FOR YOU?

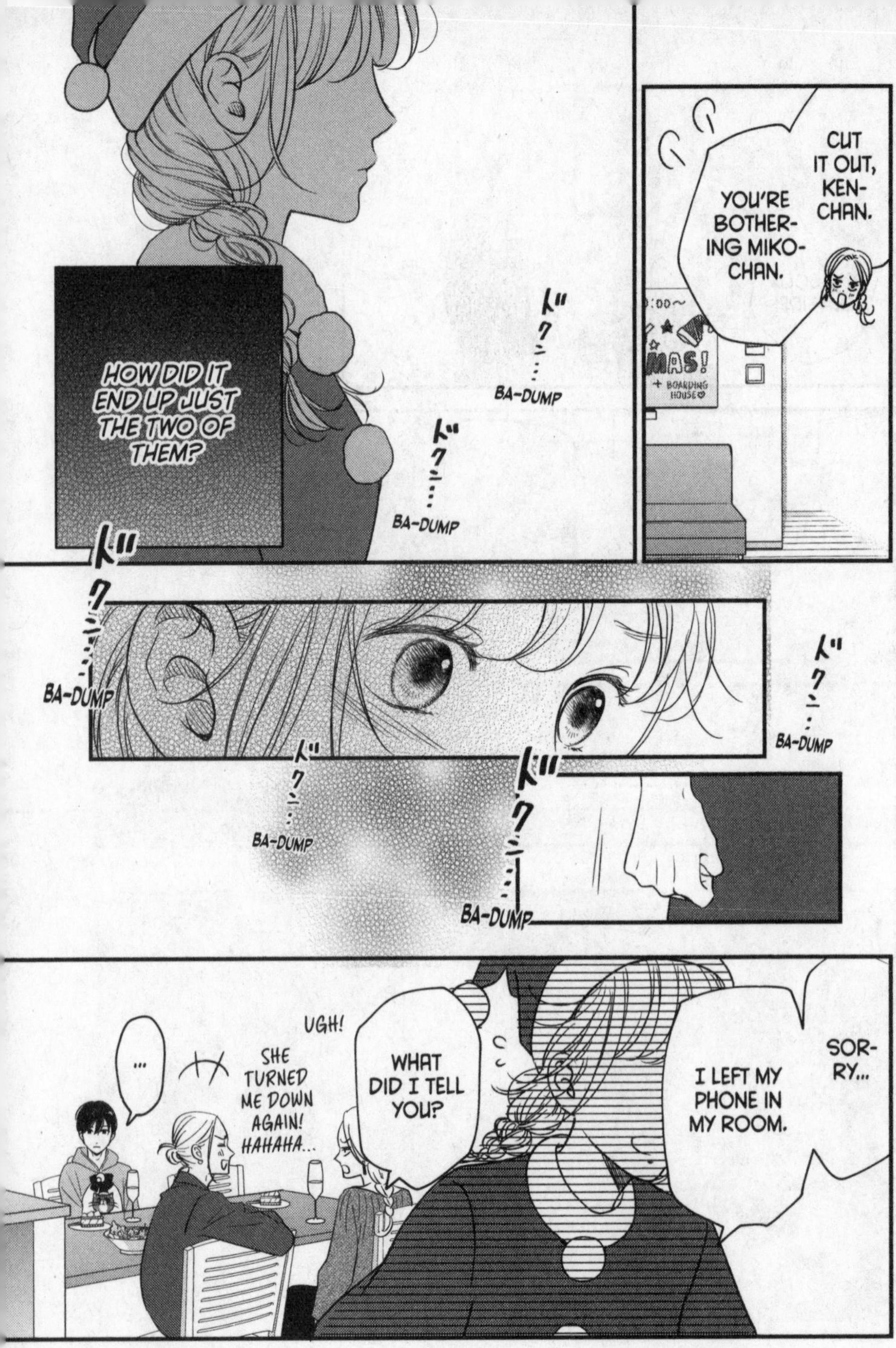
CUT IT OUT, KEN-CHAN.
YOU'RE BOTHERING MIKO-CHAN.
MAS!
+ BOARDING HOUSE♡
ドクン… BA-DUMP
ドクン… BA-DUMP
HOW DID IT END UP JUST THE TWO OF THEM?
ドクン… BA-DUMP
ドクン… BA-DUMP
ドクン… BA-DUMP
ドクン… BA-DUMP
SORRY...
I LEFT MY PHONE IN MY ROOM.
WHAT DID I TELL YOU?
UGH!
SHE TURNED ME DOWN AGAIN! HAHAHA...
...

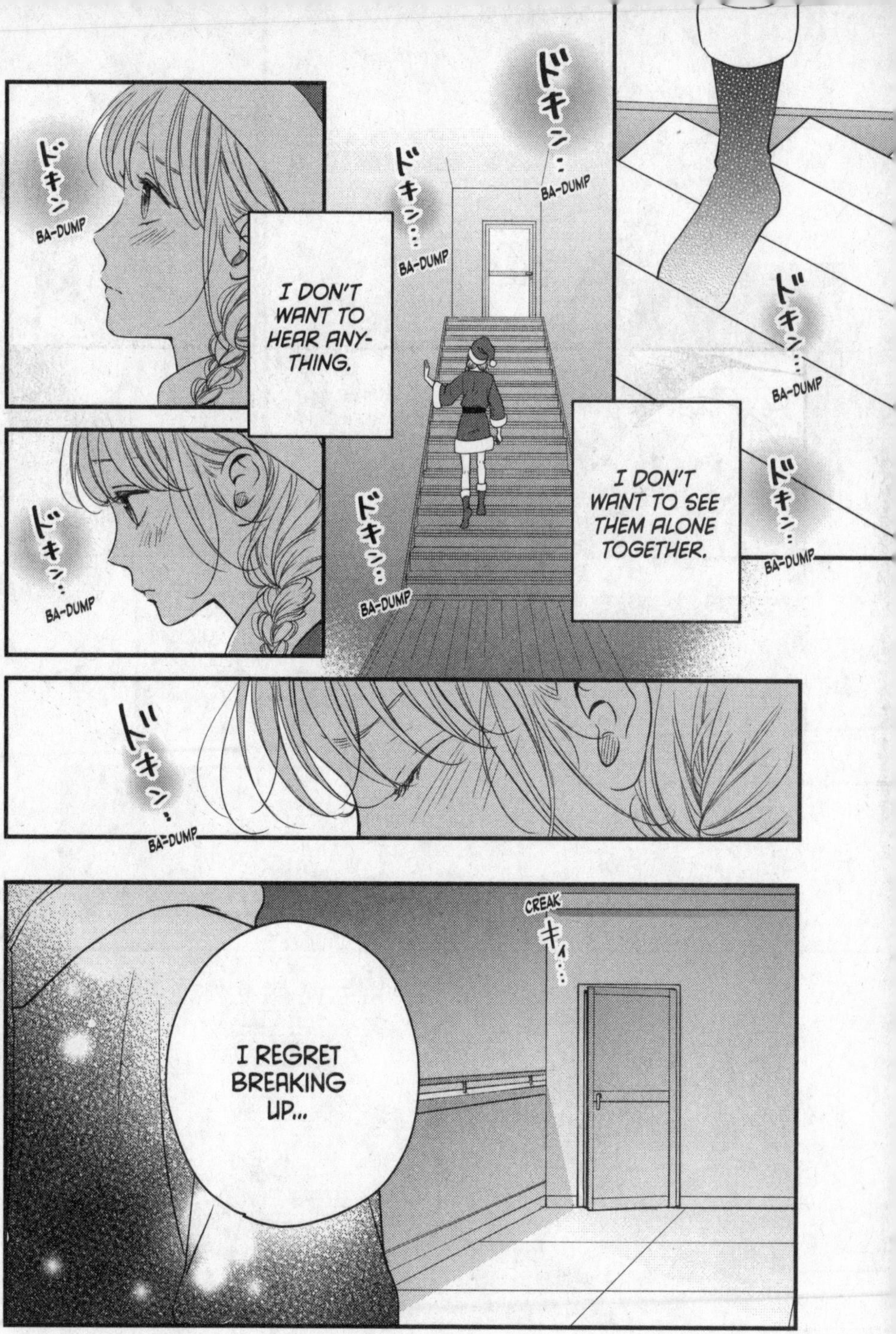
ドキン…
BA-DUMP
ドキン…
BA-DUMP
I DON'T WANT TO SEE THEM ALONE TOGETHER.
ドキン…
BA-DUMP
ドキン…
BA-DUMP
ドキン…
BA-DUMP
I DON'T WANT TO HEAR ANYTHING.
ドキン
BA-DUMP
ドキン…
BA-DUMP
ドキン…
BA-DUMP
CREAK
キィ…
I REGRET BREAKING UP...

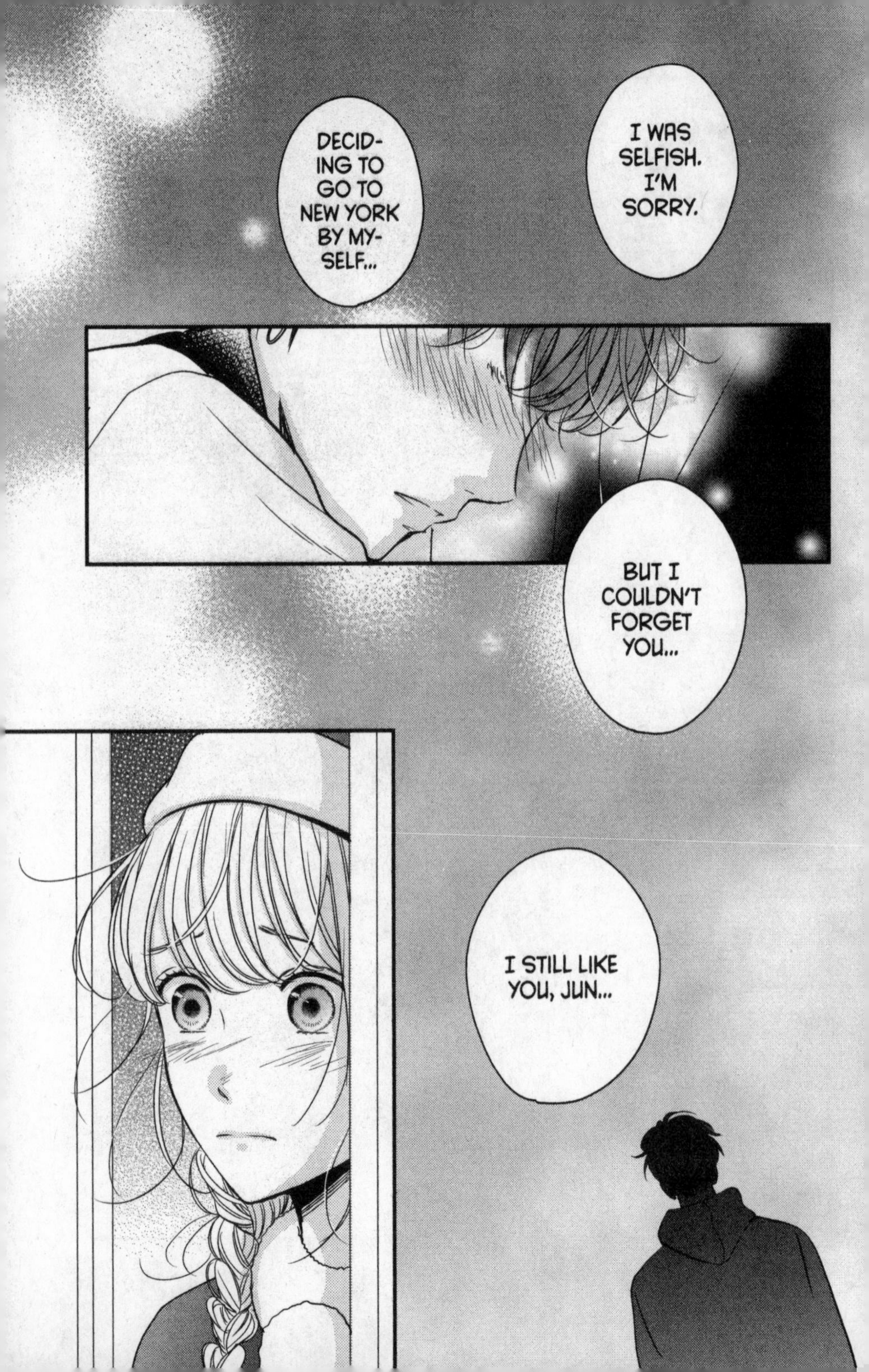
I WAS SELFISH. I'M SORRY.
DECID-ING TO GO TO NEW YORK BY MY-SELF...
BUT I COULDN'T FORGET YOU...
I STILL LIKE YOU, JUN...

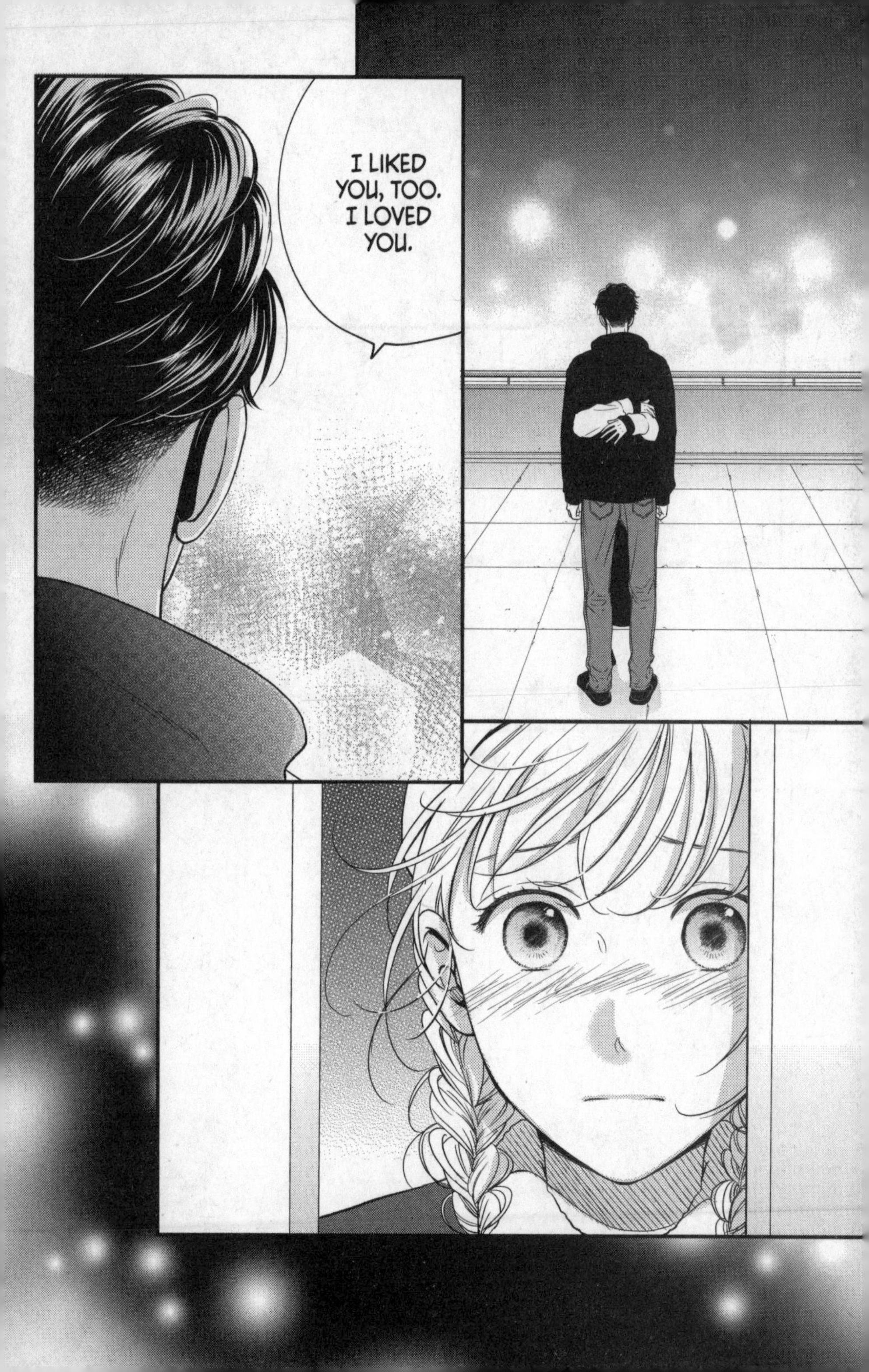
I LIKED YOU, TOO. I LOVED YOU.

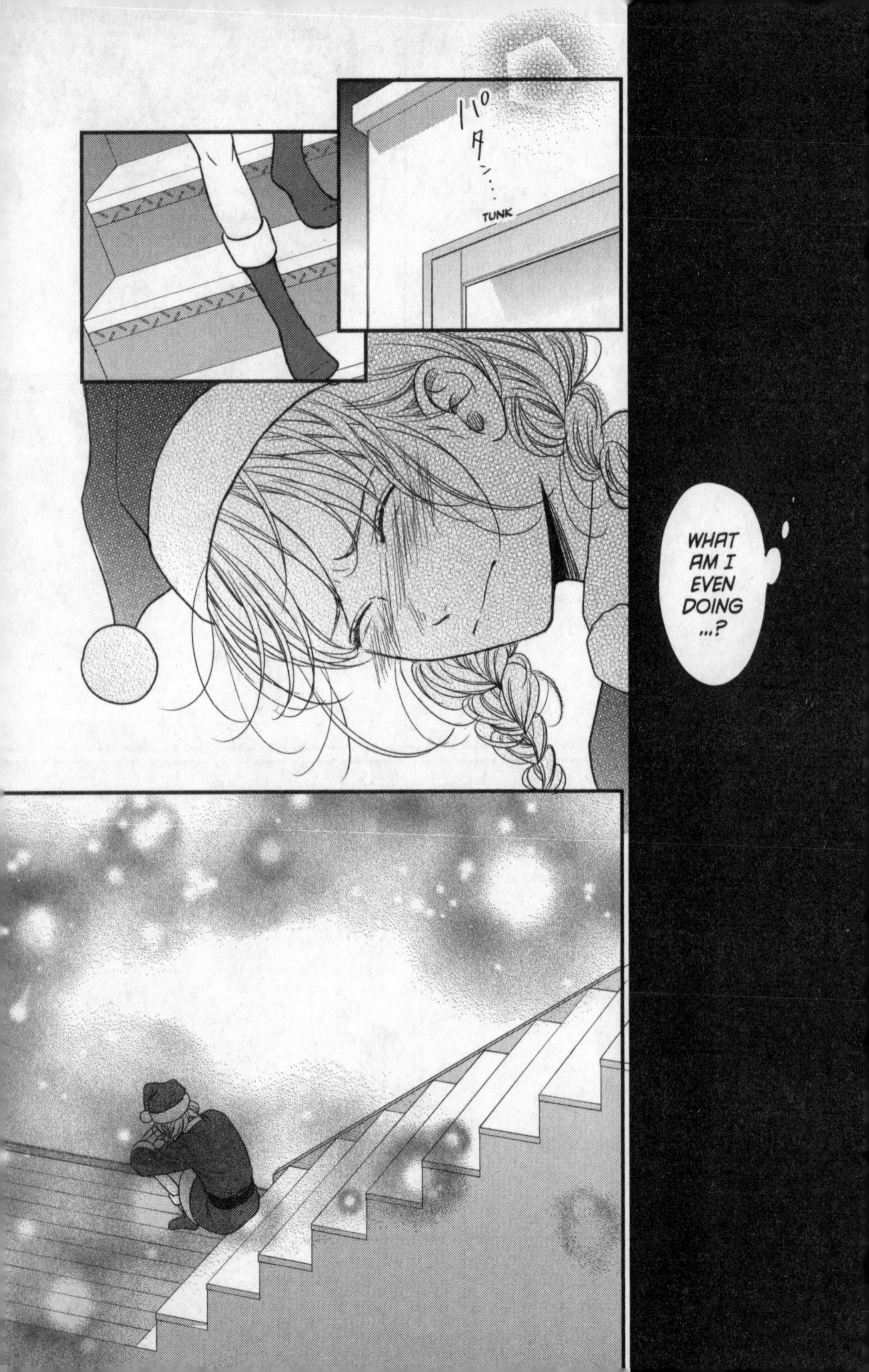
パタン…
TUNK
WHAT AM I EVEN DOING ...?

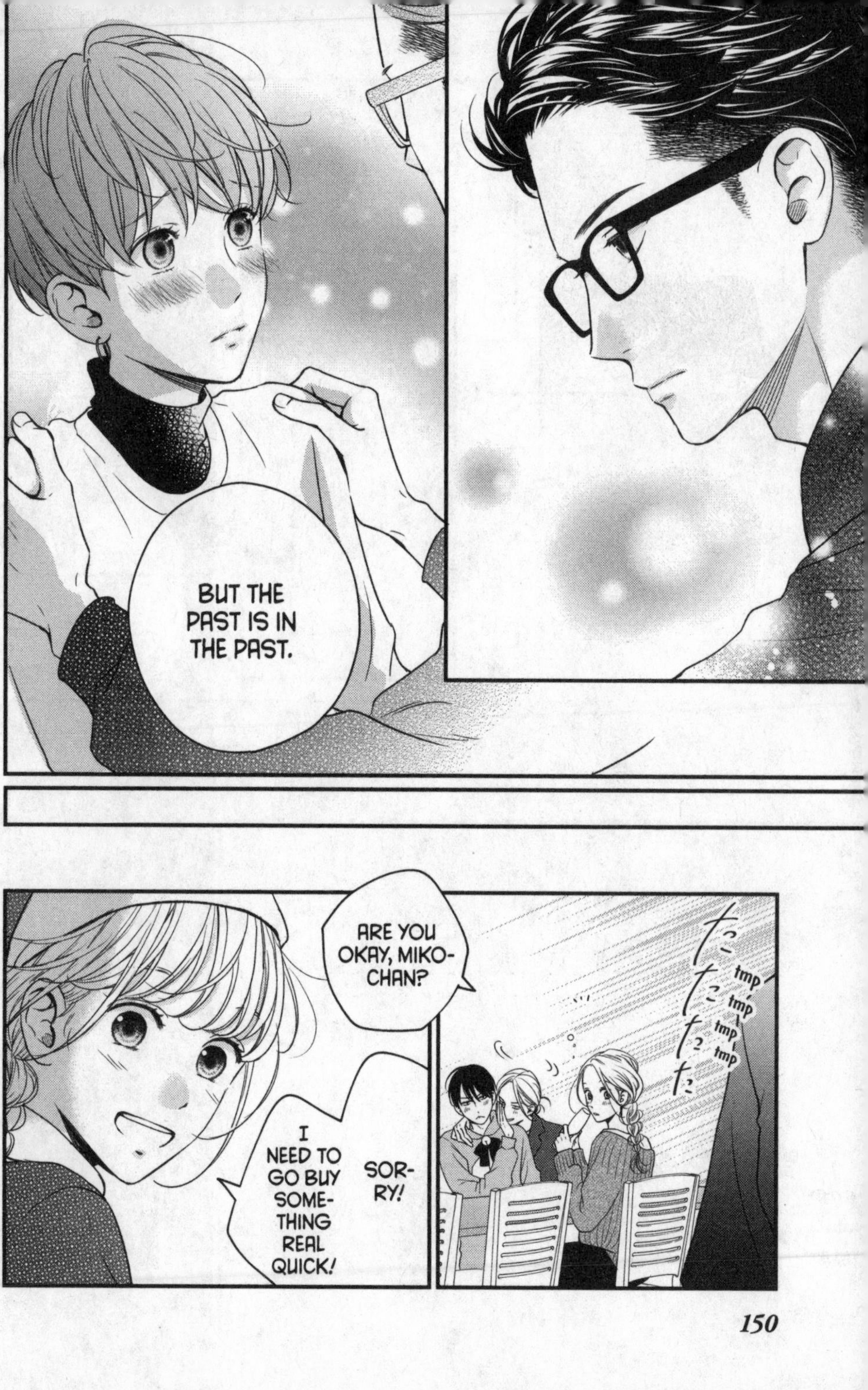
BUT THE PAST IS IN THE PAST.
たったったった
tmp tmp tmp tmp
ARE YOU OKAY, MIKO-CHAN?
SORRY!
I NEED TO GO BUY SOMETHING REAL QUICK!

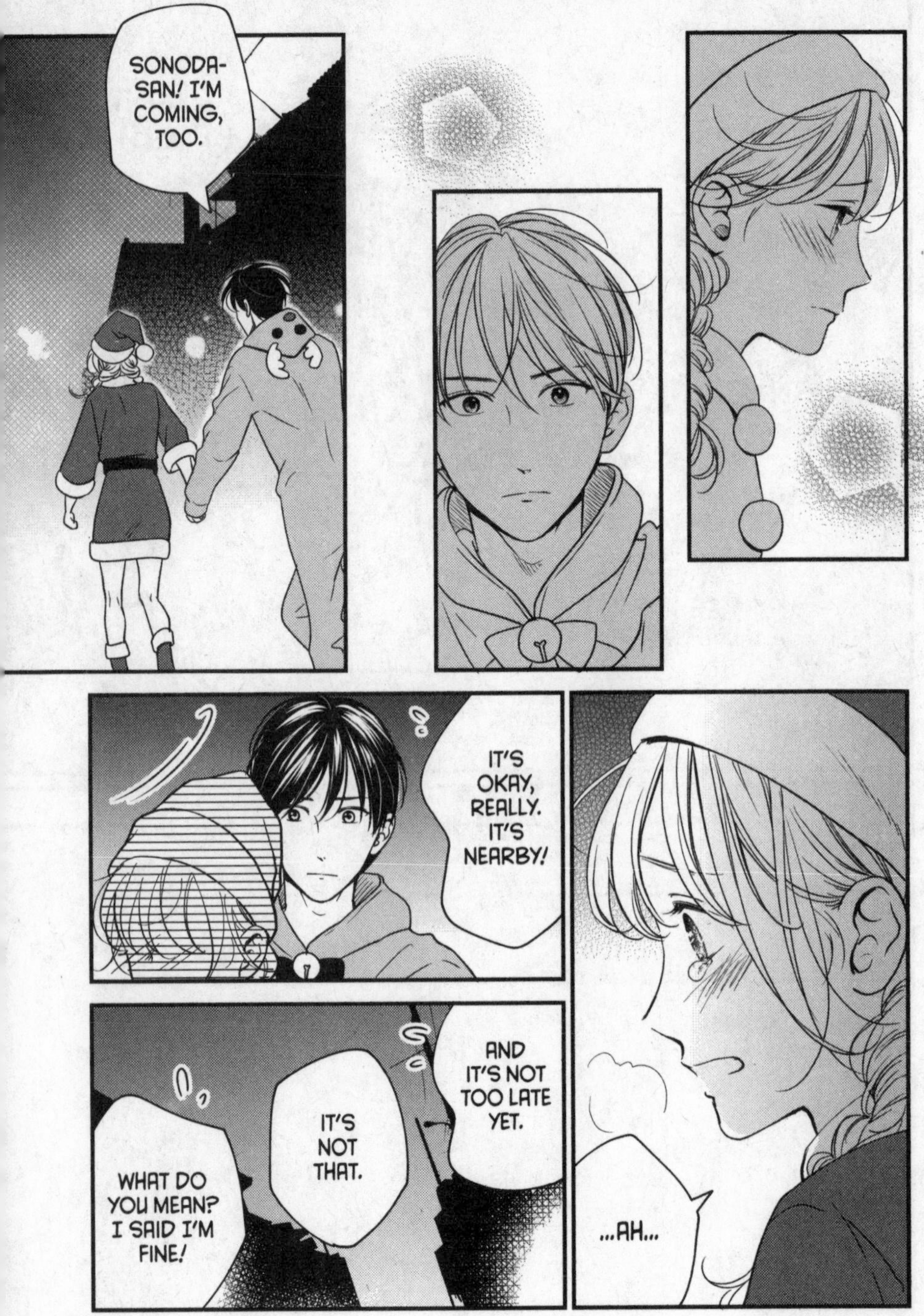
SONODA-SAN! I'M COMING, TOO.
...AH...
IT'S OKAY, REALLY. IT'S NEARBY!
AND IT'S NOT TOO LATE YET.
IT'S NOT THAT.
WHAT DO YOU MEAN? I SAID I'M FINE!

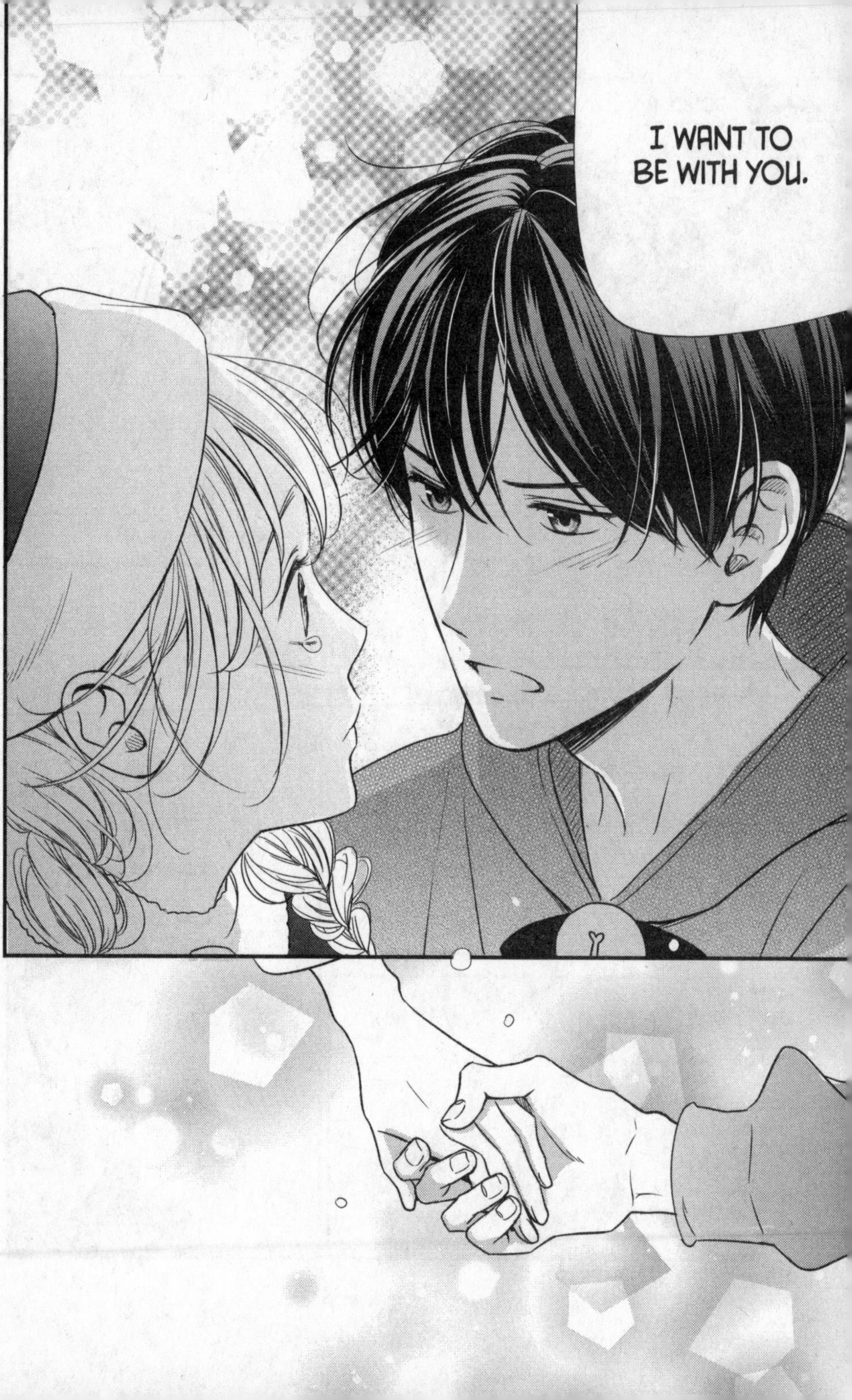
I WANT TO BE WITH YOU.

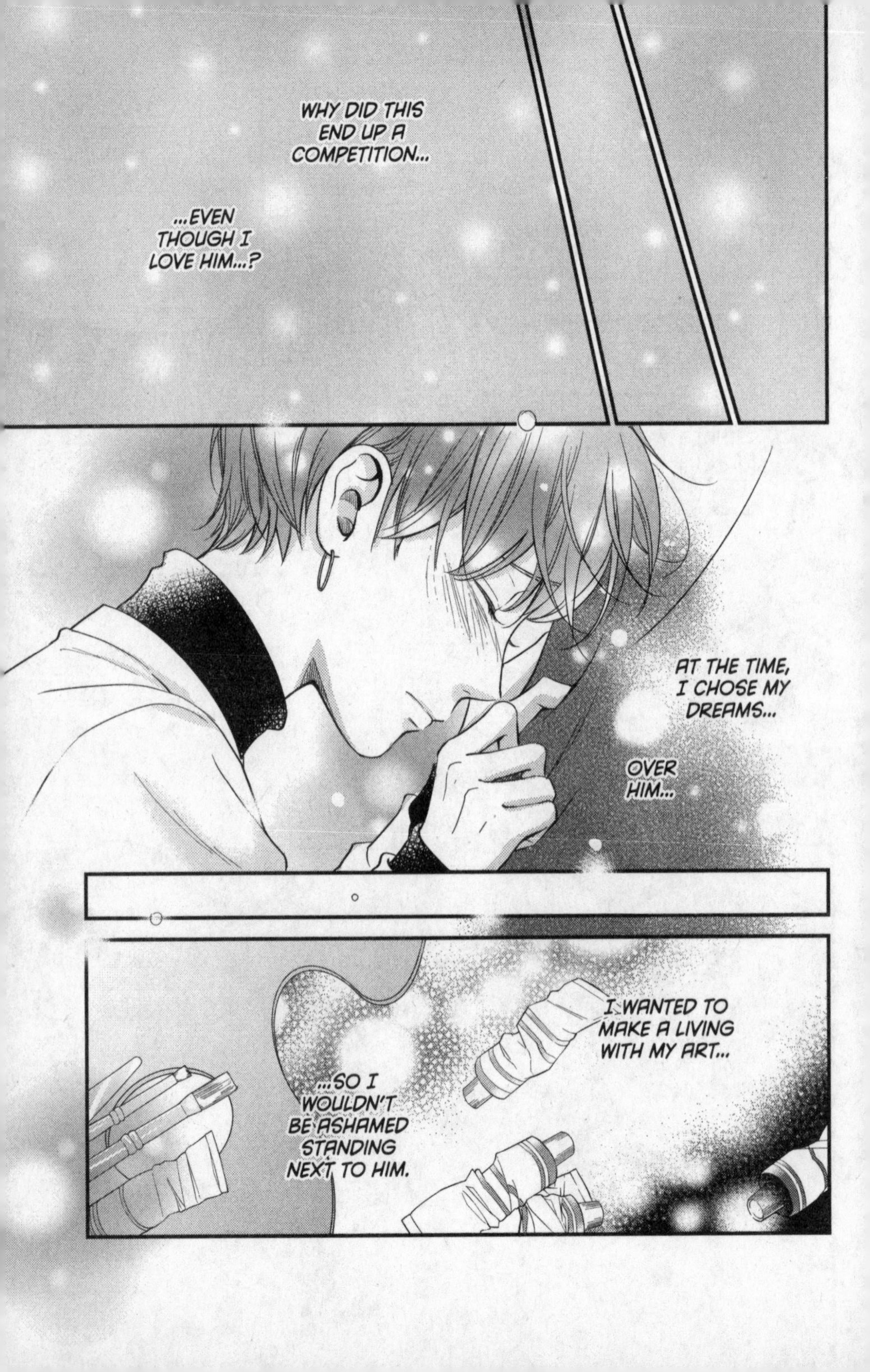
WHY DID THIS END UP A COMPETITION...
...EVEN THOUGH I LOVE HIM...?
AT THE TIME, I CHOSE MY DREAMS...
OVER HIM...
I WANTED TO MAKE A LIVING WITH MY ART...
...SO I WOULDN'T BE ASHAMED STANDING NEXT TO HIM.

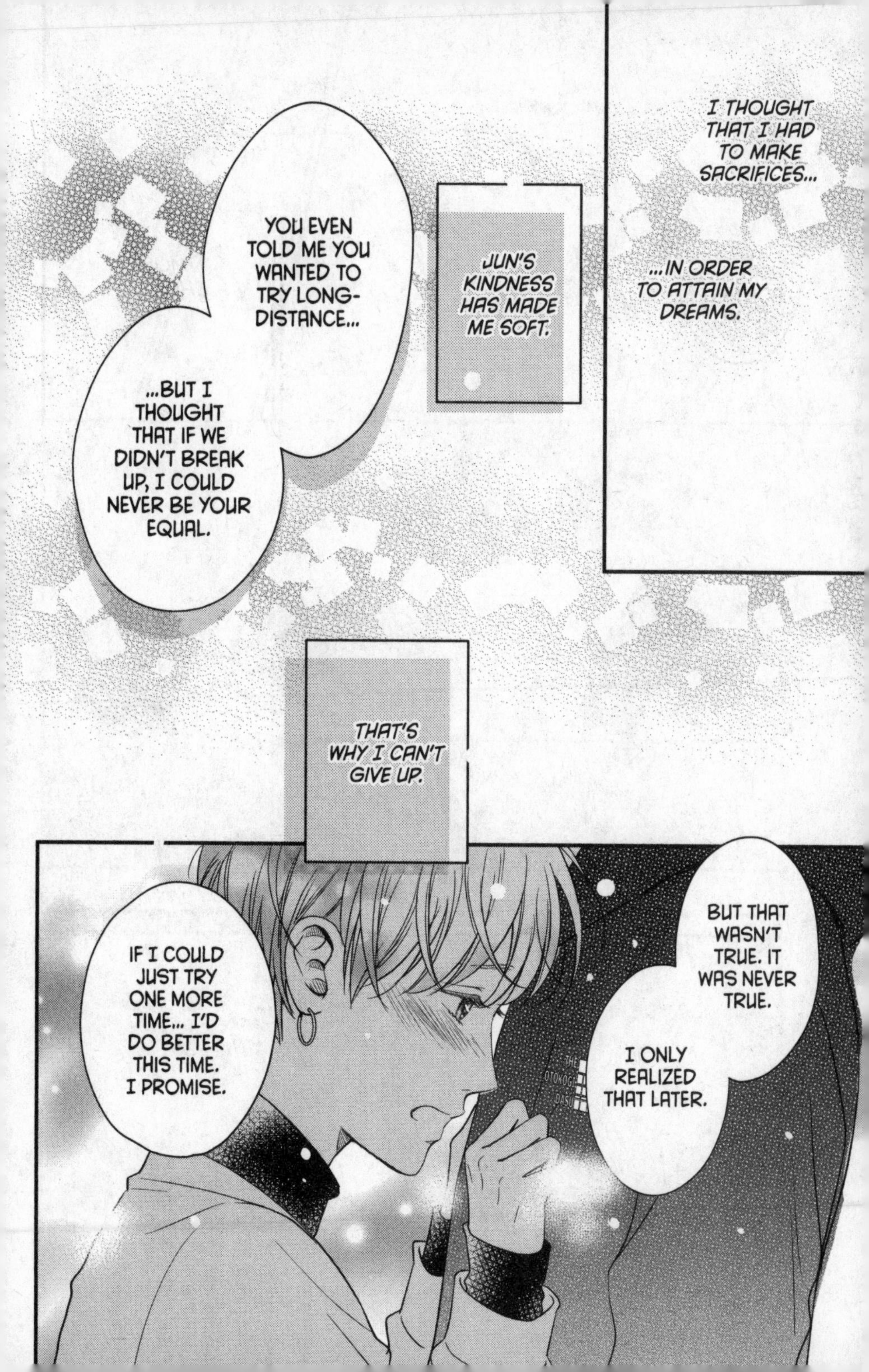
I THOUGHT THAT I HAD TO MAKE SACRIFICES...
...IN ORDER TO ATTAIN MY DREAMS.
JUN'S KINDNESS HAS MADE ME SOFT.
YOU EVEN TOLD ME YOU WANTED TO TRY LONG-DISTANCE...
...BUT I THOUGHT THAT IF WE DIDN'T BREAK UP, I COULD NEVER BE YOUR EQUAL.
THAT'S WHY I CAN'T GIVE UP.
BUT THAT WASN'T TRUE. IT WAS NEVER TRUE.
I ONLY REALIZED THAT LATER.
IF I COULD JUST TRY ONE MORE TIME... I'D DO BETTER THIS TIME. I PROMISE.

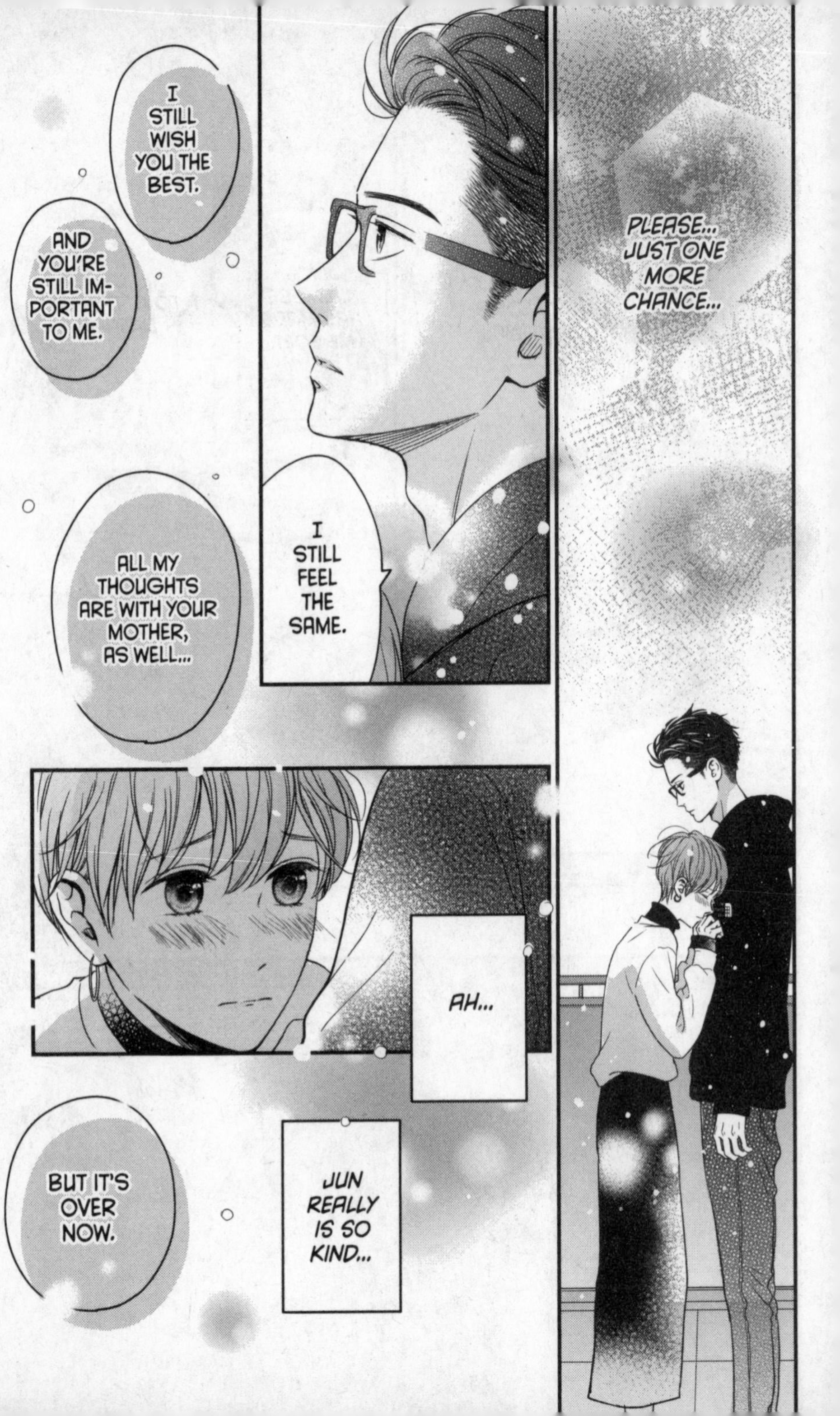
PLEASE... JUST ONE MORE CHANCE...
I STILL WISH YOU THE BEST.
AND YOU'RE STILL IM-PORTANT TO ME.
I STILL FEEL THE SAME.
ALL MY THOUGHTS ARE WITH YOUR MOTHER, AS WELL...
AH...
JUN REALLY IS SO KIND...
BUT IT'S OVER NOW.

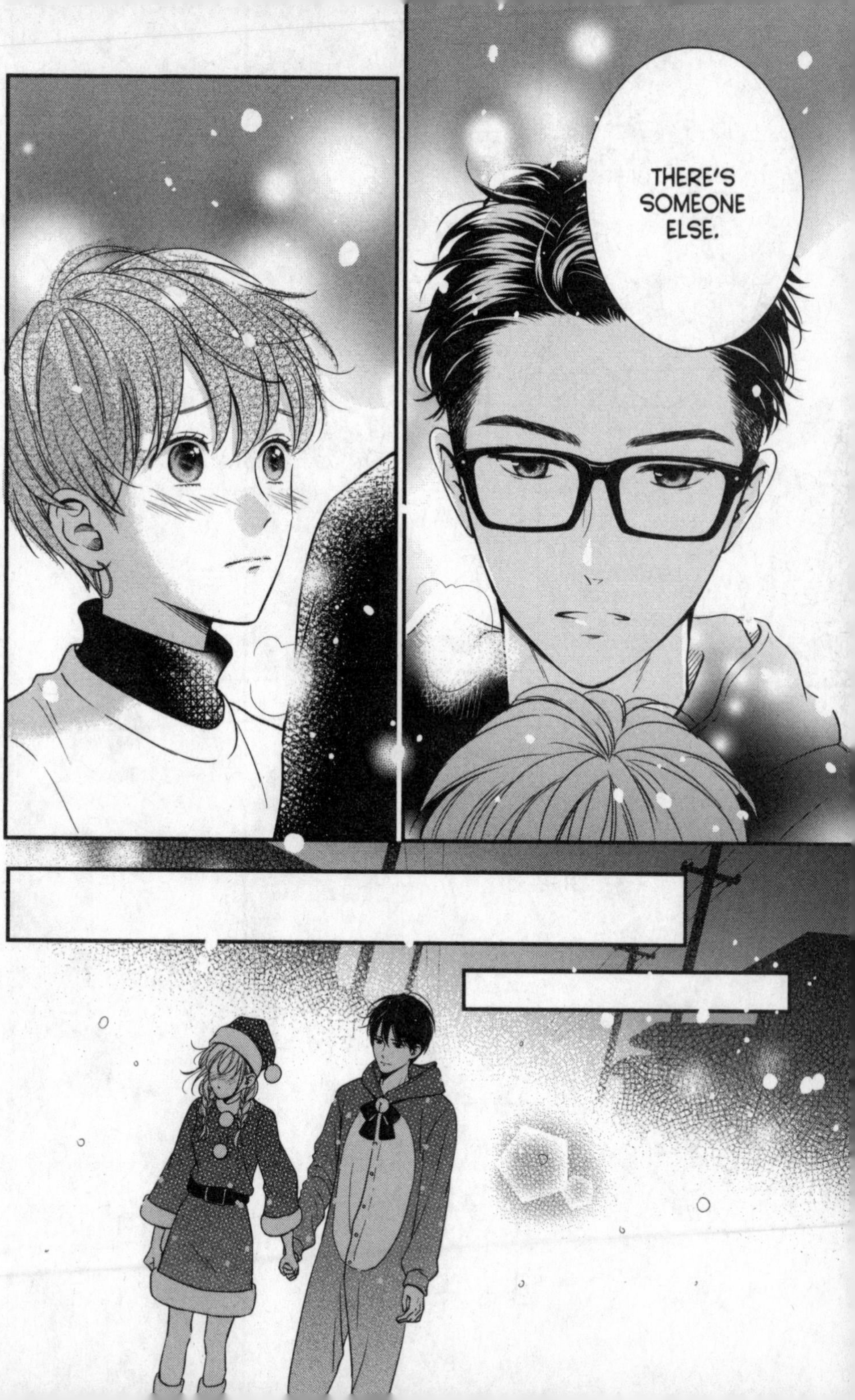
THERE'S SOMEONE ELSE.

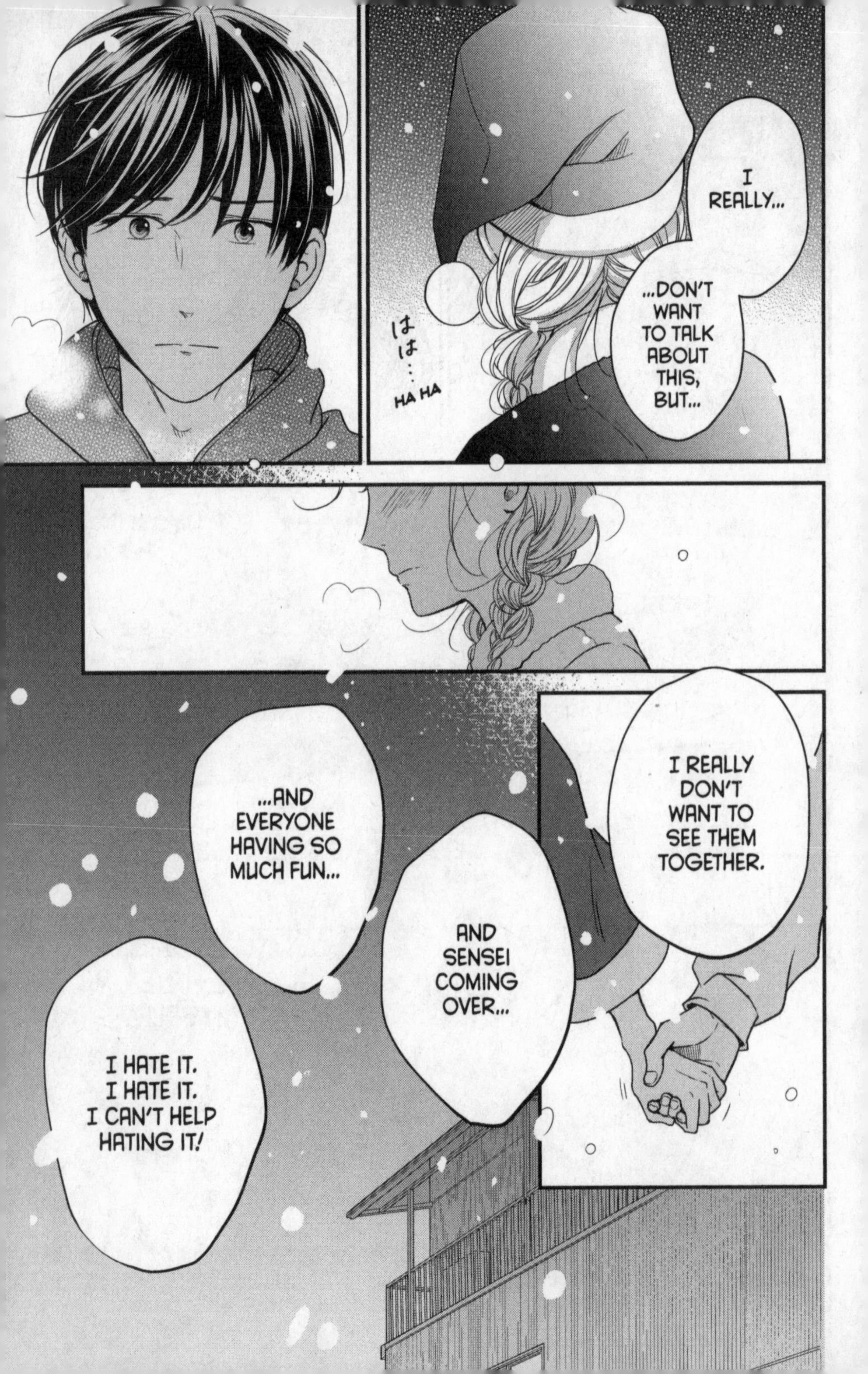
I REALLY...
...DON'T WANT TO TALK ABOUT THIS, BUT...
はは…
HA HA
I REALLY DON'T WANT TO SEE THEM TOGETHER.
AND SENSEI COMING OVER...
...AND EVERYONE HAVING SO MUCH FUN...
I HATE IT. I HATE IT. I CAN'T HELP HATING IT!

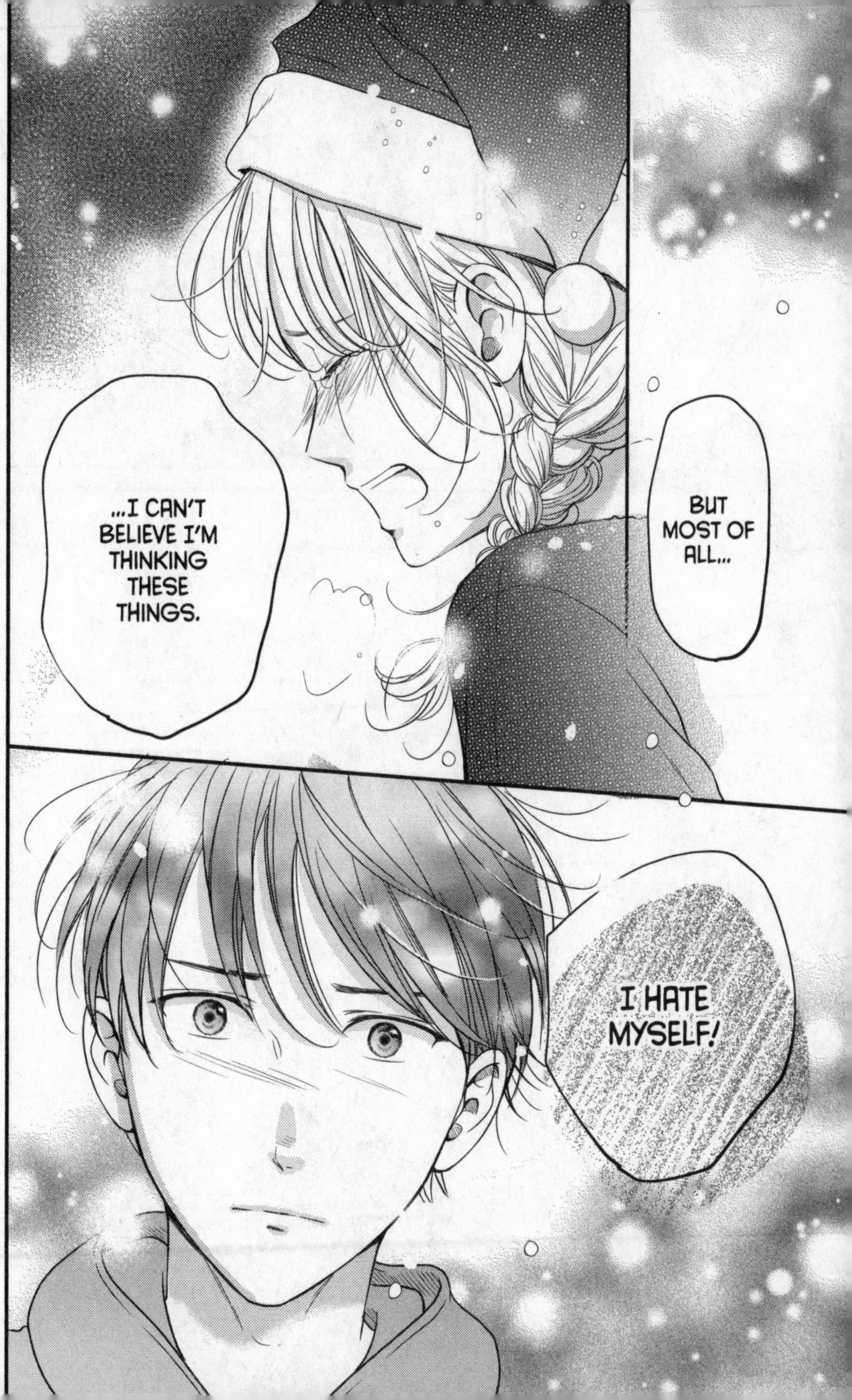
...I CAN'T BELIEVE I'M THINKING THESE THINGS.
BUT MOST OF ALL...
I HATE MYSELF!

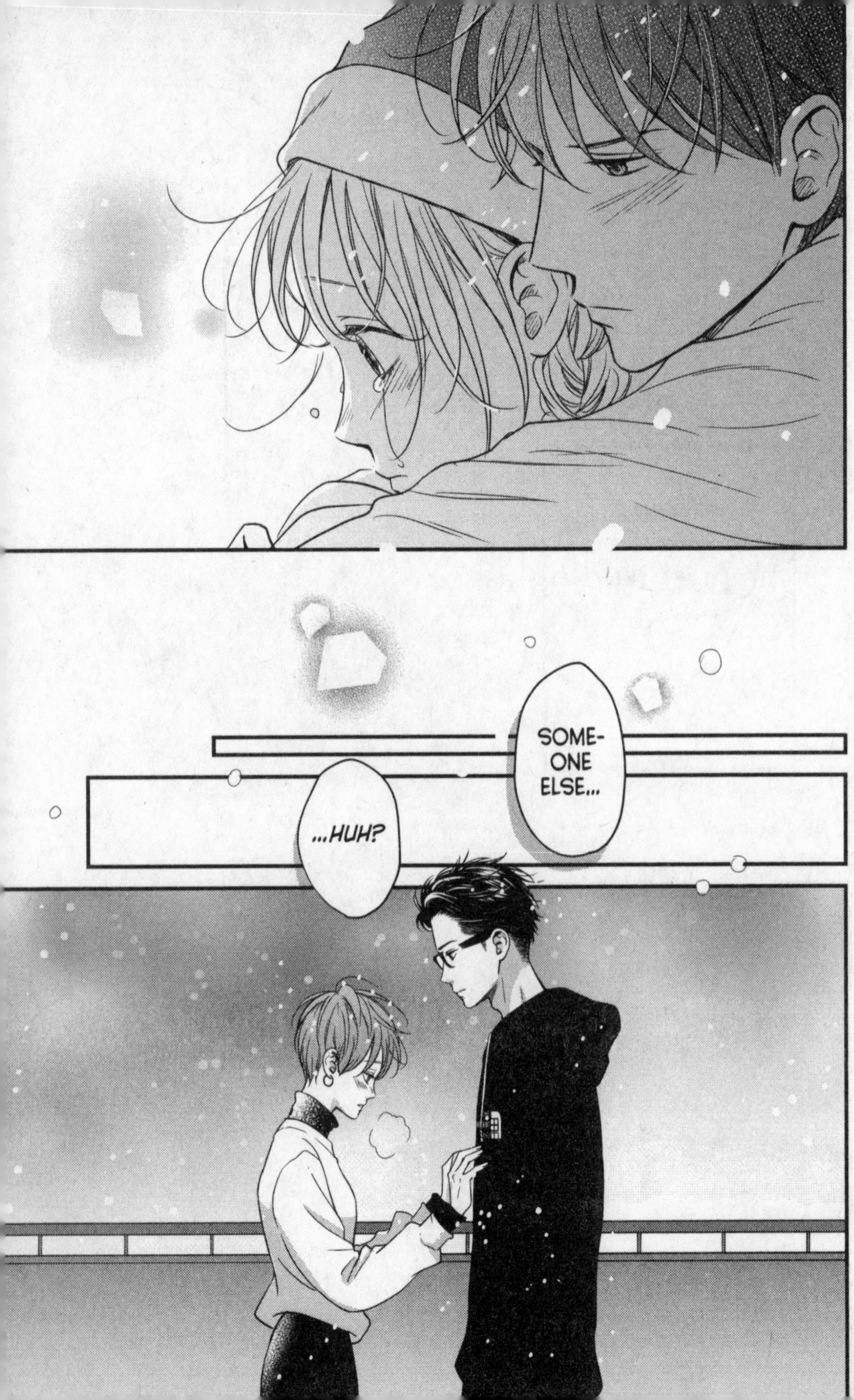
SOME-ONE ELSE...
...HUH?

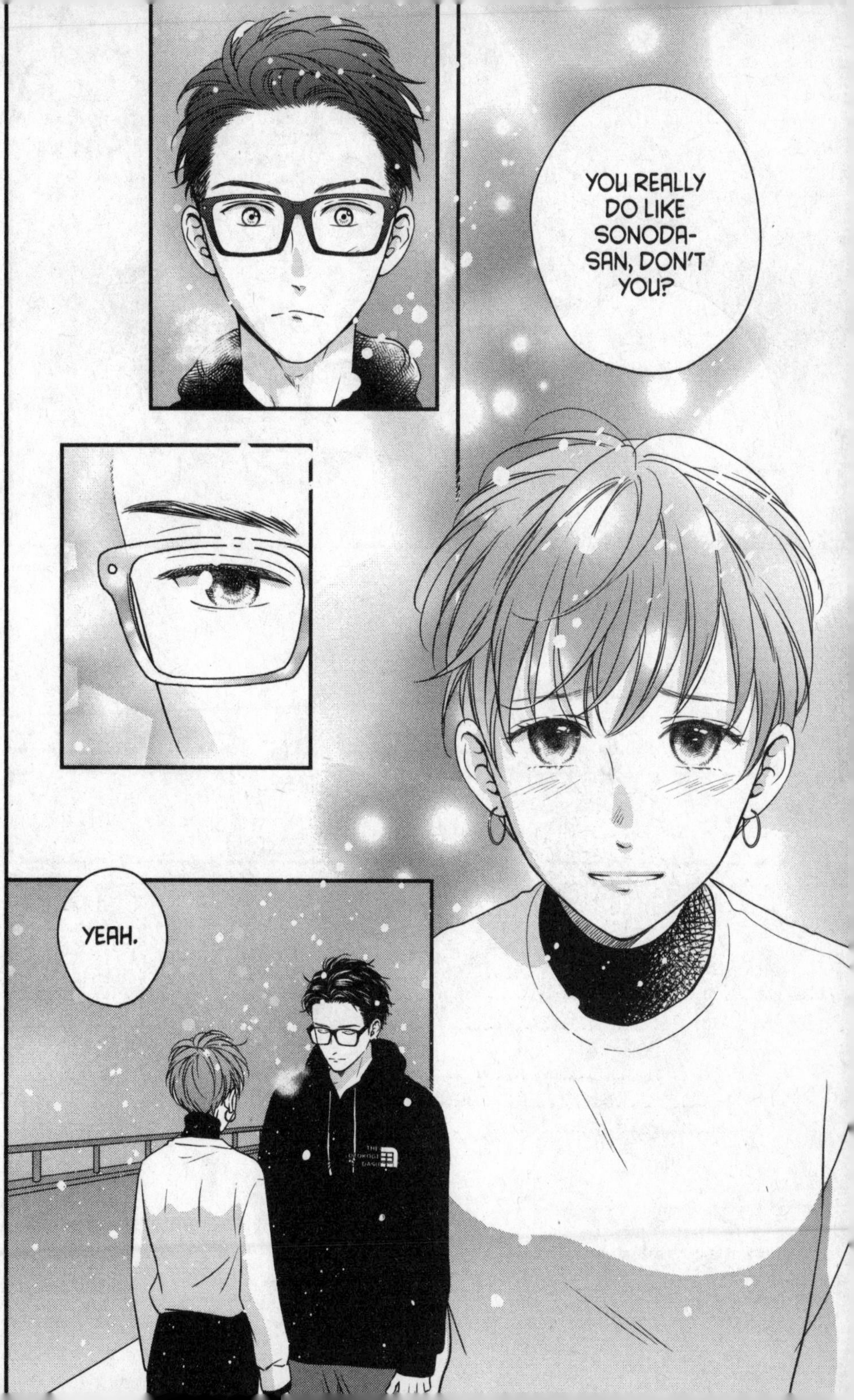
YOU REALLY DO LIKE SONODA-SAN, DON'T YOU?
YEAH.

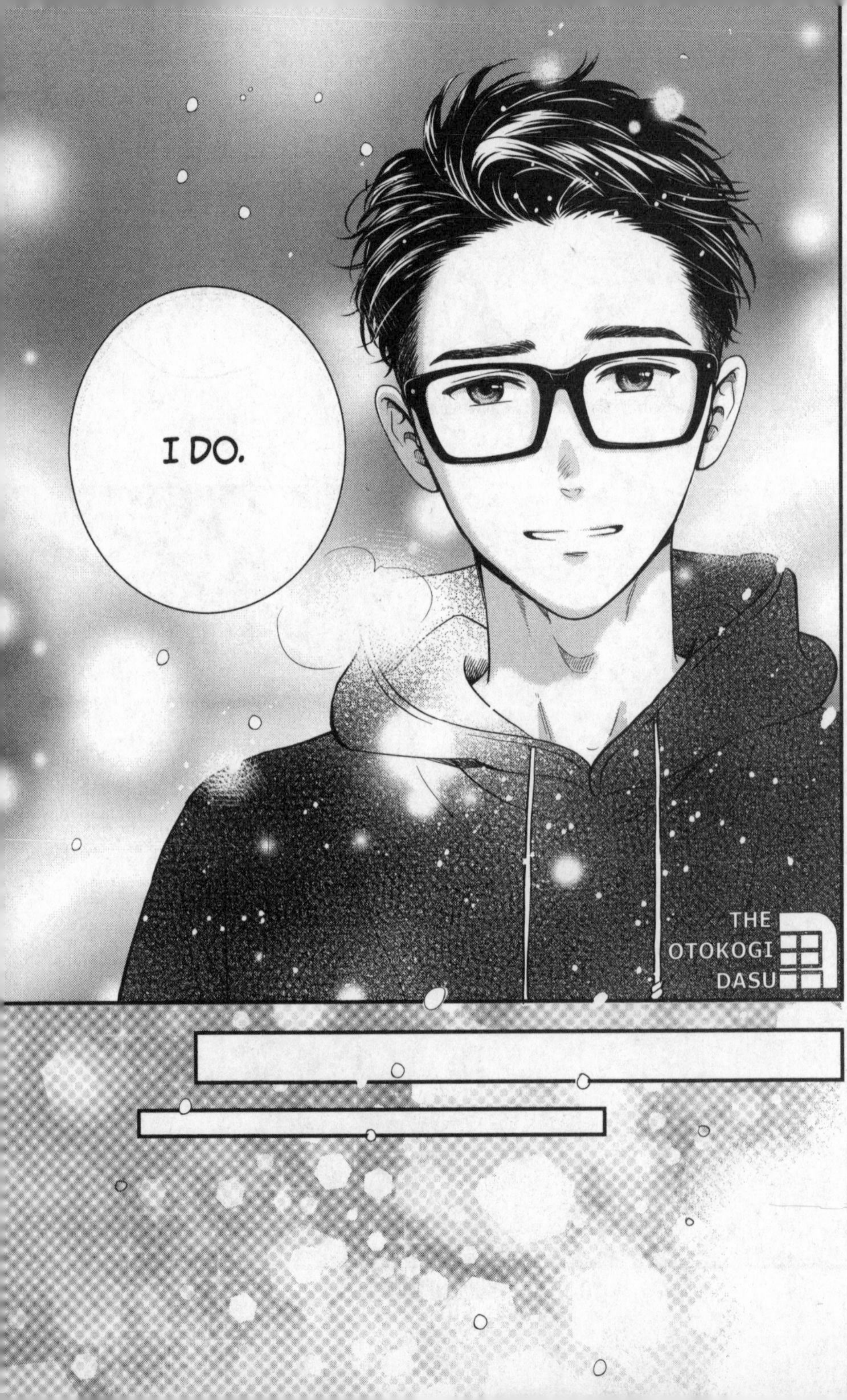
I DO.
THE OTOKOGI DASU

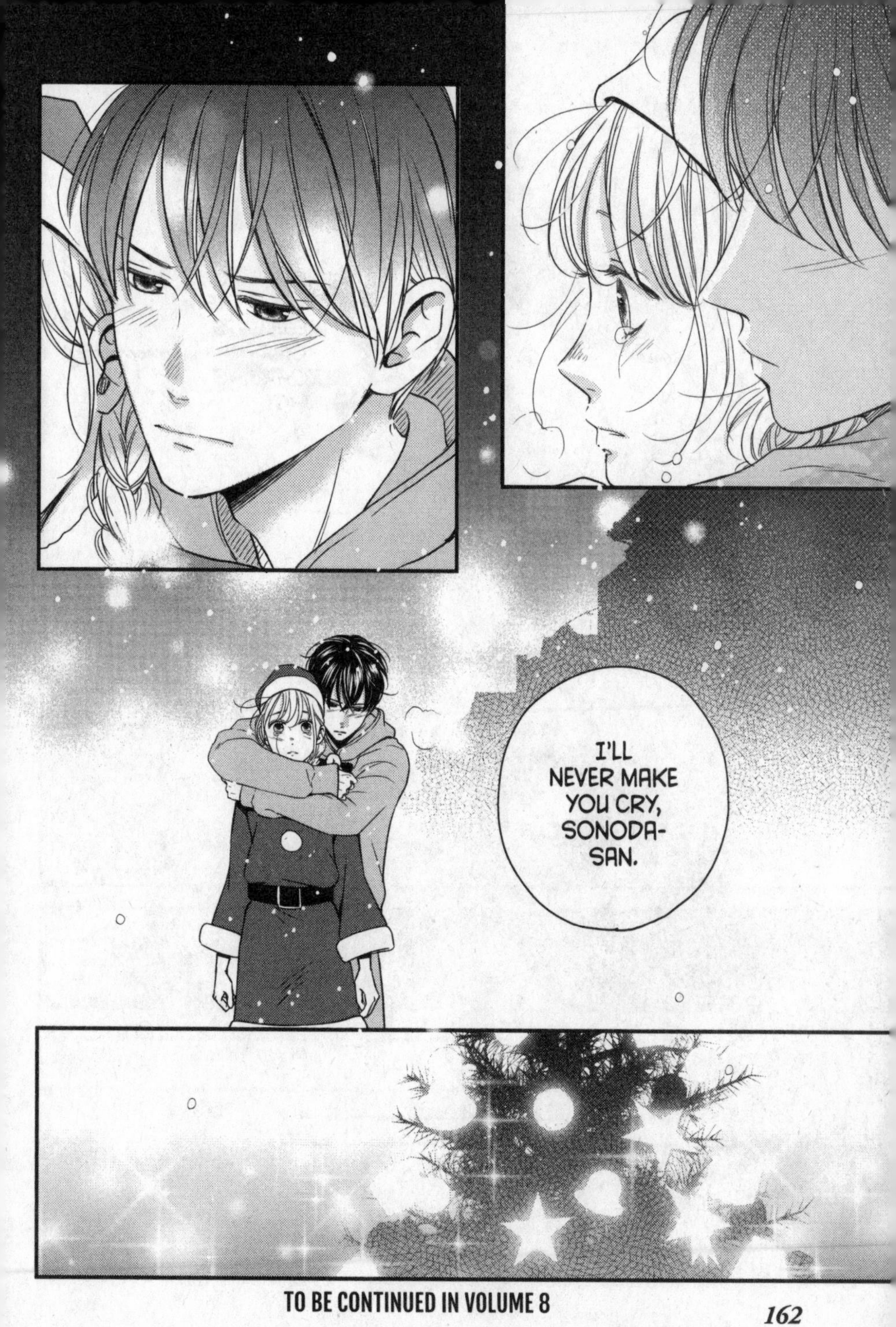
I'LL NEVER MAKE YOU CRY, SONODA-SAN.

TO BE CONTINUED IN VOLUME 8

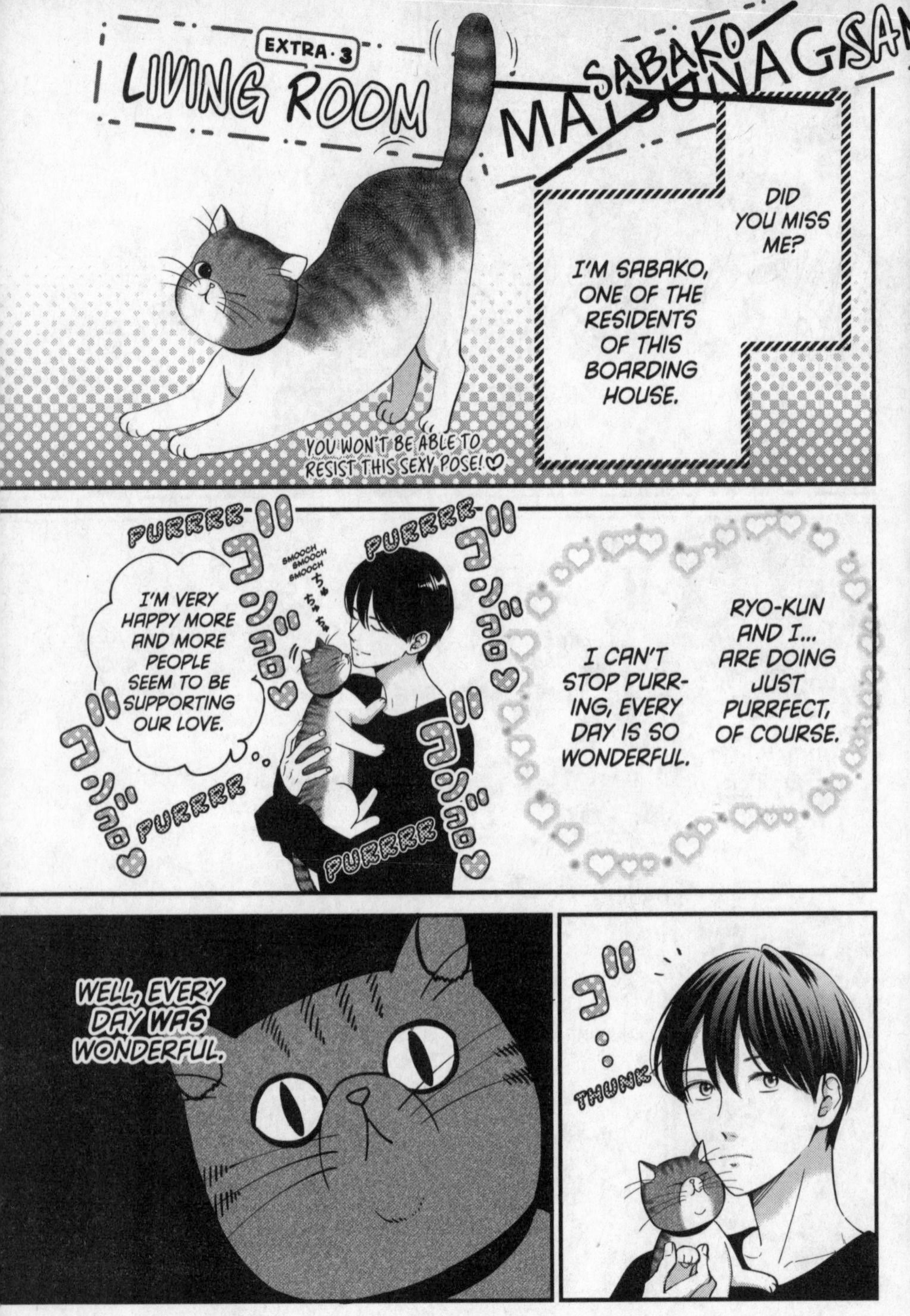
EXTRA 3
LIVING ROOM
MAISON NAGA
SABAKO-SAN
DID YOU MISS ME?
I'M SABAKO, ONE OF THE RESIDENTS OF THIS BOARDING HOUSE.
YOU WON'T BE ABLE TO RESIST THIS SEXY POSE!♡
RYO-KUN AND I... ARE DOING JUST PURRFECT, OF COURSE.
I CAN'T STOP PURR-ING, EVERY DAY IS SO WONDERFUL.
PURRRR
PURRRR
SMOOCH SMOOCH SMOOCH
I'M VERY HAPPY MORE AND MORE PEOPLE SEEM TO BE SUPPORTING OUR LOVE.
PURRRR
PURRRR
THUNK
WELL, EVERY DAY WAS WONDERFUL.

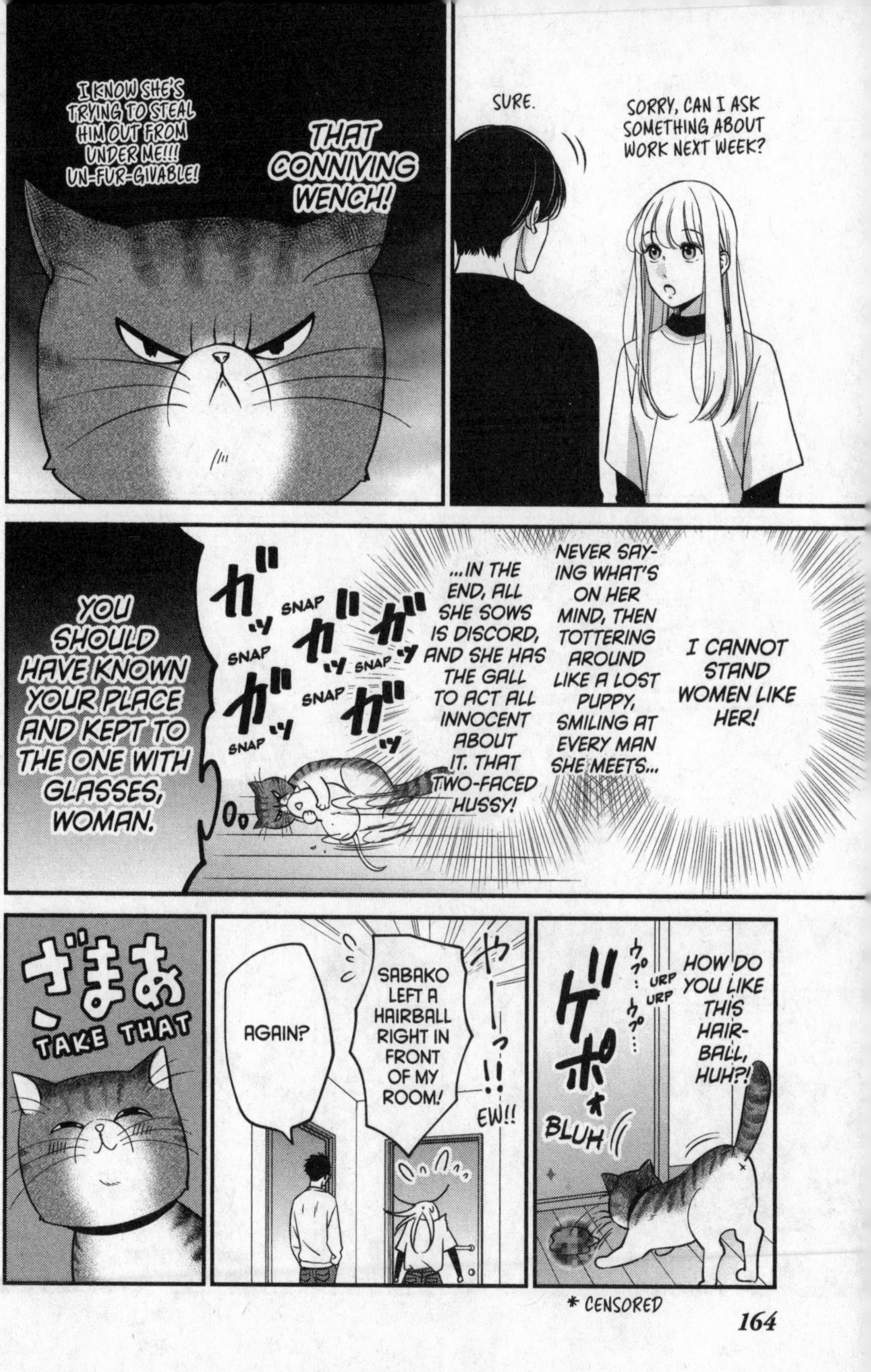
SORRY, CAN I ASK SOMETHING ABOUT WORK NEXT WEEK?
SURE.
THAT CONNIVING WENCH!
I KNOW SHE'S TRYING TO STEAL HIM OUT FROM UNDER ME!!! UN-FUR-GIVABLE!
I CANNOT STAND WOMEN LIKE HER!
NEVER SAYING WHAT'S ON HER MIND, THEN TOTTERING AROUND LIKE A LOST PUPPY, SMILING AT EVERY MAN SHE MEETS...
...IN THE END, ALL SHE SOWS IS DISCORD, AND SHE HAS THE GALL TO ACT ALL INNOCENT ABOUT IT. THAT TWO-FACED HUSSY!
ガッ SNAP
ガッ SNAP
ガッ SNAP
ガッ SNAP
ガッ SNAP
YOU SHOULD HAVE KNOWN YOUR PLACE AND KEPT TO THE ONE WITH GLASSES, WOMAN.
HOW DO YOU LIKE THIS HAIR-BALL, HUH?!
ウプ… URP
ウプ… URP
ゲポ* BLUH
やーっ!! EW!!
SABAKO LEFT A HAIRBALL RIGHT IN FRONT OF MY ROOM!
AGAIN?
ざまぁ TAKE THAT

* CENSORED

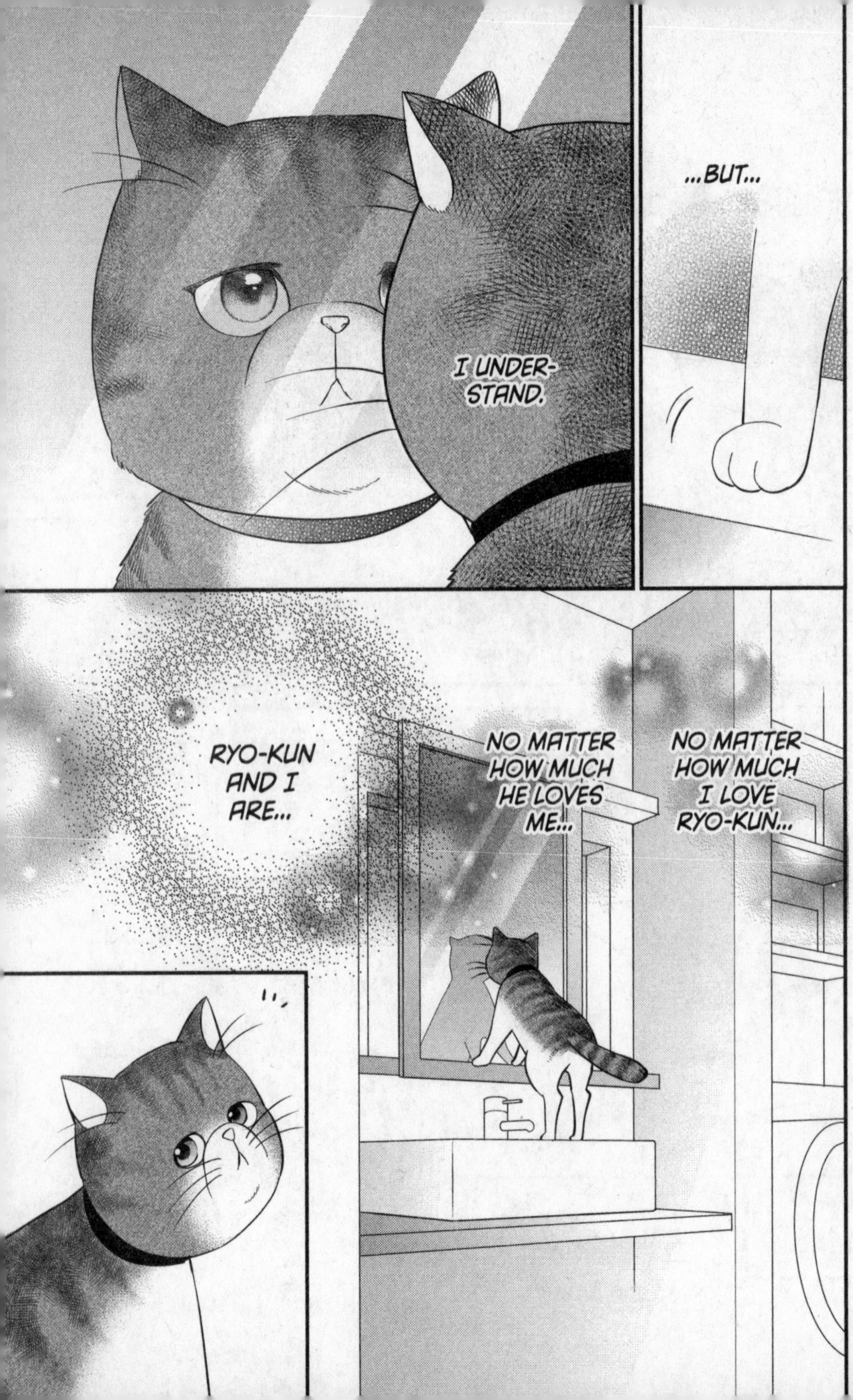
...BUT...
I UNDER-STAND.
NO MATTER HOW MUCH I LOVE RYO-KUN...
NO MATTER HOW MUCH HE LOVES ME...
RYO-KUN AND I ARE...

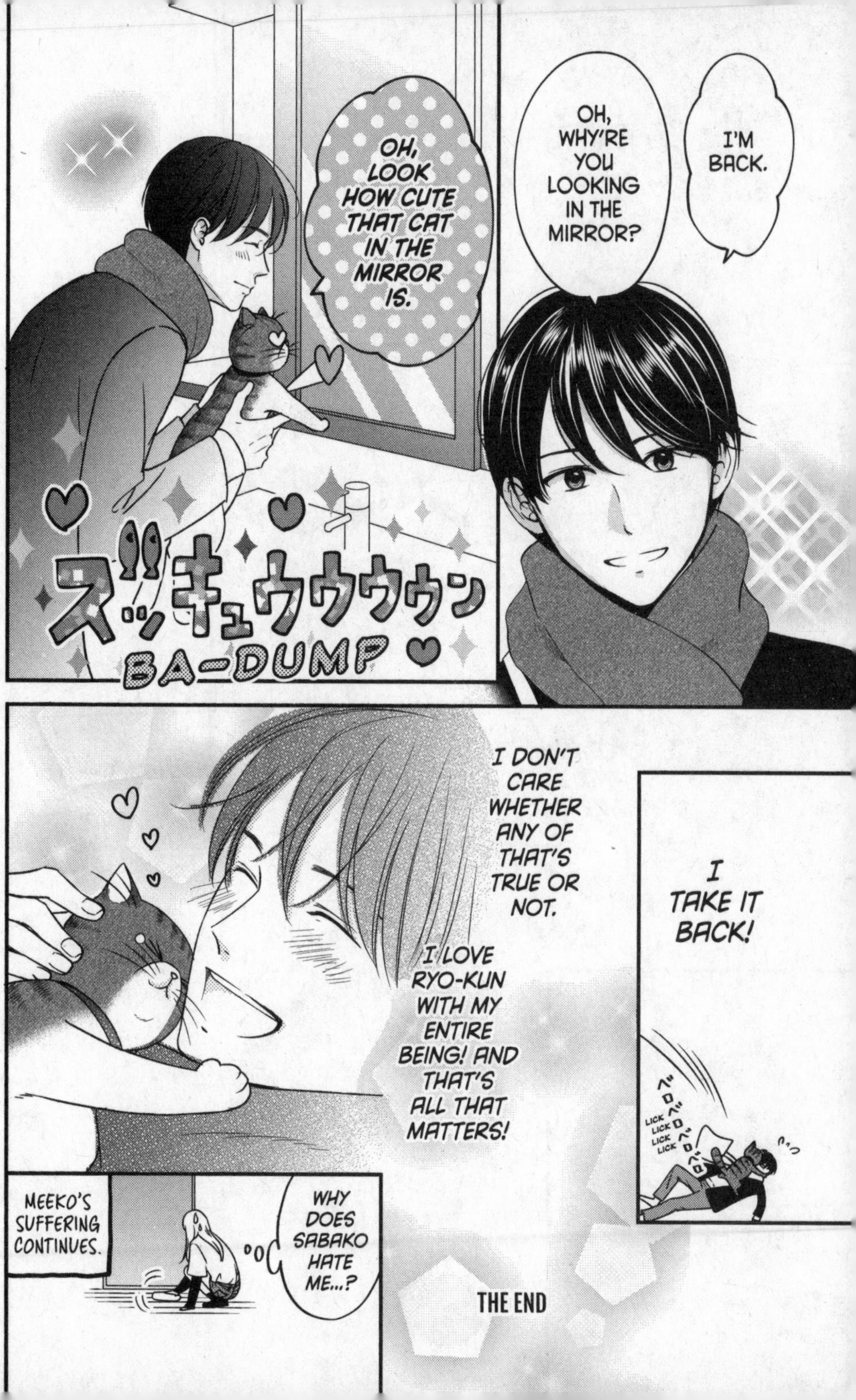
I'M BACK.
OH, WHY'RE YOU LOOKING IN THE MIRROR?
OH, LOOK HOW CUTE THAT CAT IN THE MIRROR IS.
ズッキュウウウウン
BA-DUMP
I TAKE IT BACK!
ペロペロペロペロ
LICK LICK LICK LICK
I DON'T CARE WHETHER ANY OF THAT'S TRUE OR NOT.
I LOVE RYO-KUN WITH MY ENTIRE BEING! AND THAT'S ALL THAT MATTERS!
WHY DOES SABAKO HATE ME...?
MEEKO'S SUFFERING CONTINUES.
THE END

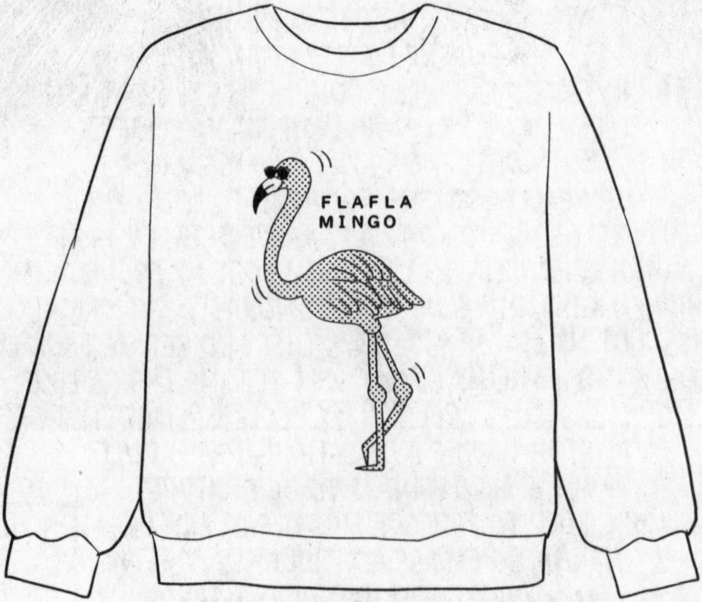
FLAFLA
MINGO

"FLAMINGO PATTERN,"
AS REQUESTED BY MK.
THANK YOU SO MUCH!
NOW REQUESTING MORE DESIGN SUBMISSIONS
FOR MATSUNAGA-SAN'S SHIRTS!
I MAY DECIDE TO USE IT BASED COMPLETELY
ON MY OWN ARBITRARY JUDGMENT...?

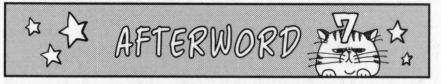

AFTERWORD 7

THANK YOU SO MUCH FOR READING
LIVING-ROOM MATSUNAGA-SAN!
SORRY FOR THE WAIT ON VOLUME 7!
I FEEL LIKE WE'RE FINALLY HERE! VOLUME 7!
THANK YOU SO MUCH FOR COMING THIS FAR WITH ME.
I FEEL LIKE I'VE FINISHED AN ENTIRE SERIES...
BUT NO! THERE'S STILL A WAYS TO GO!
I'M REALLY LOOKING FORWARD TO VOLUME 8.
IT'S BEEN PRETTY HARD TO WRITE A ROMANCE BETWEEN AN ADULT AND A HIGH SCHOOLER, SO I'VE KINDA LOST MY FOCUS AND PANICKED A BIT AND GONE IN QUESTIONABLE DIRECTIONS AT TIMES, BUT MY EDITOR IS ALWAYS THERE TO SET ME BACK ON THE RIGHT PATH. MY EDITOR WILL TELL ME THINGS LIKE, "MATSUNAGA-SAN IS CREEPY HERE" LOL. I DEFINITELY DON'T WANT HIM TO BE A LESS-THAN-IDEAL ADULT.
BUT I ALSO WANT IT TO BE EXCITING!!!
I'LL WORK HARD TO PERFECT THIS BLEND AND CREATE A FUN MANGA, SO PLEASE CONTINUE SUPPORTING
LIVING-ROOM MATSUNAGA-SAN!

♡ 11.13.2019 KEIKO IWASHITA

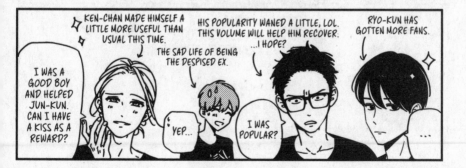

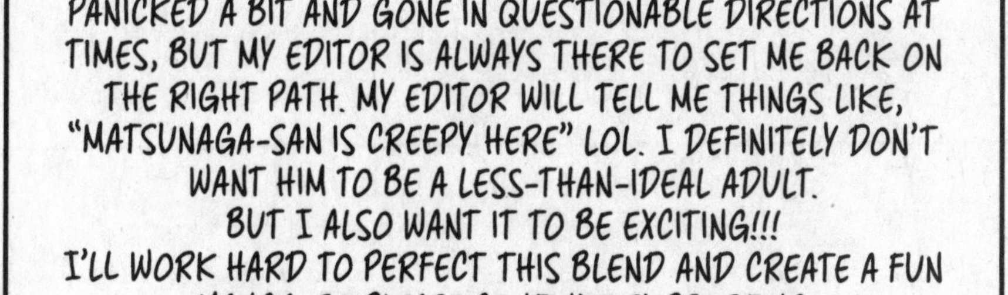

RYO-KUN HAS GOTTEN MORE FANS.
...
HIS POPULARITY WANED A LITTLE, LOL. THIS VOLUME WILL HELP HIM RECOVER.
...I HOPE?
I WAS POPULAR?
THE SAD LIFE OF BEING THE DESPISED EX.
YEP...
KEN-CHAN MADE HIMSELF A LITTLE MORE USEFUL THAN USUAL THIS TIME.
I WAS A GOOD BOY AND HELPED JUN-KUN. CAN I HAVE A KISS AS A REWARD?

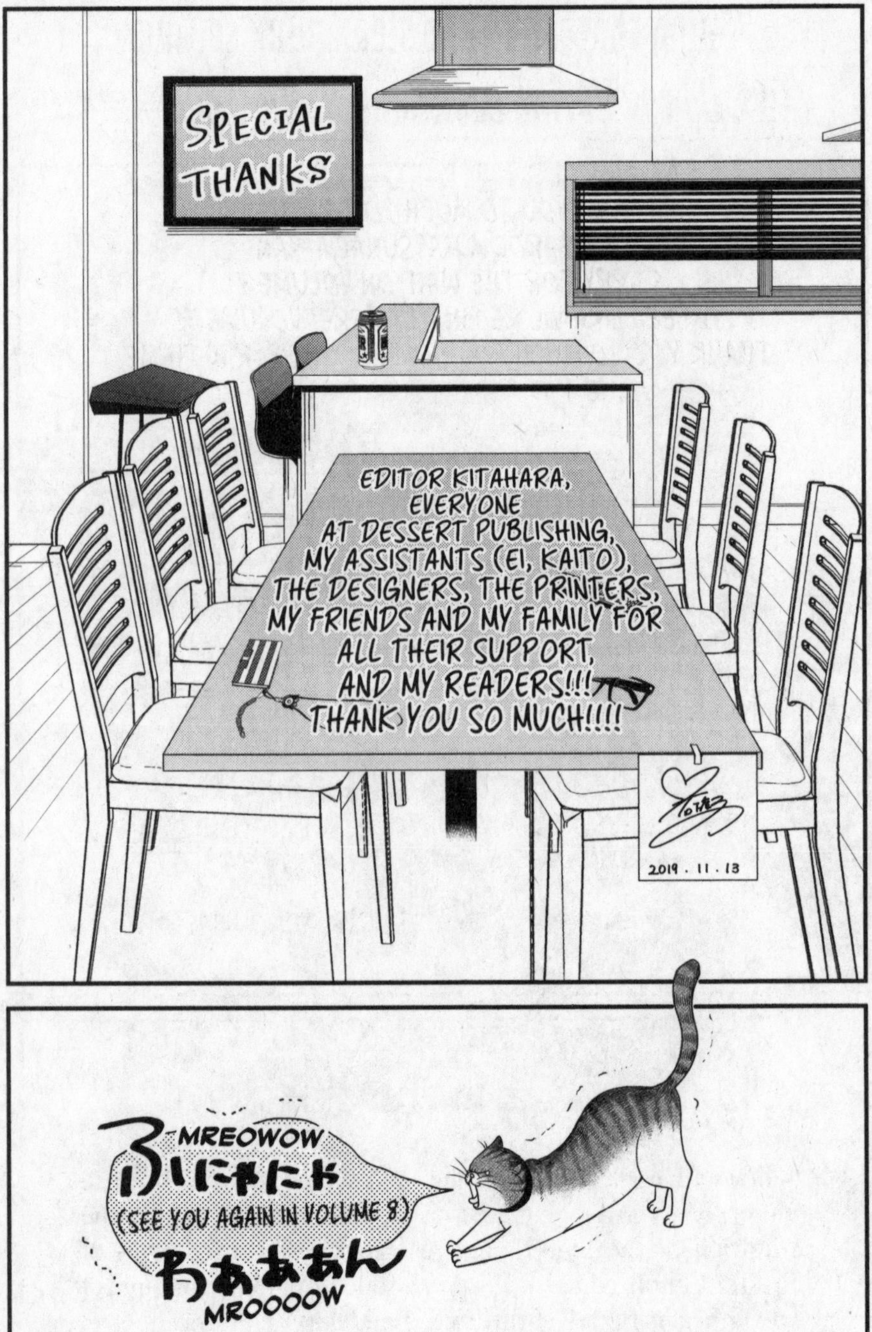
SPECIAL THANKS
EDITOR KITAHARA, EVERYONE AT DESSERT PUBLISHING, MY ASSISTANTS (EI, KAITO), THE DESIGNERS, THE PRINTERS, MY FRIENDS AND MY FAMILY FOR ALL THEIR SUPPORT, AND MY READERS!!! THANK YOU SO MUCH!!!!
2019 . 11 . 13
MREOWOW
(SEE YOU AGAIN IN VOLUME 8)
MROOOOW

Young characters and steampunk setting, like *Howl's Moving Castle* and *Battle Angel Alita*

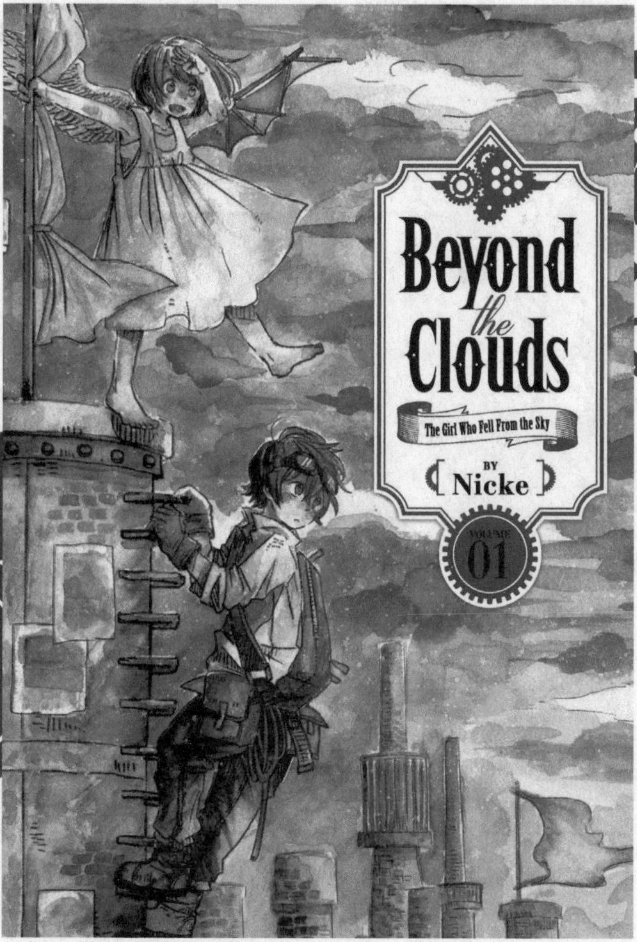
Beyond the Clouds
The Girl Who Fell From the Sky
BY
Nicke
VOLUME
01

Beyond the Clouds © 2018 Nicke / Ki-oon

KC
KODANSHA COMICS

A boy with a talent for machines and a mysterious girl whose wings he's fixed will take you beyond the clouds! In the tradition of the high-flying, resonant adventure stories of Studio Ghibli comes a gorgeous tale about the longing of young hearts for adventure and friendship!

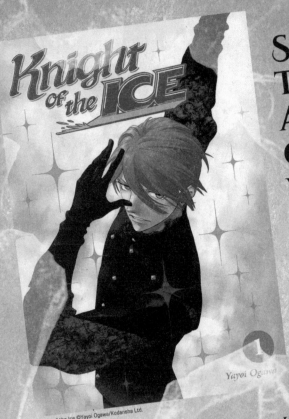

Knight of the Ice ©Yayoi Ogawa/Kodansha Ltd.

SKATING THRILLS AND ICY CHILLS WITH THIS NEW TINGLY ROMANCE SERIES!

A rom-com on ice, perfect for fans of *Princess Jellyfish* and *Wotakoi*. Kokoro is the talk of the figure-skating world, winning trophies and hearts. But little do they know... he's actually a huge nerd! From the beloved creator of *You're My Pet* (*Tramps Like Us*).

Chitose is a serious young woman, working for the health magazine *SASSO*. Or at least, she would be, if she wasn't constantly getting distracted by her childhood friend, international figure skating star Kokoro Kijinami! In the public eye and on the ice, Kokoro is a gallant, flawless knight, but behind his glittery costumes and breathtaking spins lies a secret: He's actually a hopelessly romantic otaku, who can only land his quad jumps when Chitose is on hand to recite a spell from his favorite magical girl anime!

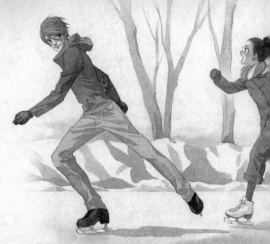

KC
KODANSHA
COMICS

PERFECT WORLD

Rie Aruga

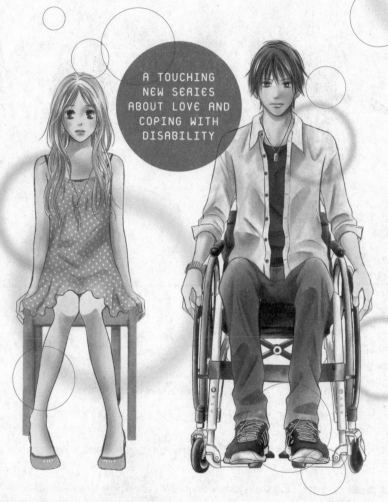

A TOUCHING NEW SERIES ABOUT LOVE AND COPING WITH DISABILITY

An office party reunites Tsugumi with her high school crush Itsuki. He's realized his dream of becoming an architect, but along the way, he experienced a spinal injury that put him in a wheelchair. Now Tsugumi's rekindled feelings will butt up against prejudices she never considered — and Itsuki will have to decide if he's ready to let someone into his heart...

"Depicts with great delicacy and courage the difficulties some with disabilities experience getting involved in romantic relationships... Rie Aruga refuses to romanticize, pushing her heroine to face the reality of disability. She invites her readers to the same tasks of empathy, knowledge and recognition."
—Slate.fr

"An important entry [in manga romance]... The emotional core of both plot and characters indicates thoughtfulness... [Aruga's] research is readily apparent in the text and artwork, making this feel like a real story."
—Anime News Network

Perfect World © Rie Aruga/Kodansha Ltd.

The boys are back, in 400-page hardcovers that are as pretty and badass as they are!

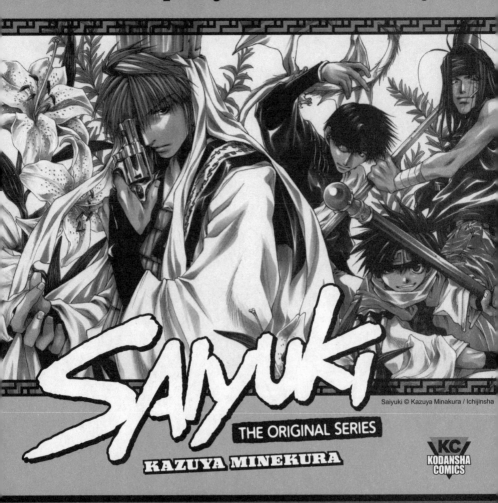

Saiyuki © Kazuya Minakura / Ichijinsha

SAIYUKI

THE ORIGINAL SERIES

KAZUYA MINEKURA

KC/ KODANSHA COMICS

"AN EDGY COMIC LOOK AT AN ANCIENT CHINESE TALE." —YALSA

Genjo Sanzo is a Buddhist priest in the city of Togenkyo, which is being ravaged by yokai spirits that have fallen out of balance with the natural order. His superiors send him on a journey far to the west to discover why this is happening and how to stop it. His companions are three yokai with human souls. But this is no day trip — the four will encounter many discoveries and horrors on the way.

FEATURES NEW TRANSLATION, COLOR PAGES, AND BEAUTIFUL WRAPAROUND COVER ART!

Something's Wrong With Us

NATSUMI ANDO

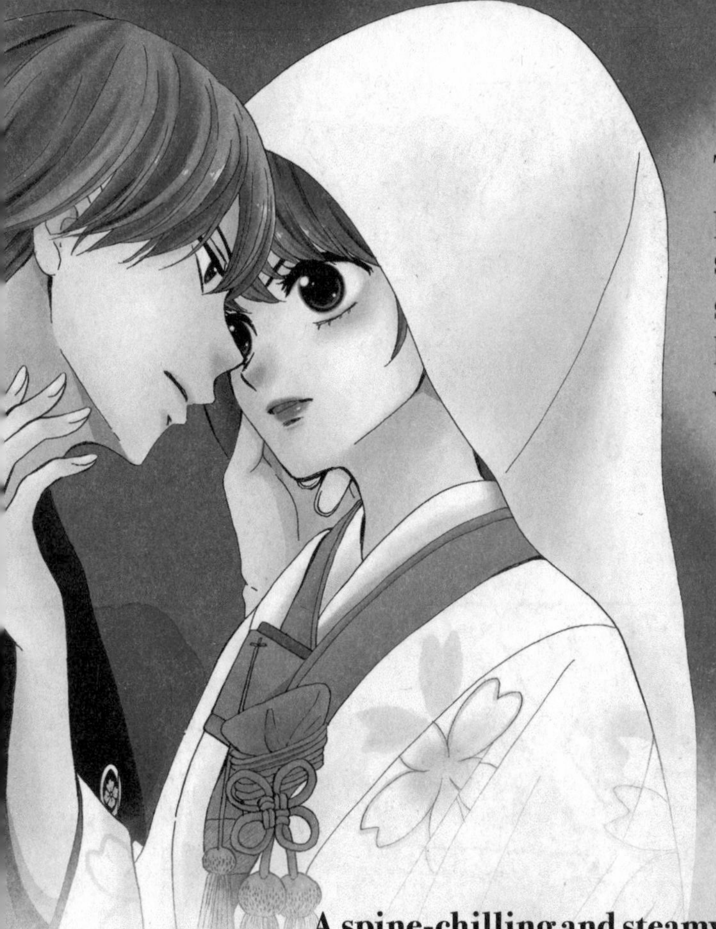

The dark, psychological, sexy shojo series readers have been waiting for!

A spine-chilling and steamy romance between a Japanese sweets maker and the man who framed her mother for murder!

Following in her mother's footsteps, Nao became a traditional Japanese sweets maker, and with unparalleled artistry and a bright attitude, she gets an offer to work at a world-class confectionary company. But when she meets the young, handsome owner, she recognizes his cold stare...

Something's Wrong With Us © Natsumi Ando / Kodansha Ltd.

KC/ KODANSHA COMICS

THE SWEET SCENT OF LOVE IS IN THE AIR! FOR FANS OF OFFBEAT ROMANCES LIKE *WOTAKOI*

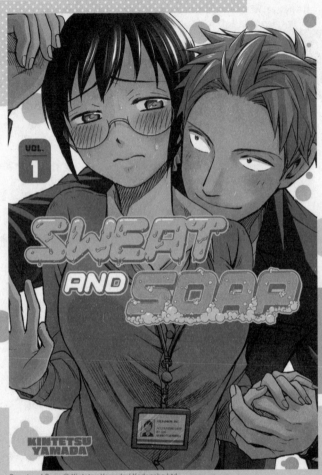

Sweat and Soap © Kintetsu Yamada / Kodansha Ltd.

In an office romance, there's a fine line between sexy and awkward... and that line is where Asako — a woman who sweats copiously — meets Koutarou — a perfume developer who can't get enough of Asako's, er, scent. Don't miss a romcom manga like no other!

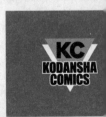

KC
KODANSHA
COMICS

Living-Roo... ...on. Names, characters, places, a... ...author's imagination or are used fictitiously. Any resemblance to actual events, locales, or persons, living or dead, is entirely coincidental.

A Kodansha Comics Trade Paperback Original
Living-Room Matsunaga-san 7 copyright © 2019 Keiko Iwashita
English translation copyright © 2021 Keiko Iwashita

All rights reserved.

Published in the United States by Kodansha Comics, an imprint of Kodansha USA Publishing, LLC, New York.

Publication rights for this English edition arranged through Kodansha Ltd., Tokyo.

First published in Japan in 2019 by Kodansha Ltd., Tokyo as *Living no Matsunaga-san*, volume 7.

ISBN 978-1-64651-056-6

Original cover design by Tomohiro Kusume and Hirotoshi Ikewaki (arcoinc)

Printed in Canada.

www.kodansha.us

9 8 7 6 5 4 3 2
Translation: Ursula Ku
Lettering: Jan Lan Ivan Concepcion
Additional Lettering: Michael Martin
Editing: Kristin Osani and Tiff Ferentini
Kodansha Comics edition cover design by Phil Balsman

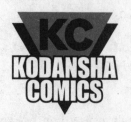

Publisher: Kiichiro Sugawara

Director of publishing services: Ben Applegate
Associate director of operations: Stephen Pakula
Publishing services associate managing editor: Madison Salters
Production Managers: Emi Lotto, Angela Zurlo